S0-CPQ-848

The Historical Bible

THE WORK AND TEACHINGS
OF THE APOSTLES

BY PROF. CHARLES FOSTER KENT

THE SHORTER BIBLE —THE OLD TESTA-
MENT.

THE SOCIAL TEACHINGS OF THE PROPH-
ETS AND JESUS.

BIBLICAL GEOGRAPHY AND HISTORY.

THE ORIGIN AND PERMANENT VALUE
OF THE OLD TESTAMENT.

HISTORY OF THE HEBREW PEOPLE.
From the Settlement in Canaan to the Fall
of Jerusalem in 586 B.C. 2 vols.

HISTORY OF THE JEWISH PEOPLE. The
Babylonian, Persian and Greek Periods.

THE HISTORICAL BIBLE. With Maps.
6 vols.

STUDENT'S OLD TESTAMENT. Logically
and Chronologically Arranged and Translated. With Maps. 6 vols.

THE MESSAGES OF ISRAEL'S LAW-
GIVERS.

THE MESSAGES OF THE EARLIER
PROPHETS.

THE MESSAGES OF THE LATER PROPH-
ETS.

CHARLES SCRIBNER'S SONS

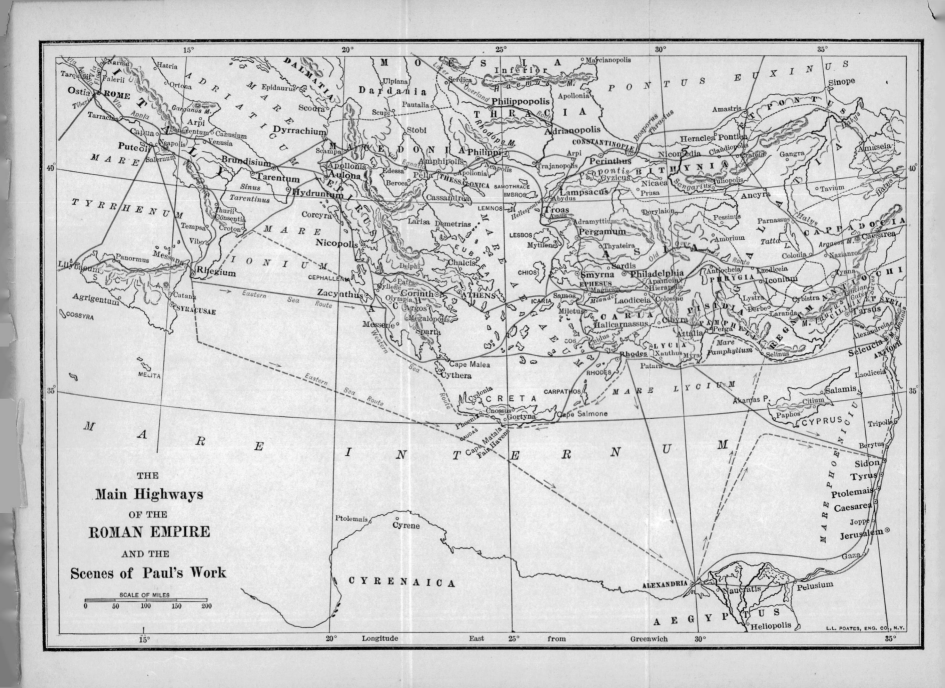

THE
Main Highways
OF THE
ROMAN EMPIRE
AND THE
Scenes of Paul's Work

SCALE OF MILES

0   50   100   150   200

Longitude   East   from   Greenwich

L.L. POATES, ENG. CO., N.Y.

The Historical Bible

THE WORK AND TEACHINGS
OF THE APOSTLES

BY

CHARLES FOSTER KENT, Ph.D., Litt.D.

WOOLSEY PROFESSOR OF BIBLICAL LITERATURE IN YALE UNIVERSITY

WITH MAP AND CHART

CHARLES SCRIBNER'S SONS

NEW YORK   CHICAGO   BOSTON

A

PREFACE

THE Apostolic Age is the most complex period of biblical history. Until the death of Jesus the interest of the biblical student is focused on the Hebrew race, but after that great turning-point in human history it suddenly becomes world-wide. Rome soon takes the place of Jerusalem as the centre of Christianity, and its historical background is the great Græco-Roman world. It is during the Apostolic Age that the relatively narrow current of Jewish thought mingles with those which flow from the ancient East, from cultured Hellas, and from Rome itself. The mingling of these currents explains the resulting complexity of apostolic life and thought. The New Testament writings vividly reflect this mingling of civilizations and ideas. As they stand these books also lack chronological arrangement. To most New Testament readers the latter part of the New Testament is a labyrinth. It is full of immortal truths and richly suggestive of the heroism and hopes of the early Christians; but, aside from the book of Acts, the New Testament writings in their present order fail to make clear the unity of the mighty, onward, first-century movement of which they are practically the only record. Therefore a chronological synthesis of the material in the epistles and Acts is an indispensable prerequisite for the intelligent study of apostolic Christianity.

The cumulative testimony of an ever-increasing body of biblical students confirms the conclusion that the most fruitful, in fact, the only satisfactory way to study biblical history and the complex literature contained in the Old and New Testaments, is by means of the source-method. When the more important passages of this ancient literature are singled out and arranged according to the scientific methods of classification, the biblical writers tell their own story and the modern student gains for the first time a clear and comprehensive knowledge of the abounding life and the vital principles recorded in the Bible. In endeavoring to lay the foundations for this study, I have been constantly helped and inspired, not only by work in the college classroom, but also by scores and hundreds of letters from men and women in various professions and activities who have been able

PREFACE

to speak from their practical experience in the larger laboratory of life. To endeavor to lay before them in each succeeding period those portions of the Bible that are the most significant and to leave out none that are of primary importance has been one of the constant aims of this series. In the present volume the task has been especially difficult, yet inspiring because of the richness of the material. In Paul's epistles the historian also possesses contemporary records which are of priceless value; but even here frequent omissions bring out in clearer relief the remaining passages which present the logical thought and the essential teachings of the great apostle to the Gentiles. Following the example of modern translators like Moffatt and Weymouth, I have broken up many of Paul's cumbersome and involved sentences into smaller and more intelligible units. By so doing the modern reader is enabled to gain a truer appreciation, not only of the apostle's thought but also of his vigorous literary style.

The large debt which I owe to the writers who have pioneered this many-sided field is suggested in the Appendix. To my former student, Professor Case, of the University of Chicago, I feel under especial obligation for his illuminating survey of the religious background of the Apostolic Age in his *Evolution of Christianity*. The study of each succeeding period of biblical history has also brought into increasing prominence the lofty yet practical social idealism of the men who inspired and wrote the Old and New Testaments. The subject is too large and too vital to be presented only fragmentarily. Its comprehensive treatment is, therefore, reserved for a separate volume on "The Social Teachings of the Prophets and Jesus."

C. F. K.

YALE UNIVERSITY,
  January, 1916.

CONTENTS

INTRODUCTION

THE RECORDS AND BACKGROUND OF THE APOSTOLIC AGE

PRIMITIVE CHRISTIANITY IN PALESTINE AND SYRIA

CONTENTS

CONTENTS

CONTENTS

CONTENTS

MAP AND CHART

INTRODUCTION

THE RECORDS AND BACKGROUND OF THE APOSTOLIC AGE

I

THE RECORDS OF THE WORK AND TEACHINGS OF THE APOSTLES

1. The Significance of the Apostolic Age. The Apostolic Age began with the death of Jesus in 29 or 30 A.D. and ended about the close of the first Christian century. This brief three-quarters of a century is significant primarily because it represented the practical application, the testing, and the crystallizing of the principles of faith and life which Jesus had set forth. Christianity then came into close contact and competition with many rival religions, such as the Roman emperor-worship, Greek Cynicism, Epicureanism, Stoicism, Judaism, many Egyptian and oriental cults, and, above all, with the popular mystery-religions. In this infinitely complex environment Christianity ceased to be based on certain simple principles proclaimed by Jesus and illustrated by his life and acts; it gradually developed an elaborate system of doctrines, rules, and institutions. This period marked the beginning of that creed-making era which culminated in 325 A.D. in the formulation and acceptance by the Western Church of the Nicene Creed. It also witnessed the spread of Christianity from the little community at Jerusalem to Rome and to the widest bounds of the Roman Empire. It saw the growth of a chain of Christian churches reaching from Babylon in the East to Spain in the West and from the Black Sea in the North to the heart of Africa in the South.

The vital questions presented by the period are historical and doctrinal. How far was the faith of Christianity based on the teachings of Jesus? How far did it come from the active mind of Paul? How far was it a composite of Jewish, Greek, and oriental ideas? Fortu-

1

nately, in answering these complex yet fundamental questions, we have as a basis of comparison the older records of Jesus' work and teachings. We can focus the search-light of these teachings upon those of Paul and of the other New Testament writers, even as the Great Teacher turned them upon those of the older prophets, priests, and sages. The historical study of the literature of the Apostolic Age gives us also a fresh vision of Jesus. Hitherto the Christian church has seen him largely through the medium of Paul's theology; but now we are beginning to distinguish in Paul three distinct elements: (1) The Pharisee and devoted student of the Jewish law; (2) The Roman citizen and heir to many of the complex religious ideas current in western Asia during the first Christian century; (3) Paul the mystic and the devoted follower of Jesus who interpreted the teachings of his Master in the light of his own rich personal experience. With a clearer knowledge of the influences which entered into Paul's vision, we are better able to-day to interpret what he actually saw and thus to see Jesus anew through the eyes of the earliest New Testament writer.

II. **The New Testament Letters and Epistles.** Fortunately, we are not dependent upon secondary sources for our knowledge of Paul. The oldest writings in the New Testament come directly from this heroic apostle to the Gentiles and furnish contemporary testimony regarding the most important movements of the first quarter century following the death of Jesus. Paul's letters and epistles were the spontaneous outgrowth of his work. When it was reported to him that false teachers were attempting to undermine his influence with the churches which he had established in Galatia, with hot indignation and earnest zeal he sat down and wrote his impassioned letter to the Galatians. Again, when he was unable to go in person and counsel his disciples in the newly established church at Thessalonica, he put into his letters known as I and II Thessalonians the words which he would doubtless have spoken could he have visited them. Later, in his absence from Corinth, he carried on an active correspondence with his fellow Christians there, which is at present incorporated in I and II Corinthians. When he found that he could not go on directly to Rome, as he had hoped, he embodied in a more general epistle the essence of his theological teaching, and added a practical application of the principles of Christianity to the every-day problems of life. Thus arose the New Testament book known as the Epistle to the Romans. Through these letters and epistles of Paul it is possible to know him almost as intimately as did those who sat under his direct teaching.

2

They introduce us to Paul as he pleads with the disciples to choose the right, or as he pours out his passionate protestations of affection and appreciation, or as he declares his faith in God and in his son, Jesus Christ, or at the high moments of his thought and experience, as when, for example, he sings his immortal hymn of love. Few characters of antiquity are revealed more clearly than is that of Paul in his ten or twelve original epistles. Even in pastoral epistles like Titus and I and II Timothy the nucleus is undoubtedly Pauline and the spirit of the great apostle transfuses them, though in their final form they probably came from the pens of later disciples. These epistles also give valuable incidental information regarding the details of Paul's work and of conditions in the Roman world, thus richly supplementing and at several points correcting the more systematic record of Acts. In these epistles, as well as in the later writings associated with the names of Peter, and James, and John, it is possible to trace clearly the growth of Christian institutions and doctrines. Epistles like II and III John and Philemon contain many personal touches which reveal the spirit and life of the early Christians. In Hebrews we listen to a great Christian preacher, setting forth the doctrines of the church as they were taught near the close of the first century. Thus through the epistles it is possible to view from many different angles the early growth and expansion of Christianity.

III. **The Aim of the Book of Acts.** The reference in the preface of the book of Acts to "my former volume" and to "Theophilus" implies that the purpose of its author was to continue the narrative of the Third Gospel and to trace the triumphs and progress of the Christian church from Jerusalem to Rome. A closer examination of Acts reveals the fact that its aim was not merely historical but irenical, practical, and to a certain extent apologetic. Its author evidently had three classes of readers in mind: (1) the Jewish and Gentile followers of Jesus; (2) the Jews who refused to accept Jesus as the Messiah; and (3) the Græco-Roman world. His practical aim therefore is threefold: First, to reconcile the differences in the early church regarding its duty to Gentiles and to show how, notwithstanding the opposition of certain narrow Judaizers in its ranks, under the guidance of the Spirit of God and through the heroism and persistency of the early apostles, and especially of Paul, it had swept over the barriers of Jewish and heathen opposition, and finally gained a firm foothold in the capital city of the empire. These facts are presented as the final, pragmatic answer to the objections of the narrow Judaistic Christians.

3

The second aim is to demonstrate that Christianity was born under the shadow of the temple or in the Jewish synagogues, and that not Christianity but Judaism precipitated the bitter hostility between the two kindred faiths. The third aim is to win a favorable reception for Christianity at Rome and from the Roman officials throughout the empire. To that end especial emphasis is placed upon Paul's Roman citizenship and on the endeavor to show that his persecutions and imprisonments came simply as the result of malignant Jewish or heathen attacks, and that the Roman officials with practical uniformity defended rather than assailed him. This aim doubtless explains why there is no mention of Paul's flogging by the Roman lictors, as recorded in II Corinthians 11[25], and why the narrative of Acts ends abruptly, saying nothing about Paul's final trial and execution. The all-embracing aim was to show how the spirit and presence of Jesus continued to inspire and direct his followers, so that all that they taught and accomplished was inspired by their living Lord and Master.

IV. **Authorship and Date of Acts.** The critical scholarship of the last century has tended to confirm the testimony of early-church tradition that Luke, the companion of Paul, was the writer of both the Third Gospel and the present book of Acts. Detailed studies of each word and phrase have demonstrated that the same literary characteristics recur throughout these books. The preponderance of medical terms, the marked interest in miracles of healing, and the evidence at every turn of the exact knowledge which only a physician could possess (cf. Hobart, *Medical Language of St. Luke*) distinguish Acts and the Third Gospel from all other New Testament writings. This remarkable unity of literary style and medical interest points clearly to Luke, the physician, as their common author. The direct statements in Acts strongly confirm this conclusion. In the accounts of Paul's journey from Troas to Philippi (16[10-17]), later from Philippi to Jerusalem (20[5]–21[18]), and from Cæsarea to Rome (27–28), the author writes in the first person, indicating that he accompanied Paul. The detailed account of their last journey to Rome implies that only two friends, Aristarchus and the author of the so-called "we" sections, were with Paul. Of the six friends whom Paul states were with him at Rome during his imprisonment (Col. 4[10-14], Philemon [23-24]) practically none except Luke the "beloved physician" (in the light of Acts 15[39], 27[2], and II Tim. 4[10]) could have been the author of this journal of travel.

Little is known regarding Luke, but that little is significant. It is clear that he was a Greek Christian. He was certainly for a time a

resident and possibly a native of Philippi, although traditio[n]
him a native of Syrian Antioch. He accompanied Paul in hi[s]
and more important journeys, probably in the capacity of med[ical at-]
tendant; but he is also mentioned by the great apostle as [a fellow-]
worker." His keen interest in all questions which concerned [the life]
and work of Jesus and the extension of Christianity througho[ut the]
Roman world is clearly demonstrated in the writings which[h have]
come from his pen. Acts 21⁸⁻¹⁰ indicates that he remained for [a time]
in the house of Philip the Evangelist and that at Jerusalem he had [the]
opportunity to converse with James, the brother of Jesus, as w[ell]
with many others of the early Christian disciples. At other [times]
he was associated with John Mark, Barnabas, and Silas, and in [fact]
was personally acquainted with practically all of the great Chri[stian]
leaders of the Apostolic Age. His opportunities, therefore, for ga[ther-]
ing information and written records regarding the facts of which[h he]
writes were unusual. The culture, the historical method, and [the]
broad interest revealed throughout his writings give to them a uni[que]
value.

The date of the book of Acts is still an open question. Its pref[ace]
indicates that it was written after the Third Gospel, and its gene[ral]
point of view is that of the last quarter of the first Christian centu[ry]
when the spirited conflicts between the Jewish and Gentile sections [of]
the church had lost much of their bitterness. Its obvious endeavor [to]
commend Christianity to the Roman world and to demonstrate th[at]
the early apostles were never hindered nor attacked by Roman officia[ls]
suggests strongly that the book of Acts was written late in the centur[y]
when Roman opposition was beginning to develop but before th[e]
violent persecutions under Domitian about 96 A.D. The book in it[s]
final form may therefore be dated with considerable assurance betwee[n]
80 and 95 A.D.

V. **The Early Sources Quoted in Acts 1¹–15³⁵.** If we did no[t]
have the original Gospel of Mark, we would not have known that Luke
in his gospel was quoting extensively from this older written source,
for his method was to reproduce the ideas and facts of the original in
his own language. This literary habit makes the discovery of the
early sources which he quoted exceedingly difficult. The evidence,
however, is convincing that in Acts, as well as in his gospel, he utilized
earlier records. Here the linguistic evidence is especially strong, for, as
Professor Torrey has shown (*The Aramaic Source in Acts*), practically
all of Acts 1⁴–15³⁵ is Luke's translation of an older Aramaic source or

5

sources. This fact is vitally important, for it strongly supports the historical value of this part of Acts. Luke's sources were not floating, popular traditions but definite, written records evidently committed to writing long before Luke completed our present book of Acts. The linguistic evidence suggests that Luke found the Aramaic original of the first part of his history of early Christianity in practically the same form as he has given it to us in his Greek translation. The internal proof, however, is cumulative that originally independent documents or traditions have been combined in this old Aramaic source. In one or two cases duplicate traditions of the same event are discernible. Thus the analogies are so many and so close between the simple, straightforward account of the imprisonment and liberation of Peter and John in Acts 4^{1-31} and the more miraculous and elaborate version in 5^{17-42}, that there is little doubt that they are older and later versions of the same incident. In Acts 9, 22, and 26 Luke also gives three distinct accounts of Paul's conversion, each of which differs in details from the others. The incompleteness of certain of the narratives also points to originally independent sources. Thus, for example, in 11^{30} and 15^2 the elders at Jerusalem are introduced without any explanation of their origin. In 12^{17} James, the brother of Jesus, suddenly appears without any account of his conversion or explanation of how he became the leader of the Jerusalem Christian community. In different parts of the book diverse points of view are also apparent. Thus in chapters 3–5, 8, and 9^{32}–11^{18}, the interest centres in Peter and to him is attributed the pioneer work in reconciling the variant views of the Jewish and Gentile Christians regarding their obligations to the Jewish ceremonial law. But in the section which begins with chapter 13 it is Paul's persistency and initiative, even in the face of strong opposition, that finally leads to the breaking of Jewish bonds. The only satisfactory explanation of these minor, yet significant variations, is that originally distinct traditions have here been combined. At least two important groups of early Christian traditions may be distinguished in chapters 3–15. The first is found in 3^1–5^{16}, 8^{5-40}, 9^{31}–11^{18}, and 12^{1-24}. The geographical background is Palestine and the events gather about Jerusalem, Cæsarea, and Samaria. Peter and Philip are the chief actors. It is possible that the facts which these stories record were gathered and written down by Philip or his daughters. The narratives found in 6^1–8^4, 11^{19-30} centre about Jerusalem and Antioch and form the natural introduction to the account of the first missionary campaign of Paul and Barnabas, found in Acts 12^{25}–15^{35}. It has been suggested that Silas, who, accord-

ing to 15^{27}, was sent as a messenger by the Jerusalem church to the Christians at Antioch, was perhaps the one who wrote this group of narratives. Whatever be their exact history, it is clear that these narratives must be regarded as the primary sources in the book of Acts. The complete absence of any reference to the destruction of Jerusalem or to the bitter persecutions which the Christians experienced under Nero favor the conclusion that the majority of them at least were written early in the second half of the first century.

VI. **Later Traditions in 1^1–15^{35}.** In addition to the material drawn from the earlier written sources certain narratives are found in the first part of Acts which bear all the marks of being secondary. The first is the account of the ascension in 1^{1-12}. In the Gospel of Luke Jesus' ascension takes place at the close of the day on which he arose from the grave (*cf.* V, 304, 305); but in the account in Acts it is at the end of forty days. Why Luke preferred to incorporate this in his later work is not entirely clear. Its presence has been one of the chief stumbling-blocks in accepting the Lucan authorship of Acts. The reason is probably because he found it already in the Aramaic source, which he quoted as a whole. As has been truly said: "Whatever involved a miracle attracted rather than repelled Luke." The account of the choice of a successor to Judas, in 1^{13-25}, evidently contains an important historical kernel. At least this narrative gives us the first glimpse into the life of the Christian community at Jerusalem. The story of the day of Pentecost resembles in literary character the nativity stories, which stand at the beginnings of the First and Third Gospels, but it clearly preserves the memory of a transcendently important event in the early history of Christianity. The later duplicate account of the imprisonment and liberation of Peter and John, contained in 5^{17-42}, bears the marks of later growth. The account of Paul's conversion in 9^{1-18} is probably based on what appear to be older accounts in 22 and 26. Occasional editorial additions, as for example, 2^{43-47}, $11^{22,\ 23,\ 30}$, 12^{25}, may be detected, but the presence of these later traditions and editorial additions only tends to confirm the conviction that the web and woof of the narratives in Acts 1–15 is very early and reliable Christian tradition.

VII. **The Journal of Travel.** The excellent historical character of the second half of the book of Acts has long been recognized. Here at every point a familiarity with details and a certainty of touch are apparent which are possible only when the author is intimately familiar with the events which he is recording, as well as with their geographical and historical setting. Recent excavations and research have signally confirmed the accuracy of the minute political, social, and religious allusions to the peculiar and rapidly changing conditions in Asia Minor and southern Europe. The explanation of these significant facts is furnished by the book of Acts itself. As has already been noted, in 16^{10-18}, 20^{5-15}, 21^{1-18}, 27^{1}–28^{16}, the author speaks not in the third but in the first person, thereby quietly setting forth the fact that he himself was a witness of the events which he records. The exactness and minuteness of detail which characterize these passages also suggest strongly that Luke is not dependent upon verbal memory but upon a journal of travel, such as it was customary for companions of important travellers to keep in order to recall their experiences. It is also probable that in the passages where the third person is used Luke was also able to draw from his own notes or from those of others who accompanied Paul, for they reveal much the same minuteness and exactness of detail as do the so-called "we" passages. This conviction is confirmed by the fact that from 15^{36} to the end of the book there is not the slightest evidence that Luke was translating from earlier Aramaic sources. The style is homogeneous throughout. In contrast to the first part of the book, where Luke is quoting from older Aramaic sources and where there are nearly a hundred quotations from the Old Testament, the second part of Acts contains only one or two quotations. The whole is written not only in a finished literary style but also from the point of view of Luke, who beyond reasonable doubt was himself the author of the journal of travel.

Thus out of a half century of radical criticism, which has been inclined at times to seriously discredit the historicity of the book of Acts, it has emerged and stands as one of the best historical documents that have come down to us from antiquity. Its faults are shared in common with the best historical writings of the period as, for example, the *Annals* of Tacitus, in which miracle stories are recounted with the greatest assurance. In using the book of Acts it is important to follow the primary sources. There is every reason to believe that these give us a remarkably faithful picture of the chief characters and events in the early history of the Christian church. While the book of Acts is excellent history, it is more than a history, it is the epic of conquering Christianity; it is the pragmatic proof of the invincible power of the spirit and teachings of Jesus.

THE HISTORICAL AND RELIGIOUS BACKGROUND OF THE APOSTOLIC AGE

I. **The Rulers of Rome.** Augustus realized his lofty ambition and brought practically all the civilized nations of the earth under one common rule. Rome in the first Christian century represented the world, and the emperor was not merely the symbol but the embodiment of all authority and government. The welfare of the world, therefore, depended as never before upon his character and policy. As a result, the citizens of the empire experienced the most varied vicissitudes of fortune during the seventy years (between 30 and 100 A.D.) which constituted the background of the Apostolic Age. Tiberius, who reigned until 37, was a stern moralist, so severe that he was regarded as a despot by the Roman nobility, whose vices he vainly endeavored to check. Caligula, who reigned from 37 to 41, was thoroughly unsound both morally and mentally. The brevity of his reign alone saved the empire from shipwreck and his Jewish and Christian subjects from terrible persecution, for in his insanity he imperatively demanded that he be worshipped as a deity by every citizen of the empire. Claudius, born in southern Gaul, proved, like Tiberius, a champion of the provinces and endeavored by a generous policy to unite in loyal citizenship all parts of the empire. He laid down the significant principle: "It is right that men should live in the religion of their country." He also instituted humane laws in behalf of slaves. For the first time in the history of Rome the killing of a slave by his master was branded as a capital offense. After a reign of thirteen years Claudius was succeeded in 54 by Nero, who came to the throne at the age of seventeen as a result of the intrigues of his mother, Agrippina. For the first eight years of his reign the direction of the government was left almost entirely to Burrus, the Pretorian prefect, and Seneca, the Stoic philosopher. Seneca favored the provinces, although he himself amassed a great fortune through the misuse of his official position. At the death of Burrus in 62 Seneca killed himself at the emperor's command, and

9

Nero assumed active control of the government. In contrast to his profligate nobles, Nero was not altogether bad but capricious. His persecution of the Christians in 64 was only one of the many mad acts of tyranny that in 68 led to a revolt of the provinces which drove Nero to suicide. In the anarchy which ensued four Roman emperors were crowned within a year, three of whom were military leaders. The last, Vespasian, the commander of the Roman army in Syria, a plebeian, succeeded in restoring peace to the empire. Setting aside the old Roman nobility, he recruited its ranks from the provinces and the cities of Italy. Thereby he gave new life to the Senate which, nominally at least, represented the people. Henceforth it supported the emperor and assisted him in the reorganization of the empire. Titus, the conqueror of Jerusalem, who in 79 succeeded his father, was kind and benevolent, intent only on promoting the welfare of his subjects. After a short reign of two years he was succeeded in 81 by his younger brother, Domitian, a scholar with high moral standards but ambitious of power and suspicious of the Senate. During his reign of fifteen years the empire prospered, but many of his subjects and especially the Christians were the victims of his tyranny and suspicions. Nerva, who in 96 was chosen as Domitian's successor by the Senate, shared his authority with his colleagues and inaugurated an era of liberty and good-will which was perpetuated by his successor, Trajan (98–117). The rulers of this period present the most striking contrasts. Claudius and Vespasian heroically endeavored to conserve the interests of all their subjects. Caligula and Nero, on the other hand, were absolutely irresponsible and vicious. Titus and Nerva were too lenient toward offenders and too lax in their rule to control the diverse elements in the empire. Tiberius and Domitian were conscientious tyrants who won the ill will of the majority of their subjects. Under these very different types of rulers Christianity in turn prospered and was persecuted.

II. **What Rome Did for Christianity.** It is an unquestioned fact that Rome alone made possible Christianity's marvellous progress during the first Christian century. The rapid spread of that local cult, an offspring of hated Judaism, until it reached the farthest bounds of the Roman Empire is unquestionably the greatest marvel in human history. The primary explanation is the personality of the Founder of Christianity and the potency of the principles which he proclaimed, but the miracle was possible because its environment was uniquely favorable. The strong hand of Augustus and of the emperors who succeeded him put an end to the destructive wars which had disrupted and devastated the states encircling the Mediterranean and for a century established practically unbroken peace. Moreover, Rome unified these diverse nations, broke down all political and racial barriers, and substituted for petty patriotism an enlarged consciousness of world citizenship. Throughout its vast domains Rome established police protection; the pirates were hunted from the sea and robbers even from the remote mountain passes. Over valleys and rivers and mountains broad highways were built which made travel in all parts of the empire relatively easy and rapid. Accommodations for travellers and traders were established in all the important cities along these highways, and imperial postal service made communication easy. Under the fostering protection of Rome, Greek traders, artists, and travelling philosophers carried the culture and language of ancient Hellas from the valleys of the Tigris and Euphrates to the Pillars of Hercules, so that Greek became the common language of communication between all the different citizens of the empire, and even in the imperial city. The great publishing houses, through the services of hundreds of slaves, were able to issue books almost as cheaply as to-day. Literature and the easy means of communication made it possible for ideas to travel with marvellous rapidity throughout the civilized world. Above all, Rome until the very close of the first century was tolerant toward all types of religion. Even in the imperial city itself scores of provincial cults had their devotees, their interpreters, and in many cases their priests and temples.

III. **Contemporary Palestinian Judaism.** The Apostolic Age was a supremely critical period in the history of Judaism. Under the rule of the Roman procurators, who in turn were under the immediate direction of the emperor, Judea felt most acutely every change in the policy of succeeding rulers. Tiberius's zeal to protect the interest of the provinces led him in 36 to banish Pontius Pilate on a charge of misgovernment. The mad Caligula figures both as a friend and a foe of the Jews. In 37 he appointed Herod Agrippa, the grandson of Herod the Great, king over the east-Jordan tetrarchy of Philip and in 39 added Galilee and Perea to his dominion. It was at this period that the personal intercession of Herod Agrippa, who had been a boon companion of Caligula, alone saved the Jews from wholesale slaughter because they refused to worship the emperor. The reign of Claudius was a golden era for his Jewish subjects. In payment of certain personal obligations to Herod Agrippa the emperor made him king over all the territory that had belonged to his grandfather, Herod the Great. For three years, 41–44, the Jews enjoyed great prosperity and privileges under his rule. Like most of the Herodian family he was a pagan at heart, but he posed as the guardian of Jewish traditions and rights not only in Palestine but throughout the Roman world. His sudden death in 44 A.D. marked the beginning of a disastrous chapter in Jewish history. His son, Agrippa II, was later made king of the kingdom of Chalcis and given charge of the Jerusalem temple and the right of appointing the high priest, but in 44 A.D. Judah was again placed under the rule of the procurators. Each succeeding ruler proved worse than his predecessor. The history of Judah from 44 to 66 is a sickening record of cruelty and rapacity on the part of the procurators and of insurrections, futile messianic uprisings, and growing hatred on the part of the Jews. After the death of Nero, and while rival emperors were struggling for the imperial throne, the Zealots precipitated the final rebellion against Rome which resulted in the complete destruction of Jerusalem and the temple. Fanaticism and civil war between the different Jewish factions made this one of the bloodiest struggles in human history. Finally, after Vespasian had been made emperor, Titus, his son, was left victor over a smouldering ruin and a devastated land. From 70 to the end of the century the intellectual capital of Judaism was transferred to Jamnia. Here its learned rabbis continued to study the law. Here also the canon of the Old Testament was completed about 90 A.D. Though mortally smitten by Rome, the Jews continued to dream their dreams of the Messiah who would yet descend from heaven, judge the heathen nations, and set up his supernatural kingdom in which the faithful would be raised from the dead to share with those who were living the glories of the messianic reign.

IV. **The Judaism of the Dispersion.** In the apostolic history the Jews of the dispersion figured more prominently than those of Palestine. Continued residence in Greek-speaking lands had produced in many ways a different type of Jew from that found under the shadow of the temple. He was equally loyal to the traditions and institutions of his race and made frequent pilgrimages to the sacred city, but his outlook was broader and his mind more open to new truth. Many of them, like Philo of Alexandria and the author of IV Maccabees, had accepted many of the principles of the Greek philosophers and were endeavoring both in theory and practice to reconcile Judaism and Hellenism. In their contemporary writings one will find many ideas that are familiar to the readers of Paul's epistles. Thus, for example, the author of IV Ezra (3^{21}) declares: "The first Adam, clothing him-

12

self with the evil heart, transgressed and was overcome; and likewise also all who were born of him." Like their Palestinian brothers, they were expecting the speedy advent of a divine messianic king to inaugurate a new era in human history. Beginning as early as the second century B.C. an earnest missionary spirit had developed among these Jews of the dispersion. The Greek translation of the scriptures had been made not only for their use but to commend the truths which these contained to the Gentile world. In such centres as Alexandria, the Greek allegorizing and spiritualizing methods of interpretation, had been applied by many Jewish scholars to these older scriptures. Israel's ceremonial institutions and even the chief events of its history were interpreted simply as symbols of spiritual realities or of future events. Under this allegorizing process the strict insistence upon obedience to the ceremonial law was gradually given up and thus the door to Judaism was opened wide to the Gentile world.

The intense zeal of these later Jewish missionaries is revealed by the volume and variety of the literature which they put forth. By means of an elastic, allegorizing method of interpretation all that was finest in Greek philosophy was read back into the Old Testament. Moses and the later prophets were proclaimed the forerunners of Plato and Aristotle. Greek philosophy was thus made the servant of the Jewish religion, for whatever the Jews of the dispersion wrote had the practical aim of winning converts and of influencing men to live a higher moral life. Imitating Homer, Philo of Alexandria wrote an epic describing in heroic terms the great events and personalities of Israel's history. These earnest missionaries even dramatized that stirring history. Fragments of the great religious epic called *The Exodus* survive as an illustration of the way in which they used the methods of the Greek drama to commend the religion of Jehovah to the Hellenic world. Their earliest efforts were rewarded. Many Greeks and Romans shared Israel's faith. A few became what were called "proselytes of righteousness," submitting to circumcision and faithfully keeping all the commands of the Jewish ceremonial law. These were freely admitted to all the services of the temple and enjoyed in full the religious privileges of native-born Jews. The majority, however, took only a partial step toward Judaism. They accepted its monotheism and its moral and social teachings but did not attempt to meet all its ceremonial requirements. Apparently these converts were welcomed by the Jews of the dispersion and were admitted freely to the services of the synagogue. These were included in the class designated in the book of Acts as the "God-fearing Greeks." They were found in almost every synagogue which Paul visited in the larger cities outside Palestine. It is probable that this class also included the open-minded students of religion, of whom there were many, who were seeking religious and ethical truth and inspiration wherever they could find them. They reveal clearly the religious conditions and spiritual needs of the world to which Christianity appealed. From their ranks came most of the early Gentile converts. Their presence in the synagogues also exerted a powerful broadening influence upon the Jews of the dispersion, preparing them for the reception of the nobler message which Christianity brought. Thus this wide-spread Jewish missionary movement must be reckoned as one of the most important forces in preparing the world for Christianity.

V. **The Greek Philosophies.** The Jewish scholars of the dispersion, in seeking to reconcile Moses and Plato, paid the highest tribute they possibly could to the Greek philosophers. Israel's practical religious teachers recognized that there was much in the intellectual life of Greece that possessed a permanent value for all mankind. They realized that the philosophers, like the Hebrew sages, approached life from the point of view of the individual. When the gods of the old Greek mythology were beginning to topple into the dust, these lovers of men strove to give their fellows certain working principles by which to live. Plato's great permanent contribution to Hellenic thought was the belief in individual immortality. In the first Christian century he was better represented by Philo, the fantastic but earnest Jew of Alexandria, than by the dilettante academicians at Rome, whose attitude on most vital questions was either negative or skeptical.

Epicureanism was still an active force in the empire. These sturdy scientists of that early age held that matter was the only ultimate reality and that their senses were the only guides to be trusted in the quest for truth. All the current superstitions they unhesitatingly threw overboard. They were ready to grant that the gods existed, but not that they exerted any influence in the earth or on the life of man. In this respect they stood directly opposed to the Stoics. The crowning virtue of the Epicureans was their sturdy loyalty to facts as they saw them. It was, however, a cold philosophy entirely devoid of spiritual inspiration.

Out of the noble teaching and example of Socrates grew the two philosophies which were potent moral and religious forces in the life of the age. Both were inspired by the same missionary zeal and the same interest in the moral welfare of the individual that had actuated the great Athenian teacher. Cynicism, whose founder was a pupil of Socrates, aimed to teach men how to live true to nature. This ideal was often carried to crude extremes. The Cynic philosophers were the early prototypes of the Franciscan friars, and they were sincerely devoted to the interests of the masses. Most of them lived lives of noble self-sacrifice and undoubtedly exerted a great influence on the people. Their basic creed was closely akin to that of the Stoics. This popular philosophy bore the stamp of its eastern origin. It taught that the ultimate reality in the universe was not matter but reason, and that the final source of reason was God. The *Logos*, or divine Reason, is what binds men to God. All men, therefore, are divine in so far as that divine Reason enters into them and they follow its guidance. Here the author of the first chapter of Genesis and the Stoic philosophers join hands. Like the Founder of Christianity, they taught that the supreme task in life was to do the divine will, and that the will of God is done by living a virtuous life in the service of man. In theory at least Stoicism was also democratic, for it taught that all men possess this divine Reason and that only those who refuse to follow its dictates and commit crimes not in harmony with the divine plan are slaves. The Stoics also believed that pain and suffering possess a positive value in developing the individual and that therefore they should be patiently and even joyously borne. In dealing with the old mythologies they, like the Jews of the dispersion, employed the allegorical method of interpretation. They also sought to retain the older forms of their religion, as long as they were helpful in developing the individual. Regarding his future immortality their teachings, especially in the first Christian century, were vague and uncertain. To the prosperous, educated man Cynicism and Stoicism had much to offer. They seemed to satisfy the facts of experience and furnished a practical basis for living. But for the outcast or the man who faced death the religion of Reason gave but cold comfort. At the same time these two philosophies were in a very real sense pioneers of Christianity. The belief that men were the children of God, that communication between him and them was possible, and that the end of existence was to do his will by living a virtuous and self-sacrificing life had been held and taught as strongly by Israel's prophets and sages as by the founders of these two philosophies. The doctrine of the *Logos*, or divine Reason, as the bond between God and men was also destined to exert a powerful influence upon certain phases of Christian thinking, and to find acceptance, as it does in the opening verses of the Fourth Gospel.

VI. **The Emperor-Worship.** Rome did not inherit from its past a native religion virile and broad enough to become the religion of the empire. Yet the need was keenly felt for a co-ordinating religious influence which would reinforce the growing consciousness of political unity. Emperor-worship attempted to meet this need. Historically it was the product of a long evolutionary process. In its origin the idea was Oriental rather than Occidental. In ancient Egypt and Babylonia the kings were believed to be incarnations of the deity. Thus the old Babylonian kings Sargon I and Naram Sin in the fourth millennium B.C. placed the sign for god before their names. Gudea, the Sumerian king of ancient Lagash, prayed to a goddess: "I have no mother, thou art my mother. I have no father, thou art my father. . . . In the sanctuary thou didst bear me." When Alexander the Great conquered the East he was soon deified and was worshipped long after his death. His successors, the kings of Syria and Egypt, were practically without exception thus worshipped. From the Orient this tendency to deify successful rulers spread to the Western world. The Greeks themselves early show an inclination to worship genius. Thus Aristotle reared an altar in Athens to Plato soon after his death. As has been well said: "The Greek theory of monarchy started with man and made of him its god; the Oriental notion started with God and made the monarch in his image" (Case, *Evolution of Early Christianity*, p. 205). Pompey was publicly proclaimed a god in Athens. Dio Cassius (XLIII, 14[6]) and Suetonius (*Julius Cæsar*, 76) both state that Julius Cæsar was styled during his lifetime "The God and Dictator and Saviour of All the World." In 42 B.C. the Roman Senate enacted that his title should be, "Divus Julius." Augustus's disapproval of this strong popular tendency repressed its public expression during his lifetime, but it did not prevent the masses from worshipping him long after his death. Henceforth it became a fixed institution in the Roman Empire. Inasmuch as it was a valuable uniting force, it was encouraged even by the better emperors. Moreover, there soon gathered about it certain national hopes that were akin to the Jewish messianic expectations. Gentiles as well as Jews were longing for a divine deliverer who would put down evil, establish justice, and inaugurate an era of prosperity. Vergil's famous prediction, found in his fourth

Eclogue, clearly voices this hope: "The last age prophesied by the sibyl has come and the great series of ages begins anew. Justice now returns, Saturn reigns once more, and a new progeny is sent down from high heaven. O chaste Lucina, be thou propitious to the infant boy under whom first the iron age shall cease and the golden age over all the world arise. . . . O child, as soon as thou shalt be able to read the praises of heroes and the achievements of thy sire and to know what virtue is, the fields shall by degrees grow yellow with ripening corn, blushing grapes shall hang on a rude bramble, and hard oaks shall drip with dewy honey. . . . Dear offspring of the gods, mighty seed of Jove, enter thy great heritage, for the time is now at hand. See how the world's massive dome bows before thee— earth and oceans and the vault of heaven!" Roman and Jew believed that the coming deliverer, whom they, like Vergil, thought would speedily appear, was to be divinely gifted and that his advent was to be attended by marvellous portents. These miracles meant more to the Orientals than to the Greeks or Romans. The latter preferred to worship a man who manifested heroic qualities rather than a God merely let down from heaven. Both Greek and Oriental believed, however, that the uniqueness of those whom they deified came through birth. "Son of God" was a common term among the Greeks and Romans and was interpreted by them in a very literal sense. Augustus bore the title *Divi filius*, and many were the traditions current regarding his divine parentage and miraculous birth (*e. g.*, Suetonius, *Aug.*, 94). Therefore the early Christian missionaries found the Græco-Roman world in an expectant attitude. Their claim seemed as natural as that of the scientists do to the men of the twentieth century. Their only task was to prove their facts. It was also inevitable that missionaries like Paul, who were Roman citizens, speaking to their Gentile audiences, should interpret Jesus in the terms not only of the Jewish messianic hope but of the larger Roman world to which they appealed. Thus it was that the emperor-worship proved an active force in opening their eyes to the fact that Jesus was not a mere Jewish Messiah but the universal Saviour of mankind. This potent influence also carried many of the early Christian theologians still further and led them to proclaim him the Creator and Ruler of the universe, as well as the Friend and Saviour of sinful men.

VII. **The Mystery-Religions.** The emperor-cult, which was simply the worship of power and success, and the Greek philosophies, with their cold appeal to reason, never fully met the deeper spiritual needs of the people. What they desired was something that would satisfy their emotions as well as their reason and would give them the consciousness of fellowship with the Deity and the assurance of personal salvation. This craving for individual protection and salvation is as old as the race. As soon as man recognized the presence of hostile forces in the world, he sought means whereby he might ally himself with some higher power or powers that would deliver him. First he felt the need of deliverance from natural forces, from wild beasts and human foes. Larger experience opened his eyes to the malignant effects of sin. Therefore he went in quest of a saviour or of a way that would deliver him from this insidious evil. Many were the ways that were devised. Scientific knowledge in time provided a partial way of deliverance from his old foes—hostile man and beast and the forces of nature. Moral laws also pointed out ways in which he might in part anticipate the malign effects of sin; but he never ceased to feel the need of the help of some power outside himself. Judaism and Stoicism put the greater emphasis on man's activity as the way of deliverance. The so-called mystery-religions put the chief stress on the help from without. They greatly attracted the masses because they claimed to make clear the way in which man might put himself into touch with this power from without and be assured of salvation. There were many types of mystery-religions in the Roman Empire, each with its exponents and its devotees. From Egypt came the mysteries of Isis; from Persia and India the Mithra cults. From Asia Minor came the Cybele-Attis mysteries. In Greece the Eleusinian mysteries, which were associated with the worship of Demeter, and the more riotous Orphic cults had long flourished. Each of these had its representatives in Rome and in many of the larger cities in the empire. Each had attracted to its shrine Romans, Greeks, and Orientals, for each had ceased to be merely a national religion or local cult. The rites differed widely. As a rule, the Oriental types were more frenzied and appealed largely to the emotions and sometimes to the passions, but they all had certain characteristics in common. They all claimed to bring their initiates into personal communion with the Deity by means of their mystic rites. They demanded of their followers, as a preliminary, ceremonial and, to a certain degree, moral purity. Thus the requirement of the candidate in the Eleusinian mysteries was that he should be able to speak the Greek language intelligently and "be pure of hand." To this was later added the requirement that he should "be pure of soul." Most of the mystery-religions also promised to give to their initiates the consciousness of deliverance from sin and of reconciliation with the Deity. To this they added the assurance of personal immortality and of dwelling happily with the gods. As a result of their primitive origin, the popular mystery-religions were a strange, almost incomprehensible combination of sensuality and idealism, often passing over into asceticism, of survivals of pagan sorcery and ritualism, combined with the loftiest conceptions of Greek philosophy, of crude beliefs, coming from barbarous ages, and divine ideals of fellowship with God and man. Notwithstanding their traditional limitations, they were not only tolerated by the emperors but received the indorsement of prominent Romans. Cicero declares (in *De Leg.*, 3[14]): "In the mysteries we perceive the principles of real life and learn not only to live happily but we die with a fairer hope." By virtue of their democracy and their appeal to universal human needs the mystery-religions proved Christianity's strongest competitor in the first century. At the same time, like Judaism and the Greek philosophies and even the emperor-worship, they did much to prepare the minds of men for the reception of Christianity. As was inevitable, when competition was so close and constant and when there was so much in them that was essentially good, they exerted a powerful influence upon Christianity, as is shown, for example, not only in the language but also in the thought of Paul and in the rites which were ultimately adopted by the Christian church.

VIII. **The Religious and Social Needs of the Masses in the Roman Empire.** Christianity in the first century spoke to a needy world. Rome had done much to promote the welfare of the masses, but it could not satisfy the deeper cravings of the individual. Men crave companionship. The many guilds and fraternities which flourished throughout the empire revealed this need. They also longed for a way of personal as well as social salvation. Amidst the wreckage of the old mythologies they longed for a worthy object of personal belief and devotion. The crimes and their consequences, which deluged and blackened society and the life of the individual, had made vividly clear the need of a faith that would unite religion and morals. The disastrous distinctions between slave and freedmen and irresponsible noble had sent the thinkers of the world in quest of a unifying faith that would bind all men and classes together. Even in imperial

Rome the great crying need was for democracy and fellowship in religion, for a faith that would make all men brothers and happy and hopeful in the common service of a common Lord and Master. In that ancient world, with its hundreds of rival cults, Christianity emerged triumphant because it met these universal needs.

CHRONOLOGY OF THE APOSTOLIC AGE

A.D.	ROME	JEWISH HISTORY AND LITERATURE	CHRISTIAN HISTORY AND LITERATURE
30	Tiberius 37 Caligula	18-36 Caiaphas high priest 26-36 Pontius Pilate procurator 20-42 Literary activity of Philo 37 Banishment of Herod Antipas 38 Persecution of Jews at Alexandria	29 or 30 Jesus' death. Day of Pentecost 31 Appointment of the Seven 32 Martyrdom of Stephen. Christianity at Antioch 32-33 Philip's preaching. 33-35 Paul in Arabia 33 Paul's conversion. 35-47 Paul in Syria and Cilicia
40	41 Claudius	40 Philo's *Contra Flaccum* and *Legatio ad Caium* 41-44 Reign of Herod Agrippa I 44 Rebellion led by Theudas 46-47 Famine in Palestine	44 Martyrdom of James the son of Zebedee 46 Paul at Antioch 47 Paul's conference with the "pillar" apostles 47-49 Paul's first missionary campaign 49 Council at Jerusalem. Peter at Antioch 49-50 Paul's work in Macedonia
50	54 Nero	50 Jews banished from Rome 50-100 Reign of Herod Agrippa II 52-55 Procuratorship of Felix 52-66 Rebellions in Palestine 56-58 Procuratorship of Festus	50 Paul's arrival at Athens and Corinth 50-51 Letters to *Thessalonians* and *Galatians* 52-54 Paul at Ephesus. Letters to *Corinthians* 54-56 Paul's arrest at Jerusalem. Imprisonment 57-58 Prisoner at Rome. *Philemon, Col., Eph., Phil.* 58 Parts of *II Timothy.* Paul's martyrdom
60	Nero 68 69	66 Jews declare war against Rome 69 False Nero in East	61 or 62 Martyrdom of James the brother of Jesus 64 Persecution of the Christians by Nero 64 Martyrdom of Peter at Rome 66 Flight of the Christians to Pella
70	Vespasian 79	70 Jerusalem and Temple destroyed 75-79 Josephus's *Jewish War*	70-75 *Gospel of Mark*
80	Titus 81 Domitian	80 Founding Rabbinic School at Jamnia 80-90 *IV Ezra* 85-96 Domitian's oppression of the Jews	75-80 *Gospel of Matthew* 80-85 *Gospel of Luke* 80-90 *Acts* 85-90 *Hebrews* 85-96 Domitian's persecutions of Christians
90 100	96 Nerva 98 Trajan	90 Synod at Jamnia 90 Canon of O.T. fixed 93 Josephus's *Antiquities*	90-95 *I Peter* 95 *Revelation* 96-110 *James. I Clement* 96-110 *I, II, III John. Gospel of John* 96-115 *Pastoral Epistle II Peter*

PRIMITIVE CHRISTIANITY IN PALES-
TINE AND SYRIA

§ CXLVI. THE ORIGIN OF THE JERUSALEM CHRISTIAN
COMMUNITY

Now when the disciples entered Jerusalem they went to the upper room where they were in the habit of staying. There were Peter, John, James, Andrew, Philip and Thomas, Bartholomew and Matthew, James the son of Alphæus, Simon the Zealot, and Judas the son of James. All these men continued with one mind in earnest prayer, together with the women, with Mary the mother of Jesus and his brothers. Return of the disciples to Jerusalem (Acts 1¹³⁻¹⁴)

Now during those days Peter, standing up in the midst of the brothers—there was a crowd of about one hundred and twenty persons all together—said, Brothers, it is necessary that the scripture be fulfilled which the Holy Spirit spoke beforehand by the mouth of David in regard to Judas, who acted as guide to those who seized Jesus. For it is written in the Book of Psalms Choice of a successor to Judas Iscariot (15-16, 20-25)

> Desolate be his habitation,
> And may no one dwell in it;

also

> Let another man take over his office.

Therefore it is necessary that of the men who have been associated with us, one should join us as a witness to his resurrection. So they put forward two men, Joseph, called Barsabbas (surnamed Justus), and Matthias. And they prayed, O Lord, who knowest well the hearts of all, do thou show clearly which of these two men thou hast chosen to take the place in this apostolic ministry from which Judas, through transgression, fell away, in order to go to his own

21

place. Then they cast lots for them and the lot fell upon Matthias, who was assigned the place with the eleven apostles.

The spiritual manifestation on the day of Pentecost (2:1-2, 4, 6a, 12, 13) Now when the day of Pentecost came, they were all together, when suddenly there came a sound from heaven like a violent rushing blast of wind which filled the whole house where they were seated. And they were all filled with the Holy Spirit, and they began to speak in other tongues as the Spirit enabled them to express themselves. Now when this sound was heard the multitude gathered; and they were all amazed and perplexed, saying to one another, What can it mean? But some others said sneeringly, They are brimful of new wine!

Peter's explanation of the action of the disciples (14-21) But Peter stood up along with the eleven, and raising his voice addressed them: Men of Judea and residents of Jerusalem, let each of you understand this and listen attentively to what I say: these men are not drunk as you suppose, for it is only nine in the morning! Rather this is what was predicted by the prophet Joel:

And it shall be in the last days, saith God,
I will pour out of my Spirit upon all flesh,
And your sons and your daughters shall prophesy,
And your young men shall see visions,
And your old men shall dream dreams,
And yea, even upon slaves and slave-girls
In those days I will pour out my Spirit,
And they shall prophesy.
And I will display wonders in the heavens above,
And signs on the earth below,
Blood, fire, and vapor of smoke;
The sun shall be changed into darkness,
And the moon into blood,
Before the great, illustrious day of the Lord comes.
And every one who calls upon the name of the Lord
shall be saved.

Jesus' death (22, 23) Men of Israel, hear these words: Jesus of Nazareth, a man accredited to you by God through miracles, wonders, and signs which God performed by him in your midst, as

22

you yourselves know, this Jesus, delivered up in accordance with God's settled purpose and foreknowledge, you by the hand of wicked men nailed to the cross and slew.

But God raised him to life by checking the pangs of death because it was not possible for him to be held by death. For David says of him: *His resurrection (24-32)*

I saw the Lord constantly before me,
For he is at my right hand lest I be shaken.
For this reason my heart is glad and my tongue exults,
My flesh also shall rest in hope,
Because thou wilt not leave my soul in the grave,
Nor let thy holy one suffer decay.
Thou hast made known to me the ways of life,
Thou wilt fill me with gladness in thy presence.

Brothers, I can speak freely to you about the patriarch David: he died and was buried and his tomb is with us to this day. Being a prophet and knowing that God had sworn with an oath to him that he would seat one of his descendants on his throne, he spoke with prophetic foresight of the resurrection of the Christ when he said that he was not left forsaken in the grave nor did his flesh suffer decay. This Jesus God raised to life as we all can bear witness.

Exalted then by God's right hand, and having received from the Father the promised Holy Spirit, he hath poured on us this which you now see and hear. For it was not David who ascended to heaven, but David himself says, *His exaltation to a position of divine authority (33-36)*

The Lord said to my Lord, ' Sit at my right hand,
Until I put your enemies under your feet.'

Therefore let all the house of Israel know beyond doubt that God hath made him both Lord and Christ, this very Jesus whom you have crucified.

Now when they heard this they were stung to the heart; they said to Peter and the rest of the apostles, Brothers, what are we to do? And Peter replied, Repent and be baptized every one of you in the name of Jesus Christ, in order that your sins may be put away; then you will receive *The effect of Peter's address upon his hearers (37-41)* the gift of the Holy Spirit. For the promise is intended for you and for your children and for all who are far off, for as many as the Lord our God may call to himself. And with many more appeals he solemnly warned and entreated them, saying, Save yourselves from this crooked generation! So those who accepted what he said were baptized and on that day about three thousand souls were added to them.

I. The Return of the Disciples to Jerusalem. "Jesus lives and reigns on high" is the triumphant note with which the Gospels end and the history of the Apostolic Age begins. However the underlying historical facts may be conceived or psychologically interpreted in the light of the widely varying records, the vivid consciousness of Jesus' presence is one of the great impelling forces throughout the apostolic period. At every point this consciousness explains what is otherwise inexplicable. It is the only sufficient answer to the question of why Jesus' disciples, who according to the oldest gospel record (cf. V, 298, 304) had fled to Galilee, terrified and heart-broken, suddenly returned, accompanied by over a hundred of his followers, to take up their permanent abode in Jerusalem. Their homes, their friends, and their occupations were all in Galilee; while Jerusalem was the centre of that Judaism which had rejected their Master and the home of the Pharisees who had hunted him out of Galilee. Here the Sadducean leaders, whose intrigues had placed him on the cross, ruled all but supreme. In returning to this city of tragic memories the followers of the crucified Nazarene had reason to expect only penury, peril, and persecution. Luke gives no direct explanation of their heroic action, for he follows the later traditions which overlook the humiliating fact that they had at first fled. Many have been the explanations offered by modern historians; but three closely related reasons appear to have influenced the disciples to take this perilous but important step. The first and chief reason was their absolute conviction that their Master was still living and in their midst. Paul declares that Jesus appeared not only to Peter and the Eleven but also to five hundred disciples. This statement is supported by the important incidental testimony of Acts 1[23]. Joseph and Matthias, in the days preceding the memorable feast of Pentecost, are selected as apparently only two of the many who were witnesses of Jesus' resurrection, and Stephen and Paul appear to be the last to share these visions. No fear of danger could deter men into whose eyes the light of heaven had shone from

24

proclaiming that fact at the centre of their nation's life. These visions also confirmed them in the growing conviction that Jesus was beyond doubt the Messiah or Christ for which their race had long waited. Henceforth they unhesitatingly interpreted every utterance of Old Testament prophet, priest, or psalmist, which seemed to look forward to the work of the Messiah, as clear predictions of their Master and of the memorable era in which they were living.

These marvellous experiences also seemed to them to confirm the popular Jewish apocalyptic beliefs, already strong in their minds, that Jesus as Messiah would soon come again with supernatural power to establish his rule on earth. The familiar prophecy of Malachi 3^1: "The Lord whom ye seek will suddenly come to his temple," undoubtedly seemed to them a direct divine promise pointing them the way to Jerusalem. It also explains most naturally why they spent so much time in those early days in the temple precincts and why the belief in the second coming of Jesus at first occupied a central place in their thought and life. It was easy for men who had just had visions of their risen and glorified Master to believe that he might at any moment appear in the heavens to proclaim and establish his visible kingdom on earth and to forget that he had declared that the Kingdom of God was not to come with observation but that it is within the hearts of his followers (Luke 17^{21}).

A third and powerful motive impelling the disciples to go back to Jerusalem was their Master's own experience and example. His ministry had made tragically clear the limitations of the Galilean field. His supreme courage and determination in going up to Jerusalem, even though well aware of the deadly perils that lurked there, were at last appreciated by his disciples in their true perspective. Now his task was theirs. Strait though the way be, they felt compelled to walk it. Only at Jerusalem could they touch the heart of their nation and bear witness most effectually to the work, the teachings, and the exaltation of their Master. Following his example, as at Capernaum, they aimed to establish a perfect brotherhood or community which would exemplify the principles of life that he had laid down and furnish the leaven needed to transform their nation. Thus their vision of their risen Master and the duty of announcing it to their nation, their expectation that he would speedily appear in the temple to inaugurate his messianic rule, and their obligation to establish at the historic place chosen by Jesus himself a miniature kingdom of God on earth were forces which drew his followers irresistibly to Jerusalem.

II. **The Choice of a Successor to Judas.** The consciousness of a great mission was evidently strong in the minds of the disciples who rallied at Jerusalem within less than a month and a half after Jesus' crucifixion. A common purpose united them: it was to make clear to all members of their race that he was indeed the promised Messiah and that his messiahship had been attested not merely by his wondrous words and deeds while on earth but by the repeated visions of him as their risen and glorified Lord. This was evidently the reason why they took steps to fill at once the place left vacant in the ranks of the Twelve by the renegade Judas, who, the variant traditions preserved in Matthew and Acts declare, had meantime met with a violent death. As far as the disciples were concerned, he had forfeited his life in the unique brotherhood the moment he betrayed their Master. The demand now was for one who had not only associated personally with Jesus, and so was familiar with his words and deeds, but was also a witness to his resurrection. This requirement also suggests the primitive definition of the term apostle, which was later applied to certain missionaries, like Paul, who were not included in the Twelve. Peter's speech on this occasion, as recorded in Acts, makes pathetically clear the perplexity of the disciples, suddenly deprived of the authoritative leadership of their Master, and the simple faith with which in their extremity they turned to the Old Testament scriptures for guidance. Any passage, which on its surface seemed to throw light on their present problems, quite regardless of its original meaning or application, was accepted as a definite guide or prediction. For example, in the original of Peter's first quotation (from Psalms 69[25]), the psalmist evidently had his many enemies in mind and prayed that their habitation might be desolate; but to adapt it to the later situation *their* is changed to *his* in Acts 1[20].

Matthias, who was chosen by lot to fill the ranks of the Twelve, shares the complete obscurity that has engulfed a majority of the disciples who were most closely associated with Jesus. One questions whether the surprising paucity of references to them in early Christian literature is purely accidental. As a whole, the men to whom Jesus intrusted his priceless teachings and example do not appear to have been gifted with marked ability. With the exception of Peter they were men of one talent. Peter's strength consisted in a simple straightforwardness and zeal rather than in statesmanship or insight. With the exception of Peter, the leading apostles, Philip, Stephen, Barnabas, Silas, Apollos, and Paul, were enlisted entirely outside the ranks of the

Twelve. The ultimate success of Jesus' work came not from the ability of his immediate followers but from the invincible power of his personality and teachings. Moreover, "the advance was not the result of design, but of the inherent universality of the new religion. It passed on from race to race by channels of its own making, and broke, with a living power, through every restriction which men had placed upon it."

It is also important to note that among the first to rally at Jerusalem were Mary the mother of Jesus and his brothers. Paul alone of all the New Testament writers gives any hint as to how the immediate members of Jesus' family were transformed into devoted followers in the few brief days that intervened between his death and the gathering of his disciples at Jerusalem. Paul in his account of the resurrection appearances states (I Cor. 15$^{1-8}$) that after "Jesus had appeared to Peter, to the Twelve, and to upward of five hundred Christian brothers at once, he appeared to James." This James was beyond reasonable doubt the brother of Jesus who later became the head of the Jerusalem church. The evident importance that Paul attributes to James's vision is significant. The order perhaps implies a certain causal relation between the visions of the older disciples and that which later came to James. In the absence of detailed records it is yet possible to supply the missing links. Up to the time of Jesus' crucifixion James did not believe that his brother was the promised Messiah. Therefore his conversion and absolute conviction that Jesus was the fulfilment of Israel's hopes and that the grave could not hold him must have made a profound impression on the other members of his family. Their presence among the disciples who gathered at Jerusalem indicates that at last even those of his own household appreciated his uniqueness.

III. The Story of the Day of Pentecost. Effects point back unmistakably to corresponding causes. The later history of Christianity is in itself convincing evidence that the day of Pentecost was the occasion of a tremendous spiritual experience. The memory of Jesus' words, of his unquenchable hope, and of his calmness in the presence of death were all fresh in the minds of the multitudes. Time and meditation had given them a perspective that enabled them to appreciate him as never before. News of the remarkable experiences that had come to his disciples had spread already among the thronging pilgrims. Among the disciples themselves the first dejection had been followed by a joyous reaction characterized by intense religious emotion. On the day of Pentecost this pent-up feeling broke out into an irresistible wave of spiritual enthusiasm that marked the beginning of the world-wide Christian missionary movement. The story in Acts 2 represents the first-century memory and interpretation of this event. Like most of the biblical narratives, which record the epoch-making moments in the development of human faith, the original account has apparently been supplemented by later additions intended to emphasize its divine character and significance.

Fortunately it bears on its face the evidences of its growth, so that it is possible to distinguish the original historical nucleus which lies back of it. The jeers of the bystanders who heard the cries of the assembled disciples, "They are brimful of new wine!" suggest that what prompted their criticism was some form of religious ecstasy rather than coherent addresses delivered in various languages. This inference regarding the historical fact underlying the story of Pentecost is confirmed by Peter's speech, in which he explains the remarkable behavior of the disciples as a fulfilment of the prediction of the prophet Joel in which there is no suggestion of speaking in foreign languages. It is clear also in the latter part of the narrative that what converted the multitudes was not miracles nor divine signs but Peter's calm, logical, convincing sermon.

In its present form three elements are traceable which apparently were not found in the original account of the event: (1) The sound from heaven like a violent rushing blast of wind which filled the whole house where the disciples were seated; (2) the tongues as of fire which appeared distributed among them with one resting upon the head of each; and (3) their speaking with foreign tongues so that their words were clearly intelligible to the pilgrims present from the various lands of the dispersion. The Bible and contemporary Jewish literature contain certain suggestive analogies which go far to explain the presence of these secondary elements in this nativity story of the Christian church. The subsequent narrative of Acts 2 implies that the sound like a violent rushing blast of wind, which filled the whole house, was the mingled ecstatic shouts and cries of the disciples upon whose waiting hearts the divine Spirit from heaven had breathed. The same dramatic mode of description recurs in 4^{31}. In the mind of the one who has given us this narrative in its present form, the analogies between the giving of the law at Sinai and the pouring out of the Holy Spirit at Pentecost were very close. In the late priestly account of the scene at Sinai we read: "As Moses came down from the mount he did not know that the skin of his face was emitting rays of light because Jehovah had been speaking with him" (Ex. 34²⁹). Just as the divine light shining in the face of Jesus at his transfiguration seemed to transfuse and transform all about him, so Acts 2 suggests that the joy and courage which filled the faces of the disciples appeared to rest like a divine radiance upon them. The statement that the disciples spoke in foreign tongues was either part of the Christian tradition or else is due to the editor's desire to picture the event in keeping with its larger historic significance. The story is apparently a reflection of the current rabbinical tradition of the giving of the law at Sinai, which states that the voice of God proclaimed the law in the seventy different languages that represented all the then known races of the earth. Back of this late account of the pentecostal experience lies the profound fact that the language of the emotions is intelligible alike to men of all races and tongues. Furthermore, Christianity from the first appealed even more strongly to the Jews of the dispersion—"Parthians, Medes, and Elamites"—who had returned as pilgrims to Jerusalem than to those of Palestine. It was this universal quality in Christianity that most interested the author of Acts 1–15 and he has dramatically set it forth at the beginning of his history.

IV. **The Coming of the Spirit.** Interpreting the secondary elements according to their deeper spiritual significance, the historical nucleus that remains in the story of Acts 2 furnishes a remarkably vivid and satisfying record of the epoch-making experience that came to the Christian community at Pentecost. It does not represent the beginning of the Christian church, for that existed at least in germ from the moment that the disciples reassembled at Jerusalem. Its separation from Judaism and its independent existence still lay in the future. The memorable day of Pentecost marked for the Christian community a new consciousness of direct divine guidance. It also demonstrated the universality and potency of the gospel of Jesus.

Modern religious psychology aids in the interpretation of this dramatic story. The feast of Pentecost had doubtless brought to Jerusalem many followers and sympathetic hearers of Jesus. The retelling of the visions which many of them had had of the risen Christ undoubtedly strengthened the faith and kindled the religious enthusiasm of all. The feast of Pentecost also recalled the never-to-be-forgotten events of the feast of the Passover only fifty days before. These national feasts during Jesus' ministry had offered rare opportunity for the presentation of his teachings, and the influence of the example of their Master on this memorable occasion must have been strongly felt by his disciples. It was in these circumstances that a divine enthusiasm seized them—an enthusiasm which henceforth for a generation at least characterized the life of the various Christian communities scattered throughout the Roman world. Paul has vividly described its manifestations in I Corinthians 14. He found it necessary at a later period to urge the Corinthian Christians, when the impulse seized them to speak with tongues, to "let two or at the most three speak at one time. Also to let some one interpret. If there is no interpreter, let the speaker keep quiet in church and speak to himself and God." He also sought to guard the early Christians from the charge which was originally flung at them by the sneering Jewish multitudes at Jerusalem, when he declared that "if at a gathering of the whole church everybody speaks with tongues, and if outsiders and unbelievers come in, will they not say, 'You are insane'?" The phenomenon was a familiar one in the ancient Oriental world. Saul, after his memorable interview with Samuel, falling in with a group of the sons of the prophets, was seized by the same divine enthusiasm. It appears to have been exceedingly common in the primitive guilds of the prophets. It is not without close analogies in the revivalistic services of modern times. Back of this experience lies the firmly established Jewish belief that the Spirit of God the Holy One, or, as it is designated in later Christian times, the Holy Spirit, took possession of certain men and women of open minds and directed their thoughts, their feelings, their words, and their very acts. Practically every extraordinary action or event not explained by ordinary causes was attributed to this direct divine influence. Jesus himself declared that by the Spirit of God he was able to perform miracles, and he appears to have quietly assumed that all that he did and accomplished was by means of the same divine power working through him. The Spirit of God in Hebrew and early Christian thought was his divine power or personality, active in nature, in human history, or working through the minds, the feelings, and the natures of his devoted followers. The great revivalistic experience at Pentecost was, therefore, not the first in Israel's history. The unique element appears to have been the intensity with which it affected the assembled disciples, and the fact that practically all of them felt its mysterious influence. It was not strange that the simple followers of Jesus lacked the vocabulary and articulate means of expressing the new and profound emotions of joy and gratitude and loyalty which filled their souls, and that they voiced them in inarticulate cries which, when heard from afar, gave the impression of a mighty, rushing wind, and evoked from bystanders the sneering words: "These men are brimful of new wine!"

V. **Peter's Memorable Sermon.** The amazement and sneers of the multitude gave Peter, the spokesman of the disciples, his opportunity. Throughout his brief address, which reflects the beliefs and ideas which were in the forefront at the beginning rather than at the end of the Apostolic Age, when the book of Acts was written, there run two parallel lines of argument and evidence. The one is drawn from Old Testament prophecy; the other is based on the actual experience of Peter and of the disciples whom he represented. Speaking to Jews, he starts from the point of view of the Old Testament and singles out the memorable prediction of the outpouring of Jehovah's Spirit upon all classes in the nation, which is found in Joel 2^{28-32a}. He follows the Greek translation, quoting rather freely and supplying the words "last days" in order to make complete the application of the ancient prediction to the events of the day of Pentecost. The latter part of the quotation shows how directly the disciples from the first drew their apocalyptic hopes from these Old Testament predictions. Then follows a remarkably vigorous epitome of Jesus' life and death condensed into one sentence. Peter's statement, "was delivered up in accordance with God's settled purpose and foreknowledge," implies that, as at later times, he had in mind the familiar portrait of the suffering servant of Jehovah in Isaiah 53. He, in common with the Jewish and Christian writers of his age, regarded David as the author of all the Psalms. In his quotation from Psalm 16^{8-11}, and in his interpretation of the promise,

> Thou wilt not leave my soul in the grave,
> Nor let thy holy one see corruption,

the logical application depends not only upon the tradition of Davidic authorship, but also upon the Greek version, which he follows and which differs widely from the Hebrew:

> Thou wilt not forsake me to Sheol,
> Nor suffer thy faithful one to see the grave.

Similarly the apostle, in keeping with the current rabbinical methods of Old Testament interpretation, cites the first verse of Psalm 110 (which is probably a Maccabean poem originally connected with

Simon the Hasmonean) as a prediction of Jesus' resurrection. In the light of our modern historical methods of interpretation the logic may be faulty, but that does not invalidate Peter's underlying argument, for this is but the way in which he sought to interpret his own spiritual experience and that of his fellow disciples. While Jesus was with them they had felt the divine inspiration of his personality and teachings. Even when death had taken him from them, the vivid consciousness of that same personality and presence had impelled them to come up to Jerusalem and face persecution. Now, not only in their own individual experiences but in a most startling and unmistakable manner they and the multitude which they addressed had seen with their own eyes the evidences of the work of the Spirit of God.

To this argument of fact Peter added a strong appeal to the multitude: "Repent and be baptized every one of you," that "you may then receive the gift of the Holy Spirit." Contrition, confession, and moral cleansing—these are the preliminary steps declared to be absolutely essential by the early prophets and John the Baptist, as well as by Jesus and his apostles, if the individual would enter into intimate spiritual relations with God. In the preaching of Peter "the name of Jesus," which stands for his character, his spirit, and his teachings, has become that which inspires contrition and public confession and gives the assurance of moral cleansing and the abounding joy and spiritual exaltation that made the day of Pentecost forever memorable. It also explains why a large number, possibly somewhat magnified, were then added to the Christian brotherhood.

VI. **The Faith of the Early Christian Believers.** Peter's speech, supplemented by those which follow in Acts, reveals the chief elements in the faith of the early Christian believers. Its fixed foundation was their personal acquaintance and association with Jesus during his life on earth and the teachings, the ideals, and the spirit with which he had filled their minds. This is the historical cornerstone upon which Christianity rests and without which it would be, like most other religions, but a system of philosophical speculations or a body of ethical teachings. The faith of the early believers was inevitably and radically moulded by the current hopes of their race and the predictions of their prophets. It had been so even while Jesus was with them to interpret this ancient heritage; it was naturally ever more so when they ceased to hear his audible voice. All the great early teachers of their race had taught them that their varied experiences as a nation were but a preparation for a glorious destiny that awaited them and that a Messiah, chosen and empowered by God, was to be the chief agent in realizing this divine purpose and in inaugurating the new era in human history. Naturally and rightly they identified Jesus as the promised Messiah or Christ. This identification at once broadened their conception of the significance of his personality and work. Hitherto they had known him simply as their personal teacher and friend and master; now the historic term Messiah, with its wealth of associations, emphasized his relation to their race and to other races. At the same time the teachings of Jesus, as well as their own interpretation of their ancient scriptures, led them to the conclusion that they, the disciples of the Nazarene, were the faithful remnant, the true Israel. Hence they were the heirs of all the Old Testament promises. Not only were they to have a central place in the new and divine order, that they believed would speedily and miraculously be established, but they had an all-important rôle in preparing the way for its consummation. All their inherited beliefs and their past and present experiences focused their attention upon Jesus as the central figure in the new divine order. Now they saw him through their spiritual vision, living and exalted, not identical with God but commissioned by him to establish this new order. Hence they called him not only Messiah but also Lord. "Jesus is Lord" was the baptismal formula of the early Christian church. Paul declares in I Corinthians 8[6]: "For us there is one Lord, Jesus Christ." On the lips of the early believers the term Lord had a far more personal and intimate meaning than Messiah or Christ. It corresponded to the older term Master, interpreted in the light of the larger perspective now attained by his disciples. It suggested a broader yet closer personal relation between him and his devoted followers. It was a term not only of adoration but of devotion and fealty. It meant the acceptance of his teachings and ideals as the absolute rule of life and his Spirit as the ever-present interpreter and guide. The first great task, therefore, of his followers was, as Peter declares, to "let all the house of Israel know beyond doubt that God hath made him both Lord and Christ."

§ CXLVII. THE LIFE OF THE PRIMITIVE CHRISTIAN COMMUNITY

Intro-
duc-
tion:
daily
life of
the be-
lievers
(Acts
2⁴⁴⁻⁴⁷)

The believers all kept together and shared all things with one another; and they would sell their possessions and goods and distribute the proceeds to all according as each man had need. Daily with one accord they resorted to the temple and broke bread in their own homes. They ate their food with gladness and single-heartedness, praising God, and were well regarded by all the people. The Lord also added daily to their number those who were being saved.

The
cure of
the
lame
beggar
(3¹⁻⁸)

Now Peter and John were going up to the temple for the hour of prayer at three in the afternoon, when a certain man who had been lame from birth was carried past, whom they used to lay daily at what is called the Beautiful Gate of the temple to ask alms from those who entered the temple. When he saw that Peter and John were about to enter the temple, he asked them for alms. But Peter looked at him intently, as did John also, and said to him, Look at us. And when he gave heed to them, expecting to receive something from them, Peter said, I have neither silver nor gold but what I have I give to you. In the name of Jesus Christ the Nazarene, walk! Then seizing him by the right hand he raised him up. Instantly his feet and ankles became strong and he leaped upright and walked about, and went with them into the temple, walking, leaping, and praising God.

Effect
upon
the
people
(⁹⁻¹¹)

And all the people saw him walking about and praising God. And when they recognized that this was the man who used to sit and beg at the Beautiful Gate of the temple, they were filled with awe and amazement at what had befallen him. And while he still clung to Peter and John, all the people rushed awe-struck to them in what was called Solomon's Porch.

Peter's
expla-
nation
of the
miracle
(¹²⁻¹⁶)

But when Peter saw this he spoke to the people: Men of Israel, why are you filled with awe at this? Or why do you stare at us as if we had made him walk by any power or piety of our own? The God of Abraham and the God of Isaac and the God of Jacob, the God of our fathers, hath glorified Jesus his servant, whom you delivered up and disowned before Pilate, even though Pilate had decided to release him. But you disowned the Holy and Just One, and you asked as a favor the release of a man who was a murderer; but the leader in the way of life you put to death. But God raised him from the dead, as we ourselves can bear witness. Moreover, through faith in his name, his name has given strength to this man whom you see and know; and it is the faith which he inspires that has made this man sound and strong in the presence of you all.

Now I know, brothers, that you have acted in ignorance, as have also your rulers; but it is in this way that God hath fulfilled the promises which he made by the mouth of the prophets that his Christ would suffer. Repent therefore and turn that your sins may be blotted out, in order that times of revival may come from the Lord, and that he may send to you Jesus the Christ, appointed beforehand, whom heaven must receive until the times of the restoration of which God hath spoken from of old by the lips of his holy prophets. Moses indeed said, 'The Lord our God will raise up a prophet for you from among your brothers, as he raised me. You must listen to whatever he may say to you; any soul that will not listen to this prophet shall be utterly destroyed from among the people.' Yea, all the prophets who have spoken since Samuel and his successors have also announced these days. You indeed are the sons of the prophets and of the covenant which God made with your fathers when he said to Abraham, 'All the families of the earth shall be blessed through your offspring.' It was for you first that God raised up his servant and sent him to bless you by turning each of you from your wicked deeds. Appeal to the people to repent and accept Jesus (17-26)

While they were speaking to the people, the priests and the commander of the temple and the Sadducees came upon them, being greatly displeased because they taught the people and proclaimed in the case of Jesus the resurrection from the dead. Arrest of the apostles (4¹, ²)

The next morning a meeting was held in Jerusalem of their rulers, elders, and scribes, at which were the high priest Annas, Caiaphas, John, Alexander, and all the members of the high priest's family. Placing the apostles in their midst, they inquired, By what power and in whose name have you done this? Then Peter, filled with the Holy Spirit, said to them: Rulers of the people and elders of Israel, if we are being examined to-day for a good act done to a man helplessly lame, as to how this man was cured, be it known to you all, and to all the people of Israel, that through the name of Jesus Christ the Nazarene, whom you crucified but whom God hath raised from the dead—through that name this man stands before you perfectly whole. This Jesus is the stone despised by you builders which has become the head of the corner. And in none other is there salvation: for neither is there any other name under heaven, that has been given among men, through which we may be saved.

Now, when they saw the boldness of Peter and John and perceived that they were uncultured and illiterate men, they were astonished; they also recognized that they had been companions with Jesus. But, seeing the man who had been healed standing beside them, they had nothing to say in reply. But when they had threatened them still further, they let them go, being unable to find any way of punishing them on account of the people, for everybody was glorifying God over what had happened; for the man was over forty years of age on whom this miracle of healing had been performed.

Now, when they were released, the disciples went to their friends and reported what the high priest and elders had said. And on hearing this, these all lifted up their voices to God and said, O Sovereign Lord, thou art he who made heaven and earth and sea and all that in them is, who said to our fathers by the Holy Spirit through the mouth of David thy servant:

' Why did the Gentiles rage,
And the peoples form futile plans?
The kings of the earth set themselves in array,
And the rulers assemble together
Against the Lord and his Christ.'

36

And now, O Lord, consider their threats and grant that thy servants may with all fearlessness speak thy word, when thy hand is stretched out to heal and to perform miracles and wonders by the name of thy holy servant Jesus.

And while they were praying the place where they were was shaken, and they were filled with the Holy Spirit and continued speaking the word of God fearlessly. And the apostles gave their testimony to the resurrection of the Lord Jesus with great power, and much grace was upon them all.

The divine answer (31, 33)

Now in the multitude of the believers there was but one heart and soul; not one of them called any of the things which he possessed his personal property, but they shared all they had with one another. There was not a needy person among them, for those who owned land or houses sold them and brought the proceeds of the things which were sold and laid them at the apostles' feet. It was then distributed to every one according as each individual had need. Thus Joseph, who was surnamed by the apostles Barnabas or, as it may be interpreted, 'Son of encouragement,' a Levite, a native of Cyprus, sold a farm belonging to him and brought the money and placed it at the apostles' feet.

Fraternal spirit in the Christian community (32, 34-37)

But a certain man by the name of Ananias who, with his wife Sapphira, had sold some property, with her connivance kept back part of the price and brought only a part of it to lay at the apostles' feet. Ananias, said Peter, why has Satan filled your heart that you should try to deceive the Holy Spirit and keep back part of the price of the land? While the land remained unsold was it not your own? And even after it was sold was it not at your disposal? How is it that you have planned this thing in your heart? You have not lied to man but to God. When Ananias heard these words he fell down and expired; and great fear came upon all who heard it. And the younger men arose, wrapped up the body, and carried it away to be buried. After an interval of about three hours, his wife came in, not knowing what had taken place. Tell me, said Peter to her, did you sell the land for such and such a sum? Yes, she said, that was the sum. But Peter said to her, How was it that you two could agree together to test the Lord's Spirit? Behold

Deception of Ananias and Sapphira (5¹⁻¹¹)

37

the footsteps of those who have buried your husband!
They are at the door and will carry you out! Instantly she
fell down at his feet and expired. And the young men
came in and found her dead, and they carried her out and
buried her beside her husband. And great awe came over
the whole church and over all who heard about these things.

Effect
upon
the
people
(12-16)

Many miracles and wonders were performed among the
people by the apostles, and they were all with one accord
in Solomon's Porch. But, although the people extolled
them, none of the rest of the people dared join them. But
instead multitudes of both men and women who believed
in the Lord were brought in, so that they even carried invalids out into the streets and laid them on beds and
mattresses, that when Peter passed, his shadow at least
might fall on some one of them. Crowds also gathered
from the towns about Jerusalem, bringing invalids and people troubled with unclean spirits; and all of them were
healed.

I. **The Historical Record.** The occasional secondary passages in
this section but serve to bring out by contrast the exact historical
character of the older source here quoted. The general statements
regarding the life of the Christian community, found in the closing
verses of Acts 2, are probably from Luke's own pen. Verse [45], in its
assertion that "they shared all that they had with one another," anticipates the detailed statement of 4^{32}–5^{14} and to a certain extent is at
variance with the testimony of this older and fuller source. The
fourth verse of chapter 4, with its statement that the Christian community numbered about five thousand, is probably also an editorial
addition, for it breaks the close connection between [3] and [5]. Verses
[15-20] of the same chapter appear to be an expansional duplicate of
[12-14], [21], [22]. The reason for the liberation of the apostles given in [21] is
the high priest's fear of a popular uprising, but in [15-20] they are represented as admitting the validity of the miracle which had been
performed in the temple. Verses [27] and [28] also break the close connection between [26] and [29], and have all the characteristics of an explana-
tory clause. Otherwise the material in this section appears to have
been taken from the early Jerusalem-Cæsarean source. It is of the
greatest historical value in portraying not only the life of the primitive
Christian community but also the faith of the early disciples, while

they still stood under the direct influence of Jesus' work and teachings and had not been fundamentally influenced by Paul's dominating ideas.

II. **The Healing of the Lame Beggar.** The book of Acts ascribes only three definite miracles of healing to the twelve disciples, and each of these is associated with the name of Peter. The gospel narratives state that miracles of healing were performed by the disciples during Jesus' lifetime, but furnish no details beyond recording the case of the epileptic (Mark 9$^{17-23}$) which had baffled them. Jesus himself appears to have anticipated that they would carry on his work of healing. The Fourth Gospel has expressed this conviction in the familiar passage: "He who believes on me also shall do the works that I do, and greater works than these shall he do" (John 14^{12}). The account of Peter's healing of the lame man in the temple is given in great detail. The situation suggests the experiences that reinforced the man's faith. Being a frequent visitor to the temple, he must have often heard the teachings and observed the acts of healing performed by Jesus. Also the news of the great spiritual experience which came to the disciples on the day of Pentecost must have filled Jerusalem. The conditions therefore were exceedingly favorable for a startling act of healing. The incident is in every respect parallel to many of the well-authenticated gospel miracles, except that Peter acted simply as the agent working in the name of Jesus. There is every reason for regarding the narrative as historical. The event was also of great importance in extending the work of the disciples. It was the credential required by the masses to prove by the testimony of their eyes that the Crucified One still lived. Peter was quick to improve the unique opportunity thus offered. Here was the supreme answer to the taunts of the people that his Master had died an ignominious death on the cross. Boldly Peter turns upon the multitude and accuses them of being the murderers of Jesus whom he designates as "the Holy and Just One," "God's servant" who had proved the "leader in the way of life." Each of these designations is rich in suggestiveness. The first is an echo of Isaiah 53 and anticipates the theme developed by Peter a little later. The second suggests the initial impression which Jesus' personality had made upon his disciples and upon all who had known him personally. The third title, with marvellous insight, describes him as the pioneer, the first to discover the boundless possibilities of life and to live it in its fulness. This phrase is nobly interpreted in the Fourth Gospel in the words attributed to Jesus: "You shall have life and that abundantly" (John 10[10]). The once helpless cripple, who now stood before the multitude sound and strong, was a convincing proof of Jesus' power to give not only spiritual but physical life to those whose faith enabled them to reach out and receive it.

III. **Peter's Interpretation of the Old Testament Prophecies.** The words with which Peter appealed to the multitude reveal great tact and, what is more important, a yearning love for them such as had filled the heart of Jesus: "Brothers, I know that you have acted in ignorance, as have also your rulers." The implied distinction between the responsibility of the common people and of their rulers was well supported by the facts. Peter's declaration that "God hath fulfilled the promises which he made by the mouth of the prophets that his Christ would suffer" is one of the many indications contained in these early records that the disciples found the explanation of the meaning of Jesus' death in the II Isaiah's portrait of the suffering servant of Jehovah. Peter reiterated John the Baptist's call to repentance, but made the motive not merely individual forgiveness but that God might send to them "Jesus the Messiah, whom heaven must receive until the times of the restoration of which God hath spoken from of old by the lips of his holy prophets." Again the impression is deepened that the apostles' firmly fixed conviction of Jesus' speedy second coming to accomplish by supernatural means what he seemed to have left undone, was derived not from their Master's words but from their perusal of the Old Testament prophecies under the influence of the current Jewish apocalyptic hopes. In Acts 3[24] Peter plainly states the principle that guided the apostles in their interpretation of these ancient scriptures: "Yea, all the prophets who have spoken since Samuel and his successors have announced these days." These typical early apostolic sermons in the opening chapters of Acts illustrate their tendency to ignore the historical background and the immediate application of these Old Testament prophecies and to apply all, which seemed apposite, to Jesus and to the age in which they were living. Their interpretation, however, of the meaning of Jesus' work and teaching to them and to all Jews who believed is of incomparable value. Peter's closing words in 3[26] are the simplest and clearest statement of primitive apostolic faith to be found in the New Testament: "It was for you first that God raised up his servant and sent him to bless you by turning each of you from your wicked deeds." Here, as in the oldest gospel records, Jesus is recognized to be the personal Friend and Teacher and Saviour of men. His saving work is done in the lives of men by delivering them from the bondage of the evil habits and ideals engendered by their past deeds.

IV. **Peter's Defense before Jesus' Murderers.** Acts is a book of striking contrasts. The event soon proved that "the disciples were not above their Lord." The conspirators and leaders of the Jewish nation who had plotted to encompass Jesus' death now interrupted Peter's earnest address. At their head was the commander of the temple police, or *segan*, who was the official representative of the high-priestly authorities. It was his duty to maintain order in the temple precincts, and the apostle's bold words gave him and the Sadducees whom he represented an excuse for silencing Peter. Deeper than their opposition to the doctrine of the resurrection, which Peter implicitly taught, was probably their recognition that he was the spokesman of the despised and crucified Nazarene. The informal meeting which was held the following morning was in many respects closely similar to the preliminary investigation of Jesus which these same high-priestly officials had instituted in order to secure data for a formal charge. It was again a packed tribunal dominated by Annas, Caiaphas, John (in the Western text D, Jonathan), and Alexander. Jonathan was a son of Annas, as was probably also Alexander; at least the narrative of Acts distinctly states that all the members of the high priest's family were present. Peter's reply to their demand that he explain by what authority he had performed the miracle was probably suggested by Jesus' reply to the Pharisees on a similar occasion: "Is it lawful on the sabbath day to do good or to do harm, to save life or to kill?" (Mark 3^{1-6}.) Psalm 118^{22} furnished Peter the figure with which he proclaimed the power of his risen Lord: "This Jesus is the stone despised by you builders which has become the head of the corner." Again it is an echo of Jesus' words recorded in Mark 12^{10}. Peter's closing assertion anticipates Paul's interpretation of the significance of Jesus' personality and work. It is probable that here, as elsewhere in the Old and New Testaments, the name is not used in a magic sense but to describe the character, aims, spirit, and methods of its possessor. Out of the depths of his own personal experience Peter declared that the spirit and teachings which his Master exemplified present the only way in which men of all races and ages may come into living and personal relations with their heavenly Father and attain the real goals of all living.

V. **The Effect of the Release of Peter and John upon the Christian Community.** The grafting high priests were naturally eager to silence the disciples of the Nazarene Teacher who had dared publicly to condemn their corrupt administration of the temple. The Sadducean nobles cared little about questions of orthodoxy. They evidently regarded the apostles as mad fanatics, followers of a Galilean Messiah, who might arouse the people unduly, and their aim was to intimidate them. There was, however, in the apostles' teaching no trace of disloyalty to the law or temple ritual or note of sedition, and for the moment they had the approval of the multitude. Hence the temple authorities, who depended largely on the support of the mob, could only let them go free. To the followers of Jesus this meant a great victory. Their leaders had openly faced the murderers of Jesus, had borne testimony to their Master's resurrection, and the crowds in the temple had upheld them. Here was another signal illustration of their conviction that the Spirit of God was working mightily in their midst. The prayer in $4^{23-26, 29, 30}$ may well have come down directly from the early Christian community. It fits most perfectly its present historical setting. Its spirit and thought are characteristic of the primitive Christians. Psalm $2^{1, 2}$, with its world-wide vision, seemed none too exalted to express their exultation and thanksgiving. The closing lines of the prayer breathe the spirit that actuated the early Christian martyrs and voice their consciousness of a mighty mission as the servants of God to proclaim the teachings and do the great work that God's holy servant Jesus had intrusted to them. As in chapter 2, Luke graphically describes the overmastering ecstasy which seized them by the statement that "the place where they were was shaken and they were filled with the Holy Spirit." This profound spiritual experience also inspired them with new zeal and courage in proclaiming the divine truth intrusted to them and in bearing testimony to Jesus' resurrection.

VI. **The Communistic Tendencies of the Believers.** The general statements at the close of chapter 2 have been popularly interpreted to mean that the primitive Christian community at Jerusalem lived together on a thoroughly communistic basis. Luke may have wished to convey this impression. He himself would probably have commended such a social organization, for his sympathies, as revealed in his gospel, are strongly communistic; but the popular interpretation is not borne out by the older sources which he has incorporated in Acts. These nowhere state that all of the believers put all of their wealth in the common treasury. Instead it is implied that those who did so wholly or in part were highly commended for their exceptional generosity. Thus Barnabas, a Jew from the Island of Cyprus, who claimed Levitical descent and who later became an active apostle, sold a farm belonging to him and turned the proceeds into the common fund. The record does not even indicate that he sold all the property that he possessed. Peter's words to Ananias also plainly and decisively indicate that no one was under any compulsion to sell his personal property or to turn any or all into the apostolic treasury. The absence of any trace of communism in the later history of Palestinian Christianity or elsewhere in the early Christian church, until the alien tendencies toward asceticism and monasticism gained a foothold within it, substantiates the testimony of Acts. All the more significant, therefore, is the spirit of generosity and practical brotherhood that inspired these primitive Christian believers. Not under the compulsion of a social compact or institution, but prompted simply by the spirit of their Master, "they called none of the things which they possessed their own, but shared all things with one another." The social ideals that Jesus had held up before his followers and tried to apply practically in the life of the closely knit community that lived around the northern shores of the Sea of Galilee were being realized. While his influence upon them was still freshest and strongest they literally did to others as they would have others do to them. What Luke records is simply a practical application of Jesus' social teachings. Undoubtedly the believers' expectation of the speedy second coming of their Master was also the background of this unique social life; but it is well that the Christian church has ever held up before it a concrete illustration of what the teachings of Jesus can do and yet will do for society, as well as for its individual citizens. Jesus saved Zaccheus, the tax collector of Jericho, by influencing him to give back in generous measure what he had stolen from society. Barnabas and other Jerusalem citizens like him represent a still higher stage in that socializing process which Jesus aimed to perfect in every man. The social leaven which he had implanted in the heart of Judaism was beginning to work silently but rapidly in an ever-widening circle.

VII. **The Story of Ananias and Sapphira.** This story has been regarded by many historians as apocryphal. In the form in which it has come to us tradition may have heightened certain details, as, for example, the immediate death of Ananias and Sapphira on the discovery of their deceit; or they may have been afflicted with acute heart-disease. One thing is certain: the narrative comes from one of the earlier sources, for it implicitly disproves the general statement of the editor that "the believers shared all they had with one another" (Acts 2^45). The apostles, like the ancient Hebrew prophets (e. g., Amos's doom upon Amaziah, Amos 7^17, or Isaiah's definite prediction of the fate of Shebna, Isaiah 22^15-19), appear to have proclaimed the doom awaiting especially guilty offenders. Thus Paul in I Corinthians 5^5 declared regarding a member of the Corinthian church who was guilty of gross social immorality: "By the power of our Lord Jesus Christ I here consign that individual to Satan for the destruction of his flesh in order that his spirit may be saved on the day of our Lord Jesus." The sin of Ananias and Sapphira appears to have been their attempt to deceive their fellow Christians by retaining part of the proceeds from the sale of the land which they had donated to the community. Confronted by this evidence of disloyalty to the teachings of Jesus, Peter could not have refrained from a scathing condemnation, and it could not have failed to make a profound impression upon the pathetic pair who were making such a disastrous attempt to serve both God and mammon. Whenever, whether at once or later, death overtook the culprits, it would be inevitably regarded as a divine judgment. It is important to note, however, that the story does not claim to recount a miracle; it simply aims to illustrate by contrast the powerful social spirit that inspired the Christian community and to point an exceedingly important moral.

VIII. **The Religious Life of the Jerusalem Christians.** Helpfulness, hopefulness, unselfishness, and joyfulness characterized the life of the early Jerusalem community. In the days immediately following the great revival at Pentecost it was in a very true sense a partial realization of Jesus' ideal of the Kingdom of God on earth. All its members were bound together by a common loyalty to their heavenly Father and a single-minded devotion to the ideals of their Master. Daily they worshipped together in the temple; each meal in their homes was apparently eaten in commemoration of their dead but risen Lord. Together they constituted one large family united by a spirit of good-will and generosity and the consciousness of a great mission. The beauty of their common life and the teachings of the apostles attracted many Jews to their ranks. The step for them was easy, for the Twelve had no thought of a break with Judaism. They regarded the scriptures of their race and the service of the temple as essential foundations of their faith. The new elements in their belief simply represented the last chapter in God's revelation to his people. Instead of separating from their fellow Jews, they sought to attract all members of their race to themselves, the true Israel. The idea of a mission to the Gentiles outside Judaism was equally alien to the thought of the Twelve, although they would doubtless have welcomed proselytes who came to them, even as did the strictest of the Jews. Acts 5^{12-16} suggests that in time they had fallen into an entanglement which Jesus in the early Galilean days had carefully avoided. The reputation which the apostles had gained through healing the lame man in the temple courts attracted to them credulous multitudes of men and women afflicted with physical and mental maladies. If the narrative be accepted as strictly historical, it is evident that this popular credulity passed over into superstition. It is significant that at this point the record of the successful preaching work of the Twelve in Jerusalem suddenly ceases. Henceforth the interest centres in the group of Hellenistic Jews, gifted with a larger outlook, whose work led ultimately to the breaking of Jewish bonds and the expansion of Christianity into a world religion. The important fact to be noted, however, is that the vital force in the life of the primitive church was not its ritual or its ceremonial forms but the common beliefs and the mutual love and spirit of service which bound all together into one great family and attracted to their ranks the many who felt the crying spiritual and social needs that Christianity, thus simply and concretely interpreted, was able to supply. The early Christian church was but an extension of the unique brotherhood which Jesus had established during his active Galilean days. What was true of Christianity at first has proved true throughout its history: its significant and lasting conquests have been won through the personal touch and through fellowship in faith, in love, and in service.

§ CXLVIII. THE WORK AND DEATH OF STEPHEN

Now during those days, when the disciples were increasing in number, the Hellenists (the Greek-speaking Jews) began to complain against the Hebrews (who were natives and residents in Palestine) because their widows were being overlooked in the daily distribution of food. Therefore the Twelve called together the main body of the disciples and said, It is not fitting that we should neglect preaching the word of God in order to serve meals. Brothers, select seven of your own number, men of good reputation, full of the Spirit and of wisdom, whom we will place in

The appointment of the seven (Acts 6^{1-6})

45

charge of this matter; but we will continue to devote ourselves to prayer and the ministry of the word. This plan
met with the approval of the whole body. Accordingly,
they chose Stephen, a man full of faith and the Holy Spirit,
Philip, Prochorus, Nicanor, Timon, Parmenas, and Nic-
olaüs, a proselyte from Antioch. These men they set before the apostles, who after praying laid their hands upon
them.

In-
crease
of dis-
ciples
(7)
The
charge
against
Ste-
phen
(8-14)
And the word of the Lord spread and the number of the
disciples in Jerusalem increased greatly and a large number
of priests became obedient to the faith.

Now Stephen, who was full of grace and power, performed
great wonders and miracles among the people. But some
of those who belonged to the so-called synagogue of the
Libyians and Cyrenians and the Alexandrians, and also the
natives of Cilicia and the Roman province of Asia began
to dispute with Stephen, and they were not able to meet
the wisdom and spirit with which he spoke. Then they
instigated certain men to say, We have heard him speaking blasphemous words against Moses and God. Thus
they stirred up the people, the elders and the scribes so
that they rushed upon him and seized him and took him
before the Sanhedrin. They also set up false witnesses
who said, This man never ceases talking against this holy
place and the law. Indeed we have heard him say that
this Jesus the Nazarene will destroy this place and change
the customs handed down to us by Moses!

His
address
before
the
Sanhe-
drin
(6¹⁵-7⁵,
8b')
Then all who were seated in the Sanhedrin fixed their
eyes on him and saw that his face shone like the face of an
angel. But the high priest said, Are these things so?
Stephen replied, Brothers and fathers, listen: The God of
glory appeared to our father Abraham while he was still in
Mesopotamia, before he dwelt in Haran, and said to him,
' Go forth from thy land and from thy kinsmen and come to
the land which I will show thee.' Then, leaving the land
of the Chaldeans, he stayed in Haran. After his father's
death, God moved him into this land where you now dwell.
But he did not give him any inheritance in it nor even a
foot of land. He did, however, promise that he would give
it as a possession to him and to his descendants after him,

46

although as yet he was childless. So Abraham became the father of Isaac, whom he circumcised on the eighth day. And Isaac was the father of Jacob, and Jacob of the twelve patriarchs.

And the patriarchs were jealous of Joseph and sold him into Egypt. But God was with him and delivered him out of all his troubles and gave him favor and wisdom in the presence of Pharaoh, king of Egypt, who appointed him governor over Egypt and over all his own household. But a famine came over the whole land of Egypt and Canaan and great misery so that our forefathers could find no food. But Jacob, hearing that there was food in Egypt, sent our forefathers there for the first time. And on their second visit, Joseph made himself known to his brothers, and Pharaoh was informed regarding Joseph's lineage. Then Joseph sent and invited his father Jacob and all his family, amounting to seventy-five persons. So Jacob went down into Egypt. *God's leadership of the people by Joseph (9-15a)*

But as the time drew near for the fulfilment of the promise made to Abraham, the people grew and multiplied in Egypt, until another king arose in Egypt who knew not Joseph. He, adopting a crafty policy toward our race, oppressed our forefathers by making them expose their infants so that they might not live. At this time Moses was born, a divinely beautiful child, and for three months he was cared for in his father's house. Then he was exposed but Pharaoh's daughter adopted him and brought him up as her own son. So Moses was educated in all the learning of the Egyptians and was a man strong in speech and action. When he had completed his fortieth year, it occurred to him to visit his kinsmen, the children of Israel. Seeing one of them being unjustly treated, he took his part and avenged the man who was being unjustly treated by striking down the Egyptian. He supposed that his kinsmen knew that by him God was going to bring them deliverance: but they did not understand. Next day he came upon two of them fighting. And he tried to make peace between them, saying, 'Men, you are brothers! Why injure one another?' But the man who was injuring his neighbor pushed him away, saying, 'Who made you ruler *Their deliverance by Moses (17-37)* and judge over us? Do you want to kill me as you killed the Egyptian yesterday?' At this speech Moses fled and became a resident alien in the land of Midian, where he became the father of two sons. At the close of forty years an angel appeared to him in the flame of a burning thorn bush in the wilderness of Mount Sinai. When Moses saw this he marvelled at the sight; but as he went up to look at it, the voice of the Lord said, 'I am the God of your fathers, the God of Abraham and Isaac and Jacob.' Trembling with fear, Moses did not dare to look. And the Lord said to him, 'Take thy sandals off thy feet, for the place where thou art standing is sacred ground. I have indeed seen the oppression of my people in Egypt. I have heard their groans and I have come down to deliver them. Come now, I will send thee back to Egypt.' That Moses whom they rejected, saying, 'Who made you a ruler and judge over us?'—that was the very man whom God sent to rule and redeem them by the help of the angel who appeared to him in the bush. He it was who led them forth, doing wonders and signs in the land of Egypt, at the Red Sea, and in the wilderness for forty years. This is the Moses who said to the children of Israel, 'God will raise up a prophet for you from among your brotherhood, as he raised me.'

Their rebellion in the wilderness (38-42)
This was the man who at the assembly in the wilderness intervened between the angel who spoke to him on Mount Sinai and our fathers; he received living words to be given to us. But our forefathers would not submit to him, but pushed him aside and in their hearts hankered for Egypt. They said to Aaron, ' Make for us gods that they may march in front of us! As for this Moses who led us out of Egypt, we do not know what has become of him!' Moreover they made a calf in those days, offered sacrifice to this idol, and rejoiced over what their own hands had made. So God turned from them and gave them up to the worship of the host of heaven.

God's provision for their worship (44-50)
In the wilderness our forefathers had the tent of testimony, made as he who spoke to Moses had instructed him to make it after the pattern he had seen. This also our forefathers in their turn brought in with Joshua when they took possession of the territory of the nations whom God

48

drove out before them. So it remained until the days of David. He found favor with God and asked that he might provide a dwelling for the God of Jacob. But it was Solomon who built him a house.

Yet the Most High doth not dwell in houses made with hands. As the prophet says:

Heaven is my throne,
And the earth is a footstool for my feet!
What kind of house will ye build for me, saith the Lord?
Or what resting place shall I have?
Did not my hand make all this?

Stiff-necked and uncircumcised in heart and ears, you are always resisting the Holy Spirit! As with your forefathers, so with you! Which of the prophets did your forefathers not persecute? They also killed those who announced beforehand the coming of the Just One, whose betrayers and murderers you have become—you who received the law given through angels and yet have not obeyed it!

The defiant, unreceptive attitude of the Jews (51-53)

When they heard this they were furious and gnashed their teeth at him. But he, full of the Holy Spirit, gazed up into heaven and saw the glory of God and Jesus standing at the right hand of God. Behold, I see heaven open, he said, and the Son of Man standing at the right hand of God. But they with a loud shriek shut their ears and rushed at him in a body. Dragging him outside the city, they stoned him. And the witnesses laid their clothes at the feet of a youth called Saul. So they stoned Stephen while he prayed, Lord Jesus receive my spirit! Then kneeling down he cried with a loud voice, Lord, let not this sin stand against them! And when he had said this, he fell asleep. But certain devout men buried Stephen and made loud lamentation over him.

Stephen's death (7⁵⁴-⁶⁰, 8²)

I. The Story of Stephen's Martyrdom. This story marks an important stage in the history of the Apostolic Age. It contains the first suggestion of a rift between the Jewish and Hellenistic elements in the Jewish Christian community. The only explanation of its presence in a writing, the irenical purpose of which is so evident as that of Acts, is that the narrative was originally drawn from an older and probably written source. The facts presented in this narrative have only the most general and loose relation to those found in the preceding chapters. The speech attributed to Stephen in chapter 7 is also the longest in the book. Its thought and argument have no close parallel in the New Testament except in the book of Hebrews. It is clearly the work of a Jew familiar with the contemporary rabbinical interpretations of the older scriptures. Thus, for example, it is stated that an angel spoke to Moses on Mount Sinai and that the law was ordained by angels (Acts 7[38, 53]). These are details of later Jewish tradition which would naturally be unknown to a Greek like Luke, except as he found them incorporated in some earlier source. Furthermore, the discourse attributed to Stephen is not closely connected with its context. It is not so much a defense as a part of a discussion such as Stephen is reported (in Acts 6[9, 10]) to have carried on in the synagogues of the Greek-speaking Jews. The only satisfactory explanation of its presence is that it was preserved and associated with the name of Stephen. These and other reasons indicate that this story of his martyrdom is one of the oldest narratives in the first part of the book of Acts. It certainly furnishes invaluable data for the interpretation of this great turning-point in the life of the early Christian community.

II. **The Appointment of the Seven.** The dramatic account of the day of Pentecost implies that many Jews of the dispersion were early attracted to the Christian community. This conclusion is confirmed by Acts 6. It was natural that the teachings and principles of Jesus should appeal more strongly to the Hellenistic Jews (that is, to the Greek-speaking Jews who had been born and reared beyond the bounds of Palestine) than to those of Palestine. Their contact with the larger Greek world had opened their minds to new truths and had developed a receptive attitude. As a whole, they were mentally more alert and better educated. Throughout all their history the Jews of the dispersion had shown themselves more friendly toward new ideas. Thus, for example, they alone accepted the so-called apocryphal books of the Old Testament, while the Palestinian Jews rejected them from their canon. Some of these Hellenistic Jews were probably temporary residents in Jerusalem, simply as pilgrims, while others, having acquired a competence, had returned, like many of the Jews to be found in Jerusalem to-day, to spend the remainder of their life under the shadow of the temple. The Jews of Palestine, on the other hand, were, as a rule, self-satisfied and inclined to look down upon the other members of their race, whom they regarded as contaminated by contact with the heathen and by long residence in foreign lands. They also viewed askance their more tolerant attitude toward Greek culture and life and the customs of the outside world. It was probably this inherited and inbred attitude that led the Palestinian Jewish Christians to neglect the needy members of the Hellenistic group. The apostles' evident ignorance of this tendency indicates that the neglect was the fault of the humbler members of the community, to whom was doubtless intrusted the task of serving food. Such differences are often more marked the lower the individuals stand in the social scale. The evil was sufficient, however, to attract the attention of the leaders in the Hellenistic group and to induce them to lay the matter before the Twelve. When it was brought to their attention, they settled it in the fairest and simplest way. They rightly maintained that they themselves should not neglect their work of preaching to serve tables. Accordingly they requested the Hellenists to select seven of their most reliable and spiritually minded leaders to look out for the interests of their group. This proposal was commended by the entire Christian community. The method adopted in meeting this difficulty also illustrates the democratic spirit that actuated the Christian believers in all their relations with each other.

The Greek names of the seven, as well as the narrative, indicate that they were probably all Hellenistic Jews by birth. It is a mistake to regard them as the prototypes of the later order of deacons. Rather they appear to have been a committee appointed to represent the Hellenistic group in the Christian community in very much the same way as the apostles represented the Palestinian group. They were chosen apparently not because of their age but for their ability. Their appointment did not establish a new office but rather met practically a pressing need. As the event proved, the men appointed were of such signal ability that they soon showed themselves qualified to do far more than serve tables. Certain of them soon surpassed the Twelve as preachers and controversialists and won a leading place among the apostles who proclaimed the teachings and works of Jesus to the Jewish and Gentile world. Their appointment is a convincing proof that the rift between the Palestinian and Hellenistic Jews, even within the Christian community, was practically inevitable, and that it was recognized long before Paul entered upon his campaign to liberate Gentile Christians from Jewish bonds.

III. **Stephen's Discussions with the Hellenistic Jews.** It is difficult to determine how much time is represented by the narrative of Acts 6 and 7. It may have been a year or more. During this period Stephen had evidently become the recognized leader and spokesman of the seven and had developed an apostolic ability which for a time even eclipsed that of Peter himself. There was apparently a tacit and amicable division of the field between the Twelve and the seven. Stephen worked where the Twelve were only partially effective, that is, among the Hellenistic Jews. The narrative indicates that, instead of confining his speeches to the temple courts, he went into their synagogues, not to preach but, after the method so much beloved by the Greeks, to engage in open discussion with their elders. The fact that he first entered the synagogues whose membership was made up of Hellenists from the Jewish colonies in northern Africa suggests that Stephen himself came originally from that part of the Roman world. This inference is strongly supported by the marked peculiarity and style of thought reflected in the speech attributed to him and recorded in Acts 7, for they are found only in writings that show the influence of Alexandria. It is exceedingly probable that in the synagogue of the Cilicians he first met, possibly in open discussion, a certain Jew from the Cilician city of Tarsus by the name of Paul. The line of reasoning which Stephen adopted is doubtless represented by the discourse in chapter 7. Starting with Jewish premises, he aimed to show the logical connection with and yet the superiority of the teachings and work of Jesus to those of the earlier teachers of his race. Apparently he triumphed over his opponents. He also aroused the bitter opposition of many of the Hellenists, so that in their rage they charged him with blasphemy. It was a charge which always stirred the wrath of the Jews. Not only did it enrage the mass of the people but evidently kindled the indignation of the Pharisaic leaders. Thus reinforced, the Hellenistic Jews lodged a definite charge against him before the national Jewish council, the Sanhedrin, before which cases of heresy were tried. The final form of the charge that they preferred against him was that his teachings had been hostile to the Jewish temple and law: "that Jesus the Nazarene will destroy this place and change the customs handed down to us by Moses." Evidently this was a popular interpretation of the intent of Stephen's teachings. It implies that he had quoted Jesus' words about the temple recorded in Mark 13[1, 2]. The discourse which follows suggests the ultimate basis of their charge. Like Jesus, Stephen aimed not to destroy the law but to show that his

DISCUSSIONS WITH THE JEWS

Master's work represented its logical fruition. This charge also suggests what would have been the conclusion of Stephen's address had not the stones flung by the infuriated mob forever interrupted it.

IV. **The Logic of Stephen's Speech.** The speech attributed to Stephen in Acts 7 is not a formal defense but a résumé of his teachings. Its logical connection is not always obvious and a certain typological undercurrent runs through it which is closely related to the contemporary writings emanating from the Alexandrian school. Its free interpretation of history and the use of scripture also recall the methods of the rabbis. He first reminds the Jews of how God called their forefather Abraham and guided their ancestors through countless perils that their descendants might ultimately realize their divine destiny. Each prophet and deliverer was a type of the deliverer that was ultimately to be revealed. The different physical resting-places to which he led his people, and, above all, the land of Canaan, were symbolic of the ultimate rest prepared for those who trust him. The tabernacle and the temple with their formal service were but primitive types of the real heavenly dwelling-place of the Almighty. Through all these various experiences God had been seeking to train his people for the reception of a greater truth, but they had consistently proved stubborn and irreceptive, resisting the influences of his Spirit. Not only they, but the men who stood before him were more intent upon persecuting and killing the prophets than of learning and accepting their messages. Little wonder then that when the Just One announced by all earlier prophets and the culmination of God's process of revelation came to them they betrayed and murdered him, for they had disobeyed the law and the divine revelation which it embodied.

It is evident that Stephen was not conscious of repudiating the Jewish law and temple ritual. Rather, like the ethical prophets of old, he felt that he was simply emphasizing their spiritual teachings. Far from desiring to bring about a breach between Judaism and Christianity, he was, like the Twelve, trying to lead the Jews to accept the teachings and work of their greatest prophet and their promised Messiah. Jesus, in the thought of Stephen, was the Just One toward whom all their earlier leaders and experiences had pointed.

V. **The Death of Stephen.** In the death of Stephen primitive Christianity lost one of its greatest interpreters. A first-hand impression of his character and work is probably preserved in Acts 6[15b]. As he stood before the hostile members of the Sanhedrin, they saw that "his face shone like the face of an angel." It is a dramatic and significant fact that Acts in its account of the martyrdom has brought Paul and Stephen together, and has left us to infer that the divine light that shone from Stephen's dying eyes proved the foregleams of the divine effulgence that beamed upon Paul on his memorable journey a little later to Damascus. Stephen manifested the same tireless energy, the same boldness, and the same utter disregard of opposition and pain as did Paul. Like Paul, his logic was destined in the end to break the narrow bonds of Judaism, though he appears to have been unconscious of that fact. If he had lived, the later history of Palestinian Christianity would probably have been very different. Certainly the break with narrow Judaistic Christianity would have come much earlier. Stephen in his preaching laid the foundations for the world-wide expansion of Christianity. In his work among the Jews of the dispersion resident at Jerusalem he apparently kindled the fire of Christianity which before long flamed up in the far-away cities of northern Africa and western Syria. Fortunately, in a very real sense the mantle which slipped from Stephen's shoulders fell upon Paul. Like Jesus, Stephen in certain ways accomplished more by his martyrdom than he did while living. Again the age-long principle was illustrated that, if a man gives his life for a cause, no one can gainsay the sincerity of his testimony. The death of Stephen was well calculated to make an indelible impression upon all who witnessed or heard of it. The narrative of Acts implies that as he was dying there was given to him one of the many visions of the risen Christ which had characterized and inspired the activity of the early Christians. His words remain the only direct testimony we have regarding the exact nature of these visions: "Behold I see heaven open and the Son of Man standing at God's right hand."

§ CXLIX. THE EXPANSION OF CHRISTIANITY AFTER THE DEATH OF STEPHEN

The scattering of the Christians (Acts 8[1b, 4]) On the day when Stephen was stoned to death a great persecution broke out against the church in Jerusalem, and all except the apostles were scattered throughout Judea and Samaria. And those who were scattered went in different directions preaching the gospel.

Philip travelled down to the city of Samaria, where he preached Christ to them. And the crowds attended with one accord to what was said by Philip, listening to him and seeing the miracles he performed. For unclean spirits came with a loud cry out of many who had been possessed, and many paralytics and lame people were healed. So there was great joy in that city.

Now for some time past a man named Simon had been practising magic arts in the city and astonishing the Samaritans, pretending he was a great person. And all sorts and conditions of people attached themselves to him, saying, This one is that Power of God which is known as 'The Great Power.' They attached themselves to him because he had amazed them for a considerable time with his magic skill. But when they believed Philip, who preached the Kingdom of God and the name of Jesus, they had themselves baptized, both men and women. Simon himself also believed, and after being baptized kept close to Philip and was astonished to see the signs and great miracles which were performed.

When the apostles at Jerusalem heard that Samaria had accepted the word of God, they sent to them Peter and John, who came down and prayed that they might receive the Holy Spirit, for it had not yet fallen upon any of them. They had simply been baptized in the name of the Lord Jesus. Then they laid their hands on them and they received the Holy Spirit. But when Simon saw that the Holy Spirit was conferred by the laying on of the apostles' hands, he brought them money, saying, Give me, too, this power, so that anyone on whom I lay my hands may receive the Holy Spirit. Peter said to him, May your money and you perish for supposing that you could buy the gift of God! You have no share nor lot in this religion, for your heart is not right in the sight of God. So repent of this wickedness of yours and pray to the Lord in the hope that your heart's purpose may be forgiven. For I see that you are a bitter poison and a pack of evil. Simon replied, Pray the Lord for me. Pray that nothing you have said may befall me.

So the apostles after bearing their testimony to the word of the Lord and preaching it, returned to Jerusalem preaching the gospel to a number of the Samaritan villages. But the angel of the Lord said to Philip, Rise and go south, along the road from Jerusalem to Gaza (this is the desert route). So he arose and went on his way. Now there was an Ethiopian eunuch, a high official of Candace the queen of the Ethiopians, who was her chief treasurer and had come to Jerusalem for worship but was on his way home. And as he was sitting in his chariot, he was reading the prophet Isaiah. Then the Spirit said to Philip, Go up and join that chariot. And as Philip ran up he heard him reading the prophet Isaiah. Do you understand what you are reading, he asked. How can I, said the eunuch, unless someone guide me? And he begged Philip to get up and sit beside him. Now the passage of scripture which he was reading was this:

> He was led like a sheep to slaughter,
> And as a lamb is dumb before the shearer,
> So he opened not his lips.
> Who will make known his generation.
> In his humiliation the justice due him was taken away,
> For his life is cut off from the earth.

So the eunuch said to Philip, Pray, of whom is the prophet speaking? Of himself or of someone else? Then Philip opened his mouth, and starting from this scripture preached the gospel of Jesus to him. As they proceeded on their way, they came to some water, and the eunuch said, there is water! What is to prevent me being baptized? So he ordered the chariot to stop, and both of them stepped into the water, and Philip baptized the eunuch. When they came up from the water, the Spirit of the Lord caught Philip away, and the eunuch saw him no longer, for he was proceeding on his way rejoicing. But Philip found himself at Azotus and he passed on, preaching the gospel in every town, until he reached Cæsarea.

Preaching the gospel to the Greeks at Antioch (11¹⁹. ²⁰, ²⁴, ²⁶b)　Now those who had been scattered by the trouble which arose over Stephen made their way as far as Phœnicia and Cyprus and Antioch, preaching the word to none except Jews. But some of them were citizens of Cyprus and Cyrene, who on reaching Antioch began preaching to the Greeks also the gospel of the Lord Jesus and considerable numbers were brought in for the Lord. In Antioch also the disciples were first called Christians.

56

Now about that time King Herod laid violent hands on some members of the church. James the brother of John he slew with the sword. Seeing that this was pleasing to the Jews, he went on to seize Peter during the days of unleavened bread. After arresting him, he put him in prison, handing him over to a guard of sixteen soldiers with the intention after the passover to bring him out to the people. So Peter was kept in prison under guard; but earnest prayer for him was offered to God by the church. Herod's persecution of the apostles (12¹⁻⁵)

Now on the very night when Herod was about to lead him forth Peter lay asleep between two soldiers, bound by two chains, with guards keeping watch before the door. And behold an angel of the Lord stood before him and a light shone in the cell; and striking Peter on the side he woke him and said, Rise quickly! And the fetters fell from his hands. Then the angel said to him, Gird yourself and put on your sandals, and he did so. Then said the angel, Throw your cloak about you and follow me. So Peter followed him out not knowing that what the angel was doing was real, but supposing that he saw a vision. When they had passed the first guard and the second, they came to the iron gate leading into the city, which opened to them of its own accord. Then passing out they proceeded through one street, when suddenly the angel left him. Peter, coming to himself, said, Now I know for certain that the Lord hath sent his angel and delivered me from the hand of Herod and from all that the Jewish people were anticipating. When he appreciated this he went to the house of Mary, the mother of John who was surnamed Mark, where a number had assembled and were praying. When he knocked at the door of the porch, a maidservant named Rhoda came to answer it, and as soon as she recognized Peter's voice, she did not open the door because of her joy, but ran and told them that Peter was standing in front of the porch. They said to her, You are mad; but she insisted that it was so. It is his angel, they said. But Peter kept on knocking. And when they opened the door they knew that it was he and were amazed. But he beckoned to them with his hand to be silent and described to them how the Lord had brought him out of prison. He Peter's escape (6-19a)

57

also said, Tell this to James and to the brothers. Then going forth, he went to another place. Now at daybreak there was no little commotion among the soldiers over what could have become of Peter. And when Herod had searched for him and could not find him after cross-questioning the guards, he ordered them away to execution.

Her-
od's
death
(19b-23)

Then Herod went down from Judea to Cæsarea and spent some time there. As he was highly incensed against the inhabitants of Tyre and Sidon, they waited on him unanimously and after having secured the good will of Blastus his chamberlain they begged the king to make peace with them for their country was dependent upon his for its food-supply. So, on an appointed day, Herod, having arrayed himself in royal robes, took his seat on the tribunal and was haranguing them. And the people kept shouting, It is the voice of a god and not of a man. Instantly an angel of the Lord struck him, because he had not given due glory to God, and, being eaten by up worms, he died.

I. The Far-Reaching Effects of Stephen's Martyrdom.

The death of Stephen inaugurated a new era in the evolution of primitive Christianity. In its background and its influence this period corresponds in many ways to the Babylonian exile out of which Judaism developed. It represented the beginning of the absolute breach between Judaism and Christianity and the birth of the Christian church as an organization independent of the Jewish temple and law. This fact was not suspected by the Palestinian Christians represented by the Twelve, who still clung to the Jewish rites. As a result, they do not appear to have been driven from Jerusalem nor to have been troubled by persecution. From Acts 8[1, 14] and Galatians 1[18] it is evident that, if they left Jerusalem at all, they soon returned to make it their permanent home. Only the Hellenistic Christians, those who had been born in the land of the dispersion and who, like Stephen, interpreted Christianity in its larger meaning, were branded as heretics by the Jews and made the object of their bitter persecution. Some were imprisoned (Acts 8[3]), others publicly beaten in the Jewish synagogues (Acts 26[11]), while others, like Stephen, suffered martyrdom (Acts 26[10]). This bitter persecution extended even to the cities outside of Jerusalem and appears to have been chiefly instigated by Hellenistic Jews, of whom Paul of Tarsus was one of the most active leaders.

EFFECTS OF STEPHEN'S MARTYRDOM

The second effect of the martyrdom of Stephen was the extension of the work of the Hellenistic Christian leaders like Philip beyond the narrow bounds of Judaism. Now began that world expansion of Christianity which Luke has dramatically recorded in the book of Acts. Hitherto the followers of Jesus have been content to remain in Jerusalem awaiting his miraculous return, but now the Hellenistic Christians took up anew his preaching mission. Many of them simply returned to their homes in the great commercial centres along the eastern Mediterranean, carrying with them the spirit and teachings of their Master. Thus Christianity, fanned into a flame by persecution, spread northward and westward along the great highways, kindling its fires in the chief cities of that ancient world. Each returning Jewish Christian became a missionary as opportunity offered. Experience soon proved, even as it had in Jerusalem, that the leaven which Jesus placed in the centre of Judaism was even more effective among the peoples living beyond the immediate pale of the temple than in Jerusalem itself.

The third effect of this first great Christian dispersion was the rapid transformation of the Palestinian type of Christianity when transplanted in new soil. It is difficult to predict what would have become of Stephen and those who accepted his point of view if they had remained under the shadow of the Jewish temple and under the influence of the conservative Palestinian Christian community. But, released from the bonds of Judaism and in close contact with the broadening influences of the Græco-Roman world, they developed the type of faith which was destined to overleap all barriers and to interpret the simple teachings and spirit of Jesus in terms intelligible to all mankind.

II. **The Samaritan Field.** There were many reasons why the Samaritan field was favorable for early Christian missionary activity. Notwithstanding the bitter fraternal hatred with which the Jews regarded the Samaritans, they looked upon them very differently than they did upon the heathen. The Jews despised the Samaritans because their forefathers had freely intermarried with the heathen, because they had shown themselves ready at all times to accept Greek and Roman culture, and because, in accepting simply the Pentateuch as their scriptures, they represented an arrested stage of spiritual, religious, and moral development. And yet even the strictest Pharisee did not object to eating with a Samaritan. Common traditions, institutions, and worship bound the two peoples together. Each shared the hopes of a coming Messiah. Jesus had set the example to his followers of freely associating with the Samaritans and even of preaching and ministering to them. Above all, in one of his great parables he had singled out a Samaritan as a supreme example of neighborliness. The Samaritans were on the whole much more open-minded and tolerant than the Jews. Samaria, therefore, was a field which appealed strongly to a Hellenistic Christian like Philip.

III. **The Results of Philip's Preaching in Samaria.** Philip's Greek name suggests that he was a Hellenist, as does also his place among the seven appointed to guard the interests of the Hellenistic section of the Jerusalem church. Acts 21[8] states that his home was in Cæsarea, a strong Græco-Roman city. Apparently his teachings stood midway between those of the native Judaizing Christians and those of the extreme Hellenists. The content of his teaching, as well as the fact that he was a resident of Palestine, strongly point to the conclusion that he had personally seen and heard Jesus. Later Christian tradition even confuses him with Philip the disciple. Another tradition makes him one of the Seventy, who, according to Luke's later version of the sending out of the Twelve, were commanded to proclaim the Gospel to the people. This tradition is probably based on the fact that Philip's teachings and method of work closely resemble those adopted by Jesus during his Galilean ministry. According to the testimony of Acts, Philip alone of all the apostolic teachers made the Gospel of the Kingdom of God central in his preaching. To this he added "the Gospel of the Name of Jesus" (Acts 8[12]). In the light of the teachings of the earlier apostles, it is evident that this peculiar phrase refers to the primitive interpretation of the character and messianic work of Jesus. With the aid of these meagre records, it is possible to reconstruct partially at least the content of Philip's addresses. Evidently his preaching consisted chiefly in a reiteration of the teachings of Jesus. On his lips may well have been preserved many of the matchless parables of the kingdom which reappear only in Luke's gospel.

The scene of his work was apparently the city of Samaria itself, the metropolis and capital of the province which bore that name. Herod the Great had encircled the hill on which this ancient city rested with a great highway, flanked on either side by stately colonnades. The top of the hill he had crowned with a great temple dedicated to Augustus, the foundations of which have only recently been laid bare. Philip had evidently stopped at this centre of Samaritan life on his way back to his home at Cæsarea, for the city of Samaria lay on the main highway which led northward and westward from Jerusalem to the sea. The Samaritans throughout their later history showed themselves a simple, childlike people, especially superstitious and susceptible to suggestion. Philip's teaching, like that of Jesus at certain periods of his ministry, was accompanied by acts of healing which appealed powerfully to the multitudes. Those who accepted his teachings were baptized. Thus Philip developed a new and effective type of evangelism which combined the teachings of Jesus and the methods of John the Baptist with a supreme devotion to the Master and the declaration that he was the fulfilment of the messianic hopes which the Samaritans shared in common with their Jewish brothers.

The passage in Acts 8^{14-25} seems to imply that the people of Samaria as a whole had been converted and that the apostles Peter and John came as the official representatives of the Jerusalem church to receive these new converts into its membership. The inference that this apostolic sanction was necessary reflects strongly the point of view and conceptions which first became prevalent during the latter part of the first Christian century. The older record implies that Philip's work was spontaneous, almost accidental, and that the results were themselves sufficient evidence of divine approval. If the apostles came to Samaria attracted by the success of his work, they probably came not in an official capacity but as fellow workers. To the same later churchly tendency is doubtless due the theory that the Holy Spirit came to the Samaritans only as a result of the laying on of the apostles' hands.

The underlying purpose of the story in Acts, however, is to illustrate the significant fact that, although Christianity doubtless often attracted impostors, its innate moral and spiritual character quickly revealed what was spurious. Philip's work among the Samaritans was new evidence of the potency and adaptability of the Gospel of Jesus and of the Gospel about Jesus that was being rapidly formulated by his followers. There was nothing in Philip's work to arouse even the most conservative Jewish Christians; and yet the prominence which the narrator gave to Philip's mission to the Samaritans indicates that it represented an important stage in the expansion of Christianity. It was apparently not in itself permanent and far-reaching largely because of the fickle character of the Samaritans. Possibly it was also because neither Philip nor Peter had Paul's organizing and pastoral skill.

IV. Philip's Conversation with the Ethiopian Eunuch. The early apostles inherited from the Hebrew prophets and from Jesus the consciousness of acting at each important crisis in their lives under direct divine guidance. This conviction is everywhere apparent, not only in Acts but in the writings of Paul. The terms by which this guidance is described vary, as in the present narrative. In Acts 8[26] it is stated that an angel of the Lord gave the command to Philip. In [29] it is simply the Spirit, and in [39] the Spirit of the Lord that directed his evangelistic activity. In each case the impulse evidently came from within. The account of Philip's memorable conversation with the Ethiopian eunuch implies that the impulse to follow him came after the evangelist had already returned with the apostles to Jerusalem. The visit of a prominent proselyte, such as the treasurer of Candace, the queen of the Ethiopians, to Jerusalem must have been quickly known to all of its inhabitants. Doubtless as a worshipper he also brought rich gifts to the temple. Ethiopia was the vast, mysterious region to the south of Egypt, whence in the days of Augustus had emerged a queen by the name of Candace who had attempted to drive the Romans out of the Thebiad, but who had been defeated by the Roman general Petronius in 24 B.C. and her capital, Meroë, captured. According to the testimony of Pliny the name Candace was regularly borne by the queens of Ethiopia, and probably corresponded to the Egyptian term Pharaoh. As early as 300 B.C. Greek culture had penetrated Ethiopia, and this fact explains how the Ethiopian eunuch was able to read the Greek version of the Old Testament which Philip found in his hands. It also reveals the influences which led him to make a pilgrimage of fully one thousand miles to the Jewish sanctuary at Jerusalem.

The fact that he was reading from Isaiah 53[7, 8], which describes the suffering of Jehovah's servant, and questioning the meaning of this passage, strongly suggests that while at Jerusalem he had come in contact with the teachings of the apostles and their interpretation of this passage as a direct reference to Jesus. A knowledge of this fact may well have come to Philip and, if so, it constituted one of the chief elements in the impulse which led him to follow the returning pilgrim. It was a case which must have appealed strongly to Philip's instincts as an evangelist. A late tradition places the spring where the Ethiopian official was baptized on the narrow road, practically impassable for chariots, which leads southwestward from Jerusalem. An older and more probable tradition, however, identifies it with the copious spring a little north of Bethzur on the main road southward through Hebron and Gaza. The latter corresponds more perfectly to the desert road definitely mentioned in Acts 8[26]. In a mind already prepared Philip sowed the seeds of the Gospel and thereby added to the rapidly growing ranks of the believers one whose influence may go far to explain why before the end of the first Christian century in distant Abyssinia there was a strong and flourishing Christian community. The conversion and baptism of the Ethiopian was not contrary to the narrow traditions accepted by the Palestinian Christians, for, as a proselyte, he had already been accepted within the ranks of Judaism. The incident, however, represents the gradual opening of the door to the Gentiles and was evidently reported for this reason.

With the true spirit of the evangelist, Philip, as he set out again for his home at Cæsarea, stopped at Azotus on the coast, about twenty miles north of Gaza, and at the other towns on his way and preached the Gospel at every point until he finally carried it to his home city.

V. **The Spread of Christianity to Antioch.** The interest of the author of Acts 2[1]–15[36] in Paul and Peter led him to introduce immediately after the story of Philip's baptism of the Ethiopian eunuch the accounts of the way in which these two leading apostles were divinely led to see that God's gracious purpose included Gentiles as well as Jews. In developing the symmetrical plan of his history, the author recorded the mission of the apostles first to the Jews, then to the Samaritans, then to the Gentiles. Out of deference to Paul and Peter and in keeping with his point of view, it was also natural that he should give Paul and Peter the precedence; although Acts 9[31] plainly states that the events underlying the account of Peter's vision and baptism of the Roman centurion Cornelius were not immediately after the death of Stephen but during a period of peace, after the church had been extended widely "all over Judea, Galilee, and Samaria." Fortunately, however, Luke has cited definite evidence of what Paul states in his letter to the Galatians (cf. 2[8, 9]), namely, that the pioneer in proclaiming Jesus to the Gentiles was not Peter. It was not even Paul but certain Hellenistic Christians, natives of Cyprus and Cyrene, who at Antioch, soon after the death of Stephen, "told the Greeks also the Gospel of the Lord Jesus." This reading is supported by excellent texts and is clearly implied by the context, although in the accepted version it reads *Hellenists* (Greek-speaking Jews) instead of *Hellenes* (Greeks). Probably Luke wrote *Hellenists*, although his source read *Hellenes*. It was this significant step in the extension of Christianity to the whole world which led the author to add in Acts 11[22, 23] that, when the news of this preaching of the Gospel to the Gentiles reached the church in Jerusalem "they despatched Barnabas to Antioch. When he came and saw the grace of God he rejoiced and encouraged them all to remain loyal to the Lord with hearty purpose, for he was a good man, full of the Holy Spirit and faith." The narrator has apparently forgotten for the moment that Barnabas was a Hellenist and therefore among those who had fled from Jerusalem after Stephen's martyrdom. The next verse, evidently quoted from an early source, states that "Barnabas went off to Tarsus to look for Saul." Barnabas was the leading spirit in the Antioch church. It is exceedingly probable that this Cypriot was the leader of "the citizens of Cyprus" who first preached the Gospel to the Greeks. Lucius, another leader at Antioch, was a native of Cyrene (Acts 13[1]). To these generous, noble-hearted Hellenistic Jews, Barnabas and Lucius, beyond reasonable doubt belongs the honor of first breaking the bonds of Judaism and of establishing the important precedents which Paul later made an accepted principle.

While Jerusalem was the first home of Christianity, profligate, cosmopolitan Antioch was the birthplace and cradle of Gentile Christianity from which it radiated to all the great cities of the Graeco-Roman world. It is significant that here the followers of Jesus, who had hitherto called themselves "brothers" or "believers" or "the saints" and by the Jews had been known as the "Nazarenes" or "the sect of the Nazarenes," were first called Christians. The presence of Greeks in the ranks of the new sect called for a broader designation. The term is akin to those which the Greeks of Asia coined to designate different parties, so that there is little doubt of its Hellenistic and Antiochian origin. It also indicates that the Christians of Antioch used the Greek language (for Christ is the Greek equivalent of the Hebrew word Messiah) and that the doctrine that Jesus was the promised Messiah was a distinctive element in their teaching.

Thus within less than five years after the death of Jesus his teachings had overleaped the narrow bounds of Judaism and Palestine and were the accepted rule of life for a large body of Gentiles as well as Jews in the ancient capital city of Antiochus Epiphanes, the arch-persecutor of the Jewish race. From the first the Antioch church appears to have been strong in numbers and leadership and to have almost overshadowed the Jerusalem community. The gifts of the Antioch Christians at the time of the great famine of 46 A.D. still further strengthened their position.

VI. The Persecution of the Jerusalem Christians by Herod Agrippa I. Luke or an earlier editor has arranged his material in Acts 9–12 not chronologically but according to a definite plan. Thus the account of the famine of 46 A.D. is introduced in 11²⁷⁻²⁹ before the record in 12¹⁻²³ of the persecutions instigated by Herod Agrippa, which culminated in the death of James the apostle, probably at the Passover of 44 A.D. The editor's object is to complete his history of the Jerusalem church that he may devote the remainder of his narrative to a detailed account of Paul's missionary work. He also aims to give to the apostle Peter the prominence that he deemed fitting. To this end he introduces the popular stories in Acts 9³¹–11¹⁸, which represent Peter as a pioneer in proclaiming the Gospel to the Gentiles, before the record of Paul's first missionary campaign.

The first persecution of the Christians was about 32 A.D. and was directed chiefly against the Hellenistic Christians. In the second persecution of 44 the chief victims were the Twelve and especially James, the son of Zebedee, and Peter. The years 41–44 were a bright spot in the otherwise gloomy, tempestuous history of Judaism under the rule of Rome. Among the profligate princes who had been educated at the imperial city was a son of Aristobulus, the ill-fated offspring of the marriage of Herod the Great with Mariamne the Maccabean princess. Herod Agrippa I was therefore not only a grandson of Herod the Great but also a prince of the Jewish royal line. As a youth at Rome, he had plunged deeply into all forms of vice which that great city presented. At forty he was bankrupt and in extreme disfavor even with the dissolute emperor Tiberius. To escape imprisonment for his debts and for his crimes, he fled to Palestine and through the intercession of his wife was saved from starvation by his relative, Herod Antipas, who appointed him superintendent of markets at Tiberias. He soon incurred the suspicion of Antipas and fled to Damascus, where he was caught in the act of accepting graft from its citizens. Thence he returned to Rome, where he was soon thrown into prison by the Emperor Tiberius, but on the accession of Caligula he was made king over the tetrarchy of Philip. When Claudius, Agrippa's boon companion, came to the throne in 41, he not only showed special favor to the Jews, giving them full rights as citizens and many privileges, but paid a debt that he owed Agrippa by giving him all the territory in Palestine once held by his grandfather, Herod the Great. To this concession he added the right of appointing the high priest at Jerusalem. Although a Hellenist and immoral at heart, Herod Agrippa assumed while at Jerusalem the rôle of an apostle of strict Pharisaic Judaism. His zeal to figure as the champion of his people led him to attack Christianity and to kill James the apostle. Peter was also thrown into prison, but he was probably not put to death because of his well-known regard for Jewish law and institutions. James, the brother of Jesus, who was a still more ardent supporter of the Jewish law, was apparently not even imprisoned. The weight of Herod's persecution seems to have fallen simply upon the leaders of the Jerusalem church.

Acts 12⁴⁻¹⁹ contains the popular account of Peter's remarkable escape from prison. The form of the story is probably determined by the current Jewish belief that each man had his own guardian angel which interposed in his behalf at critical moments in his life. The detailed character of the narrative leaves little doubt that it rests on historical facts and that Peter was enabled, to the utter surprise of his fellow Christians, to make his escape from Jerusalem on the night preceding the day set for his trial before Herod Agrippa. Possibly the angel of death that smote Herod was the divine agent that liberated Peter. In any case, the sudden death of Agrippa at Cæsarea put an end to the persecution of the Jerusalem Christians by the Jews, for Judea again came under the control of a Roman procurator. Herod paid the penalty for his earlier vices while attending one of the great Hellenic games which he had instituted at his capital and of which he was very fond.

VII. **Peter's Changed Attitude Toward the Gentiles.** The narrative in Acts 12 indicates that Peter fled from Jerusalem and probably took refuge in some city outside the large kingdom which Herod Agrippa then ruled. Antioch with its strong Christian church would be the most natural place of refuge. Unfortunately, the narrative in Acts leaves many gaps which can be filled in only conjecturally. It is probable, however, that when the sudden death of Herod Agrippa put an end for a time to the active persecution of the Jerusalem Christians Peter ventured to return to the borders of Palestine and to take up his abode at Joppa. There he would naturally come into contact with Gentiles and Gentile Christians and was subject to the broadening influences of an important seaport town. There he faced the great Western world even as Paul later did at Troas. It is probable, therefore, that the combined influence of his recent personal experience, his contact with the Greek Christians at Antioch, and his new appreciation of the needs of the Græco-Roman world were all effective in preparing the way for the vision recorded in the terms of popular tradition in Acts 10 and 11. Doubtless the problem was presented to him in concrete form in the person of the Roman centurion Cornelius. The narrative in Acts implies that Cornelius, like the Ethiopian eunuch, was already a sympathizer with, if not a proselyte to Judaism. It is possible that he had listened to the preaching of Philip the Evangelist, whose home was at Cæsarea, and that Peter with his characteristic zeal and good sense could no longer resist this appeal, although it was contrary to all his earlier Jewish training. In the minds of Luke and of the Palestinian Christians, among whom this tradition grew up, this change in Peter's attitude was evidently regarded as pre-eminently important. In the larger perspective of apostolic history it was one of the many indubitable proofs of the potency and universality of the Gospel of Jesus and of its ability, not only to transform the minds and characters of the Gentiles, but to broaden those who were rigorously trained under the Jewish law.

VIII. **The Limitations and Significance of Early Palestinian Christianity.** There is much that is discouraging in the development of the Jerusalem church and of the Palestinian Christianity which grew up about it. Most of the members of the Jerusalem church appear to have sunk into poverty and to have been largely dependent for subsistence upon the gifts of the Western churches. In their thinking and life they were still largely bound by the fetters of Judaism and shared to a great extent the series of calamities which overtook the Jews of Palestine and culminated, in 70 A.D., in the destruction of the temple. The Jewish persecution had also driven from the capital city the virile leaders in the Christian church, leaving it sadly depleted. One great and inestimable service, however, was performed by the Jewish Christians who still clung to the temple and to places so full of rich associations: they collected and faithfully preserved the records of the teachings and deeds of Jesus. Without this service Christianity would have gone forth to its world-task sadly handicapped. If the Jewish Christians of Palestine failed to appreciate the larger significance of the work and teachings of Jesus, they faithfully cherished the words and memories of the great Teacher and in so doing have transmitted to us those vivid portraits of the historical Jesus without which Christianity would lack a definite, concrete historical foundation.

PAUL'S WORK AND TEACHINGS

§ CL. PAUL'S EARLY TRAINING AND CONVERSION

Paul's education (Acts 22³)

I am a Jew, born at Tarsus of Cilicia, brought up in this city, educated at the feet of Gamaliel in the strictness of our ancestral laws, zealous for God.

His zeal for his racial traditions (Gal. I¹³, ¹⁴, Acts 26⁹⁻¹¹)

You know the story of my past career in Judaism. You know how bitterly I persecuted the church of God and made havoc of it and how in zeal for my ancestral traditions I surpassed many of my own age and race. I indeed believed it was my duty to do many things in opposition to the name of Jesus the Nazarene. This I did in Jerusalem. Armed with authority from the high priests, I shut up many of the saints in prison. When they were about to be put to death, I voted against them. In all the synagogues I often punished them and forced them to blaspheme, and in my insane fury I persecuted them even to foreign cities.

His vision of Jesus (Acts 26¹²⁻¹⁸, Gal. I¹⁵,¹⁶ᵃ)

I was travelling to Damascus on this business with authority and a commission from the high priest, when at midday on the road I saw a light from heaven more dazzling than the sun flash around me and those who were travelling with me. We all fell to the ground, and I heard a voice saying to me in Hebrew, ' Saul, Saul, why dost thou persecute me? It is painful for thee to kick against the goad.' ' Who art thou?' I asked, and the Lord said, ' I am Jesus and thou art persecuting me. Now arise and stand on thy feet, for I appeared to thee in order to appoint thee to my service as a witness of what thou hast seen and of the visions thou wilt have of me. I will deliver thee from the Jewish people and also from the Gentiles, to whom I send thee, that their eyes may be opened and that they may turn from darkness to light, from the power of Satan to God, in order that they may receive the forgiveness of their sins and an inheritance among those

68

sanctified by faith to me.' Thus the God who had set me apart from my birth and called me by his grace chose to reveal his son in me that I might proclaim the good news concerning him to the Gentiles.

Forthwith, instead of conferring with any human being or going up to Jerusalem to see those who had been apostles before me, I went off into Arabia, and I came back again to Damascus. Then I proceeded to preach first to those at Damascus. At Damascus the ethnarch of King Aretas set guards in the city of the Damascenes to arrest me, but I was lowered in a basket through the wall and so escaped from his hands. *His first three years (Gal. 1 16b, 17, Acts 26 20a, II Cor. 11 32, 33)*

Then after three years I went up to Jerusalem to become acquainted with Cephas (Peter). I remained a fortnight with him. I saw no other apostle except James the brother of the Lord. I swear to you before God that I am telling the truth in what I write to you. *Visit to Jerusalem (Gal. 1 18-20)*

Then I went to the districts of Syria and Cilicia. I was personally quite unknown to the Christian churches of Judea; they only heard that ' our former persecutor is now preaching the faith of which he once made havoc,' which made them praise God for me. *Work in Syria and Cilicia (21-24)*

I. **Paul's Inheritance.** "A man small in size, baldheaded, bandy-legged, well built, with eyebrows meeting, rather long nose, and with motions full of grace"—such is the traditional description in the late Christian story of Paul and Thecla of the man who, next to Jesus, has done more than any to shape the religious faith of the human race. The familiar passage in II Corinthians 4 7 implies that in appearance Paul was weak and insignificant. At Lystra he was worshipped as Hermes, the small, beardless god. The reference in II Corinthians 12 7 indicates that he was the victim of some chronic disease, which he dramatically describes as "a thorn in the flesh." Galatians 6 11 suggests that it was an affliction of the eyes: "See with what letters I am writing to you with my own hand." This implication is confirmed by the fact that otherwise Paul apparently always dictated rather than wrote his letters. Furthermore, in referring to his illness in his letter to the Galatian Christians he writes: "I can testify that you would have torn out your very eyes, if you could, and given them to me." From his statement that "my flesh was a trial to you" it

69

would seem that intense sick headaches was one of the accompanying symptoms of his eye trouble. This was probably "the stake in the flesh" to which he elsewhere refers. Thus it would appear that Paul's physical inheritance was insignificant. It was indeed a fragile "earthen vessel" in which his indomitable spirit abode.

Paul was probably born about the same time as Jesus. His family belonged to the tribe of Benjamin. He himself bore the Jewish name of Saul, Israel's first great king. His Roman name was Paulus, or Paul. In the book of Acts this is used uniformly and appropriately as soon as the description of his active mission to the Græco-Roman world begins. He evidently sprang from the well-to-do working class. His spontaneous interests were with the manual laborers rather than with the rich or learned. His father doubtless taught him his trade of tent-maker. Weaving the wool of the Cilician goats and making it into tents was an important industry for the inhabitants of Tarsus. From Acts 23[16] we learn that Paul had a married sister and a nephew at Jerusalem. Like Jeremiah, he declares in Galatians 1[15, 16]: "It was the good pleasure of God that separated me from my mother's womb and called me through his grace and revealed his Son in me." The Jewish colony at Tarsus, like most of the similar communities in the great cities of the eastern Mediterranean, was a small Jewish world in itself in the midst of the complex Greek and pagan civilization which surrounded it. Here the youthful Saul grew up a strict Jew, familiar with all the customs of his race and zealous for its institutions.

II. **Paul's Personality.** Paul possessed a versatile, mercurial temperament. He was subject to frequent reactions, but, on the whole, his spirit was that of buoyant optimism. In his religious life he was a mystic, given to frequent visions, which to a great extent determined his thought and action; and yet in his teachings and methods of work he was intensely practical. To his versatility and remarkable adaptability was added the characteristic persistency of his race. Nothing in heaven or earth could deter him from the realization of his purpose. Over burning deserts and bleak mountain passes, through perils of sea and perils of land he goaded on his weak body until he made it his obedient slave (I Cor. 9[27]).

In his letters and in his acts he shows himself not only courageous, strong, and enthusiastic but a hard fighter, whenever he was sure that he had a just case. He was absolutely fearless and outspoken in his denunciation of corruption and wrong-doing of every kind. He was governed by a high sense of personal honor and an intense moral earnestness. Like the great earlier prophets of his race, he was ready for the sake of the cause which he served to give up everything: family, wealth, reputation, scholarship, ease. He deliberately chose arduous toil, privation, taunts, and danger, and at times active persecution and ultimate death rather than be disloyal to the highest interests of the Master whom he served. Through certain of his more personal letters it is possible to look into the very soul of the man. There we find a playful humor, warm feelings, deep sympathies, and strong friendships. Love is the impelling power. As he declares: "Love it is that constrains me." With these emotional qualities Paul combined a splendid organizing ability. He was unquestionably the greatest statesman of the primitive Christian church. Broad in his grasp of the world situation and master of details as well as of men, able to execute as well as to plan—the present generation is beginning to realize that Paul was even greater in his personality and work than in his teachings.

III. **Paul's Early Environment at Tarsus.** Paul shows clearly the influence of the many and varied educational forces with which he came in contact during his diversified career. He ever remained a Hebrew of the Hebrews; but to the powerful racial influences which surrounded the young Jew of Tarsus were added those of the cosmopolitan city in which he was born. This great metropolis of fully half a million inhabitants was situated on the River Cydnus, ten miles north from the coast, under the shadow of the Taurus mountains, which rise to the north. It commanded the famous southern gateway to Asia Minor which led northward through the Cilician passes. Tarsus was by virtue of its natural situation a great commercial and intellectual centre, where the ideas and civilization of the East and West met and mingled as in no other Mediterranean city, except possibly in Ephesus. It contained an exceedingly enterprising, cosmopolitan population, in close touch with all the Roman world, exceedingly proud, as was Paul, of their Roman citizenship. It was also the seat of a great university, which for generations had been an important centre of Stoic and Cynic philosophy. Strabo's list of the famous philosophers who had either been born or who had studied here is a long one. Chrysippus, the great Stoic, was a native of Tarsus, and the teacher of Cleanthes, whose noble utterance Paul aptly quoted in his famous address at Athens before the court of the Areopagus. The Stoic philosopher Athenadorus, the teacher and friend of Augustus, had been appointed by his royal patron ruler of his native city, Tarsus.

The principles which guided him in his effective rule are quoted by Seneca (*Concerning the Peaceful Mind*, III): "So it is requisite for us in order to prepare our minds for the managing of the civic affairs, to be always active. For if one is determined to make himself useful to his fellow citizens, yea, and to all men, one accomplishes two things at once. He who places himself at the centre of affairs and administers them according to his faculties benefits both the public interests and his own affairs." Nestor, also a well-known philosopher, succeeded Athenadorus and was probably at the head of the government at Tarsus during Paul's boyhood. The University of Tarsus was chiefly attended by natives of that city. This seat of learning apparently exerted a powerful influence not only upon the government but upon the life and thought of all the citizens. They were famous for their ability to speak on practically any subject without previous preparation. Strabo declares: "Even the natives do not remain but travel abroad to complete their studies, and having completed them reside in foreign countries" (XIV, 5[13, 14]). Tarsus to a unique degree produced citizens of the world and sent forth many itinerant preachers of the Stoic and Cynic philosophies. These facts shed a new light on Paul's declaration: "I am debtor both to the Greeks and to the barbarians, both to the wise and to the foolish" (Rom. 1[14]). It is clear, however, that although he was indirectly and inevitably influenced by the intellectual and cultural environment in which he spent his early youth, the attitude of the young Jew of Tarsus toward Greek learning was, on the whole, one of distrust, if not contempt. The Judaism of the dispersion was always self-sufficient. Though a part of the Græco-Roman world, the Jews stood apart. Hence, the most powerful influences in Paul's early youth were unquestionably those of his Jewish home. As at Jesus' home at Nazareth, the traditions and laws of his race were closely interwoven with the every-day life of the family. Among the earliest words which fell upon his childish ears were those which voiced Israel's confession of faith: "Hear, O Israel, for the Lord our God is one Lord." Every waking hour was filled with reminders of his people's remarkable past and of the presence of the supreme Ruler and Father whom they revered. His studies in the local synagogue school, to which he probably went at about the age of seven, further intensified the strong religious influence of his home. Here he was probably taught Hebrew and Aramaic, although most of his quotations from the Old Testament come from the Greek version, which was by this time in

common use among the Jews of the dispersion. His words in Galatians
1^{15} strongly suggest that, although he was taught the trade of tent-
making, from his earliest childhood he was consecrated by his parents
to the rabbinate. This conclusion is confirmed by his appearance in
Jerusalem a little later. Thus from his boyhood years the consciousness of a definite calling gave an especial interest and objective to all
his studies. It doubtless also exerted a powerful influence on his
daily life so that he was able to declare that as regards the righteousness which was in the law he was blameless (Phil. 3^{6-7}).

IV. **Paul's Training at Jerusalem.** Probably at about the
age of fifteen Paul went to Jerusalem to complete his preparation as
a rabbi. In the Jewish world Jerusalem was the great central university, the home of advanced religious study. It was to Judaism
what Athens had long been to the Græco-Roman world. The breadth
of Paul's home training is indicated by the fact that he went to sit at
the feet of Gamaliel, the most progressive and prominent Jewish teacher
of his age. This famous rabbi is said to have been the grandson of
Hillel. He was then the head of the liberal school which that great
teacher had founded. He it was who said: "Appoint for yourself a
teacher; thus you will avoid what is doubtful." He was one of the
very few Jewish teachers who dared depart from the traditions of his
race and make use of Greek literature. In Paul's earlier years the
master was probably much broader and more tolerant than his disciple, but his example later bore rich fruit in the memorable address
on the Areopagus. In the schools of Jerusalem Paul was instructed
not only in the current interpretations of the scriptures of his race
but also in the peculiar rabbinical methods which he frequently used in
his later discourses and letters. These methods were intuitive rather
than logical; often fanciful rather than inductive. Real or imaginary
analogies were employed more often than strictly scientific processes
of reasoning. Allegorical interpretations were freely adopted, even
though they had no support in the original. Paul's tendency to employ
these methods explains many of the most troublesome passages in his
epistles, for notwithstanding his complete conversion to the principles
of Christianity, he ever remained in his methods of thought an oriental
Jew.

V. **Paul's Zeal as a Persecutor.** It was not only the teaching
which he received in Jerusalem but its atmosphere which powerfully
affected Paul. There he became a Pharisee of the Pharisees (*cf.*
Phil. 3^5 for his own testimony). In him the intense devotion, the

aspiration, the zeal, and the intolerance of his race was sublimated. His was also in part the zeal and intolerance of youth. These were strengthened by his own natural characteristics. He never did anything half-way. The result was that, according to his own testimony, Paul, the youthful candidate for the rabbinate, became the ardent persecutor of the Galilean sect which had suddenly taken root not only in Jerusalem but also in certain other Syrian cities. In him the Sadducean high priests, Ananus and Caiaphas, ever suspicious of this sect with its messianic leanings, found a valuable agent. They appear to have given him an open commission to accuse of blasphemy— a capital offense in the Jewish law—any whom he might suspect. Unfortunately, Paul gives no details concerning the inner development which resulted thus tragically. The account of Stephen's work and martyrdom implies that he first came into contact with the followers of Jesus in the open discussions led by Stephen in the synagogues of the Hellenistic Jews in Jerusalem. As has been already noted, the report of Stephen's speech in Acts 7 suggests the nature of these discussions. The rabbinical methods employed in interpreting the Old Testament scriptures were accepted as valid by Paul as well as by Stephen. The great question at issue, the character, work, and appearance of the promised Messiah, was of the keenest interest to every member of the Pharisaic party. About it were focused their most cherished political and social and religious hopes. In the light of our later knowledge of Paul, it requires little imagination to picture the fiery zeal with which he entered into these discussions. The claim of Stephen and of the other followers of Jesus that he was indeed the Messiah seemed not only preposterous but blasphemous. There is no clear evidence that Paul had ever seen Jesus in the flesh. The references in his letters are evidently to his spiritual vision. He had doubtless often heard about Jesus and his work from the Pharisees who had dogged the footsteps of the Galilean Teacher; and their reports would be far from favorable. It was the very leaven of the Pharisees, against which Jesus had so earnestly warned his disciples, that filled the mind of Paul. Jesus' critical attitude toward much of the Mosaic law and especially toward the traditions of the fathers was enough in itself to condemn him in the eyes of an enthusiastic young Pharisee. Instinctive antagonism explains why Paul, even if he had the opportunity to see and hear Jesus, probably never improved it. So to one like Paul, familiar with the Deuteronomic law, which declared that "he who is hanged is accused of God" (Deut.

74

21[23]) Jesus' ignominious death was in itself absolute proof of the flagrant impiety as well as folly of those who claimed that he was the Messiah. That this very passage was earlier one of Paul's chief stumbling-blocks is indicated by the way in which he refers to it in his letter to the Galatians (3[13, 14]). To their seeming impiety the followers of Jesus added the still more blasphemous claim that he yet lived and had been exalted to the right hand of God, and they adduced as proof the astonishing statement that since his crucifixion he had repeatedly appeared to them. The old law of Deuteronomy seemed to point the way of duty very clearly to Paul: "If thy brother, the son of thy mother, or thy son, or thy daughter or the wife of thy bosom, or thy friend, who is as thy own life, teach heresy, thou shalt not listen to him nor pity him, but thou shalt surely kill him; thy hand shall be first upon him to put him to death and afterward the hand of all the people. And thou shalt stone him to death with stones." To one who was taught to believe, as were the disciples of the rabbis, that "he who asserts that the law is not from Heaven has no part in the future world," the command of God seemed clear though its execution was repugnant to all the best impulses implanted in the heart of man. Some such process of thought alone explains why the naturally kind-hearted, impulsive, conscientious Jew of Tarsus became an arch-persecutor of the humble followers of Jesus. Possibly the bitter heat engendered by the discussions in the synagogue of the Cilicians also explains why Paul first consented to the stoning of Stephen, the leader of the opposition, and then, having thus committed himself to an extreme position, threw himself into the persecution with his characteristic vehemence.

VI. **The Four Accounts of Paul's Conversion.** It is significant that the New Testament contains four variant accounts of what was in its far-reaching consequences the most important event in the history of the early Christian church. The author of Acts has preserved three of them, although no one agrees with another in all details. Here the analogies are close with the stories which gather about the important events of Old Testament history, as, for example, Moses' prophetic call or the exodus from Egypt. The oldest account is the briefest and comes directly from Paul: "God, who set me apart from my birth and called me by his grace, chose to reveal his Son in me that I might proclaim the good news concerning him to the Gentiles" (Gal. 1[15, 16]). To this he adds in connection with his account of the resurrection visions of Jesus in I Corinthians (15[1-8]): "And last of all, as to

75

a child untimely born, he appeared to me also." Paul's words leave no doubt that his conversion was a real spiritual experience, as is evinced by his changed activity and attitude. The account in Acts 26 is evidently the oldest of the three traditions presented by Luke. It agrees substantially with Paul's own testimony, but it makes the revelation more objective. The time and place are indicated and, as in the account of the call of Isaiah or Jeremiah, the divine revelation takes the form of a dialogue. The entirely new element is the statement that a marvellous flashing light was seen not only by Paul but also by his companions. The second account in Acts 22 agrees substantially with that in Acts 26, except that it states that, while Paul's companions saw the light, they did not hear the voice that spoke to him. It also adds that Paul was divinely commanded to go to Damascus, where he would be told what he was destined to do and that this promise was fulfilled through the instrumentality of a certain Ananias, who baptized him and in the presence of whom he regained his lost sight. It also states that he returned to Jerusalem, where he had another divine vision and a renewal of his commission to go to the Gentiles. The third account in Acts 9 is evidently in part a composite of the two accounts in 22 and 26. It differs, however, in stating that Paul's companions heard the divine voice but saw no one. It adds that a special vision was vouchsafed Ananias very similar to that attributed to Peter in Acts 10. It also states that after conducting an active mission in Damascus he went up to Jerusalem and entered into open discussions with the Hellenistic Jews. Paul's own testimony, however, is that he remained but fifteen days in Jerusalem and saw no apostle except Peter and James, the brother of Jesus. The minor variations in these versions indicate clearly that in the later tradition imagination has furnished many details. The tendency in each succeeding generation was to interpret Paul's inner vision more objectively and supernaturally.

VII. **Paul's Transforming Psychological Experience.** Paul and the early Christian historians inevitably described his conversion in terms of the first-century psychology and belief. Greek and Roman, as well as Jew, then firmly believed that the spirit of the departed could become visible to the human eye and exert a powerful influence in the affairs of men (cf. Morley, *Greek and Roman Ghost Stories*). They also believed that the gods could enter in and dwell in men and direct their thoughts and words and acts. Thus they interpreted the acts of the priestess at the Delphic oracle and the ecstatic deeds and utterances of the devotees of the various mystery religions. This idea was already an established tenet in Judaism, as well as in other oriental religions. While these beliefs naturally determine the form in which Paul describes his experience, they do not conceal the ultimate reality. The task of the modern age is to interpret it into the terms of present-day psychology. In his epistles, and especially Romans, Paul throws much light upon the inner struggle that preceded his conversion. In the first eight chapters of Romans he tells of the bitter dissatisfaction which came to him when he discovered that even the law which he so ardently championed could not free him from sin. In the face of the dying Stephen he saw reflected the peace and joy which he himself passionately coveted. The fierce zeal with which he persecuted the Christians suggests the acts of a fanatic, dimly conscious of the weakness of his position. Like a refractory ox, he was kicking against the goad. Not being an ox but an intelligent being, the knowledge of how unreasonable was his action only added to his fury. Moreover, Paul was not governed primarily by his intellect but by his intuition and emotions. The devotion and forbearance of Stephen and of other Christian martyrs, who followed his heroic example, undoubtedly appealed powerfully and in the end irresistibly to the naturally tender heart of Paul. Here was something that Pharisaism lacked. Could it be that the teacher, in loyalty to whom his followers serenely faced death, was indeed the promised Saviour of the race? Was the way of the cross, after all, the way of salvation? If, as his disciples claimed, Jesus still lived, then he had indeed broken the power of the ancient curse upon any one that hangs upon a tree and had the unmistakable approval of God himself. Such thoughts must have been in the mind of Paul when the great transformation came to him. Later tradition is probably right in stating that this came suddenly. This rapid transformation was in perfect keeping with Paul's temperament and character. It is closely analogous to the epoch-making moments in the life of the ancient prophets like Isaiah and Jeremiah. It came as a sudden, marvellous vision of the crucified and risen Lord. What the disciples had seen, Paul now beheld. Possibly in keeping with the psychology of his day, he himself believed that he saw and heard a visible, objective personality. Certainly those to whom he related his experience soon believed that he had. But the essential fact in Paul's experience was, as he declares, that God "had revealed his son in him." Henceforth the Spirit of Jesus became the abiding, guiding force in Paul's life. All of his subsequent career bears testimony to the reality of this fact. He clearly had in mind his own transforming experience when he declared: "We all with unveiled face, reflecting as a mirror the glory of the Lord, are transformed into the same likeness as himself from glory to glory." To a man with Paul's earnest, devoted spirit, such a revelation was an imperative, divine call to service, "for God who said, 'Let light shine out of darkness,' has shone within my heart to illuminate men with the knowledge of God's glory in the face of Christ." Paul also saw further than Jesus' disciples, for he recognized that through him the old law was set aside and a new way of finding God and the richness of life was provided for Gentile as well as Jew. Paul's personal interests, as well as the divine will, impelled him to proclaim that Gospel to the great world that lay outside of Palestine which he knew so well and which, like himself, was craving and seeking for that fellowship with the eternal Father, that sense of brotherhood with the human race, and that ideal of service which Jesus had not only taught but realized.

VIII. **Paul's First Fifteen Years of Missionary Activity.** The narrative of Acts is almost silent regarding the fifteen years immediately following Paul's conversion. The chief interest of the writers which Luke quotes regarding this period is in the Jerusalem church and the authority of the apostles. Luke does cite certain traditions which represent Paul as working at Jerusalem in conjunction with the apostles, but this is belied by Paul's own testimony. The one point in which Luke's evidence is supported by that of Paul is that he labored during the latter part of this period in his native province of Cilicia. Meagre though his allusions are, Paul is practically our only informant regarding these early years. From the references in his epistles it is possible to develop at least the order of events with reasonable assurance. Paul's conversion must have taken place before 36 A.D., when Caiaphas was deposed. The year 33, three or four years after the death of Jesus, is a most probable date. Three years he appears to have worked in the neighborhood of Damascus before his expulsion by the ethnarch of the Arabian king Aretas IV. The exact way in which this was accomplished and the extent of the power of Aretas are not known. Paul's hasty, secret visit to Peter at Jerusalem evidently followed closely after his escape from Damascus. The next important conference with Peter fourteen years later (Gal. 2¹) would therefore be about 47 A.D., immediately before his first missionary campaign. This conclusion in perfect harmony with the data in Acts, which indicates that 46 was the year spent by Paul at Antioch before he set out on that campaign.

The period of retirement in Arabia was clearly a period of reconstruction, spent not with men or apostles, but alone with God. Then Paul adjusted himself to his new vision of Jesus and to his new task. Immediately after this he began his missionary work in Damascus, preaching undoubtedly to Gentiles as well as Jews. That he did so and that his work met with some success alone explain the attempt of the ethnarch of the Arabian king to arrest him. The two weeks spent quietly at Jerusalem with Peter and James, the brother of Jesus, gave to an alert, devoted disciple like Paul a marvellous opportunity to become intimately acquainted with the facts regarding the life and especially with the teachings of Jesus. It, as well as later interviews, furnishes the explanation of that consciousness of speaking on the basis of Jesus' direct authority which is evident throughout Paul's letters.

The next twelve years were devoted to missionary work in Syria and Cilicia. Gradually Paul worked back to his native city Tarsus. These years appear to have been rich in experience. In II Corinthians (11[23-27]) he has given a word-picture of the trials and deeds of heroism which belong chiefly to these years: "I have often been at the point of death. Five times I have received forty lashes (all but one) from the Jews, three times have I been beaten; once I was stoned, three times shipwrecked; I have been adrift on the sea a night and a day, in many journeys, in perils from rivers, in perils from robbers, in perils from Jews and Gentiles, in peril of town and desert, in perils on the sea, in perils among false brothers, through labor and hardships, through many a sleepless night, through hunger and thirst, often starving, cold and ill-clad." It was in this school of strenuous, heroic service that the world's greatest missionary was trained. During these arduous years Paul does not seem to have met with large success. Nowhere in his letters does he refer to the results of this work. At least it was not sufficient to arouse the alarm of the conservative Jewish Christians at Jerusalem. Only to their ears had come the vague, though cheering report that "our former persecutor is now preaching the faith of which he once made havoc." This early work was significant because it was an earnest of greater things. Like his Master, Paul found joy in the midst of pain and persecution. In II Corinthians (12[1-4]) he tells of one of the glorious visions that illumined his arduous way. He dates it about 40 A.D., when he was in the midst of his work in Syria and Cilicia. He declares that he was caught up into the third heaven. He frankly confesses that he does not know whether it was in the body or not that he was thus transported up to paradise, but he does know that he heard sacred secrets which no human lips can repeat. That this experience was to him of profound spiritual import is clear from the way in which he refers to it and from its effect upon him and upon his life-work. In the same connection he speaks of his superabundance of visions, indicating that these experiences were frequent. They reveal the mystical side of Paul's nature, that capacity for personal fellowship with God which was the perennial source of his power. The vivid consciousness of God working in and through him was the irresistible force that drove him on through seemingly insuperable obstacles and perils. Even though its manifestations reflect the unscientific psychological ideas of the age, it was supremely vital and real to Paul and through him to the human race, for it meant personal redemption, liberty, and life.

§ CLI. PAUL'S FIRST MISSIONARY CAMPAIGN

Paul at Antioch (Acts 11 25, 26)

Now Barnabas went off to Tarsus to try to find Saul. And when he found him, he brought him to Antioch, where for a whole year they were connected with the church there and taught a large number of people.

Contributions to the famishing Christians in Judea (11 27-30, 12 25)

During these days certain prophets came down from Jerusalem to Antioch. One of whom, named Agabus, showed by the Spirit that a great famine was about to come throughout the whole world (the famine which came in the reign of Claudius). So the disciples, each as he was able, decided to send relief to the brothers living in Judea. This they did, sending their contributions to the elders by Barnabas and Saul. After Barnabas and Saul had performed their mission, they returned from Jerusalem bringing with them John, surnamed Mark.

Commission of Barnabas and Saul as missionaries (13 1-3)

In the church at Antioch there were prophets and teachers, Barnabas, Symeon (called Niger) and Lucius the Cyrenian, besides Manaen (a playmate of Herod the tetrarch) and Saul. As they were worshipping the Lord and fasting, the Holy Spirit said, Set me apart Barnabas and Saul for the work to which I have called them. Then after fasting and praying and laying their hands on them they let them go.

80

WORK OF BARNABAS AND PAUL IN CYPRUS

So they, being thus sent by the Holy Spirit, went down to Seleucia and from there they sailed to Cyprus. On reaching Salamis they proclaimed the word of God in the Jewish synagogues, and they had John [Mark] as their assistant. And when they had gone through the whole island as far as Paphos, they met with a Jewish sorcerer and false prophet called Bar-Jesus; he was with the proconsul Sergius Paulus, an intelligent man, who called for Barnabas and Saul and asked to hear the word of God. But Elymas the sorcerer (for that is the translation of his name) tried to divert the proconsul from the faith. So Saul (who is also called Paul), filled with the Holy Spirit, looked intently at him and said, You son of the devil, you enemy of all that is right, full of craftiness and cunning, will you never stop diverting the straight paths of the Lord? See, even now the Lord's hand will fall on you, and you will be blind, unable for a time to see the sun. Instantly a mist and a darkness fell upon him, and he groped about for someone to take him by the hand. Then the proconsul, when he saw what had happened believed, being astounded at the teaching of the Lord.

Their work in Cyprus (4-12)

Setting sail from Paphos, Paul and his companions came to Perga in Pamphylia. John left them and went back to Jerusalem, but they, passing on from Perga, arrived at Pisidian Antioch.

Journey to Antioch (13, 14a)

On the sabbath they went into the synagogue and sat down; and, after the reading of the law and the prophets, the rulers of the synagogue sent word to them, Brothers, if you have any word of encouragement for the people, say it. So Paul stood up and, motioning with his hand, said, Listen, men of Israel and you who revere God. The God of this people Israel chose our fathers; he made the people great during their stay in the land of Egypt and with uplifted arm led them out of it. For about forty years he fed them as a nursing mother in the desert, and after destroying seven nations in the land of Canaan, he gave them their land as an inheritance for about four hundred and fifty years. After that he gave them judges down to the time of the prophet Samuel. Then it was that they asked for a king, and God gave them for forty years Saul, the son of

Paul's address to the Jews of Antioch (14b-41)

Kish, who belonged to the tribe of Benjamin. After deposing him, he raised up David to be their king, to whom he bore this testimony: ' In David the son of Jesse I have found a man after my own heart, who will obey all my will.' From his offspring God brought to Israel, as he had promised, a Saviour, even Jesus, before whose coming John had already preached a baptism of repentance for all the people of Israel. And as John was closing his career he often said, What do you consider that I am? I am not he. But there is one coming after me. I am not worthy to unloose the sandals on his feet! Brothers, sons of Abraham's race and all among you who revere God, the message of this salvation has been sent to us. The inhabitants of Jerusalem and their rulers, by condemning him in their ignorance, fulfilled the words of the prophets which are read every sabbath. Though they could find him guilty of no crime that deserved death, they asked Pilate to have him put to death. After they had carried out all that had been written of him, they took him down from the cross and laid him in a tomb. But God raised him from the dead. For many days he was seen by those who had come up with him from Galilee to Jerusalem; they are now his witnesses to the people. And we preach to you the glad news that God hath fulfilled the promise made to our forefathers by raising up Jesus. As it is written in the second psalm:

Thou art my son,
To-day have I become thy father.

And as a proof that he has raised him from the dead, never to return to corruption, he hath said, I will give you holy and trustworthy promises made to David; in another psalm he saith:

For thou wilt not let thy Holy One see corruption.

Of course David, after serving his own generation in accord with God's purpose, died and was laid beside his fathers; he saw corruption, but he whom God raised did not see corruption. Therefore you must understand, my brothers, that forgiveness of sins is proclaimed to you through him, and that by him everyone who believes is absolved from all that the law of Moses could not absolve you. Beware then lest the prophetic saying applies to you:

Behold, ye who are disdainful, be astonished and perish,
For in your days I am carrying out a work—
A work which you will never believe, though one were to
    explain it to you.

As Paul and Barnabas were going out, the people begged to have all this repeated to them on the following sabbath. And when the synagogue broke up, a number of the Jews and the devout proselytes followed Paul and Barnabas who talked to them and urged them to hold fast to the grace of God. *Its immediate effect (42, 43)*

And on the next sabbath nearly all the city gathered to hear the word of the Lord. But when the Jews saw the crowds, they were filled with jealousy; they began to contradict what Paul said and to abuse him. So Paul and Barnabas spoke out boldly. The word of God, they said, had to be spoken to you first; but since you spurn it and judge yourselves unworthy of eternal life, well, here we turn to the Gentiles. For this is the Lord's command to us: *Opposition of the Jews and the proclamation of tho Gospel to the Gentiles (44-52)*

I have set you to be a light for the Gentiles,
To bring salvation to the end of the earth.

When the Gentiles heard this they rejoiced and glorified the word of the Lord and believed, that is, all who had been ordained to eternal life; and the word of the Lord was spread abroad throughout the whole country. But the Jews incited the devout women of high rank and the leading men in the town, who stirred up persecution against Paul and Barnabas and drove them out of their territory. But they shook the dust off their feet as a protest against them and went to Iconium. The disciples, however, were filled with joy and the Holy Spirit.

At Iconium the same thing happened. They went into the synagogue of the Jews and spoke in such a way that a great number both of Jews and Greeks believed. But the refractory Jews stirred up and exasperated the feeling of the Gentiles against the brothers. Yet they spent a considerable time, speaking boldly about the Lord, who attested the word of his grace by allowing signs and wonders to be performed by them. The populace of the town, however, was divided; some sided with the Jews, some with the apostles. But, when there was a hostile movement of Gentiles and Jews along with their rulers to insult and stone them, the apostles escaped to the Lycaonian towns of Lystra and Derbe and the surrounding country; there they continued to preach the gospel.

The
effect
of the
curing
of the
lame
man
at
Lystra
(8-18) At Lystra there was a man sitting, who was powerless in his feet, a lame man unable to walk from birth. He heard Paul speaking, and Paul, gazing intently at him and recognizing that he had faith enough to make him well, said in a loud voice, Stand upright on your feet. So he sprang up and began to walk. Now when the crowds saw what Paul had done, they shouted in the Lycaonian language, The gods have come down to us in human form! Barnabas they called Zeus, and Paul Hermes, since he was the chief speaker. Indeed the priest of the temple of Zeus in front of the town brought oxen and garlands to the gates, intending to offer sacrifice along with the crowds. But when the apostles, Barnabas and Paul, heard this they tore their clothes and rushed out into the crowd, shouting, Men, what is this you are doing? We are but men, with natures like your own! The gospel we are preaching to you is to turn you from these unreal things to the living God who made the heaven, the earth, the sea, and all that in them is. In past ages he allowed all nations to go their own ways, though as the bountiful giver he did not leave himself without a witness, giving you rain from heaven and fruitful seasons, giving you food and joy to your heart's content. Even by words like these they could scarcely keep the crowds from sacrificing to them.

But Jews from Antioch and Iconium arrived, who won over the crowds and stoned Paul and dragged him out of the city, thinking he was dead. But, as the disciples gathered round him, he arose and went into the city.

Next day he went off with Barnabas to Derbe; and after preaching the gospel to that city and making a number of disciples, they turned back to Lystra, Iconium and Antioch, strengthening the disciples, encouraging them to hold by the faith, and telling them, We must enter the Kingdom of God through many afflictions. They ordained elders for them in every church, and with prayer and fasting commended them to the Lord in whom they had believed. Then, passing through Pisidia they came to Pamphylia; and after speaking the word of the Lord in Perga they went down to Attalia. Thence they sailed for Antioch, where they had been commended to the grace of God for the work they had now completed. *Revisiting the Galatian churches (21-25)*

On their arrival they gathered the church together and proceeded to report how God had worked with them, and how he had opened a door of faith for the Gentiles. They spent a considerable time there with the disciples. *The report to the church at Antioch (26-28)*

I. **Paul's Work at Antioch.** Antioch, the old Syrian capital, was not only the city where the term "Christians" was coined, but also the point from which Christianity set out on its deliberate conquest of the Roman world. Here it was that the Gospel of Jesus had first been proclaimed to the Gentiles. As a result, many Greeks were already found in the membership of the Antioch church. Antioch was also the Syrian gateway through which ran the main highway that led across Asia Minor and Macedonia to Rome. Its natural position, as well as its history, fitted it for its lofty rôle. The wisdom and foresight of the Antioch Christians and especially of Barnabas, their leader, were revealed by taking Paul into their ranks. It was a most significant recognition of the man and his work in Tarsus and Cilicia. Barnabas even went in person to bring Paul to Antioch, thus giving to the act an official authority. For Paul the year spent in teaching at Antioch must also have been of great value. Here amidst most favorable conditions he faced many of the problems that he later met single-handed in the other great cities of the empire. Here he worked side by side with Barnabas, whose earlier years as a follower of Jesus had been spent at Jerusalem in closest contact with the Twelve. Here Paul must have absorbed many of the beliefs and hopes of the primitive Jerusalem church, although, as he repeatedly asserts, his own faith rested on more personal grounds—his experience of the risen Christ and of the divine Spirit working in his life and in that of the converts who responded to his preaching.

The date of Paul's work at Antioch is indicated by Luke, for he connects it with the terrible drought and famine that came according to Josephus during the procuratorship of Tiberius Alexander, 46–48 A.D. Jerusalem suffered especially. The needs of its inhabitants were in part relieved through the generous gifts of a Jewish proselyte, Queen Helena, of Adiabene. Her example was followed by the Christians of Antioch. Barnabas and Paul, the leaders in the mission to the Gentiles, were chosen to bear these evidences of the good-will and devotion of the Gentile Christians to the members of the Judean churches. This Christian act undoubtedly did much to heal the threatening breach between these two branches of the church. It also opened the way for the memorable interview between Paul and the authorities at Jerusalem, recorded in Galatians 2 (*cf.* § CLII), which established the freedom of the Gentile Christians. It is also significant that the one condition then insisted upon by the Jerusalem authorities was that the benefactions of the Gentile Christians be continued. Another important result of the mission to Jerusalem was that Paul and Barnabas brought back with them to Antioch Barnabas's nephew, John Mark, who, according to early Christian tradition, had been closely associated with Peter and who later wrote the earliest surviving life of Jesus. Thus the two very different types of churches, that at Jerusalem and that at Antioch, were closely bound together by the bond of mutual service and the way prepared for the great forward step that came on the return of Paul and Barnabas to Antioch.

II. **The Sending Forth of Barnabas and Paul.** The narrative in Acts implies that the impulse to enter upon the first foreign missionary campaign came not from one man but from the collective body of Antioch Christians. Paul by his teachings and example had undoubtedly sown the seed. It requires little imagination to detect his personal influence in the memorable meeting when the great decision was made. Those who suggest are usually chosen to execute, and Barnabas and Paul were the two appointed to initiate the work. The success of the Jerusalem mission may also have led the Antioch Christians to seek a larger field. They probably had large resources at their command. Barnabas formerly held land in Jerusalem; Manaen, one of their number, had been a playmate of Herod, the tetrarch. Antioch was an opulent city and the Jews were among its most prosperous citizens. It is probable, therefore, that Barnabas and Paul went forth on their foreign mission supported not only by the prayers and benedictions but also by the gifts of the Antioch Christians, for "freely you have received, freely give" was a fundamental tenet of their faith. The missionary spirit was not a later growth but a fundamental principle of primitive Christianity.

III. **The Work of Barnabas and Paul in Cyprus.** It is significant that when they went forth Barnabas was the leader; when they returned Paul, the younger, was the commanding spirit. Barnabas first led Paul and Mark to his native island of Cyprus, but before the two leading apostles returned they had carried the Gospel of Jesus many miles beyond Paul's native city, Tarsus. The author of this section of Acts deliberately condenses his account of the missionary campaign in Cyprus. His reason is in keeping with his purpose, which was to describe the victorious advance of Christianity from Jerusalem to Rome and to show that it was protected rather than opposed by the Roman authorities. Cyprus, as well as Egypt, was aside from the main line of that advance. At Salamis, the chief eastern port of Cyprus, the Christian missionaries found a large Jewish colony and were doubtless freely admitted to the synagogues, for it is probable that in this distant outpost little opposition between Judaism and Christianity had as yet developed. Luke's narrative does not expand until Barnabas and Paul come into contact with the Roman proconsul who ruled the island from its capital, Paphos. This was the new Paphos on the coast ten miles northeast of the ancient city of Paphos which had long been famous for worship of the Paphian goddess, whose shrine was there. The Roman proconsul, Paulus, was evidently a man of culture, interested in the various current philosophies. Pliny mentions him among the Roman writers of the day. In his train was a Jew who had grafted on to his inherited faith many of the heathen ideas and practices that had come from the East, especially from Persia. This half philosopher and half fakir had also won a reputation as a prophet or public preacher. He was one of the many missionaries in that strongly missionary age. The mother goddess of Phrygia, the Egyptian goddess Isis, as well as the Cynic and Stoic philosophies, all had their emissaries, like the Pharisees "encompassing sea and land to make proselytes." In Asia Minor, Macedonia, and Rome Paul met and contested with them for the faith of men. In the presence of the cultured Roman proconsul it is not Barnabas nor Saul the Jew, but Paulus the Roman citizen who suddenly stands forth and from this time on holds the central place not only in the book of Acts but in the missionary work of the Christian church. The scene in Acts is symbolic of the victorious contest that Christianity was destined to wage with the heathen cults and philosophies of the ancient world.

IV. **The Mission Field in Southern Asia Minor.** The activity of Paul and Barnabas in Cyprus does not appear to have been very fruitful. The narrative in Acts implies that they confined their work chiefly to the Jews. It is not even claimed that the Roman proconsul definitely aligned himself with the Christian beliefs. No discouragements or obstacles, however, could daunt Paul or deter him from the realization of the aim which he henceforth set before him. This aim alone explains why he left Cyprus and struck northward into Asia Minor. It was because he was eager to carry the Gospel of Jesus the next stage westward of Cilicia toward the heart of the Roman Empire. Perga, near the southern coast, was left behind, for it was strongly pagan and aside from the great world currents. There also, John Mark turned back, while Paul, sick in body but fearless and determined, dragged Barnabas with him up over the almost impassable southern headlands of Asia Minor, facing untold hardships, "perils of rivers and perils of robbers," to the commercial cities that lay on the great highway which led from the East to Rome. Here Paul the cosmopolitan again found himself at home. Here, as at Tarsus, Roman organization, Greek culture, and Jewish religious zeal were found side by side, even though they did not blend. Here was a field that appealed to the great missionary statesman of early Christianity.

V. **At Galatian Antioch.** Antioch, one of the two chief cities of the Roman province of Galatia, was an important eastern outpost of the imperial city. It lay on an isolated plateau over thirty-six hundred feet above the sea-level and two hundred feet above the western plain. It was guarded on the eastern side by the swift, deep-flowing River Anthios. Augustus, recognizing its strategic importance, had made it a Roman colony about the beginning of the Christian era. It dominated the surrounding region to which the narrative of Acts refers and was a most favorable centre in which to plant the Gospel seed. Here was evidently a large Jewish colony which had attracted to its ranks many thoughtful Greeks as well as Jews. The official abolition of the local religion increased the possibilities of this new mission field. Through the medium of the local synagogue Paul

PAUL AT GALATIAN ANTIOCH

and Barnabas easily gained a hearing from the more religiously minded citizens of this important metropolis. The sermon which the author attributes to Paul contains many echoes of Stephen's earlier address. In its use of the Old Testament it reflects the current rabbinical methods. While its form may be due in part or largely to the author of this section of Acts, it is an excellent illustration of the sermons which carried conviction to the minds of earnest Jews and Gentiles seeking the way of salvation. The success of Paul and Barnabas in Galatia and Antioch was most marked. The Jews and devout Greeks gathered about them with eager questions. Not only the city itself but the surrounding region which it commanded was stirred by the message of the apostles until the opposition of the more conservative Jews was aroused. The author here as elsewhere represents the apostles as speaking first to the Jews and then to the Gentiles, but the account itself indicates that from the first the appeal was to both classes. Recognizing the universality of Jesus' work, Paul in his own teaching and activity had long since broken the bond which still fettered the Palestinian Christians.

VI. The Apostles' Work at Iconium and Lystra. A positive character and message such as Paul's inevitably aroused opposition and he was soon driven with Barnabas to find refuge elsewhere and a new field of work. They left behind, however, a devoted group of disciples whose joy and spiritual exaltation testified to the divine transformation which had been worked in their lives. Eighty miles east of Antioch lay another important Galatian city. Iconium, unlike Antioch, was on a fertile, level plain on the western side of a lofty mountain range from whose sides rushed the stream which irrigated the great plain about the city. The almost constant danger of floods and foreign invasion had developed in highest measure the energy and resourcefulness of its inhabitants. Here the apostles found a flourishing colony and Jewish synagogue. Jews and Greeks alike responded to their teaching, although certain of the Jews bitterly opposed them. Here for weeks and probably months they conducted a successful mission, but its very success in time aroused the rulers, so that at last the apostles departed amidst taunts and pelting stones.

Wearied by constant opposition and in quest of a quiet place of refuge, Paul and Barnabas turned westward to the native town of Lystra, twenty miles from Iconium. It was situated in a peaceful valley, watered by two streams from the western hills. In the midst of the valley rose the acropolis, a steep hill, a hundred and fifty feet in height. Here the apostles were among a simple peasant people of the old Lycaonian stock. A kindly work of healing, wrought upon a lame man whose faith was equal to the task, almost instantly won the adoration of the populace. The narrative well illustrates the common popular belief of the day that the gods in human form frequently came down and walked among men. Barnabas, the taller and more commanding figure, was identified as Zeus; Paul, the smaller and alert and more gifted speaker, with Hermes, the spokesman and messenger of the gods. Not understanding the native language, the apostles apparently did not at first understand that the people were about to worship and offer sacrifices to them; but as soon as they appreciated the situation they loudly protested and improved the opportunity to tell them of the one living God, whence came all their blessings. Lystra, however, was under the control of the Galatian Antioch and so near Iconium that the Jewish persecutors of the apostles soon overtook them and turned the zeal of the populace into mad rage, so that Paul barely escaped death at their hands. Derbe, the next place to which the apostles turned for refuge, was on a great plain about forty-five miles south of Iconium. Here amidst the native population they met with little opposition. This point, however, marked the eastern limit of their campaign, for it was near the eastern bounds of the province of Galatia. Paul, instead of going eastward along the direct road to his boyhood home at Tarsus and to the field of his earlier activity in Cilicia, was evidently eager to return and perfect the organization of the Christian communities which they had established in the important cities of Galatia. The lapse of time and in many cases the change of rulers and the abatement of opposition made this possible. Hence they retraced their steps, in each place strengthening the disciples. Out of the ranks of each Christian community they selected certain presbyters or elders to direct and instruct the individual members. Evidently Paul was seeking not to build up a hierarchy but a democratic brotherhood akin to that which Jesus himself had established during his ministry in Galilee. Thence they returned through Pamphylia to the sea at Attalia and from there by ship to Antioch, where they reported the results of their work to the church which had sent them forth and the great fact that the Gentile world was waiting eagerly to receive the message of their risen Lord. Within less than two decades after the death of Jesus Christianity had entered upon its world conquest, so great was the potency of the personality and teachings of him who taught as never man taught before.

§ CLII. THE BREAKING OF JEWISH BONDS

[Paul himself states that] Fourteen years after my first visit with Peter I went up again to Jerusalem accompanied by Barnabas. I also took Titus with me. I went up in obedience to a revelation. And I laid before them the gospel which I preach to the Gentiles; I did this in private before the authorities lest by any means I should be running, or should already have run in vain. But even though Titus, who was with me, was a Greek, he was not obliged to be circumcised. The opposition came through certain traitorous false brothers who had crept in to spy out the freedom we enjoy in Christ Jesus in order that they might enslave us again. But, in order that the truth of the gospel might hold good for you, we did not consent for an instant to submit to them. Indeed from the authorities—whatever they are it makes no difference to me; God payeth no respect to persons—these authorities had no additions to make to my gospel. On the contrary, when they saw that I had been intrusted with the gospel for the uncircumcised just as Peter had been for the circumcised (for he who equipped Peter to be an apostle to the circumcised equipped me as well for the Gentiles), and when they recognized the grace that had been given me, James and Cephas and John, who were considered the pillars of the church, gave to me and Barnabas the right hand of fellowship that we should go to the Gentiles, they to the circumcised. One thing they urged, that we should remember the poor, which I myself was exceedingly eager to do.

Paul's interview and agreement with the apostles (Gal. 2¹⁻¹⁰)

When Cephas came to Antioch, I opposed him to his face, because he stood condemned. For before certain persons came from James, he ate with the Gentile Christians; but when they came, he withdrew and held aloof for fear of the circumcision party. The rest of the Jewish Christians also played false along with him, so that even Barnabas was carried away by their false play. But when I saw that they were not acting uprightly in the true spirit of the gospel, I said to Cephas in the presence of them all: If you who are a Jew live like the Gentiles and not like the

Paul's later rebuke of Peter for inconsistency (11-16)

Jews, why do you oblige the Gentiles to become Jews? We may be Jews by birth and not ' Gentile sinners,' but, knowing that a man is justified by faith in Christ Jesus and not by doing the things which the law commands, we ourselves have believed in Christ Jesus so as to be justified by faith in Christ and not by doing the things that the law commands, for by doing those things which the law commands no human being shall be justified.

The Christians' obligations to the Mosaic law (Acts 15¹, ²)

Now certain individuals came down from Jerusalem and taught the brothers: Unless you are circumcised after the custom of Moses you cannot be saved. Inasmuch as there was a sharp dispute and controversy between them and Paul and Barnabas, it was arranged that Paul and Barnabas, along with some others of their number, should go up to Jerusalem to consult the apostles and elders at Jerusalem about this question.

The deputation to Jerusalem (3. 4)

So they set out, being accompanied for a distance by members of the church. And they passed through Phœnicia and Samaria, telling about the conversion of the Gentiles. And they inspired all the brothers with great joy. When they arrived at Jerusalem, they were received by the church and the apostles and elders. And they reported all that God had done through them.

Peter's speech in the council (5-11)

But some of the believers who belonged to the Pharisaic party got up and said, Gentiles must be circumcised and enjoined to observe the law of Moses. Then the apostles and the presbyters met to investigate this question, and a keen controversy sprang up; but Peter rose and said to them, Brothers, you know well that from the earliest days God chose among you that by my mouth the Gentiles were to hear the word of the gospel and believe. The God who knows all hearts attested this by giving them the Holy Spirit just as he gave it to us; in cleansing their hearts by faith he made no distinction at all between us and them. Well now, why are you trying an experiment upon God by imposing a yoke on the neck of the disciples which neither our fathers nor we ourselves could bear? No, it is by the grace of the Lord Jesus that we believe and are saved, in the same way as they.

92

Then the whole assembly was silent and listened to Barnabas and Paul recounting the signs and wonders God had performed by them among the Gentiles.

When they had finished speaking, James replied, Brothers, listen to me. Simeon has told how God originally sought to secure a people from among the Gentiles to bear his name. This agrees with the words of the prophets; as it is written,

After this I will return and rebuild David's fallen tent,
Its ruins I will rebuild and set it up again,
That the rest of men may seek for the Lord, that they
    may possess the remnant of Edom
Even all the Gentiles who are called by my name,
Saith the Lord, who maketh this known from of old.

My judgment therefore is that we ought not to put fresh difficulties in the way of those who are turning to God from among the Gentiles, but enjoin them to abstain from whatever is polluted by idols, from sexual vice, from the flesh of animals that have been strangled, and from blood; for Moses has had his preachers from earliest ages in every city, where he is read aloud in the synagogues every sabbath.

Then the apostles and the elders, together with the whole church, decided to select some of their number and send them to Antioch with Paul and Barnabas. The men selected were Judas (called Barsabbas) and Silas, leading members of the brotherhood. They bore the following letter: The apostles and the elder brothers send greeting to the brothers who belong to the Gentiles throughout Antioch and Syria and Cilicia. Since we have learned that some of our number, without being authorized by us, have disturbed you with their teaching and upset your souls, we have decided unanimously to select some of our number and send them to you along with our beloved Barnabas and Paul who have risked their lives for the sake of our Lord Jesus Christ. We therefore send Judas and Silas, who will also tell you these things by word of mouth. The Holy Spirit and we have decided not to impose any extra burden on you, except these essential requirements: abstain from food that has been offered to idols, from tasting blood, from the flesh of animals that have been strangled, and from sexual vice. Keep clear of all this and it will be well with you. Farewell.

Its
recep-
tion
(30-35)
When the messengers were despatched, they went down to Antioch and, after gathering the whole assembly, they delivered the letter. On reading it the people rejoiced at the encouragement it brought. And as Judas and Silas were themselves prophets, they encouraged and strengthened the brothers with many a discourse. Then after they had spent some time there they were dismissed with a greeting of peace from the brothers to those who had sent them. Paul and Barnabas, however, stayed on in Antioch, teaching and preaching the word of the Lord along with a number of others.

I. **The Burning Problem in the Christian Church.** The extension of Christianity far beyond the bounds of Palestine, and especially the work of Paul and Barnabas among the Gentiles, presented to the Christian church its first great and insistent problem. Fortunately, it did not become a pressing issue until the work of the Hellenistic Christians had furnished a large body of facts born of experience. The problem involved three distinct issues and it is important not to confuse them. The first and most insistent was, Were the Gentile Christians to be compelled to follow the demands of the Jewish law? Second, What were the obligations of the Jewish Christians to their inherited law? The third question, fortunately, came to the forefront a little later, What were to be the mutual obligations of each when Jewish and Gentile Christians ate and associated together? According to the testimony of Paul (Gal. 2⁴), the problem was precipitated by certain Jewish Christians "who had crept in to spy out the freedom" that the Antioch Christians were enjoying in Christ Jesus and who aimed to enslave again the Gentile members of that great and growing church by compelling them to satisfy all the detailed demands of the Jewish law.

II. **The Accounts of the Way in Which the Problem Was Solved.** Fortunately, in the second chapter of Paul's letter to the Galatians he has given a brief but straightforward and clear statement of the issue and its outcome. It reveals not merely Paul's position but that of the "pillars" at Jerusalem and unquestionably must be regarded as the primary historical source. Acts 14^{28}–15^{35} contains what is generally regarded as a parallel record of the same vital controversy. In the outstanding facts the two accounts are in substantial agreement. That in Acts, however, makes it a public rather than the distinctively private conference described in the second chapter of Paul's letter to the Galatians. The influence of the author's harmonizing purpose is also apparent in the absence from his account of any reference to the radical issue between Peter and Paul regarding the obligations of Jewish and Gentile Christians where the two were associated together in the same church. To the formal decision of James and the Jewish Christians at Jerusalem Paul makes no reference in Galatians 2. The only satisfactory explanation is that Paul's private interview with the "pillars" at Jerusalem took place when he went up to Jerusalem with Barnabas to present the gift of the Antioch Christians. This date is supported by Paul's clear implication that he had made no other visit to Jerusalem since his first meeting with Peter, fourteen years before his memorable interview. Paul and Barnabas, therefore, set out on their first missionary campaign with the assurance that the leaders at Jerusalem approved of their action. The public council at Jerusalem apparently came after their return two years later. This chronological arrangement solves many difficulties and brings the testimony of Paul and of Acts into substantial agreement.

III. **Paul's Interview with the " Pillars " at Jerusalem.** The date of Paul's memorable interview with the leaders of the Jerusalem church was probably in 47 A.D., and therefore antedated by two years the conference reported in Acts. Paul tells us that, as frequently in the great decisive moments in his life, he was led to go up to Jerusalem as the result of a special revelation, although in the same connection he speaks of the subversive influence of certain traitorous false brothers in the Antioch church who had precipitated the issue. He plainly felt that the time had arrived for decisive action. To make the question absolutely clear and concrete, he took with him Titus, a Greek Christian who had not submitted to the Jewish rite of circumcision and who, presumably because of his Gentile origin, observed none of the detailed Jewish laws. Frankly and fully Paul described to the authorities at Jerusalem the Gospel which he had been in the habit of preaching to the Gentiles and asserted its universality and applicability freed from all Jewish limitations. In the light of the facts, the "pillars" of the Jerusalem church, including the disciples Peter and

John and James the brother of Jesus (who had probably been chosen to fill the vacancy in the ranks of the Twelve due to the martyrdom of James the son of Zebedee), fully accepted Paul's position and gave him the right hand of fellowship. It was decided that Paul should be allowed to preach the Gospel to the Gentiles without any limitations. The account also implies that the Twelve were to continue to preach the Gospel to the Jews and to require that the Jewish Christian converts should continue to observe the demands of their law. The only obligation laid upon Paul was the request that he remember the needs of the poor Christians at Jerusalem—a request that he declares himself eager to grant. This request was probably prompted by the actual needs of the Jerusalem Christian community, many of whom had no direct means of support, and who after the period of famine that had just preceded were in great want. It also aimed to bind together the Jewish and Gentile sections of the Christian church by practical acts of service. Furthermore, it implied a certain obligation, if not subjection, of the Gentiles to the Jews. This obligation is frankly admitted by Paul himself at the close of his letter to the Romans: "Macedonia and Achaia have decided to make a contribution for the poor among the saints at Jerusalem. Such is their decision, and it is a debt they owe them, for if the Gentiles have shared their spiritual blessings they owe them a debt of aid in material things" (15[26, 27]).

Paul says nothing about the public announcement of the results of this interview to the Jerusalem Christians, but it may be inferred that it was made, for the later opposition that Paul had sought to allay by his visit to the historic home of the church came not from the apostles but from certain ardent Pharisaic Christians. Paul states in Galatians 2[6-9] that Peter and James defended the rightness of his claims. He in turn confirmed the wisdom of this decision by telling of the significant work that he had already accomplished (in Syria and Cilicia) among the Gentiles. Paul's vivid record of his interview with the Twelve does not suggest that the slightest limitation was placed by them upon his mission to the Greek world. They simply agreed to divide the Jewish and Gentile fields and not to intrench on the work of the other. Throughout the interview the spirit of their common Master guided them in dealing with this most delicate and important question, so that without a rupture in the church the ancient Jewish bonds were thrown aside and Christianity went forth unfettered to its world conquest.

IV. Problems Arising from the Association of **Gentile Christians.** One vexed question remained unso before long demanded an answer. In the early church it portentous proportions; but in the perspective of history it ap relatively unimportant. It became insistent in the mixed Jew and Gentile churches, where the division between the mission to the Gentiles and that to the Jews could not be rigidly observed. Paul, on the basis of his earlier experience, fully recognized this fact. At the beginning he asserted his conviction as to what was the only satisfactory solution by taking the uncircumcised Greek Titus with him to Jerusalem and by freely associating with him. In the private interview the apostles tacitly accepted Paul's position and made no additions to it, although certain Jewish Christians opposed it from the first (Gal. 2[4-6]). When Peter later came to Antioch, he also at first accepted it in practice as well as theory. This attitude was perfectly natural in a disciple of a Master who had freely eaten with sinners and tax-collectors and who had shown in all his career a calm unconcern for all ceremonialism. Peter needed no special vision to convince him on this point. The fraternal spirit manifest among the Antioch Christians was also indubitable evidence that their faith was rooted in something far deeper than mere ceremonial forms. It is evident, however, that during his absence on his first missionary campaign the narrow Judaizers in the Jerusalem church had been active. They were doubtless the same men who had protested against associating with the Greek Christian Titus. Reports of what Peter had been doing at Antioch had probably reached them. Their protests even influenced James to send messengers to Peter with the result that he withdrew from associating closely with the Gentile Christians. Even Barnabas yielded to the pressure of the Judaizers. Luke in Acts 15[23-29] has probably embodied the essence of their demands. In any case, Paul's explicit testimony in Galatians 2 indicates that these specific regulations were issued not only after his interview with the "pillars" at Jerusalem but also after Peter's visit to Antioch. They stipulate that all Gentile Christians should abstain from things contaminated by contact with idols, from sexual vice, from the flesh of animals that had been strangled, and from tasting blood. According to the Jewish law found in Leviticus, chapters 17 and 18, these were the exact limitations placed upon foreigners resident in Palestine. While there is no evidence that Peter publicly insisted that the Gentile Christians of Antioch should observe these injunctions, his ceasing to eat

…mplied a tacit acceptance of the principle
…oubtless to maintain peace and harmony
…d to avoid destroying his influence with
…is strong Jewish inheritance and Jeru-
…egarded Peter's position as tenable. It
…actical considerations which influenced
…illing that Paul should preach the Gospel
…tion but, recognizing that his own mis-
…he deemed it unwise to openly repudiate
… of the Jewish law.

The incident recorded in Galatians 2 may antedate certain of the
facts underlying the story of Peter's vision in Acts 10, which aims to
show how he was led to see that in the eyes of God there was no validity
in the legal distinction between clean and unclean (10^{9-16}), and that he
was to associate freely without restriction with Gentiles as well as Jews
and to call no man "common or unclean" (10^{28}). His later mission
to the Gentiles, to which Paul refers in I Corinthians 9^5, implies that
in time Peter repented of the backward step which he had taken at
Antioch and joined with Paul in his mission to the Greek and Roman
world.

V. **Paul's Controversy with Peter.** The reason for Paul's
indignation and public arraignment of Peter is obvious. He was conscious that the great apostle agreed with him in principle, but that his
action was a deadly blow at the Christian liberty which Paul so ardently championed. He argued also that the work of Christ was
sufficient for the salvation of both the Jew and the Gentile and that
insistence upon the observation of the law was evidence of lack of
faith in the Gospel. At the same time, Paul in his later writings and
in his own practice strongly advocates consideration for the religious
scruples of his Jewish brothers. "Therefore, if food is any hinderance
to my brother's welfare, rather than injure him I will never eat flesh
as long as I live" (I Cor. 8^{13}). "To the Jews I have become like a
Jew to win over Jews. To those outside the law I have become like one
of themselves" (I Cor. $9^{20a, \ 21a}$). The fundamental difference between
Paul's position and that of Peter and the Jerusalem apostles was that
they proposed to impose definite rules upon all Gentile Christians,
thus breaking the agreement into which they had entered at the
memorable interview at Jerusalem, while Paul demanded for each man
individual liberty, although even in his letter to the Galatians with
all its protests against the Judaizing Christians, he urges: "Brothers,

98

you are called to be free; only do not make your freedom an opening for the flesh, but serve one another in love" (Gal. 5[13]). The principle involved in this great controversy was long debated in the early Christian church. Revelations 2[14, 20] simply emphasizes the importance of having all Christians abstain from eating things offered to idols. Not until the latter half of the first century, when Christianity broke entirely with Judaism, was the broad yet considerate position advocated by Paul universally adopted by the Christian church. Even as late as 120 A.D. the *Teaching of the Twelve* directs: "But as concerning foods bear that which thou art able; however, abstain by all means from meat sacrificed to idols, for it is the worship of dead gods."

VI. The Significance of the Breaking of Jewish Bonds. Viewed in the broad perspective of history, the incidents recorded in Galatians 2 mark a new epoch in the history of Christianity. What had hitherto been accepted in practice outside of Palestine was now formulated in a definite principle. Christianity stood before the Græco-Roman world completely free from the swaddling-clothes of Judaism. Henceforth the apostles to the Gentiles entered upon their noble task of interpreting the principles of Jesus into forms attractive and intelligible to that world. Paul, conscious of the strong opposition against himself and his teachings in the Palestinian church and at variance even with certain leaders like Barnabas of the Antioch church, henceforth faced with undivided zeal the Gentile mission field. The consciousness of fighting for a great principle spurred him on to still greater endeavors. It also led him to seek fields beyond the immediate pale of Jewish influence in which he could demonstrate in broader and larger measure the efficacy of the Gospel of Jesus for Gentile as well as Jew. The unfortunate by-products of the great controversy were destined to pursue him and undermine to a certain extent his work not only in Asia Minor but even in distant Corinth. At the same time it called forth some of his greatest utterances and tended to confirm him in his broad position. It was clearly the chief cause of the breach between himself and Barnabas; but the fact that he lost the companionship of his earlier co-laborer led him to rear up a group of faithful disciples who ultimately multiplied manyfold the work of the great apostle to the Gentiles. Thus out of the bitterness of the struggle came rich fruits and the Christian liberty which is man's most cherished possession.

AUL'S SECOND VISIT AND LATER LETTER TO THE CHURCHES OF GALATIA

Paul's departure with Silas (Acts 15³⁶⁻⁴¹)

After remaining certain days in Antioch, Paul said to Barnabas, Let us now go back to visit the brothers in all the cities where we have proclaimed the word of the Lord and see how they are doing. But while Barnabas wanted to take along John (who was called Mark), Paul did not deem it desirable to take with them a man who had deserted them in Pamphylia instead of going on with them to the work. So there was a serious disagreement with the result that they parted company. Barnabas, taking Mark with him, set sail for Cyprus, while Paul selected Silas and went off, commended by the brothers to the grace of the Lord. He passed through Syria and Cilicia strengthening the churches.

Selection of Timothy as a helper (16¹⁻³)

He also came to Derbe and Lystra. At Lystra there was a disciple called Timothy, the son of a believing Jewess and of a Greek father. He was well spoken of by the brothers at Lystra and Iconium. Paul, desiring to have him accompany him, took and circumcised him on account of the Jews who were in those parts, for they all knew that his father was a Greek.

Greeting (Gal. 1¹⁻⁵)

[Paul also wrote to the churches of Galatia]: Paul, an apostle, sent not by man, nor commanded by any man, but by Jesus Christ, and God the Father, who raised him from the dead, and all the brothers who are with me, to the churches of Galatia: Grace and peace to you from God our Father, and the Lord Jesus Christ, who gave himself for our sins, to set us free from the present evil world, in accordance with the will of our God and Father, to whom be glory for ever and ever. Amen.

Thesis (6-9)

I am astonished that you are so hastily deserting him who called you by the grace of Christ and going over to another gospel. It simply means that certain ones are unsettling you and desire to pervert the gospel of Christ. Now, even if we or some angel from heaven preach a gospel different from that gospel which I preached to you, may God's curse be on him! As I have said it before, so I

100

say it now: whoever preaches a gospel to you different from the gospel you have received, let God's curse be on him!

O foolish Galatians, who has bewitched you—you, before whose eyes Jesus Christ the crucified has been vividly presented? One thing only I wish to learn from you: did you receive the Spirit by doing what the law commands, or by believing the gospel message? Are you so foolish? Did you begin with the Spirit to end now with the flesh? Have you had all that experience in vain—if it has really been in vain? When he supplieth you with the Spirit and worketh miracles in you, is it because you do what the law commands, or because you believe the gospel message? It is as it was with Abraham, who had faith in God and it was reckoned to him as righteousness. Know then that those who have faith are the real sons of Abraham. *The gift of the Spirit, conditioned on faith, is the only valid evidence of being a son of Abraham (3¹⁻⁷)*

Before faith came, we were confined by the law and limited to the faith that was to be revealed. Thus the law was our tutor until Christ should come, that we might be justified by faith. But since the faith has come, we are no longer under a tutor; for you are all sons of God by your faith in Christ Jesus, for as many of you as have been baptized in Christ have taken on the character of Christ. There is no longer Jew nor Greek, slave nor free, male and female; for you are all one in Christ Jesus. Now, if you are Christ's, then are you Abraham's offspring; by virtue of the promise you are heirs. *Faith in Christ makes all men sons and heirs of God (²³⁻²⁹)*

What I mean is this. As long as an heir is under age, there is no difference between him and a slave, although he is lord of all things: he is under guardians and stewards until the time fixed by his father. So with us also. When we were under age, we lived under the bondage of the elemental spirits of the world; but, when the fullness of time had come, God sent forth his son, born of a woman, born under law to ransom those who were under the law, in order that we might receive our right of sonship. Because you are sons, God has sent forth the spirit of his son into our hearts, crying Abba! Father! So you are no longer a slave but a son and, as son, also an heir through God. *Jesus through his spirit of sonship liberates from bondage to the law and to heathen gods (4¹⁻⁷)*

The return of the Galatians to the bondage of the law (8-11)

But in those days, when you did not know God, you were in bondage to those who by nature are no gods; but, now that you know God, or rather are known by God, how is it that you are turning back again to the weak, poverty stricken, elemental spirits? Why do you wish to be enslaved all over again by them? You observe days, and months, and festal seasons and years! You make me afraid that I may have spent my labor on you in vain!

Their changed attitude toward Paul (12-20)

I beg of you be as I am, for I was even as you, brothers. You did me no wrong, although you knew it was because of an illness that I preached the gospel to you on my former visit. And, though my flesh was a trial to you, you did not despise nor scoff at me but received me as an angel of God, like Christ Jesus. Now what has become of all your congratulations? For I can testify that you would have torn out your very eyes, if you could, and given them to me. Have I become your enemy because I have spoken the truth to you? These men seek you zealously but not honestly; rather they desire to shut you out from me in order that you may zealously seek them. Now it is a fine thing for you to be zealously sought for at all times in the right manner—not only when I can be with you. My little children, you for whom I am again in travail until Christ be formed within you, would that I might be with you at this time and alter my tone, for I am at my wit's end about you!

Circumcision now evidence of lack of faith in Christ (5²-6)

See! I, Paul, say to you: if you let yourselves be circumcised, Christ will be of no use to you. I assert again to everyone that lets himself be circumcised that he is under obligation to carry out the whole of the law. You who seek justification in the law are done with Christ. You have fallen from grace, for it is by faith that we wait in the Spirit for the hope of righteousness. For in Christ Jesus neither circumcision nor uncircumcision avails anything, but only faith and love.

The law of liberty (13-15)

Brothers, you were called to be free; only do not make your freedom an opportunity for the flesh, but serve one another in love. For the entire law is summed up in one word, You must love your neighbor as yourself. But, if you bite and devour one another, take care lest you be destroyed by one another.

THE GUIDANCE OF THE SPIRIT

I mean, walk by the Spirit; then you will not satisfy the inclinations of the flesh. For the inclination of the flesh is against the spirit, and the inclination of the spirit is against the flesh; for these two are opposed to each other, so that you are not free to do as you please. But, if you are led by the spirit, you are not under the sway of the law. The guidance of the spirit (16-18)

Now the deeds of the flesh are quite evident, such as sexual vice, impurity, sensuality, idolatry, sorcery, quarrels, contention, jealousy, anger, rivalry, factions, party spirit, envy, drinking bouts, revelry, and the like. I tell you beforehand, as I have told you already, that those who do these things will never inherit the Kingdom of God. But the fruit of the spirit is love, joy, peace, forbearance, kindness, generosity, fidelity, gentleness, self-control—there is no law against those who do these things. The fruits of the flesh and of the spirit (19-23)

Now those who belong to Christ have crucified the flesh with its passions and inclinations. If we live by the spirit, let us walk also in the spirit. Let us not be vain nor given to provoking or envying one another. Even if anyone is caught in some wrong act, brothers, you who are spiritual must set such a one right in a spirit of gentleness. Let each one of you look to himself lest you be tempted. Bear one another's burdens and so fulfill the law of Christ. If anyone imagines that he is somebody when he is nobody, he is deceiving himself. Let everyone test his own work and then he will have something to boast about on his own account, and not in comparison with his neighbor. For everyone will have to bear his own load. Each one who is taught should share all the good things of life with those who teach him the word. The Christian way of living (5:24-6:6)

Be not deceived; God is not to be mocked: for whatever a man sows, that shall he also reap. He who sows for his own flesh shall from the flesh reap destruction, and he who sows for the spirit shall reap from the spirit life eternal. And let us not grow weary of doing what is right, for in due season we shall reap if we faint not. So then, as we have opportunity, let us do good to all men and especially to those who are of the household of the faith. The harvest of life (7-10)

See what big letters I make when I write with mine own hand! These men who are seeking to compel you to be

Paul's
auto-
graph
and
bene-
diction
(11-18) circumcised desire to make a fine show in the flesh. It is simply that they may not be persecuted for the cross of Christ. For even they who have been circumcised do not keep the law themselves; but they desire to have you circumcised so that they may boast over your flesh! But far be it from me to glory except in the cross of our Lord Jesus Christ, by which the world has been crucified to me and I to the world. For what counts is neither circumcision nor uncircumcision, but the new creation, and on as many as will walk by this rule may peace and mercy rest, even upon the Israel of God.

Henceforth, let no man interfere with me, for I bear branded on my body the marks of Jesus.

The grace of our Lord Jesus Christ be with your spirit, brothers. Amen.

I. **Date and Aim of Paul's Second Missionary Campaign.** Paul probably set out on his second missionary campaign in the early autumn of 49 A.D. He was eager to get away from the dissensions raised by the Judaizers at Jerusalem and Antioch. Acts states that his primary purpose was to visit the Galatian churches, doubtless with a view to strengthening them (Acts 16⁵). He also aimed to prepare them for the problems that he saw before them. His ultimate purpose was to carry the Gospel of Jesus westward throughout the provinces of Asia Minor immediately beyond the Roman province of Galatia which had been the scene of his earlier work. The great metropolitan city of Ephesus, the commercial and religious capital of the province of Asia, was clearly Paul's definite objective. His comprehensive aim even at this period was evidently to conquer the great Gentile world that had been assigned to him at the memorable interview at Jerusalem. Paul sought not only to extend his conquests to the great political and social centres of this Gentile world, but also, at this critical stage, to make each field in which he preached and planted churches the base for the next advance.

II. **Revisiting the Galatian Churches.** Paul was evidently the one who originally proposed to Barnabas that they face the perils of Asia Minor and penetrate again to the heart of the Roman province of Galatia. Throughout this arduous but successful enterprise Paul had taken the initiative. The reason given in Acts why Barnabas did not accompany Paul in his second visit to this field is their disagreement about taking John Mark with them. Probably a deeper reason was their disagreement regarding the right and wisdom of letting Jewish and Gentile Christians freely associate together without imposing on either any ceremonial limitation. Moreover, Barnabas's interest lay in his homeland, Cyprus; Paul's in the unconquered territory beyond his native city, Tarsus. Paul's later references to Barnabas indicate that there was no permanent alienation (I Cor. 9[6], Col. 4[10]). The separation of these two pioneer apostles to the Gentiles appears to have resulted in a tacit, or possibly definitely defined division of the Gentile field. Tradition says that Barnabas not only went to Cyprus but also to Egypt, which early became an important Christian centre. Egypt also had a great Jewish population and might well be regarded as belonging to the sphere of activity set aside for the Twelve. At least some such implied division of territory best explains why Paul with his world-wide outlook and tireless zeal never visited nor even alludes in his letters to the populous land of the Nile and the flourishing cities on the southern Mediterranean.

Starting from Antioch and taking Silas, who was an influential member of the Jerusalem church and likewise possessed Roman citizenship (Acts 16[37]) and was therefore a Hellenist, Paul set out northward on the great highway that led through Asia Minor to Rome. On the way he probably strengthened the Christian churches which he had established during the first thirteen years of his ministry in northern Syria and Cilicia. Unfortunately, Luke has not preserved the names of these churches. That there was one at Tarsus is reasonably certain. Thence, following the great Roman highway, they passed through the cities which Paul had visited together with Barnabas. Paul's circumcision of the half-Jewish youth Timothy, whom he wished to accompany him on his visit to the strongly Jewish churches at Iconium and Galatian Antioch, is not a repudiation of the principles for which he contended at Jerusalem but rather an illustration of his avowed purpose, with the Jews "to become like a Jew to win over Jews." Unfortunately Luke, instead of giving details regarding the visit to these churches, has simply introduced one of his general summaries (Acts 16[4, 5]). In keeping with his assumption that Paul had accepted the resolutions of James and the other authorities at Jerusalem, he states that Paul formally transmitted these to the different churches. What Paul actually did can best be learned from his own testimony in his letter to the Galatians.

III. **The Occasion of Paul's Letter to the Galatians.** The interpreter of Paul's letter to the Galatians is at once confronted with a much-debated question. Did Paul write this letter to the churches in the Roman province of Galatia, which he and Barnabas had established during their first missionary campaign, or was it written to Christian churches farther north organized by Paul in the old province of Galatia during his second missionary campaign? Volumes have been written in defense of each of these positions and New Testament scholars are about equally divided. Fortunately, our appreciation of Paul's vigorous letter to the Galatians and of the superb spirit and personality which it reveals is not dependent upon the answer to these questions. The chief corner-stone of what is known as the "North Galatian theory" is Luke's statement in Acts 16[6], following his summary of Paul's work in Derbe, Lystra, and Iconium, that "they crossed the Phrygian and Galatian region, the Holy Spirit having stopped them from preaching the word in Asia; when they got as far as Mysia they tried to enter Bithynia, but the spirit of Jesus would not allow them, and so they passed by Mysia and went down to Troas." Many hold that the most natural interpretation of this statement is that, having passed through the Derbe, Lystra, and Iconium, which were in ancient Phrygia, they turned northward to the old province of Galatia and from thence westward to the seaport of Troas. It is difficult, however, to explain why Luke is absolutely silent regarding Paul's activity in this northern province, if it had been significant enough in its results to call forth the powerful letter to the Galatians. In view of Paul's avowed purpose, we naturally anticipate that, after leaving Iconium, he would go directly to Antioch in Pisidia, which also lay in the Roman province of Galatia—in fact, it is almost impossible to believe that he failed to visit this important scene of his earlier work. The absolute absence of any reference or suggestion, either in Acts or in Paul's own letters, that implies a period of successful missionary activity in the old province of Galatia leaves to the "North Galatian theory," to say the least, a very uncertain and indefinite basis. On the other hand, the churches founded by Paul and Barnabas in their first campaign were on the direct highway from Syria to Rome, and therefore most exposed to the influence of the Judaizers to which Paul frequently refers in his letter to the Galatians. It is also exceedingly probable that Paul the traveller and Roman citizen would use the term Galatia in its contemporary Roman rather than in its older local application. This conclusion is supported by his custom at other times. In any case, the definitely known conditions and problems of the south Galatian cities furnish a thoroughly satisfactory explanation of the many detailed allusions contained in Paul's famous letter, so that there can be little doubt that the churches at Antioch, Iconium, Lystra, and Derbe were in his mind as he wrote.

If Galatians was written to these churches, it must have been after Paul had revisited them at the beginning of his second missionary campaign. His inability to visit them again, to which he alludes at the beginning of his letter, suggests strongly that he was not in Antioch nor the East, but already actively engaged in his work either at Corinth or Ephesus. Apparently the Judaizers, to which he refers, followed close in his footsteps after leaving Antioch and had worked quietly and almost unknown to him while he was busy in the western field. At the same time the questions involved are the direct aftermath of the interview at Jerusalem and the reaction at Antioch to which Paul refers. It is probable, therefore, that the Epistle to the Galatians is one of the three earliest of Paul's letters and was probably written during the earlier part of his ministry at Corinth.

IV. **The Literary Structure and Contents of Galatians.** Paul's letter to the Galatians falls naturally into four divisions, with an impassioned introduction found in 1^{1-9}. Chapters $1^{10}-2^{21}$ contain Paul's masterful declaration of independence and authority. Rapidly and evidently under the pressure of great feeling, he marshals the important events in his own career and especially his relations to the "pillars" at Jerusalem, concluding the description with a statement of the terms agreed upon in his famous interview at Jerusalem and their later interpretation at Antioch. The second main division of the letter, $3^{1}-5^{12}$, contains his defense of his gospel of freedom from the law and of justification by faith through Jesus Christ. In $5^{13}-6^{10}$ he corrects the possible misinterpretations of his gospel of freedom by defining the moral responsibility of those that hold the Christian faith. The epilogue, 6^{11-18}, recapitulates in short, forcible sentences the chief points for which he was contending and concludes with the usual benediction. This epistle has been appropriately likened to one of the dashing mountain torrents, which in many of the fields of Paul's activity leap from the heights above, at first sweeping away all opposition, but in time gradually broadening out to water the plain below. As Sabatier has said, here "unfinished phrases, daring omissions, parentheses which leave us out of sight and out of breath, rabbinical subtleties, dashing paradoxes, vehement apostrophes pour on like surging billows." Here Paul writes as he would doubtless have spoken could he have stood in the presence of the faltering and much-confused Christians of Galatia. It is Paul the militant who is here revealed, the man who quickly proved himself the master of every situation into which Providence led him.

He is fighting here not merely for the faith of the Galatian Christians but also for the fundamental principles of Christian liberty. It was the age-long issue between the authority of accepted tradition and ceremonialism and the authority of the Spirit of God in the heart and life of the individual. The principle was the same for which Jesus contended against the Pharisees, Luther against the Catholic Church, and modern Christianity against ecclesiastical and literalistic conservatism.

V. **Paul's Interpretation of the Significance of the Jewish Law and of the Work of Jesus.** It is evident that Paul's opponents made a strong and plausible appeal to the Galatian Christians. They had the whole weight of Jewish tradition back of them. Their charge that Paul was an iconoclast, who rejected as useless the greater part of the Jewish law, was valid. In comparison with the definite way of salvation presented by that law, Paul's gospel must have seemed to many minds somewhat vague. In supporting his position Paul reveals in this letter his marvellous skill in appealing to the intellects as well as to the hearts of men. His first appeal is to the inner spiritual experience of the Galatian Christians themselves. Was it the teachings of the Judaizers or Paul's gospel which had given them the consciousness of the presence of the divine Spirit in their hearts and lives? The phenomena of speaking with tongues and miracles had further attested the divine origin of his gospel. In Paul's mind this evidence of spiritual experience transcended all others. His next line of evidence was historical. Abraham, the forefather of his race knew nothing of the later law, but to him had been given the divine promises of which the work of Jesus was the fruition. These promises had been given not only to the descendants of Abraham, but to all, both Jew and Gentile, who shared his faith. What, after all, had the law accomplished? In answering this question, Paul evidently drew from his own personal experience. It developed, he declared, a consciousness of sin, which, on the one side, pointed only to death as its just penalty, but, on the other hand, in opening the minds of men to the need of divine forgiveness, it prepared the way for the fulfilment of God's promises and the accomplishment of the work of Jesus. Gentiles and Jews alike were subject to the laws of nature, which they believed to be controlled by elemental spirits. Hitherto men had been like immature children, under the tutelage of the law or of their imperfect religious beliefs; but now at last humanity was about to enter into its heritage. Through Jesus, whose central teaching had been the fatherhood of God and man's divine sonship, man had been delivered from its old bondage. "He was no longer a slave but a son and as son also God's heir." Therefore he assures the Galatian Christians that their inner spiritual experience, the consciousness, "of Christ formed within them," was the only and supreme evidence that they were the heirs of the promises given to Abraham and indeed the sons of God. To adopt the rite of circumcision and to go back to the observance of the Jewish ceremonial law would be to substitute form for the Spirit and to repudiate the divine heritage which had come to them through the work of Jesus.

VI. **The Responsibilities of Spiritual Liberty.** To Paul, faith and life in Christ had brought liberty. Christian liberty is one of his favorite themes; but Paul always guarded against its interpretation as license. He strongly asserts that freedom from the law does not mean liberty to follow one's wayward caprices. It means rather, constant loyalty to the guidance of the Spirit. Indeed, those who "belong to Christ have crucified the flesh with its passions and inclinations." Furthermore in Paul's vocabulary, liberty is a synonym for responsibility. Not only is the Christian to bear the fruits of the Spirit (which he defines) but also "to bear one another's burdens and so fulfil the law of Christ"—that higher spiritual law which has taken the place of the old Jewish law. The one supreme principle, he declares, in that new law is love: "For the entire law is summed up in one word, 'You must love your neighbor as yourself.'" Thus the epistle opens with powerful invective, which merges into impassioned argument and then in conclusion strikes Paul's ever-dominant note, that of love.

§ CLIV. PAUL'S MISSIONARY WORK IN MACEDONIA

Paul and his associates crossed the Phrygian and Galatian country, but were prevented by the Holy Spirit from preaching the word in the province of Asia. When they reached Mysia, they tried to enter Bithynia, but the Spirit of Jesus would not allow them, and so, passing by Mysia, they went down to Troas.

The journey to Troas (Acts 16⁶⁻⁸)

109

The appeal to go to Macedonia (9, 10)

There a vision appeared to Paul by night: a man in Macedonia was standing and appealing to him and saying, Come over into Macedonia and help us. As soon as he saw the vision, we immediately made efforts to go on to Macedonia, inferring that God had called us to preach the gospel to them.

Arrival at Philippi (11, 12)

Then setting sail from Troas, we ran straight to Samothrace and on the next day to Neapolis, thence to the Roman colony of Philippi, which is the foremost city of the district of Macedonia. In this city we spent some days.

Lydia's conversion (13-15)

On the sabbath we went outside the gate by the river, where we had reason to believe there was a place of prayer; and we sat down and talked to the women who had gathered. Among our hearers was a woman by the name of Lydia, a dealer in purple, who belonged to the city of Thyatira and was a worshipper of God. The Lord opened her heart to attend to what Paul was saying. When she and her household had been baptized, she begged us, saying, If you are convinced that I am a believer in the Lord, come and stay in my house. And she compelled us to come.

The healing of a slave girl (16-18)

Now it happened as we were going to the place of prayer that a slave girl met us who had a spirit of ventriloquism and brought great profit to her owners by telling fortunes. She kept following Paul and the rest of us crying aloud, These men are servants of the Most High God; they proclaim to you the way of salvation. This she did for many days. Then Paul, completely worn out, said to the spirit, In the name of Jesus Christ I order you to come out of her. And it came out of her immediately.

The arrest of Paul and Silas (19-24)

But when her owners saw that their hope of profit was gone, they caught hold of Paul and Silas and dragged them into the forum before the magistrates. Bringing them before the prætors they said, These are Jews who are making a disturbance in our city; they are proclaiming customs which we Romans are not allowed to adopt or observe. The crowd also joined in the attack upon them, while the prætors, after having stripped them, ordered them to be flogged. After they had inflicted many lashes upon them they put them into prison, charging the jailer to keep them safe. He, on receiving such an order, put them into the inner prison and secured their feet in the stocks.

About midnight, as Paul and Silas were praying and singing to God and while the prisoners were listening to them, there was suddenly such a great earthquake that it shook the very foundations of the prison. All the doors immediately flew open and the fetters of all the prisoners were unfastened. The jailer, starting up from sleep and seeing the prison wide open, drew his sword and was about to kill himself, supposing that the prisoners had made their escape. But Paul said with a loud voice, Do not harm yourself, for we are all here! So, calling for lights, the jailer rushed in, fell trembling before Paul and Silas, and brought them out of the prison. Sirs, he said, what must I do to be saved? Believe in the Lord Jesus Christ, said Paul, and both you and your household will be saved. And they spoke the word of the Lord to him and to all his house. Then he took them at that very hour of the night and washed their wounds. And he and all his family were immediately baptized. Then taking them to his house, he put food before them and rejoiced with all his household at having believed in God. *The jailer's conversion (25-34)*

The next morning the prætors sent the lictors with the order, Release these men. The jailer announced these words to Paul, saying, The prætors have sent to release you. So now come out and go in peace. But Paul replied, They flogged us in public without trial, we who are Roman citizens! They put us in prison, and now they are going to eject us secretly! Far be it! Rather let them come here themselves and take us out. The lictors reported these words to the prætors, who, on hearing that the men were Roman citizens, were filled with alarm, and came to appease them, and, after taking them out of prison, begged them to leave the city. So leaving the prison, they went to Lydia's house, where they saw the brothers and encouraged them; then they departed. *The release of the apostles (35-40)*

Then travelling on to Amphipolis and Apollonia, they reached Thessalonica, where there was a Jewish synagogue. And, as was his custom, Paul went in to them and *Paul's preaching in Thessalonica (17¹⁻⁴)*

111

for three sabbaths argued with them from the scriptures, explaining and quoting passages to show that the Messiah had to suffer and rise from the dead, and that the Jesus I proclaim to you is the Messiah. Some were persuaded and attached themselves to Paul and Silas, including many devout Greeks and not a few of the leading women.

The riot kindled by the Jews (5-9)

But the Jews, stirred by jealousy, called to their aid some idle fellows and formed a mob and set the city in an uproar. Attacking Jason's house, they endeavored to bring Paul and Silas out before the people, but failing to find them, they dragged Jason and some of the brothers before the politarchs, shouting, These men, who have raised a tumult through the whole world, have come here too! Jason has welcomed them! These all violate the decrees of Cæsar by declaring that there is another king called Jesus. Great was the excitement among the crowd and the politarchs when they heard this; but after binding Jason and the others over to keep the peace, they released them.

Paul and Silas at Berœa (10-12)

Then the brothers at once sent off Paul and Silas at night to Berœa. And they, on arriving there, went to the Jewish synagogue. The people there were more noble than at Thessalonica, for they very readily received the word and daily studied the scriptures to see if it really was as Paul said. As a result many of them believed, together with a large number of prominent Greeks, both men and women.

Paul's journey to Athens (13-15)

But as soon as the Jews of Thessalonica heard that the word of God was being proclaimed at Berœa as well, they came to create a disturbance there and a riot among the crowd at Berœa. Then the brothers at once sent Paul down to the sea coast, while Silas and Timothy remained there. Those who accompanied Paul brought him as far as Athens and left with orders that Silas and Timothy were to come to him as soon as possible.

I. **Paul's Quest of a New Mission Field.** The narrative of Acts 16[6-8] is exceedingly condensed and leaves us in uncertainty regarding many questions. The inference is that Paul, all the way from Iconium until he finally found himself at Troas, was seeking vainly for a suitable field for missionary activity. The phrases "forbidden by the Holy Spirit" and "the Spirit of Jesus would not allow them" are already familiar to the reader of the book of Acts. In Acts 21⁴ it is stated that the disciples "told Paul by the Spirit not to set foot in Jerusalem." This statement apparently points to a prophetic utterance under the influence of ecstasy, and the same psychological phenomena probably lie back of the statements in Acts 16. According to Acts 15³², Silas, Paul's companion, already had a reputation as a prophet. It is possible that he was the spokesman of the Spirit on these occasions. The analogy of Galatians 2² points, however, to a decision in Paul's own mind made under the influence of a careful consideration of the facts involved. This was apparently the way in which he made most of the important decisions of his life. Facts and truths, which were more or less central in his thought, were suddenly and, as it seemed to him, miraculously crystallized into an absolute conviction which he regarded as divinely inspired and which he henceforth followed unfalteringly. Even though the narrative of Acts at this point is meagre, it is possible to conjecture what were the underlying reasons which led Paul to turn aside from the Roman province of Asia and its chief city Ephesus, which evidently from the first had been the objective of his second missionary campaign. It is probable that already a small Christian community was found at Ephesus and therefore to go there was to break one of Paul's fundamental rules, namely, not to "build on another man's foundation" (Rom. 15²⁰). It was also the seat of an exceedingly popular and strongly intrenched heathen cult. When Paul ultimately visited it, it proved a very difficult field. The province of Bithynia, from which he was also turned aside, was situated in the northwestern corner of Asia Minor. Pliny the Younger in his famous letter to Trajan, written near the beginning of the second Christian century, indicates that Christianity at a very early period had gained a strong foothold in this province. It is not at all improbable that when Paul drew near to Bithynia he learned that already other Christian missionaries had anticipated him. From a topographical point of view it was also a difficult field to traverse, and it is probable that the effects of the illness, to which Paul refers in his letters, still deterred him from doing what his indomitable spirit longed to accomplish. Thus hemmed in on every side, he at last found himself at the end of the great Roman highway which led from Syria to Europe. Troas was the door that led across the Ægean to Europe and to Rome itself, the ultimate goal of Paul's ambition. Should he abandon his well-established policy of pressing on from province to province, leaving no important strategic centres behind him, and follow instead the great Roman highway across the sea? Would he succeed, if he left behind him the more distinctly Jewish background and entered the very different Greek world?

II. Paul's Vision at Troas. It is significant that at this point in Acts the history is written in the first person. This personal testimony continues until Paul reaches Philippi and again appears when he comes back to Philippi on his way to Jerusalem and ultimately to Rome. The most natural explanation of these facts is that Luke lived at Philippi, and that either by chance or previous arrangement he first met Paul at Troas. Ramsay's suggestion that the prototype of the man of Macedonia, who figures in Paul's vision, was Luke himself has much to commend it. The words which came to Paul in his vision from the lips of the man in Macedonia, "Come over into Macedonia and help us," suggest strongly that the one who uttered them was already a follower of Jesus and eager to secure the co-operation of the great apostle to the Gentiles. The fact that Paul went directly to Philippi and began there rather than at Thessalonica his mission to the Macedonians strongly indicates that the words of Luke lay in the background of Paul's consciousness when he had his epoch-making vision. Such incidents, as well as the vision itself, were in perfect harmony with similar experiences in Paul's life. Even as the young patriot Isaiah, laboring under a sense of personal responsibility, suddenly beheld a vision of Jehovah in his temple and was thereby consecrated and committed to his life-work, so Paul in one significant moment left behind all uncertainty and recognized that he was divinely committed to the evangelization of Macedonia.

III. Paul's Work in Philippi. Paul on landing on the northern shore of the Ægean passed through the seaport of Neapolis and pressed nine miles northward to Philippi, not the metropolis of Macedonia as the author of Acts states, but the chief city on the southern end of a great plain. This was bounded on the east by a river which lost itself in a huge marsh to the south of the city. Here in 42 B.C. Octavian and Anthony fought their great decisive battle against Brutus and Cassius. Here the ideal of a republic fell before that of an empire. Octavian in his gratitude for the victory made Philippi a Roman colony and gave it a thoroughly Roman form of government. Here Paul found a small Jewish community, too small to support a synagogue but accustomed on the Jewish Sabbath to meet for worship by the riverside. In this group Paul found Greek proselytes as well as Jews. Chief among them was a certain Lydia from the Lydian city of Thyatira. She was evidently a woman of great ability and possessed of considerable wealth, for she appears to have had a bazaar, as well as a home in Philippi. To her Paul's preaching appealed so strongly that she offered her home as a centre for his work. There he apparently remained for some months.

Certain details in Paul's experience at Philippi stand out clearly and are obviously based on the extracts from the journal of travel. The story of the slave girl, "who had a spirit of ventriloquism," gives a vivid impression of the religious and social environment amid which Paul worked. Evidently the girl possessed a keen mind, like many of the slaves to be found during that period throughout the broad bounds of the Roman Empire, for her success in predicting the future of those who appealed to her for a divine response was clearly due to her power of insight and inventive genius. Her attitude toward Paul and his fellow workers indicates that she appreciated the truth of their teaching and that she was apparently eager to help them. Her words and deeds, as reported, are a public confession of faith in their teaching. Paul, however, was evidently annoyed by the fact that that confession seemed to come through the medium of heathen divination. His words to her were therefore of the nature both of a command and of a rebuke. They produced the desired result. Evidently she had hitherto believed in her miraculous powers; but now Paul's words through suggestion had acted as an inhibition. Therefore she could not go on as formerly. Her silence is possibly an index that she accepted the apostle's teaching. That Paul believed that she was possessed of an unclean spirit cannot be doubted in the light of his assertion in I Corinthians 10[20]. The terms in which he addressed her recall Jesus' rebuke to the man possessed of an unclean spirit in the synagogue at Capernaum (Mark 2[25]). Furthermore, that Paul believed that he had performed a miracle cannot be doubted, for he plainly asserts his conviction that he possessed this power in II Corinthians 12[12]. The slave girl's masters, in their mad frenzy, at first succeeded in playing on the prejudices of the Roman rulers of Philippi. Hatred of everything Jewish was then common throughout the Roman Empire, and Philippi was especially jealous of its Roman citizenship. Paul's personal appearance may have also aroused this race antagonism. Soon the city mob was seized with the same fanatical frenzy.

In these circumstances it was futile for Paul to urge in defense his Roman citizenship. Without waiting for the formality of a judicial trial, the prætors gave the cruel command to flog him and his associates. While Paul does not refer to this experience in his later letter to the Philippians, he does declare in II Corinthians 11[25] that he was "thrice beaten with rods," indicating that on two other occasions his Roman citizenship was not sufficient to deliver him from this horrible indignity.

It is possible that the account of the imprisonment of Paul and Silas has been influenced by the late tradition of Peter's imprisonment found in Acts 5[17-42]. The present narrative, however, does not claim that the disciples were supernaturally liberated but simply states that a violent earthquake shook the very foundations of the prison, loosening the bars from the prison doors and the chains which bound the prisoners. In view of the insecure construction of prisons in this part of the world even to-day the phenomena described are not without analogies. Paul's action in this crisis is characteristic. As later, when shipwrecked, the prisoner suddenly becomes the master of the situation. Out of sheer admiration and gratitude the jailer, who doubtless had previously heard Paul's preaching and been impressed by his personality, voiced spontaneously the need and the belief that was already germinating within him. Paul throughout all his ministry revealed a marvellous adaptability to every change of circumstance. Dramatic indeed is the picture of his preaching in the darkness of the earthquake-shaken prison to the frightened jailer and his prisoners. Possibly the earthquake was effectual in restoring the judicial prudence of the Roman prætors, for at dawn they sent the command to loose the prisoners whom they had so unjustly treated. Thus it is that Paul was able to gain a hearing for his assertion that he and Silas were Roman citizens, with the result that the Philippian judges came in person to beg their prisoners to leave the town and that they were thankful thus to escape the consequences of their rash action.

Paul left behind him at Philippi a small but exceedingly devoted band of Christians that during the rest of his life was an unceasing source of joy to him. Their personal devotion to him was most marked. At least twice they sent funds for the support of his work at Thessalonica (Phil. 4[16]); again at Corinth he was cheered by their gifts (II Cor. 11[10]); and the one supreme love-letter that comes down to us from his lips was prompted by a similar evidence of their affection when he was a prisoner, facing death at Rome (Phil. 4[10, 18]).

IV. **The Founding of the Church at Thessalonica.** Paul left Philippi, not as a fugitive, but at the request of the magistrates. His plan of campaign is again illustrated by the fact that he passed by the smaller cities of Amphipolis and Apollonia and went directly to Thessalonica, the metropolis of Macedonia. It was majestically situated at the head of the Theramic Gulf in a great natural ampitheatre and looked southeastward toward the Ægean Sea. Here the Egnatian Way met the highways of commerce that radiated from the northern Ægean through the rich plains to the north. Commercially and strategically it resembled Corinth in many ways. It was a free Greek city, ruled by politarchs and proud of its independence and prestige. The opportunities of trade had attracted here a strong Jewish colony. The Jewish faith had also won many Greek proselytes.

As usual, the author of Acts emphasizes Paul's public preaching, especially in the Jewish synagogue. Fortunately in Paul's letters to the Christians of Thessalonica he has given vivid pictures of his work and experiences there. He found living in this great commercial city expensive. Night and day he worked at his trade of tent-making, while he told his fellow workmen about Jesus (I Thess. 2⁹). The majority of the converts were from the poorer classes (II Cor. 8²). Most of them were Greeks, for he states that his chief task was to turn them from idols to the service of the living and real God and to prepare them for the coming of his son Jesus, who would deliver them from the wrath that threatened (I Thess. 1⁹, ¹⁰). The idea of the *parousia* or coming of Antiochus or of Augustus or of a god was familiar to the devout Greeks, as we now know from many contemporary inscriptions. Eagerly they entered into the expectation of a speedy coming of the divine king whom Paul proclaimed. Indeed, as the event proved, they were too eager, for their expectations in time affected unfavorably their ordinary activity (II Thess. 2).

Paul's teaching regarding the coming of Jesus was apparently also the basis of the charge which the Jews preferred against him and Silas. While Paul does not directly refer to it in his letters, this is probably the reason for his reference to the Jews as those "who offend God and oppose all men by hindering us from speaking words of salvation to the Gentiles" (I Thess. 2¹⁶). Here, as at Philippi, Paul's assailants did not trust to a fair judicial trial but aroused the mob to support their indefinite charge. Warned by previous experience, Paul and Silas had found refuge in concealment. Jason, at whose house they had been received, and certain others of the Christian converts

117

resident at Thessalonica were dragged before the politarchs on the hysterical charge of having entertained "these upsetters of the whole world" who were treasonably proclaiming that not Augustus but Jesus was king. The charge is an echo of that which was brought by the Jewish high priests against Jesus himself. Although the rulers of Thessalonica were especially sensitive to a charge of this kind, they evidently recognized its absurdity and simply put Jason and his associates under bond to keep the peace. The incident, however, marked the end of the personal work of Paul and Silas at Thessalonica. Even though their sojourn there had been limited to a few months, Paul emphatically declared: "Our visit to you was no failure" (I Thess. 2¹). The foundations were laid for a strong, democratic, loyal Christian church, which was one of the crowns of his missionary activity.

V. Paul's Work at Berœa. The public attack upon Paul and Silas led the Christian brothers to send them off by night to Berœa, fifty miles southwest of Thessalonica. This secluded Greek town was on the western side of a fertile plain that extended eastward to the Ægean Sea. It was flanked on the west by Mount Bermius, from whence came cool, flowing streams to water the groves and fields that encircled it. It proved a quiet haven of refuge for the apostles. While Paul would naturally have chosen a more important centre, he again illustrated his zeal and marvellous adaptability. In a short time he gathered about him an earnest band of Christian believers. The narrative of Acts states that he found here a better class of Jews than at the great commercial city of Thessalonica. It also states that his method was not so much that of public preaching as teaching. Here, as at Philippi and Thessalonica, he was doubtless working out with his fellow converts the doctrines that he later incorporates in his letters to the Corinthians and Romans. The majority of the Christian converts at Berœa were evidently Greeks, and numbered many prominent men and women. This is implied by the narrative of Acts and confirmed by the fact that Sopater, the son of Pyrrhus, clearly a Greek, was the representative of this church, who later accompanied Paul to Jerusalem (Acts 20⁴).

VI. The Results of Paul's Work in Macedonia. The chronological data in Acts are at this point indefinite, but it is probable that Paul's missionary campaign in Macedonia did not extend over more than a year. It represented days and weeks of intense physical and religious work. Much of it was done in the face of strong opposition; but on the whole it was for him a period of great joy and exaltation.

Here at last he demonstrated beyond all question the adaptability of the Gospel of and about Jesus to the purely Greek world. He must also have been profoundly impressed at this time by the readiness of the Gentiles for that new religion. Christianity was no longer the faith of a little Palestinian sect, but was rapidly becoming a universal world religion. At this time Paul also succeeded in planting the leaven of Christianity in two of the most important cities of southern Europe, which lay on the main highway that led directly to Rome. The Jewish element in these Macedonian churches appears to have been insignificant. Jason (the Greek form of Joshua and Jesus) of Thessalonica is the only distinctively Jewish name that appears in the record. Otherwise the relatively long list of converts mentioned in Acts and in Paul's letters all bear unmistakably Greek names. During his work in Macedonia Paul succeeded in establishing especially strong personal relations with the individual converts. As he faced new and more difficult fields, their love and warm friendship, as well as help, were his constant inspiration. During this period also he was training an efficient body of assistants. With the exception of Timothy they appear to have all been enlisted from this new field. We know the names of at least four who were native Macedonians: Sopater, Aristarchus, Secundus, and Gaius (Acts 19[29], 20[4]). To this list should perhaps be added the name of Luke. In Paul's later letter to the Philippians he mentions two women and three other men who were his active co-workers. In Macedonia Paul also realized in fullest measure his purpose to make each new Christian community the basis for the extension of the Gospel to other centres. Apparently in no other field did he succeed so well in implanting his intense missionary spirit. Until the very end of his life gifts to the "saints" in Jerusalem and to Paul himself were sent forth by the poor Christians of Macedonia whom he had helped so effectually.

§ CLV. PAUL'S LETTERS TO THE CHRISTIANS AT THESSALONICA

Paul, Silas and Timothy to the Church of the Thessalonians in God the Father and the Lord Jesus Christ: grace and peace to you.

Salutation (I Thess. 1[1])

We always thank God for you all when we make mention of you in our prayers. We never fail to remember your works of faith and labor of love and steadfast hope

Paul's
gratitude
for the
fidelity
of the
Thessalonians
(2-10)

in our Lord, Jesus Christ, before our God and Father.
O brothers, beloved by God, we know that he hath chosen
you. For our gospel came to you not with mere words but
with power and with the Holy Spirit and with great conviction. For you know what sort of men we were among
you for your sakes. And you are imitators of the examples
set by us and by the Lord, receiving the word amidst great
affliction, with joy inspired by the Holy Spirit. Thus you
became a pattern to all the believers in Macedonia and
Achaia; for the word of God has resounded from you not
only through Macedonia and Achaia, but your faith in God
has reached every place, so that we have no need to speak
about it. People tell us of their own accord how we were
received by you and how you turned to God from idols to
serve a living and real God and to await the coming of his
Son from heaven, whom he raised from the dead, Jesus who
rescues us from the wrath to come.

The
spirit
and
conduct
of the
apostles
(2¹-¹²)

For you yourselves know, brothers, that our visit to you
was not a failure. But, as you know, although at Philippi
we had been ill-treated and outraged, we took courage in our
God to tell you the gospel of God under great strain. For
our appeal does not spring from any delusion, nor from an
unclean motive, nor is there any fraud in it. Rather we
have been tested by God that we may be intrusted with
the gospel. Therefore, we speak not to please men, but
God who tests our hearts; for as you well know we have
never resorted to flattery nor to any pretext for self seeking.
God is witness; we never sought honor from men, from
you, nor from any others, though as apostles of Christ we
might have claimed authority. On the contrary, while we
were among you we were as gentle as a mother, nursing her
own children. Since we were thus drawn to you by affection, we would gladly have imparted to you not only the gospel of God, but have given our very lives also, for you have
become very dear to us. Brothers, you remember our hard
labor and toil, how we worked at our trade night and day
so as not to become a burden to any of you, while we preached
the gospel of God to you. You are witnesses and so is
God how pious and upright and blameless we acted toward
each one of you, even as a father toward his own chil-

dren, beseeching you, encouraging you, and charging you to live lives worthy of the God who calleth you to share his own kingdom in glory.

And for this we also thank God unceasingly, that when you received God's message from us, you embraced it, not as a human word, but for what it really is, the word of God, which also works in the hearts of you who believe. For you, brothers, have followed the examples of the churches of God in Christ Jesus which are in Judea in that you have suffered from your fellow countrymen just as those churches have suffered from the Jews who killed the Lord Jesus and the prophets. Your countrymen now persecute us and are not pleasing God, but oppose all men by preventing us from preaching to the Gentiles that they may be saved. Thus they continually fill up the measure of their own sins; but the wrath has come upon them at last! *The bravery of the Thessalonians under persecution (12-16)*

Brothers, when we were separated from you for a little time (out of sight, not out of mind!), we were the more intently eager to see you, for we did want to come to you—I did, I, Paul, more than once—but Satan hindered us. For who is ' our hope, our joy, our crown ' of which we boast? Is it not you yourselves in the presence of our Lord Jesus at his coming? Yes, you are our glory and joy! *Paul's loving solicitude (17-20)*

So when I could bear it no longer, I decided to remain behind at Athens alone, and I sent Timothy, our brother and minister of God in proclaiming the gospel of Christ, for your strengthening and encouragement in the faith that none of you might be disturbed by these present troubles; for you yourselves know that they are our appointed lot. And this is so, for even when we were with you, we forewarned you, saying that, ' We are soon to suffer affliction,' and so it proved as you know. I on this account, being unable to bear it any longer, sent to find out about your faith, lest perchance the tempter had tempted you and our labor had been lost. *The sending of Timothy (3 1-5)*

But now that Timothy has just come back to us from you and has brought us the good news of your faith and love and how you always remember me affectionately, longing to see us, as we also long to see you, we have been comforted about you, brothers, in all our distress and trouble *Timothy's report (6-8)* because of your faith. For now we live indeed, if you but stand firm in the Lord.

Paul's
grati-
tude
and
prayer
for the
Thes-
salo-
nians
(9-13)

How can we give thanks enough to God for you in return for all the joy which we experience because of you in the presence of our God? Night and day we pray most earnestly that we may see your faces and supply whatever is lacking in your faith. May our God and Father and our Lord Jesus direct our way to you, and may the Lord make you increase and excel in love to one another and to all men, even as is our love toward you, so as to strengthen your hearts and make them blameless in holiness before our God and Father at the coming of our Lord Jesus with all his holy ones.

The
moral
and
social
obliga-
tions
of the
Chris-
tian
(4¹-12)

Finally, brothers, we beg and beseech you in the Lord Jesus to follow our instructions about the way you ought to live in order to please God. You are indeed leading that life, but I write that you may excel in it still more. For you know the commands we laid upon you on the authority of the Lord Jesus. For it is God's will that you should be pure, that you abstain from sexual vice, that each of you learn to take for himself a wife, who shall be his own, in purity and honor, not to gratify sexual passion as do the Gentiles who have no knowledge of God; and that in this matter there be no encroaching on or over-reaching the rights of his brother, for the Lord avengeth all these sins, as we have already taught you and soundly warned you. For God did not call us to an unclean but to a pure life. Therefore, he who disregards this disregards not man but the God who gave you his Holy Spirit. There is no need that I should write you in regard to brotherly love, for you yourselves are taught by God to love one another, as indeed, is your practice toward all the brothers in all of Macedonia. We beseech you, brothers, to excel in this more and more and to endeavor to live peacefully, to attend to your own business, and, as we charged you, work with your own hands, so that you may live worthy lives in your relations to those about, and not be a burden to anyone.

We do not wish you to be ignorant, brothers, regarding those who sleep the sleep of death, lest you should mourn as others do who have no hope, for if we believe that Jesus died and rose again, we also believe that God by means of Jesus will bring with him those who have fallen asleep, for we tell you, as on the Lord's own authority, that we who are alive and survive until the Lord comes will by no means take precedence of those who have fallen asleep. The Lord himself will descend from heaven with a shout, with the voice of an archangel and with the trumpet of God. Then the dead in Christ will rise first, afterwards we who are alive and survive will be caught up along with them in the clouds to meet the Lord in the air, and so we will be with the Lord forever. Therefore encourage one another with these words. _{The future of those who have died in the faith (13-18)}

But as to times and dates, brothers, it is unnecessary that anything be written to you. For you know perfectly well that the day of the Lord comes as a thief in the night. When men are saying, Peace and safety, then all of a sudden destruction is upon them, like birth pangs on a pregnant woman, and escape there is none. But you, brothers, are not in darkness that the day should surprise you like a thief. You are all sons of the light and sons of the day. We do not belong to the night nor the darkness. So then let us not sleep like the rest of men, but let us keep awake and be sober; for sleepers sleep by night, while drunkards drink at night. But we who belong to the day must be sober, clad in faith and love as our coat of mail and the hope of salvation as our helmet. For God destined us not for wrath but to attain salvation through our Lord Jesus Christ, who died for us that waking or sleeping in death we should live together with him. Therefore encourage one another and let each edify the other, as indeed you are doing. _{The Lord's coming (5 1-5)}

Brothers, we beg you to show respect for those who are laboring among you and are your leaders in the Lord and advise you. Hold them in special esteem and love on account of the work they are doing. Be at peace among yourselves. We beseech you, brothers, admonish the unruly, comfort the faint-hearted, sustain the weak, be patient toward all. See that no one of you pays back evil for evil, but always seek for opportunities of doing good to one another and to all men. Rejoice at all times, pray _{Concluding exhortation (12-28)}

unceasingly. In every circumstance be thankful, for this is God's will in Christ Jesus respecting you. Do not quench the Spirit, do not disdain prophetic utterances, but test them all, retain what is good; abstain from every form of evil.

Bene-
diction
and
closing
saluta-
tion
(23-28)

May the God of peace entirely consecrate you. May you be kept spirit, soul, and body, complete and blameless until the coming of our Lord Jesus Christ. He who calls you is faithful and he will do it. Brothers, pray for us. Salute all the brothers with a holy kiss. I solemnly charge you by the Lord to have this letter read aloud to all the brothers.

The grace of our Lord Jesus Christ be with you.

Super-
scrip-
tion of
Paul's
second
letter
(II
Thess.
1¹, ²)

Paul, Silas and Timothy to the church of the Thessalonians in God our Father and the Lord Jesus Christ. Grace and peace to you from God the Father and the Lord Jesus Christ.

Paul's
grati-
tude
(3-5)

We are bound unceasingly to thank God for you, brothers; it is appropriate that we should because your faith is growing greatly and the love of each of you for all the others is increasing. The result is that throughout the churches of God we are proud of you, because of your steadfastness and faith amidst all the persecutions and troubles which you are enduring. They are plain proof of God's justice; you are suffering for the Kingdom of God and he means to make you worthy of it.

The
time of
Jesus'
second
coming
(2¹-⁷)

As regards the coming of our Lord Jesus Christ and our being gathered to meet him, we beg you, brothers, not to let your minds become easily unsettled or disturbed by any spiritual revelation, or any declaration, or any letter purporting to come from me to the effect the day of the Lord is now here. Let no one in any way deceive you. It will not come until the great act of apostasy first comes and the appearing of the man of sin, the son of perdition, the adversary who vaunts himself against and above every so-called god or object of worship so that he seats himself in the very temple of God, proclaiming himself to be God. Do you not remember that I used to tell you these things when I was still with you? Therefore, you now know what restrained him from being revealed before his appointed time. For the secret force of lawlessness is already at work, only it cannot be revealed until he who restrains it is removed.

Finally, brothers, pray for us that the word of God may spread rapidly and be glorified, as in your own case, and that we may be delivered from unreasonable and evil men, for the faith is not shared by all. But the Lord is faithful; he will surely strengthen you and guard you from the evil one. Now, we have confidence in you in the Lord that you are doing and will do what we command. May the Lord direct your hearts in the love of God and the patience of Christ. *Paul's request for prayer (3¹⁻⁵)*

We command you, brothers, in the name of the Lord Jesus Christ to shun any brother who is an idler and not living according to the teaching which he received from us. For you yourselves know that it is your duty to follow our example; we did not act disorderly in your midst nor did we eat any one's bread without paying for it. Rather we labored and toiled hard day and night so as not to be a burden to any of you. This was not because we have no right; it was simply that we might give you an example that you might imitate us. For even while we were with you, we laid down this rule: 'If a man is not willing to work, he shall not eat.' But we hear that some of your number are idlers and mere busy-bodies. Now by the authority of the Lord Jesus, we command and exhort such to work quietly and eat their own bread. But you yourselves, brothers, must not grow weary of doing what is right. If any one will not obey our command in this letter, mark that man, do not associate with him so that he may be made to feel ashamed. Do not regard him as an enemy, caution him as a brother. *The Christian's obligation to work quietly and faithfully (6⁻¹⁵)*

May the Lord of peace himself, continually grant you peace in every sense. The Lord be with you all. The salutation is in my own hand, Paul's. This is a mark in every letter. This is how I write. The grace of our Lord Jesus Christ be with you all. *Farewell blessing (16⁻18)*

I. **The General Structure of Paul's Letters.** Deissmann (*Light From the Ancient East*, pp. 218–221) has drawn a sharp distinction between a letter and an epistle. Recent excavations have disclosed many examples of these two types of literature and have thrown much light upon the literary form of Paul's writings. The epistle was frequently used by the philosophers and teachers of the period to set forth their doctrines. These were essentially essays or discourses set in the epistolary form. Of this type of literature Paul's Epistle to the Romans is an excellent example. Of the simple letter his personal note to Philemon or the short note to the Ephesian Christians, found in the last chapter of Romans, are good illustrations. It is difficult, however, to rigidly classify the rest of Paul's writings either as letters or epistles, for the one almost insensibly merges into the other. It is clear, however, that Paul's epistles grew out of his habit of making public addresses and of writing personal letters. His first letter to the Thessalonians illustrates excellently the way in which a personal letter naturally developed into an epistle. With the exception of his letter to the Galatians, which was written to meet an imperative situation and under the influence of hot indignation, Paul's letters all possess the same general literary structure. They open with the salutation, giving the names of those to whom they are addressed and conclude with the Greek word *grace* and the equivalent of the ancient Hebrew word *peace*. It probably corresponds to the blessing which opened every Jewish synagogue service and suggests the corresponding order in the early Christian service, which was clearly modelled after the Jewish. The salutation was followed by words of thanksgiving and of commendation of the virtues of those whom he addressed and a prayer that these might continue. Being a wise teacher, Paul appreciated the value of sincere appreciation as a premise, even to the most severe condemnation. The third element in his letters was a statement of the thesis or doctrine which he wished to emphasize. This represented the heart of each epistle. It was followed in turn by practical moral applications of the principle stated and by earnest exhortations. When Paul wished to add personal notes or directions, these were introduced at this point and the letter or epistle concluded with a benediction, even as did the Jewish synagogue service. Sometimes Paul places greater emphasis on the doctrinal teachings and sometimes on the direct applications and exhortations, but with practically no exceptions each epistle contains these distinctive elements and in the same general order.

II. **The Literary Characteristics of Paul's Letters.** The contents, as well as his frequent statements, leave little doubt that

LITERARY CHARACTERISTICS OF PAUL'S LETTERS

Paul usually dictated his letters. It is fortunate that he did so, for the epistles which have come down to us are as a result faithful representations of the exact way in which he talked or preached. All that is lacking are his intonations and gestures, and these are sometimes implied by the context. It is possible that the scribes to whom Paul dictated his letters were masters of the short-hand system of writing which was well known at this period. As a rule the dictation was taken down on waxed tablets in a cursive script. If the letter was short, the wax impression was sent. If it were long, as were most of Paul's letters, it was carefully copied on rolls of papyrus. In one case we know the name of Paul's scribe. In the short letter to the Christians at Ephesus, which is now found in the sixteenth chapter of Romans, we find this postscript: "I, Tertius, who write the letter, salute you in the Lord."

It has been suggested that Paul, coming from the ranks of the laboring class, was not himself a fluent writer and that he avoided whenever possible the mechanical work of writing. The postscript to II Thessalonians ends with the statement: "The salutation is in my own hand, Paul's. That is a mark in every letter of mine. This is how I write. Let the grace of Jesus Christ be with you all." It implies that he never added more than a line or two and this simply for the purpose of confirming the genuineness of his letters. His literary style reveals at points the results of his habit of dictating, for evidently the ideas often followed each other so rapidly that the amanuensis had difficulty in transcribing them. This characteristic is especially marked in his passionate epistle to the Galatians (2^{6-10}). Like Jesus, he was fond of striking paradoxes, as for example: "When I am weak, then am I strong." Many passages in his epistles are characterized by certain rhythmical accents and balanced syllables which are clearer in Greek, yet apparent even in an English translation. Thus, for example, in I Corinthians $15^{22, 23}$ we read: "And so it is with the resurrection of the dead:

> It is sown corruptible,
> It rises incorruptible;
> It is sown inglorious,
> It rises in glory;
> It is sown in weakness,
> It rises in power;
> It is sown an animate body,
> It rises a spiritual body."

Paul was also a master of the rhetorical climax, as is well illustrated in the classical passage, I Corinthians 16$^{50-54}$. In this respect there is a striking contrast between Paul the cosmopolitan, with his varied culture, acquainted with the complex life of the city, and Jesus the peasant, a keen lover of nature, reared amidst the simple life of Palestine. Jesus' literary style is simple, direct, and limpid; Paul's is complex, often involved, and in some cases even turgid. Jesus drew most of his illustrations from the life of the country; Paul from the teeming life of the city. Both, however, revealed the powerful influence of the earlier wisdom teachers of their race and both employed the epigrammatic method in presenting their teachings. Thus, for example, in I Corinthians 3^6 Paul declares:

> I planted, Apollos watered,
> But God made the seed grow;
> So neither planter nor the waterer is important,
> But God who maketh the seed grow.

The Old Testament which Paul used was the Septuagint or Greek translation. To him all written therein was practically of equal authority. Like the Jewish rabbis of his day and most of the early Christian teachers, he employed at times the literalistic and allegorizing methods in interpreting these older scriptures. Freely he used whatever seemed to be adapted to the point which he was endeavoring to prove. As a result his logic often depended upon the superficial rather than the fundamental meaning of the earlier biblical passages. His method of reasoning is intuitive rather than logical. His literary style is that of a religious mystic rather than that of the cold, dogmatic theologian. It appeals primarily to the heart rather than to the reason. It is also suffused with a brilliant, glowing imagination and profound emotion. It is inspired by the wide experiences and the deep feelings of the great apostle. Through it all one feels his intense zeal, his kinetic personality, his heroic devotion, and his warm love for his fellow men. The famous hymn to love in I Corinthians 13 is beyond question the crown of Paul's literary efforts. Of it the classical Greek scholar von Norden has said: "Since the hymn of Cleanthes nothing at once so heartfelt and magnificent had been written in Greek." The perennial charm of Paul's literary style, however, is not his logic nor finished literary form but the man himself and the heroic devotion to a great cause which are revealed in every sentence which comes from his lips.

III. **The Occasion of Paul's First Letter to the Thessalonians.** Paul had taken temporary refuge in Berœa in the hope that he might be able to return to his friends and converts at Thessalonica; but developments there rendered this impossible. Hence he turned southward, first to Athens and then to Corinth, from which he watched intently the course of events in Thessalonica. Great was his relief, therefore, when Timothy came bringing direct news. It is evident that Timothy also brought to Paul a letter from the Christians at Thessalonica and that the wording of his first letter to them is largely determined by what they had said to him. Thus, for example, in I Thessalonians 2^{13} he replies, "We *also* thank God constantly for you," implying that they had said the same of Paul and Silas. His statement, "You are our glory and joy" (in $2^{19, 20}$) probably also echoes the protestations of the loyal Thessalonians who were eager to repudiate the position taken by certain of their number who had openly questioned Paul's sincerity on account of his failure to return to them. The dramatic way in which Paul repeatedly emphasizes and develops the idea of imitation in this letter (1^6, 2^{14}; *cf.* II Thess. 3^{7-9}) strongly suggests that they had also declared their determination to imitate Paul in bearing the troubles that were overtaking them. Such loyal statements fully explain the note of thanksgiving and mutual confidence that runs through Paul's first epistle to the Thessalonians and which beyond reasonable doubt is the earliest of his extant letters. On the whole, the report which Timothy brought to Paul was favorable, but there were some in the church at Thessalonica who had become idle and intemperate (5^7) and had shown an inclination to go back to the worship of heathen gods (4^{3-5}). Paul, therefore, wrote to strengthen those who were loyal, to warn the weak and wavering, and to emphasize the more important teachings which he had set before them during his initial work in their midst. There is every reason to believe that in this first epistle to the Thessalonians we have precisely the words which Paul would have spoken, could he have stood in person in the midst of his Thessalonian friends and converts.

IV. **The Contents of Paul's First Letter to the Thessalonians.** The thought of this letter is remarkably clear. It is evident throughout that Paul is dealing with definite conditions and needs in the Christian community at Thessalonica. Hearty commendation and thanksgiving are expressed in 1^{2-10}. In declaring that the faith of the Thessalonian Christians had been reported throughout the world, Paul was using justifiable hyperbole. It was the Western

Christian world which he clearly had in mind. In 2^{13}–3^{13} he ardently professes his love for them and his eagerness to revisit them and explains why it was impossible for him to do so. In the remainder of the letter (4^{1-12}) he stresses certain of his earlier teachings, the importance of which he more fully appreciates in the light of the information which has come to him. As occasionally elsewhere in his letters, he speaks on the basis of the direct authority of Jesus (4^2). It is significant that where Paul stands most squarely on Jesus' teachings the social note is strongest. Chapter 4^{1-12} is an important supplement to our gospel records, for it ranks in date and authority with the early collection of the teachings of Jesus attributed by tradition to the Apostle Matthew. The teachings here present the lofty standard of social morality that Jesus held up before his followers. It does not teach asceticism but absolute fidelity to the marriage relation. It demands still more: the marriage bond was not to be made an excuse for gratifying the sensual passion, but each man is enjoined to treat his wife purely and honorably as a divine creation. This passage is a luminous reflection of Jesus' chivalrous attitude toward the weaker and more dependent members of society and especially toward women. The ideal here set forth is as important and certainly as valid to-day as when Paul contrasted Jesus' standard with the gross and brutal sensuality of the contemporary heathen world. Paul also emphasizes Jesus' law of brotherly love and each man's obligation quietly to attend to his own business as his first and fundamental contribution to the welfare of society.

Paul then discusses in 4^{13}–5^{11} the much-debated question of what would become of those who died before Jesus' second coming and how soon that appearing would be. In 4^{15} he quotes Jesus as the authority for the statement that, "we, the living, who survive until the Lord comes are by no means to take precedence of those who are fallen asleep." Nowhere in the gospels do we find the exact basis of this statement. Possibly Paul had in mind Jesus' declaration that "he who loses his life for my sake and the gospel's shall find it" (Mark 8^{35}), or perhaps the allusion may be to Jesus' mild rebuke of James and John, who asked to have the first place in the coming kingdom. In his general teaching regarding Jesus' second coming, Paul clearly reflects his Jewish inheritance and reiterates the current apocalyptic hopes which are found in the contemporary writings of the Sibylline Oracles, the apocalypses of Enoch, Baruch, and IV Ezra. In his two letters to the Thessalonians, Paul's expression of his belief in Jesus' second coming reaches its climax—in fact, II Thessalonians marks the beginning of its subsidence. When a decade later Paul finally faced death, he spoke not of Jesus' coming, but of his going to Christ (Phil. 1²³).

V. The Contents and Authenticity of II Thessalonians. Paul's second letter to the Thessalonians is little more than an appendix to I Thessalonians. It has, however, all the characteristic divisions of a typical letter. Chapter 1 contains Paul's words of greeting and thanksgiving for the steadfastness of the Thessalonian Christians. In 2¹⁻¹² he aims to correct certain misunderstandings regarding his teaching about the second coming of Christ. In 2¹³⁻¹⁷ he expresses his strong confidence in the Thessalonians. Chapter 3¹⁻¹⁵ consists of concluding exhortations, and 3¹⁶⁻¹⁸ contains his blessing, personal autograph, and farewell. Throughout this second letter he repeats and emphasizes the same points as in the first. The parallelism is so close that many scholars have regarded II Thessalonians as the work of another hand. The mark of Paul's style and thought are, however, indelibly stamped upon it. While it deals with the same conditions that are reflected in I Thessalonians, it nevertheless marks progress. In I Thessalonians Paul had poured oil on the fiercely burning expectation of Jesus' speedy coming. Now he aims to hold in check that over-ardent hope. In so doing he voices certain popular beliefs which clearly antedate the destruction of Jerusalem in 70 A.D. It is, therefore, far easier to hold that they came from the lips of Paul than from the pen of a later editor. Paul probably wrote his second letter to the Thessalonians only a few months after the first. Intimations had evidently come to him that his first letter had been in part misinterpreted and he therefore wrote in haste in order to correct the false inferences which had been drawn from it.

VI. Paul's Aim in II Thessalonians. A recent writer (Harnack) has suggested that in this second letter Paul had especially in mind the Jewish Christians in Thessalonica. They, rather than the Gentile Christians, would naturally be most interested in the apocalyptic hopes which in their origin were distinctly Jewish rather than Greek. Possibly they had intimated that in his first letter Paul had reflected only a part of the current hopes which gathered about the doctrine of Jesus' second coming. In his second letter he adds what was a constant factor in Jewish eschatology. It is the allusion to the arch-enemy of God, the Anti-Christ, whose activity it was believed would reach its climax before the appearance of the Christ to overthrow this foe and to establish his visible kingdom on earth. In Paul's

mind the one who still held in restraint the secret forces of lawlessness was evidently Rome. It has even been suggested that here is a
play on the name of the then reigning emperor, Claudius. Evidently
Rome had not yet assumed in the minds of the Christians its later
rôle of the Anti-Christ. Nowhere is Paul's good sense as a pastor
and leader better illustrated than in this second epistle to the Thessalonians. Like every progressive Jew, he still held, as firmly as, for
example, we to-day hold the theory of evolution, that the Messiah's
work would not be complete until he established a visible kingdom on
earth. It is through these letters of Paul, as well as through the influence of the books of Daniel and Revelation, that the old, popular
Jewish apocalyptic hopes gained such a firm hold on Christianity that
they constantly crop out to-day, not only in the cults of the Millerites
and Second Adventists, but even in the earnest exhortations of certain of our most popular evangelists. In the face, however, of all his
Jewish inheritance and firm beliefs, Paul strove in his second letter
to the Thessalonians to counteract the evil effects of this hope, which,
we see, was a mistaken one, and to deliver the church from the perils
which threatened it. In the first place, he called their attention to
the fact that the present situation did not supply all the conditions
which were popularly supposed to precede the advent of the Messiah.
In the second place, he held up before them his own example and teaching, how he toiled hard at his trade, working night and day, even
though he shared with them the hope of Jesus' early reappearance.
Finally, he enunciated a great and far-reaching economic law: "If a
man will not work, he shall not eat." This is the heart of Paul's
social philosophy, and it is one of his great contributions to the science
of society. It is even more striking, because it was set forth at a
moment when he expected even in his own lifetime to behold the end
of the present social order. Time and deeper knowledge have demonstrated the futility of the old Jewish apocalyptic hopes, the practical
evils of which Paul himself appreciated, but the great social and
economic principle which he laid down abides awaiting full acceptance
and application.

§ CLVI. PAUL'S WORK AT ATHENS AND CORINTH

While Paul was waiting at Athens for Silas and Timothy, his spirit was stirred within him as he beheld the
idols that filled the city. So he argued in the synagogue

with the Jews and the devout proselytes and also in the market place daily with those whom he happened to meet there. Some of the Epicurean and Stoic philosophers also came across him and certain of them said, What has this worthless picker-up of scraps of learning to say? Others said, He seems to be a herald of foreign deities. This was because he preached Jesus and the resurrection. Then taking him up to the Areopagus they said, May we know what this new teaching of yours is? For certain things that you are saying sound strange to us; therefore, we want to know what they mean. (For all the Athenians and the foreign visitors to Athens spent their time at nothing else than telling or hearing about something new.) Paul's discussions with the Jews and Greeks (Acts 17 16-21)

So Paul standing in the midst of the Areopagus said, Men of Athens, I observe that in every respect you are most religious. For as I passed along and saw the objects which you worship, I even found an altar with the inscription, Paul's speech to the court of the Areopagus (22-31)

TO AN UNKNOWN GOD.

Now I proclaim to you that which you worship in your ignorance. The God who made the world and all things in it, he, being Lord of heaven and earth, doth not dwell in shrines made by human hands. He is not served by human hands, as if he needed anything, for he it is who giveth life and breath and all things to all men. He hath created all nations from a common ancestor that they may inhabit all the surface of the earth. He hath also fixed for them their allotted periods and the boundaries of their abodes that they may seek for God on the chance of finding him in their groping for him, although he is not far from each one of us; for it is in him that we live and move and exist, as certain of your own poets have said, For we also are his offspring. Therefore, as the offspring of God, we ought not to imagine that the divine nature resembles gold or silver or stone, the product of human art and invention. These ages of ignorance God overlooked, but he now commandeth men that they are all everywhere to repent, since he hath fixed a day on which he will judge the world justly by a man whom he hath destined for this.

And he hath given proof of this to all by raising him from the dead.

Its effect (32-34) But when they heard of the resurrection of the dead, some sneered, while others said, We will hear you again on this matter. So Paul withdrew from their midst. Certain men, however, joined him and believed, among whom were Dionysius, the Areopagite, a woman called Damaris, and some others with them.

Paul's preaching at Corinth (18 1-6) After this Paul left Athens and went to Corinth. There he found a Jew named Aquila, a native of Pontus, who had recently come from Italy with his wife, Priscilla, for Claudius had ordered all Jews to leave Rome. Paul visited them and, as he was of the same trade, he remained with them and they all worked together, for by trade they were tent-makers. On every sabbath he argued in the synagogue and tried to persuade both Jews and Greeks. By the time that Silas and Timothy came down from Macedonia, Paul was engrossed in preaching the word, testifying to the Jews that Jesus was the Messiah. But as they opposed and abused him, he shook out his garments in protest, saying, Your blood be on your own heads! I am not responsible; after this I will go to the Gentiles.

Paul's activity in Corinth (7-10) Then Paul went to the house of a devout proselyte called Titus Justus, which adjoined the synagogue. But Crispus, the president of the synagogue, believed in the Lord, together with all his household; and many of the Corinthians hearing, believed and were baptized. And the Lord said to Paul in a vision at night, Have no fear, speak on and do not stop, for I am with you and no one will attack you to injure you; I have many people in this city. So Paul settled there a year and six months, teaching among them the word of God.

Paul's defense before Gallio (11-18a) But when Gallio became proconsul of Achaia, the Jews with one accord rose against Paul and brought him before the tribunal saying, This man is inducing people to worship God contrary to the law. But when Paul was about to begin his defense, Gallio said to the Jews, If it had been a misdemeanor or wicked crime, I might reasonably listen to you, O Jews; but as these are merely questions of words and names and your law, you yourselves can attend

to them. I do not wish to pass judgment upon such matters. So he drove them from the tribunal. Then all the
Greeks, seizing Sosthenes, the president of the synagogue,
beat him before the tribunal; but Gallio did not take the
least notice of these things. Then after waiting for a
number of days, Paul took leave of the brothers and sailed
for Syria, accompanied by Priscilla and Aquila.

I. **The Athens of Paul's Day.** Finding the door of Macedonia
temporarily closed to him, Paul naturally turned to the original home
of Greek culture. The goal of his journey from Berœa was evidently
the great commercial city of Corinth, but Athens, like a loadstone, attracted him irresistibly. Curiosity and his natural itinerary, rather
than missionary zeal, apparently carried him thither. Although
stripped of all political power and much of its intellectual prestige,
Athens still stood at the height of its material splendor. It contained
much that must have been of keenest interest to Paul. During his
sojourn of several days he probably found his way to the great Stadium,
on the hills at the east of the city, which had only recently been completed. Here were held the Panatheniac games—a type of sport with
which Paul was well acquainted and in which he probably was keenly
interested. In the centre of Athens arose the stately Acropolis,
crowned by the Parthenon, the chief glory of Athenian art and the
home of Pallas Athena, the goddess of wisdom. About it were grouped
the marvellous temples and public buildings which made Athens ar-
chitecturally the most beautiful city in the ancient world. Paul's
attention was probably arrested by the massive temple of Olympian
Zeus, standing southeast of the Acropolis, which had been reared by
Antiochus Epiphanes, the arch-persecutor of Judaism. Below the
Acropolis on the southwest was the Agora, the centre of Athens's commercial and intellectual life. On the west was the Royal Porch in which
the court of the Areopagus at this period usually held its sessions.
On the south was the Senate house, the Hall of Zeus, and the Stoa
Pœcilé. Immediately to the west of the Agora was the Areopagus, or
Hill of Mars, originally separated from the Acropolis by a deep, narrow
chasm.

II. **Paul's Attitude Toward the Intellectual and Religious
Life of Athens.** In the cosmopolitan university atmosphere of
Athens the Jew from the university town of Tarsus found himself in
part at least at home. He apparently spent most of his time in the

Agora. Its intense business and intellectual activity fascinated this cosmopolitan city dweller. In the Stoa Pœcilé, Zeno, the founder of the Stoic philosophy, had lived and taught about three centuries earlier. It was still the favorite place where the Stoic philosophers met their disciples and from whence their influence radiated to distant Tarsus and dominated the intellectual life of that great commercial city. Here also Cleanthes, the illustrious pupil of Zeno, had sung his immortal hymn to Zeus, from which Paul quotes in his famous address to the men of Athens:

> O God, most glorious, called by many a name,
> Nature's great King, through endless years the same;
> Omnipotence, who by thy just decree
> Controllest all, hail Zeus, for unto thee
> Behooves thy creatures in all lands to call.
> We are thy children, we alone, of all
> On earth's broad ways that wander to and fro,
> Bearing thy image wheresoe'er we go,
> Therefore with songs of praise thy power I will forth show.

Three centuries earlier also in this same city Epicurus had lived for a considerable period and founded the philosophy which bore his name. The most prominent among the lecturers and students from all parts of the Roman Empire who thronged the Agora were the followers of Zeno and Epicurus. Paul in the midst of this throng appears to have arrested attention both by his appearance and by his actions. In the university slang of the day he was soon contemptuously characterized as "a worthless picker-up of scraps of learning." In this intellectual life of Athens Paul found much which he could approve. In its strong emphasis on the moral life and in its growing belief in one supreme God back of all phenomena, which Cleanthes so nobly voices in his hymn to Zeus, he found many points of contact. The deeply religious spirit of the city also impressed him. The Roman writer Petronius says sarcastically that it was easier to find a god in Athens than a man! Pausanias a century later said there were more gods in Athens than in all the rest of the country. Recent excavations have disclosed a broken altar which apparently bore the inscription:

> "To the Unknown Gods
> Capiton
> Torchcarrier."

136

PAUL'S ATTITUDE TOWARD ATHENIAN CULTURE

The beauty of the Athenian temples and the peerless statues may have appealed to Paul, for his repeated use of building figures reveals a certain interest, but what impressed him most and at the same time irritated him was this evidence on every side of the idolatry regnant in this most cultured city. Luke's Macedonian point of view is evinced in his general criticism in Acts 18²¹, and yet it was on the whole true of the life of the city at the period when Paul visited it: "For all the Athenians and the foreign visitors to Athens occupied themselves with nothing else than with repeating and listening to the latest novelty." Apparently the common people, as well as the foreign students that thronged the city, were confirmed lecture tasters but lacked the depth of conviction and emotion necessary for fundamental transformations in character and life. The attitude of the Athenian university crowd toward Paul seems to have been thoroughly contemptuous. Here was a voluble Jew who promised them certain entertainment—a religious sensation. Although Socrates had been condemned to death by the court of the Areopagus on the charge of introducing the worship of new gods, the Athenians had since the days of Socrates outgrown their intolerance and prided themselves instead on welcoming teachers of all religions. It is probable, however, that the court of the Areopagus, the duties of which in earlier days appear to have been the regulation of morals and education, still exercised a certain supervision over the lecturers who were allowed to present their teachings in the Agora. The evidence is clear that Paul was not placed on trial under a definite charge but that rather he was given an opportunity to present his new teachings in order that the members of the court might determine whether he should be permitted to continue to teach in their midst.

III. **Paul's Address to the Athenian Crowd.** The scene of Paul's memorable address, as reported in Acts 17, was evidently the Agora, and very probably in or near the Royal Porch, where the court of the Areopagus held its sessions. Paul's introductory words, as well as the contents of his address, indicate that his audience consisted not merely of philosophers and members of the court but also included the Athenian mob, the "worthless pickers-up of scraps of learning," whose decisions, like that of every Oriental mob, carried weight with the ruling authorities. To them, as the more hopeful elements in his audience, Paul seems to have primarily addressed his speech. As Professor Ramsay has said (*St. Paul*, p. 150): "There is nothing in the reported words of Paul at Lystra and Athens (with a possible exception of 'the man whom he hath ordained') that several Greek philosophers might not have said." With marvellous skill he adjusted himself to his environment and established a common point of contact between himself and his hearers. In many respects the principle contained in his address as here reported was the same as is found in his letter to the Romans in 1¹⁹⁻³². The passage from the hymn of the Stoic poet Cleanthes, to which Paul alludes, was one of the noblest expressions of the growing belief among the Greek philosophers that one supreme personality was back of the phenomena of nature and therefore the ultimate object of all worship. Equally significant is the similar hymn to Zeus that comes from Aratus, the poet of Soli, in Cilicia, Paul's native province, whom the apostle possibly also had in mind:

> Zeus fills all the city streets
> Of the nation's crowded marts; fills the watery deeps
> And heavens. Every laborer needs the help of Zeus.
> His children are we. He, benignant,
> Raises high signals, summoning man to toil,
> And warning him of life's demands.

Here, as at Thessalonica, Paul's aim was to turn the Gentiles from the worship of idols to the one living God. In his broad attitude toward the Gentile world and in his declaration that the earlier ages of ignorance God overlooked, Paul reveals the influence of the Jewish Stoic who has given us the Wisdom of Solomon, which reads in 11²³: "Thou overlookest the sins of men to the end that they may repent." Paul's Athenian audience followed him until he began to set forth the Jewish doctrine of a final judgment-day and to tell of the resurrection of him whom God had destined to sit on the seat of judgment. True to their well-known characteristics, the Athenian audience was divided in its judgment; but contempt or general indifference prevailed. Paul's immediate departure from the city also suggests strongly that the court of the Areopagus, if it passed formal judgment upon his address, refused him the rights of the Agora. The author of Acts, although elsewhere inclined to magnify the results of the work of the early apostles, is evidently here faithful to his data, for he emphasizes simply the fewness of those who responded to Paul's preaching. Paul himself speaks later of Stephanas of Corinth as the first-fruits of Achaia (I Cor. 16¹⁵), implying that he regarded his earlier work in Athens as practically fruitless. This outcome of his brief sojourn at the historic centre of Greek culture is not so much a demonstration of Paul's limitations as a revelation of the character of the class to which he spoke.

IV. **Paul's Skill as an Orator.** It is not probable that the author of Acts has preserved a verbatim report of Paul's addresses; but he has given us an exceedingly vivid impression of the consummate skill, as well as devotion, which made Paul the great apostle to the Greek world. In appealing to his Gentile audiences he was handicapped by the strong prejudices then felt toward his race, by his rather unattractive personal appearance, by his involved literary style, by his rabbinical methods of thought, and, above all, by the fact that in his appeal he spoke more to the heart than to the mind. Notwithstanding these seemingly impossible handicaps, he reached and won many of the most thoughtful and cultured men of his age by his words and by his personality. He was like a rushing mountain torrent that carried all before it. The source of his irresistible strength was his absolute conviction of the truth of what he spoke and of his divinely given authority to proclaim it. Apparently, never for a moment did he question his call or the certainty of his convictions. To this assurance was added an intense earnestness, accentuated doubtless by his belief that the end of the present order was at hand. Like the old Hebrew prophets, he was ever dominated by an overwhelming sense of responsibility and a passionate desire to save men from the appalling calamity which he felt to be imminent. While on the one side he shared the Jewish apocalyptic expectations, he felt the deep craving of the Gentile world for personal salvation and for the consciousness of fellowship and friendship with the Infinite. Hence, his words appeal to universal human needs. He was keen to appreciate these needs but he was equally skilful in adapting his message to his audiences. He had the rare art of "being all things to all men." He was also conscious of this art and deliberately exercised it: "To the Jews I become like a Jew, in order to win Jews. To those outside the law, I become as one outside of the law, in order that I may win those outside of the law. To the weak I become as one weak myself, in order to win over the weak." He met the pagan peasants of Lystra and the cultured students of Athens on the common ground of universal religion. Having established a close point of contact, he led them on tactfully to the appreciation and acceptance of his own point of view. To the Jews he appealed on the basis of the promises contained in their ancient scriptures. To use his own figure, he never planted his blows as one who beats the air. To his earnest and consummate tact he added a profound sympathy for those whom he sought to reach. His method, like that of Jesus, was not negative and destructive, but prevailingly positive and constructive. His aim was not merely to interest and convince men, but to save them. The motive power in Paul, the orator, therefore, was not mere logic, but love for men and loyalty to the Master whom he served. Back of his words was his heroic personality. He spoke from personal experience, directly out of his own heart to the hearts of men. To these strong qualifications were added a wide and varied knowledge of the world and of human nature, a bold originality and unusual ability in using apt and popular figures of speech and illustrations. These he drew from the life of the merchant, the farmer, the traveller, the sailor, and even the athlete. Colloquial phrases, current in the agora, the forum, and the temple, were constantly on his lips, for Paul was supremely skilful in interpreting the Gospel into the every-day life and thought of the exceedingly varied audiences to which he spoke.

V. **Paul's Problems and Methods at Corinth.** The great metropolis of Corinth lay on the "Bridge of the Sea," the isthmus which separated the Corinthian from the Saronic Gulf. This narrow neck of land cut straight across the shortest natural highway from Rome to Ephesus and the East. Every cargo sent on this route must here be transshipped. Hence it was one of the most important commercial centres in the Roman world. The city was built on a broad natural terrace above which its acropolis rose to a height of about eighteen hundred feet above the sea-level. Corinth had been a Roman colony since the days of Julius Cæsar. To it had gravitated the most varied population. It was opulent, cosmopolitan, corrupt, and profligate. Into it had poured, not only the gold and the ideas, but the vices of the East and West. Strategically, it was of the greatest importance, for ideas implanted here would readily spread through the Roman world. Corinth was a city well calculated to appeal powerfully to the sympathies, to the heroic daring, and to the broad statesmanship of Paul. Fortune, or rather seeming misfortune, drove him here. Hunted from Philippi, Thessalonica, and Berœa, baffled at Athens, anxious, harassed by poverty and weakened by sickness, Paul about 50 A.D. entered upon his work in this capital and metropolis of Achaia. For about a year and a half he lived and worked here. To support himself he took up his occupation as a tent-maker. His earliest friends and fellow workmen were Aquila and his wife, Prisca, or, as she is better known by the diminutive form of her name, Priscilla. They were natives of Pontus, but had lived in Rome until they had recently been expelled by the edict of Claudius, which is dated by Orosius in 49 B.C. Suetonius declares that this expulsion of the Jews was due to a certain riot led by one Chrestus. Apparently this is a popular corruption of the name Christ, and the remark of Suetonius suggests that at this early date the Christians already formed a strong community in the capital city. The fact that Paul early made his home with Priscilla and Aquila and that he never includes them among his converts indicates that they were Christians before they found refuge in Corinth. Paul's intimate relations with them undoubtedly put him in close touch with conditions in Rome and must have contributed to his growing desire to visit the imperial city. Following his usual custom, Paul first sought through the Jewish synagogue to gain a public hearing. Silas and Timothy aided him in his work, but soon they experienced the usual reaction. A majority of the Jews rejected Paul's claim that Jesus was the Messiah; but at least one devout proselyte, and probably several, opened their hearts and their homes to Paul's message. With his usual persistence and boldness, Paul chose the house of Titus Justus, which adjoined the synagogue, as the new centre of his work. Crispus, a high official in the synagogue, accepted Paul's teachings and his example exerted a strong influence on all classes in Corinth. So successful was Paul's work that it aroused the usual persecution, especially on the part of the Jews. In their blind rage they dragged Paul before the Roman proconsul, Gallio, a brother of the famous Stoic philosopher Seneca. Recognizing that the case was simply a quarrel between the partisans of different religious sects the proconsul summarily dismissed the case and drove them from the tribunal. It is not entirely clear whether it was hatred of the Jews or interest in Paul and his teachings which led the mob to seize Sosthenes, the president of the Jewish synagogue, and beat him. Their action certainly did not reflect the spirit of Paul's teachings. It is possible, however, that this was the same Sosthenes to whom Paul refers later as a devoted convert. In his correspondence with the Corinthians Paul tells us that at Corinth he abandoned all philosophical discussions and terminology and devoted himself solely to proclaiming in simplest terms the Gospel of the cross.

VI. **The Results of Paul's Work in Corinth.** The eighteen months spent at Corinth were among the most critical and fruitful in Paul's ministry. The transformation of the ignorant and corrupt Greeks of this voluptuous city into worthy Christians was the greatest miracle in Paul's ministry, if not in the early history of Christianity. Here he was battling with the most seductive and brazen form of immorality which, under the guise of the old pagan religions, had permeated the whole life of Corinth. To this deep-seated immorality was added the gross materialism of a strongly commercial city and the fickleness which has always been a characteristic of the Greek race. In the face of all these odds Paul established a strong Christian church at Corinth. The so-called First Epistle of Clement, which was written near the close of the first Christian century by the Church of Rome to the Corinthian Christians, speaks of their name as venerable and famous and worthy of all men's love. Elsewhere in the same epistle is found this high commendation: "Who ever dwelt even for a short time among you, and did not find your faith to be as fruitful of virtue as it was firmly established? Who did not admire the sobriety and moderation of your godliness in Christ and who did not rejoice over your perfect and well-rounded knowledge?") It is from Corinth also that Paul sent his letters to the Macedonian churches and, through the frequent visits of his assistants, strengthened and confirmed them in the Christian faith. Here also he met the attack of the narrow Judaizers who sought to undermine his work in Galatia and even found their way to Corinth itself. Paul's ministry at Corinth appears to have been one long battle, and the battle by no means ceased when he went on to Ephesus; but in the end he won a victory which marked a great and signal advance in Christianity's conquest of the Roman world. *Purpose* —

§ CLVII. PAUL'S CORRESPONDENCE WITH THE CORINTHIAN CHURCH

The superscription to Paul's second letter (I Cor. 1¹⁻³)

Paul called to be an apostle of Christ Jesus through the will of God, with brother Sosthenes, to the church of God at Corinth, to those who are consecrated in Christ Jesus, called to be saints, as well as to all who in every place call on the name of our Lord Jesus Christ, their Lord as well as ours: grace and peace to you from God our Father and the Lord Jesus Christ.

His reasons for thanksgiving (4-6)

I thank my God continually in your behalf for the divine grace which has been bestowed on you in Jesus Christ, in that through him you have been so richly blessed with all power of speech and with all knowledge. Thus in you the testimony which we bore to Christ has been confirmed.

Brothers, in the name of our Lord Jesus Christ, I beg of you that you all speak in harmony. There must be no divisions among you, but rather you must be united with the same mind and by the same point of view. For I have been informed regarding you, brothers, by Chloe's people, that there are dissensions among you. What I mean is this: each of you is saying, 'I belong to Paul,' and 'I to Apollos,' and 'I to Cephas' [Peter], and 'I to Christ.' Is Christ divided? Was Paul crucified for you, or was it in Paul's name that you were baptized? I am thankful that I baptized none of you except Crispus and Gaius, so that no man can say that you were baptized in my name. Yes, I did baptize the household of Stephanus, but I baptized no one else as far as I know. For Christ sent me not to baptize, but to preach the gospel. *Appeal to drop party strife (10-17a)*

For when the world with its wisdom failed to know God in his wisdom, God was pleased, through the foolishness of the message which we proclaim, to save those who believe. The Jews demand miracles and the Greeks seek wisdom. We, however, proclaim Christ, the crucified, a stumbling block to the Jews, mere foolishness to the Gentiles, but to those who are called, whether Jews or Greeks, a Christ who is the power of God and the wisdom of God. For the foolishness of God is wiser than men and the weakness of God is stronger than men. *The simple message of the cross (21-25)*

For, brothers, look at those of your number whom God hath called: not many wise according to human judgment, not many mighty, not many of noble birth have been called. Rather, God hath chosen the foolish things of the world, to put to shame the wise; God hath chosen the weak things in the world, to put to shame the strong; God hath chosen the base and despised things of the earth—things which are not—to bring to naught the things which are, that no mortal man may boast in the presence of God. *Illustrated in the Corinthian church (26-29)*

And so when I came to you, my brothers, I came not to proclaim to you with excellency of speech or wisdom the mystery of God. Rather I determined while among you to know nothing except Jesus Christ and him crucified. It was in weakness and in fear and with much trembling that I came to you. My language and my message did not de- *Paul's aim at Corinth (2:1-5)*

143

pend on persuasive words of wisdom, but on the demonstration of the Spirit and of its power, that your faith might not rest on any wisdom of men but on the power of God.

The source of the Christian's wisdom (11-16)

Who among men knows a man's thoughts, except the spirit of the man within him? So too, no one knows the thoughts of God except the Spirit of God. But we have not received the spirit of the world, but the Spirit which comes from God, that we may know the blessings which come from God. And of these things we speak, not in language taught by human wisdom, but taught by the Spirit, interpreting spiritual things in spiritual terms. The unspiritual man does not receive the truths of the Spirit of God, for they are folly to him and he cannot know them, since they must be spiritually appreciated. The spiritual man, on the contrary, can appreciate all things, although he himself is appreciated by no one. For who has known the mind of the Lord, so as to instruct him? But we have the mind of Christ.

The evidence of the lack of spiritual insight among the Corinthians (3:1-7)

But I, brothers, was not able to speak to you as spiritual persons. I had to speak to you as worldlings, as babes in Christ. I fed you with milk, not solid food, for you were not strong enough, and you are not even strong enough now; you are still worldly. For with jealousy and quarreling in your midst, are you not worldly? Are you not acting like ordinary men? For whenever any one says, 'I belong to Paul' and 'I to Apollos,' are you not like ordinary men? Who then is Apollos? Who is Paul? They are simply servants through whom, as to each the Lord gave power, you learned to believe. I planted and Apollos watered, but God made the seed grow. So neither the planter nor the waterer is important, but God who maketh the seed grow.

Responsibility of the teacher (9-11)

We are fellow workers with God. You are God's field, God's building. According to the grace of God which was given me as the wise master-builder, I laid the foundation; but another builds on this foundation. Let each be careful how he builds, for no one can lay any other foundation than that which is laid, namely, Jesus Christ.

Do you not know that you are God's temple and that God's Spirit dwells within you? If anyone destroys God's temple, God will destroy that one, for God's temple is sacred, and that is what you are. Therefore, let no one boast about men. For all things are yours: Paul, Apollos, Cephas, the world, life, death, the present, and the future—all are yours and you are Christ's and Christ is God's.

You are satisfied already, are you? You are rich already! You reign without us! Would, indeed, that we might reign with you! For I think God hath set forth us apostles last of all, as men doomed to death! We are made as spectacles to the world, to angels, and to men. For Christ's sake we are fools, but you are wise in Christ! We are weak but you are strong! You are honored, we are dishonored! To this very hour we hunger and thirst, we are scantily clad and knocked about. We are homeless. Wearily we toil with our own hands. When reviled, we bless. When persecuted, we put up with it. When slandered, we try to conciliate. We have come to be regarded as the scum of the earth, the refuse of the universe, even until now.

I am not writing this to make you ashamed, but to counsel you as my beloved children. For if you had ten thousand instructors in Christ, you could not have many fathers. I, it was, who in Christ Jesus became your father by means of the gospel. I beg of you, therefore, imitate me. To this end, I am sending you Timothy, who is my beloved and faithful son in the Lord. He will remind you of my methods in Christ Jesus by which I teach everywhere, in every church. Some of you have been puffed up, as if I were not coming to you. Indeed, I will come to you quickly, if the Lord willeth, and then I will learn from those who are puffed up, not what they say, but what power they have. For the Kingdom of God is not a thing of words but of power. What do you wish? Shall I come to you with the rod, or with a loving and gentle spirit?

It is actually reported that there is immorality among you, immorality such as is not even practised among the Gentiles—that a man has taken his father's wife! And yet you are puffed up! You should rather mourn, in order that the perpetrator of such a crime might be expelled from your midst. I, indeed, though absent in the body, but

145

present in spirit, have already come to a decision as though present, namely, that by the power of our Lord Jesus, when you are assembled in the name of the Lord Jesus and my spirit is with you, that individual be delivered over to Satan for the destruction of his flesh in order that his spirit may be saved in the day of our Lord Jesus.

The treatment of those who are deliberately immoral (9-13)

I wrote you in my letter that you were not to associate with the immoral, not that in this world you are to keep entirely aloof from the immoral or the avaricious or the thievish or from idolaters, since in that case you would have to leave the world altogether. What I now write is, that you are not to associate with any so-called brother who is immoral or avaricious or idolatrous or given to abusive language or hard drinking or robbery. With such you ought not even to eat. For what business have I to judge outsiders? Is it not for you to judge those who are within the church? God will judge outsiders. Remove the wicked from among you.

The prevailing doubt regarding the resurrection of the dead (15:12-19)

If Christ is preached as having risen from the dead, how is it that some of you say that there is no resurrection of the dead. If there is no resurrection of the dead, then Christ did not rise; and if Christ did not rise, then our preaching has been in vain and your faith also is vain. We also are detected bearing false witness about God, because we have testified concerning God that he raised Christ, whom he did not raise, if after all the dead do not rise. For if the dead do not rise, Christ did not rise; and if Christ did not rise, your faith is futile; you are still in your sins. Furthermore, those who sleep in Christ have perished. If we have only a hope of Christ in this life, we are, of all men, the most to be pitied.

Christ's resurrection the pledge for all (20-28)

But Christ in reality did rise from the dead. He was the first to be gathered of those who sleep; for since death came through man, by man also came the resurrection of the dead. Just as all die in Adam, so shall all be made alive in Christ. But each in his own order; Christ, the first to be gathered, then all who belong to Christ at his arrival. Then comes the end, when he is to surrender the kingship to God, the Father, when he has put down all other authority, rule and power, for he must reign until he has placed

146

all of his foes under his feet. Death is the last enemy to be overthrown, for God hath put everything under his feet. When it is said that everything has been put under him, it plainly excludes him who putteth everything under him. And when all things are put under him, then, the son himself will be put under him who subjected everything to him, that God may be all in all.

But some one will say, how can the dead rise? With what kind of body do they come back? Foolish man! What you yourself sow does not come to life unless it dies; and what you sow is not the body which is to be, but a mere grain of wheat it may be, or some other seed. God giveth it a body as he pleaseth, even to each kind of seed a body of its own. So it is with the resurrection of the dead: it is sown corruptible, it rises incorruptible; it is sown inglorious, it rises in glory; it is sown in weakness, it rises in power; it is sown an animate body, it rises a spiritual body. Thus, as we have borne the likeness of the earthly man, so we are to bear the likeness of the heavenly man.

The nature of the resurrection (35-38, 42-44, 49)

This I tell you, brothers: flesh and blood cannot inherit the Kingdom of God, nor can the corruptible inherit incorruption. Behold I tell you a mystery: we shall not all sleep, but we shall all be changed in a moment, in the twinkling of an eye at the last trumpet call. For the trumpet will sound and the dead will be raised incorruptible, and we shall be changed. For this corruptible body must be clothed with incorruption and this mortal body clothed with immortality. But when this corruptible body has been clothed with incorruption, and this mortal body clothed with immortality, then the words of the scripture will be fulfilled:

The victory over death through Christ (50-58)

> Death is swallowed up in victory.
> O Death, where is your victory?
> O Death, where is your sting?

Thanks be to God who giveth us the victory through our Lord Jesus Christ! Therefore, my beloved brothers, be firm, immovable, excel at all times in the work of the Lord, knowing that your work in the Lord is never in vain.]

The collection for the poor in Jerusalem (16¹⁻⁴)

With regard to the collection for the saints, you must do just as I directed the churches in Galatia. On the first day of the week, let each of you put aside whatever gain has been granted him, so that the money will not have to be collected when I come. When I am with you I will send credentials to those whom you select, to bear your gracious gift to Jerusalem and, if it is worth while for me to go too, they will accompany me.

Paul's future plans (5-7, 10-12)

I shall come to you after I go through Macedonia, for I am going to pass through Macedonia. Perhaps I will spend some time with you, or even pass the winter, that you may speed me forward, wherever I am going. I do not wish to see you now merely in passing, for my hope is to stay some time among you if the Lord doth permit. If Timothy arrives, see that he is quite at home among you, for he is engaged in the Lord's work, even as I am. Therefore, let no one slight him, but send him on his way in peace in order that he may come to me, for I am awaiting him along with the other brothers. As for our brother, Apollos, I begged him most earnestly to go to you with the brothers, but it was not at all his wish that he should come now. He will come, however, when he has a good opportunity.

Concluding exhortation (13, 14)

Watch, stand firm in the faith, be men, be strong! Let all that you do be done in love.

Paul's defense in his third letter (II Cor. 10¹⁻⁶)

I, Paul, myself, entreat you by the gentleness and consideration of Christ—the Paul 'who is humble enough to your face, when he is with you, but outspoken enough when he is away from you!' I beg of you that when I do come that you will not compel me to make a bold display of my confidence with which I am determined to show my courage toward certain people who consider that we act in accordance with worldly principles. For though we still live in the world, we do not fight with worldly weapons. The weapons of our warfare are not worldly weapons, but divinely strong to overthrow fortresses, overthrowing theories and every stronghold raised up against the knowledge of God, and we take captive every project, to make it subject to Christ. We are ready to pass judgment upon every act of disobedience, when once your submission is complete.

PLEADING FOR THE LOYALTY OF THE CORINTHIANS

I wish you could have put up with a little foolishness on my part. Do bear with me, for I feel jealous for you, even as God is jealous. I betrothed you as a chaste maiden, to present you to your one husband, Christ; but I am afraid that, even as the serpent with its craftiness beguiled Eve, so your thoughts are being seduced from a single devotion to Christ, for you bear it well when some one comes proclaiming another Jesus whom we have not proclaimed, or when you receive another Spirit than that which you have received, or a different gospel from that which you have already welcomed! For I consider myself not in the slightest inferior to the most eminent apostles! In speech, I may be defective, but not in knowledge. We have in every way made that fully evident to you. ^{His pleading for the loyalty of the Corinthians (11 1-6)}

Here I am ready to visit you for the third time; and I will not burden you, for I desire not your money, but you yourselves; for children are not under obligations to store up money for their parents, but parents for their children. I will gladly spend all I have and be utterly spent for your souls. Am I to be loved the less because I love you so intensely? ^{Plan to visit Corinth (12 14, 15)}

I forewarned you and now warn you in advance, as I did on my second visit when present and do now when absent, both you who sinned before and all the rest, that if I come back again, I will spare no one, since you seek proof that Christ speaks through me—he who is not weak toward you but powerful in you. For though he was crucified in weakness, he lives by the power of God. For though we are weak as he was weak, yet with him we shall be alive toward you by the power of God. Test yourselves to see if you are in the faith; examine yourselves. Do you not know that Jesus Christ is in you or else you are failures? For this reason I am writing these things to you while absent, that when I do come I may not have to deal severely with you by the authority which the Lord hath given me, for the purpose of building you up and not of pulling you down. ^{The object of his visit (13 2-5)}

Paul, an apostle of Christ Jesus by the will of God, and brother Timothy to the Church of God at Corinth as well as to all the saints who are in the whole of Achaia: Grace and ^{Salutation in Paul's fourth letter (II Cor. 1 1, 2)}

149

peace to you from God our Father and the Lord Jesus Christ.

Thanks-
giving
(3, 4)

Blessed be the God and Father of our Lord Jesus Christ, the Father of tender mercies and the God who comforteth us in all our affliction, so that we are able to comfort those who are in any affliction, by the comfort with which we ourselves are comforted by God.

Paul's
refer-
ences
to his
former
visit
(23, 21-4)

I call God to witness against my soul that it was to spare you that I did not revisit Corinth. I decided I would not come to you again to bring you pain, for if I pain you, who is there then to give me joy except the very people I am paining? And I write this to you in order that when I come, I may not receive pain from those who ought to give me joy, being assured regarding all of you that my joy is a source of joy to you all. For I wrote you in great affliction and misery of heart, with many a tear, not to give you pain, but in order that you might know how my heart is overflowing with love for you.

For-
give-
ness
for the
peni-
tent
of-
fender
(5-10a)

If a certain individual has caused pain, he has caused it not only to me, but in some degree (that I may not exaggerate) to all of you. The censure from the majority is sufficient for that individual, so that, on the contrary, you should rather now forgive and comfort him, lest he be overwhelmed by excessive grief. Therefore, I beg of you to reinstate him in your love. For I wrote you with the aim that I might know your mind, whether you were absolutely obedient. If you forgive the man, I will forgive him also.

Appeal
for
confi-
dence
(611-13,
72-4)

O Corinthians, our mouth is unsealed to you! Our heart is wide open for you! There is no restraint in our love; yet you restrained your feelings for us; but let it be a fair exchange. I speak as to my children, Open wide your hearts to us. Make room for us. We have wronged no one, ruined no one, taken no selfish advantage of anyone. I speak, not in order to condemn you, for I said before that you are our very heart, whether we die with you or live with you. I have great confidence in you; great is my boasting over you. I am filled with comfort. I am overflowing with delight amidst all our affliction.

Now, brothers, we would have you know the grace of

God, which has been given to the churches of Macedonia, how while passing through a most trying ordeal, their boundless joy and their deep poverty have overflowed in a flood of generous liberality. I can testify, that according to their means, and even beyond their means, they have given freely; with much entreaty, they begged us for the favor of sharing in the service in behalf of the saints. They have also done more than we hoped, for first of all they gave themselves to the Lord and to us in accordance with the will of God. This led us to urge Titus, inasmuch as he had been the one who had commenced the work, also to complete this work of beneficence among you. Indeed it is superfluous for me to write to you about this service to the saints. For I know your willingness, on account of which I boasted about you to the Macedonians, saying that Achaia was ready last year. And your zeal has spurred on the majority of them. *The generosity of the Macedonians (8¹⁻⁶, 9¹, ²)*

He who furnisheth the seed for the sower and bread to eat will supply you with seed and multiply it and will increase the fruits of your charity. You will be enriched in every way, so as to show all liberality which through us makes men give thanks to God. For the service rendered by this sacred gift, not only supplies the wants of the saints, but in addition causes many a cry of thanksgiving to God. By the practical proof of this service you cause God to be praised for the fidelity of your allegiance to the gospel of Christ and for the liberality of your contribution to them and to all. They also with supplication in your behalf are bound to you in love because of the surpassing grace which God has bestowed on you. Thanks be to God for his unspeakable gift! *The fruits of liberality (10-15)*

I. **Conditions in the Church at Corinth That Called Forth Paul's Letters.** At least a year had elapsed since Paul had concluded his initial work at Corinth. From I Corinthians 16¹ we learn that meantime he had made a visit to the Galatian churches; already a strenuous period of work at Ephesus lay behind him. Apollos, the brilliant Alexandrian disciple of John the Baptist and later a convert to Christianity, had labored for a time at Ephesus, together with Aquila and Priscilla, and then had gone on to Corinth to take Paul's place.

151

When I Corinthians was written he had returned to Paul at Ephesus. Notwithstanding his Greek name, Apollos was clearly a Jew by birth, learned in the scriptures of his race, and a gifted orator. Alexandria, Tarsus, Ephesus, and Rome were the chief centres at this period in which the culture and learning of the East and West mingled and found prominent public expression. The Jewish community at Alexandria was still dominated by the personality and teachings of the famous Jewish scholar Philo, many of whose disciples survived. Here Apollos would be trained equally in Greek and Jewish thought and in the allegorical method of interpretation which the Jews had learned from the Greeks. To the Greek Christians of Corinth Apollos evidently appealed very strongly. His eloquence, his learning, and his methods of interpretation fascinated them and suggested to these rather ignorant, uncultured members of the Christian community invidious comparisons with Paul the humble tent-maker. Even though Apollos and Paul were in heartiest accord and recognized no rivalry, as is clearly shown by the fact that Paul urged Apollos later to return to Corinth (I Cor. 16^{12}), a factious spirit broke out in the ranks of the Greek Christians at the commercial metropolis of Achaia. News of this reached Paul and was one of the chief themes in his Corinthian correspondence. The Christians of Corinth were also especially exposed and susceptible to the social immorality which characterized the life of that ancient maritime city. The case of incest was tolerated even within the church itself and the prevailing standard of morality was low. Questions of church discipline and of individual responsibility also agitated the members of the Christian community. To Greeks trained to accept Plato's doctrine of spiritual immortality, the Jewish belief in bodily resurrection and of a final judgment day, in which the righteous should rise to share in the messianic kingdom with those still living, presented great difficulties. These were the major problems which are the occasion of the voluminous correspondence between Paul and the church which he first planted in Achaia. Apparently he received two letters from them and himself sent four to them. Twice he visited them. Twice he was informed of conditions there by Christian travellers from Corinth and twice he appears to have despatched Timothy to them with direct messages. This correspondence represents a period of intense activity and apprehension on the part of Paul and at the same time reveals with remarkable clarity his spirit and teachings.

II. **Paul's First Letter to the Corinthian Christians.** In I Corinthians 5^9 Paul writes: "In my letter I wrote you that you are not to associate with those who are immoral." From this reference it is clear that our present epistle known as I Corinthians is not the first in Paul's correspondence with the Corinthians. In the heart of the second epistle to the Corinthians is a section (6^{14}–7^1) which is evidently alien to its present context and begins: "Avoid all unnatural ties with unbelievers. What have righteousness and iniquity in common or how can light associate with darkness?" Through six verses he emphasizes the importance of Christians not associating with those who are immoral. It is exceedingly probable that this is a fragment of the missing first letter to which Paul refers. It and the evils of which it speaks probably led three of the Corinthian Christians, Stephanus, Fortunatus, and Achaicus, of whom Paul speaks in I Corinthians 16^{17}, to visit him in Ephesus and to lay before him the concrete problems which he discusses at length in his second letter, now found in I Corinthians.

III. **Paul's Second Letter to the Corinthians.** First Corinthians is the longest and in many ways the most beautiful letter which Paul has bequeathed to us. Here is pre-eminently revealed the pastor dealing with the definite question which his Corinthian converts had propounded to him in person and with the unfortunate conditions which had arisen in Corinth during his absence and which had been brought to his attention by the members of the household of a certain Christian woman by the name of Chloe. His broad aim is to teach the Corinthian Christians how they, in their individual and communal life, may realize the ideal of Jesus. The structure of the letter is clearly defined. The first nine verses contain his formal greeting and the rather measured note of thanksgiving in which he refers to the virtues of those to whom he was writing. Chapters 1^{10}–4^{21} contain a kindly but sharp rebuke of the factious tendencies of the Corinthians. Here Paul's breadth is strikingly illustrated. The individual leaders and their early doctrines are unimportant; loyalty to Christ and his cross are alone essential. Here he contrasts the Greek philosophies and sophistries, which certain of the Gentile Christians of Corinth are inclined to esteem most highly, with the simple spiritual message of the Gospel which he had proclaimed. Argument, gentle irony, and personal appeal are here united in Paul's characteristic way. In 5–7 he deals with the lax moral conditions that prevailed in the Corinthian church and more concretely with the special case of incest which had been reported to him. Here and in the succeeding chapters Paul's fundamental principles of living are dramatically set forth. In 8^1–11^1 he defines the proper Christian attitude toward idol sacrifices and feasts. In 11^2–14^{40} he discusses questions of public worship and the relative values of the different types of religious activity then prevalent in the church. Chapter 15 takes up the question of personal immortality, and 16 contains Paul's concluding instructions, salutations, and benediction. Paul throughout these burning chapters aims to lead his Corinthian converts to look beyond parties and teachers and doctrines to the vital spiritual life within the individual, which is the essence of Christianity and of all true religion.

IV. **Paul's Third Letter to the Corinthians.** Students have long noted the dramatic and fundamental contrast in spirit, content, and literary style between the first nine chapters of II Corinthians and the concluding four chapters. The spirit in the first part of the epistle is that of thanksgiving and commendation; in the second part Paul sometimes ironically, sometimes appealingly, expresses his surprise and bitter disappointment at the attitude of those to whom he is writing. The glaring inconsistencies of the epistle disappear when we recognize that 10–13 probably contain a part of Paul's third letter to the Corinthians which has been appended, by a later editor or as the result of displacement, to the fourth and final letter now found in 1–9. In his second letter Paul speaks of Timothy's impending visit and urges the Corinthians to receive him with open mind. The apostle also expresses the hope that he himself may visit them soon. It is evident from II Corinthians 10–13 that Timothy did visit them but met with a most unfavorable reception, for Paul's kindly but strong rebuke of their party strife and lax morality had aroused their resentment. When the news of this reached Paul, he had apparently gone to Corinth, only to meet with rebuff. It was undoubtedly one of the most tragic moments in his life. He could endure patiently and even joyously the perils of land and sea, but the disloyalty of the Corinthian church cut him to the heart. Evidently certain Judaizers, possibly the same who had dogged his footsteps in Galatia, had reached Corinth and had poisoned the minds of the Corinthian Christians, already smarting under Paul's just rebukes. For the moment they were inclined to distrust him and to attribute to him mercenary motives. One of the bolder wrong-doers had openly insulted him, and the better-minded members of the church had failed to rebuke the offender. Paul evidently left Corinth baffled and heart-sick. As has been truly said, when he wrote his third letter to the Corinthians:

PAUL'S THIRD LETTER

"He was fighting with his back to the wall." Its labored style speaks plainly of the deep emotion that almost overmastered him as he wrote. Hesitatingly and yet under the compulsion of a great necessity, he casts aside his modesty and boldly asserts his apostolic authority. But gradually, as he writes, his indignation abates and the irony with which he opens passes into open appeal and a tender expression of the fatherly love which he felt, even toward the disloyal Corinthians.

V. **Paul's Fourth Letter to the Corinthians.** The letter contained in II Corinthians 1–9 is so full of personal detail that its date and setting can be determined with great assurance. After writing his third letter to the Corinthians, Paul had evidently sent Titus to note its effect upon them and to report to him. With keenest apprehension he awaited this report. When Titus's return was delayed, Paul went to Troas and then on to Macedonia, where at last he found him. Titus's report removed from Paul's shoulders the heavy burden which had so oppressed him. From II Corinthians 1–9 it is possible to reconstruct that report. Paul's third letter had evidently aroused the troubled consciences of the Corinthians and their old loyalty to him asserted itself. Inspired by the good news, Paul wrote in hot haste this fourth letter to the Corinthians. It opens with greetings in 1$^{1, 2}$. The first main section (1^3–2^{17}) is an explanation of his personal plans and an expression of his joy over the loyal action of the Corinthians. Chapters 3^1–4^6 are a defense of his teaching, while 4^7–5^{10} contain the pathetic justification of his own physical weakness and of the great misfortunes which had overtaken him and which in the eyes of the ignorant were still regarded as evidences of divine disfavor. Chapters 5^{11}–6^{10} contain a defense of his methods of work. In 6$^{11-13}$, 7$^{2-16}$ is found a joyous song of thanksgiving, prompted by the love and loyalty of the Corinthians. Chapters 8 and 9 contain a concluding plea for a liberal collection in behalf of the poor saints at Jerusalem. This letter is one of the most personal and noble epistles ever penned by Paul. It is full of deep emotion and lofty aspiration. It reveals with remarkable clarity the exalted motives which inspired him. It is the convincing proof of his absolute sincerity and his deep personal affection for the men whose lives he was seeking to transform. Here the spirit of Jesus again finds expression and enables even the reader in this far-away age to appreciate the charm which drew men to Paul and made his words a miracle-working force in their lives.

§ CLVIII. PAUL'S PRINCIPLES OF CHRISTIAN LIVING

The settlement of disputes between Christians (I Cor. 6¹⁻⁶)

If one of you has a grievance against another, does he dare to go to law before sinful pagan judges and not before the saints? Do you not know that the saints are to sit in judgment upon the world? If the world is to come under your jurisdiction, are you incapable of deciding petty questions? Do you not know that you are to sit in judgment upon angels, to say nothing of the things of this life, and yet, when you have things of this life to decide, do you refer them to the judgment of men who are of no account in the church? I speak in order to put you to shame. Has it come to this that there is not one wise man among you who is able to decide between a man and his brother instead of one brother going to law with another, and that before unbelievers?

The futility of litigation between Christians (7-10)

Therefore, the fact that you have lawsuits with one another is convincing evidence of a defect in you. Why not rather let yourself be wronged? On the contrary, you inflict injustice and practise fraud, and that upon your brothers. Do you not know that the wicked will not inherit the Kingdom of God? Be not deceived: neither the immoral nor idolaters, nor adulterers, nor any who are guilty of unnatural crimes, nor thieves, nor avaricious people, nor the drunken, nor the abusive, nor robbers, will inherit the Kingdom of God.

The limitations of Christian liberty (12-20)

All things are lawful for me, but all things are not profitable for me. All things are lawful for me, but I will not let anything master me. Foods are for the stomach and the stomach for foods, but God will cause the one and the other to perish. The body is not for immorality, but for the Lord, and the Lord is for the body. Even as God raised up the Lord, so he will also raise us by his power. Do you not know that your bodies are members of Christ? Shall I then take away the members of Christ and devote them to a harlot? No, indeed. Do you not know that he who joins himself to a harlot is one with her in body (for the two, it is said, shall become one flesh), while he who joins himself to the Lord is one with him in spirit? Shun immorality! Every other sin that a man commits is outside the body, but the immoral man sins against his own body. Do you not know that your body is the temple of the Holy Spirit within you, which you have received from God, and that you are not your own. For you were bought for a price. Therefore, glorify God with your body.

For married people, my instructions are—yet not mine but the Lord's—a wife is not to separate from her husband, or if she has separated, let her remain single or be reconciled to her husband. Also a husband must not put away his wife. To other people I say—I, not the Lord—if any brother has a wife who is not a believer and she consents to live with him, let him not put her away. And if any woman has a husband who is not a believer and he consents to live with her, let her not put her husband away. For the unbelieving husband is consecrated through his wife and a woman who is not a believer is consecrated through union with the Christian brother; otherwise your children would be unholy instead of being holy, as they now are. If, however, the unbeliever is determined to separate, let him do so. In such cases the Christian brother or sister is not bound as a slave. God has called you to a life of peace. O wife, how do you know that you may not save your husband? O husband, how do you know that you may not save your wife?

The evil of divorce (7$^{10-16}$)

Let each man continue in the condition of life which the Lord has assigned to him, just as when God called him. Thus I laid down the rule to all the churches. Was a man already circumcised at the time when he was called? Let him not efface the marks of it. Has any man been called when he was uncircumcised? Then let him not be circumcised. Circumcision is nothing and uncircumcision is nothing, but obedience to God's commands is everything. Each man must remain in the condition of life in which he was when he was called. Were you a slave when you were called? Do not mind that; but if you are able to get free, make use of the opportunity. But a slave, when he is called to be in the Lord, is a freedman of the Lord. In the same way a free man who is called is a slave of Christ, for you have been bought for a price. You must not become slaves

Contentment with one's lot (7$^{17-24}$)

157

to men. Brothers, each one must remain with God in the condition in which he was when he was called.

Consideration for others' scruples (8:1-4, 7-9, 12, 13)

Now as to food which has been sacrificed to idols. 'We know about this for we all possess knowledge!' Knowledge puffs up, but love builds up. Whoever imagines that he has some knowledge has not as yet attained the knowledge which he ought to have attained. But if anyone loves God, that man is known by him. Now in regard to food which has been offered to idols: we know well that an idol is nothing in the world and there is only the one God. But this knowledge is not shared by all. Some through their relation with idols even now eat that which has been sacrificed to idols as such, and their conscience being weak is polluted. Food itself will not bring us any nearer to God, nor do we lose anything if we do not eat; while, if we do eat, we do not gain anything. But take care lest this liberty of yours prove a stumbling block to the weak. By thus sinning against the brothers and wounding their weaker consciences, you are sinning against Christ. Therefore if such food causes my brother to fall, I will never eat it again as long as I live, lest I should cause my brother to fall.

Paul's right and practice as an apostle (9:13-18)

Do you not know that those who perform the temple rites get their food from the temple and that the attendants at the altar share the sacrifices? In the same way the Lord also directed that those who proclaim the gospel are to get their living from the gospel. But I have not availed myself of any of these rights, nor do I now write in order to secure any of these rights for myself; for I would rather die than have anyone render this boast of mine an empty one. For if I go on preaching the gospel, that is nothing for me to boast of, for the necessity is imposed upon me. Yes, woe to me if I do not preach the gospel. For only if I preach it willingly, do I receive a reward. If I do it simply because I must, it only means that I have a stewardship intrusted to me. How then do I get a reward? In that I preach the gospel free of charge, that I refrain from using my full rights as a preacher of the gospel.

For though I am free from all, I have made myself the slave of all in order to win the more converts. To the Jews

I have become like a Jew in order to win Jews. To those
under the law I have been as if I were under the law in
order to win those under the law. To those outside the
law I have become as one outside of the law—though I
am not outside the law of God, but under Christ's law—in
order that I may win those outside the law. To the weak
I have become as weak myself in order to win over the
weak. To all men I have become all things in order to save
some in all of these ways. And I do all of these things for
the sake of the gospel in order that I may share in it.

His
eager-
ness to
win all
men by
all
means
(19-23)

Do you not know that in a race, though all run, only one
receives the prize? So run that you may get the prize.
Every athlete practises restraint in all ways; but while
they do this to receive a fading wreath, we do it for the
sake of one that will not fade. Therefore, I thus run with
no uncertainty. I plant my blows not as one who beats the
air; rather I maul and master my body lest I, after preaching to others, might myself be disqualified.

The
goal
(24-27)

So then, let him who thinks he stands securely take care
lest he fall. No temptation has waylaid you that has not
come to man. God, indeed, is faithful and will not permit
you to be tempted beyond what you can stand; but when the
temptation comes, he will also provide a way of escape, so
that you will be able to bear it.

How to
resist
temp-
tation
(10¹²,¹³)

Whether you eat or drink or whatever you do, do all to
the glory of God. Do not be causes of stumbling either to
the Jews or the Gentiles or to the church of God. Thus I
seek to satisfy all men in all points, aiming not at my own
advantage but at that of the many in order that they may be
saved. Imitate me, just as I imitate Christ.

Com-
plete
conse-
cration
to the
service
of God
and
man
(31-33)

As the human body is one, yet has many members, and
all the members form one body, though they are so many,
so it is with Christ. For by one Spirit we have all been
baptized into one body, whether Jews or Greeks, slaves
or freedmen. We have all been nourished by one Spirit.
For even the human body does not consist of one member
but many. If the foot were to say, Because I am not the
hand, I do not belong to the body, that would not make it
any less a part of the body. If the ear were to say, Because
I am not the eye, I do not belong to the body, that would

The
organic
unity
of the
Chris-
tian
broth-
erhood
(12¹²⁻²⁰)

not make it any less a part of the body. If all the body were an eye, where would the hearing be? If all the body were an ear, where would the smell be? But as it is, God hath placed the members in the body, each as he pleased. If they are all but one member, where would the body be? As it is, there are many members and one body.

Each part essential to the whole (21-31)

The eye cannot say to the hand, I have no need of you, nor again the head to the feet, I have no need of you. No, it is decidedly otherwise. Even those members of the body which are considered weaker are indispensable, and the parts which we deem less honorable, we invest with special honor, while our indecorous parts receive a special attention which it is not necessary to pay to our more decorous parts. Rather, God hath built up the body and bestowed a special attention on the parts that lacked, so that there might be no disunion in the body but that the parts might have a common concern for one another. And if one member suffers, all members suffer with it. If one member is honored, all the members share its honor. You, indeed, are Christ's body and individually members of it. Thus God hath set people in the church, first as apostles, second as prophets, third as teachers, then workers of miracles, then those who are able to cure diseases, helpers, administrators and those who speak in tongues of various kinds. Are all apostles? Are all prophets? Are all teachers? Are all workers of miracles? Are all able to cure diseases? Are all able to speak in tongues? Are all able to interpret? But always seek the highest gifts. And now I will point out to you a still higher way.

The supreme gift: love (13:1-3)

Though I speak with the tongues of men and of angels,
But have not love,
I am become like sounding brass or a clanging cymbal.
Though I have the gift of prophecy,
And know all mysteries and all knowledge,
And have such faith that I can remove mountains,
But have not love, I am nothing.
Though I distribute all my goods to the poor,
And give up my body to be burned,
But have not love, it profits me nothing.

160

LOVE'S WAY

Love is patient and kind,
Love knows no jealousy,
Love is neither boastful nor conceited,
It is not shameless nor self-seeking,
It is never provoked nor resentful,
It rejoices not in evil,
But rejoices in the truth.
It covers all faults,
It believes all things,
It hopes all things,
It endures all things.

Love's
way
(4-7)

Love never fails;
As for prophecies, they shall be set aside,
As for tongues, they shall cease,
As for knowledge, it shall be set aside,
For we know in part,
And we prophesy in part,
But when that which is perfect comes,
That which is imperfect shall be set aside.
When I was a child,
I talked as a child,
I thought as a child,
I argued as a child,
But now that I am become a man,
I have put away childish things.
For now we look in a mirror and are puzzled,
But then we will meet face to face.
Now I know only in part,
But then I will fully know,
Even as I have been fully known.
And so these three abide:
Faith, hope, and love.
But the greatest of these is love.

Its
eternal
and
pre-
emi-
nent
char-
acter
(8-13)

Follow after love and zealously seek spiritual gifts, but most of all that you may prophesy. For he who speaks in tongues is not speaking to men but to God, for no one understands him. He is speaking of divine secrets in the Spirit. But he who prophesies, speaks to men that which is

Superi-
ority of
proph-
ecy
to re-
ligious
ecstasy
(14 1-5,
13, 18, 19)

edifying, encouraging, and comforting. He who speaks with tongues edifies himself, but he who prophesies, edifies the church. I would like to have you all speak with tongues, but I would prefer to have you prophesy. The man who prophesies is superior to him who speaks with tongues— unless, indeed, the latter interprets, so that the church receives edification. Therefore, let a man who speaks in tongues pray that he may be able to interpret it. Thank God, I speak in tongues more than any of you; but in church I would rather say five words with my own mind, in order that I might instruct other people, than ten thousand in tongues.

The use of spiritual gifts (26-33a, 37-40) What then, brothers? Whenever you meet together each has something to contribute: a song of praise, a teaching, a revelation, a speaking in tongues or an interpretation; but let all things be for edification. If there is speaking in tongues, let two or at the most three speak, one at a time. Also let someone interpret. If there is no interpreter, let the speaker keep quiet in church and speak to himself and God. Let only two or three prophets speak, and let the rest use their judgment. If a revelation comes to one who is seated, let the first speaker be silent. You can all prophesy, one after another, in order that all may learn and all be encouraged, for the spirits of the prophets are subject to the prophets, for God is not a God of disorder but of harmony. If anyone considers himself to be a prophet or gifted with the Spirit, let him recognize that what I write to you is a command of the Lord. If anyone ignores this, let him be ignored. To sum up, my brothers: zealously seek to prophesy and do not check speaking with tongues; but let everything be done in a decorous and orderly manner.

I. **Paul's Teachings Regarding the Christian's Duty in His Economic Relations.** The heart of Paul's second letter to the Corinthian Christians (now found in I Cor.) contains detailed answers to certain practical questions which they had raised in a letter that Paul had recently received. In the light of the answers it is possible to determine the character of these questions. Each question and its answer must be interpreted in the light of its peculiar Corinthian background. Corinth, because of its geographical position and resulting commercial activity, was the scene of constant and doubtless bitter litigation. This tendency was intensified by the mixed character of its population. After its destruction by the Romans Julius Cæsar had recolonized it with Italians and dispossessed Greeks. Both of these races, and especially the Greeks, were given to quarrels and lawsuits, and the population of Corinth largely consisted of the pioneer spirits who had settled there, or their descendants. Evidently the Corinthian Christians could not quickly throw off their inheritance, especially in the contentious atmosphere in which they lived. Apparently the question raised by the leaders of the Corinthian church was whether disputes between Christians should be referred to the Roman courts. Paul answered: "No." He argued that certainly there was enough justice and legal insight within the Christian community to settle all petty disputes. He also called their attention to their belief that the Christians, as heirs to the promises originally given to the Jewish race, were ultimately to sit in judgment upon the heathen. This belief is clearly one of Paul's Jewish inheritances, and yet back of it lies the great fact that, inasmuch as the true Christians embodied the higher principles of their Master, the injustice and crime of the Gentile world were to be revealed by comparison with the righteous and pure lives of Jesus' followers. This teaching, however, was only preliminary to Paul's more fundamental treatment of the question. His ultimate argument rested upon Jesus' law of love. He who defrauds or wrongs another, or even entertains hate against another, thereby excludes himself from participating in God's rule in the world, for such acts and feelings are evidence that God is not ruling in his life. If Jesus' principle of considering first the best interests of the other is applied, the very causes of lawsuits are removed. The existence of such lawsuits, therefore, is evidence that they have reverted to the old condition from which Paul's preaching and the Gospel of Jesus had temporarily lifted them. Thus, by kindly irony, plain logic, and an appeal to the lofty social ideals of Jesus, Paul endeavored to lift the ignorant and sorely tempted Corinthian Christians to the high level of social living demanded by their Master.

II. **Paul's Advice Regarding Sex Questions and Divorce.** It was inevitable that insistent sex problems should come to the forefront in ancient Corinth. The city was steeped in social immorality. We are told that in the great temple of Venus, which stood on its acropolis, there were to be found one thousand courtesans. Gross immorality stalked abroad under the guise of religion. There is little wonder that Paul said with vehemence to his Corinthian converts: "Shun immorality." Licentious feasts and immoral practices confronted and allured them at every turn. This deadly leaven was even working within the Christian community itself. Some of its members were interpreting Paul's own words, "All things are lawful for me," as an excuse for mere license. They also insidiously urged that, as it was right to gratify the appetite for food, so also the grosser appetites. With his usual skill, Paul met this seductive reasoning. "Yes," he declared, "all things may be lawful, but all things are not good." Waving aside all appeal to the Jewish or Roman law, he declared that the analogy drawn between the bodily appetites was not valid. The body is not for self-gratification but for the glorification of God. It is the dwelling-place of God's Spirit. Social immorality means the pollution of the body, the lowering of the individual to the level of the harlot, and hence the destroying of the seat of the spiritual life. The figure which he employs to crystallize this fundamental teaching was especially effective with the Greek Christians at Corinth. The glory of Greece and of Corinth was its temples. The temple was the symbol of the abiding presence of the Deity. For centuries among all ancient peoples its sanctity had been jealously guarded by laws and institutions. Therefore, when Paul declared that the human body was the temple of the Spirit of God, he set forth in a way never to be forgotten one of the most fundamental teachings of Christianity.

Paul answers questions of social morality in the light of the peculiar conditions existing in Corinth. He nowhere suggests that he is laying down universal rules for the Christian world. On only one point is he absolutely certain and that is regarding divorce and remarriage. Here he reiterates in clearest terms Jesus' command, as recorded in Mark 10⁹⁻¹². No husband or wife is to break the marriage bond and remarry another. The wife may separate from her husband for sufficient grounds, but is to remain single. On his own authority Paul advises Christians married to unbelievers not to separate. If the unbelieving partner insists upon separation, Paul grants that the Christian brother or sister is thereby freed from the marriage bond; but in the same breath he earnestly exhorts all Christian husbands and wives to spare no effort to save their unbelieving partners. The entire aim in Paul's teaching is to preserve the sanctity of the marriage relation even in the most desperate cases.

MARRIAGE AND DIVORCE

In his advice to the Corinthian Christians Paul undoubtedly reveals a slightly ascetic tendency which is one of the chief bases of mediæval monasticism and similar modern movements. He frankly states, however, that it is not on the authority of Jesus, but simply to insure the freedom of the individual Christians in the Corinthian church and to "secure decorum and concentration upon a life of devotion to the Lord" ($7^{25, 35}$). He also says that the chief reason why he counselled those who are able to remain unmarried is the distress that he deems imminent and because he believes the interval until Christ comes again is short. At the same time he does not forbid marriage nor say that it is in any sense evil. In Ephesians 5^{21-23} we have his true convictions regarding marriage expressed under more normal conditions. He there uses the figure of the marriage relation to describe Christ's intimate relation to the church. He reaffirms, as did Jesus (in Mark 10^9), its divine foundation as set forth in Genesis 2^{24}. Far from condemning it, he simply endeavors to make its bonds so strong that nothing can sever them. He exhorts all wives to reverence and be subject to their husbands. Even though Paul lacks Jesus' supremely chivalrous attitude toward woman, he does assert in Galatians 3^{28}: "There is no room for slave or freeman, there is no room for male and female; you are all one in Christ Jesus." To his exhortation to wives in Ephesians 5 (which reflects his oriental conception of woman) he adds the ringing command to husbands: "Let every man of you love his wife as himself." In I Corinthians $7^{3, 4}$ he also places the intimate obligations of the husband to his wife and of the wife to her husband on an absolute equality. Here again we recognize the direct reflection of Jesus' absolute democracy and knightly chivalry which have exalted woman to her rightful place.

III. **Paul's Practical Application of Jesus' Law of Love.** The detailed problems of the tempted and perplexed Corinthian Christians precipitated some of Paul's noblest and most practical teachings. One of these questions was: "Shall we eat food that has been offered to heathen idols?" It is evident that much of the food, and especially the meat thus offered, was later exposed for sale in the public markets of Corinth. Hence it was almost impossible for the Christians to be sure that any food which they might buy had not been thus polluted. This insistent question had evidently developed two parties in the Corinthian church. One echoed Paul's teachings and asserted: "We all possess knowledge; belief is the essential thing. Mere ceremonial questions are entirely unimportant. As long as our faith is clear and true, it makes no difference what we eat." The other party—possibly the Cephas party—had not yet broken away from their traditional regard for ceremonial distinctions. Obviously the more broad-minded Corinthian Christians found great difficulty in satisfying the demands of these two antithetic positions. Paul meets the situation in his characteristic practical way. "Yes," he declared, "knowledge is all right but it puffs up. There is a higher principle and that is love, for it builds up." Here again he used a word which appealed with peculiar power to the Greek mind. To build was their dominant ambition and genius. Knowledge, Paul declares, is individualistic but love is social and constructive. Thus early in his epistle he strikes that lofty note which forever immortalizes it. His application of the principle of love is as clear as it is convincing. It is the guide of individual liberty. Liberty and knowledge thus guided by love will never permit a brother to ride roughshod over the conscientious scruples of a fellow Christian. In eating food offered to idols, therefore, each man will be governed not only by his own conception of what is right but by the effect of his act upon his less enlightened brothers. Back of Paul's teachings lay his own life and example, which he repeatedly cites with great effectiveness. Forgetting his own individualistic point of view and selfish wishes, he had become all things to all men to win them to Christ. Again adopting a figure very dear to the inhabitants of a city long famous for its Isthmian games, he urges the Corinthian Christians to keep this high goal ever in view and, like trained athletes, make everything else subservient to attaining it. At the conclusion of this discussion stands Paul's great social confession of faith: "Thus I seek to satisfy all men in all points, aiming not at my own advantage but at that of the many that they may be saved." In this practical way Paul interpreted by example, as well as by word, Jesus' supreme command: "Do to others as you would have them do to you."

IV. "The Body of Christ." In setting forth his social teachings, Paul employed a figure already used by the Stoic philosophers. They, however, spoke of all humanity as one body. Paul had in mind, when he used this pregnant phrase "the Body of Christ," the collective group of Christian believers. It was the objective social realization of Jesus' ideal of the Kingdom of God. It recognized that in this more ideal social group each had his own peculiar gift and task. If one member suffers, all the members share his suffering. As each contributes faithfully to the rest, the whole body prospers. The fidelity of each individual member is, therefore, essential to the welfare of the whole. Hence each individual gift must be consecrated to the common social good. It was from this higher vantage-point that Paul approached the problems presented by the jealousy between the different members of the Corinthian church and the heartburns caused by the fact that some appeared to possess higher spiritual gifts than others. It is evident from his statements that the intellectual and emotional life of that church was intense. Paul recognized the danger that it might become merely individualistic, merely emotional, and therefore shallow. The picture which he gives of its life is exceedingly illuminating. In his recapitulation he places first the more intellectual gifts: the power to speak words of wisdom and knowledge by the Spirit; second, the gift of faith and the corresponding power of healing; third, the more intuitive gift of prophecy, which is evidently here used in the sense of preaching and exhorting; and, fourth, the unconscious gift of tongues or ecstatic utterance and the power of interpreting the meaning of these emotional ejaculations. Each, Paul declares, is inspired by the same divine Spirit. Each is of value simply as it is made to conserve the common good. The one supreme aim must be the edification, that is, the building up of the Christian body.

V. **Paul's Immortal Hymn in Praise of Love.** It was while Paul was struggling to emphasize the importance of the motive that should lie back of these various expressions of the religious life that there dawned upon him the immortal principle which is crystallized in his matchless hymn in praise of love. It is one of his wonderful digressions, and yet it was the culmination of all of his thinking in the early part of the epistle and the embodiment of his own life and experience. He calls it the still higher way in which these spiritual gifts are to be used. With a remarkable breadth and insight he declares that all those gifts that were so highly esteemed in the early church, and even the most passionate self-sacrificing devotion, were absolutely useless unless inspired and guided by brotherly love. Then follows the familiar description of the characteristics of love's way in I Corinthians 13[4-7]. Its background is the personal ambitions, the jealousy, the self-glorification, the backbiting, the factiousness, and the discouragement of the Corinthian Christians. Clearly Paul sees the intellectual and moral perils that confront them. Only as they are lifted into the higher levels of faith and feeling can they hope to realize the ideals which he set before them. Childish, indeed, seemed their bickerings. Like a father, he yearned to lead them on from imperfection to perfection, to teach them step by step until they might attain a perfect vision of truth. In meeting all these universal needs, he declared that not human knowledge but faith and hope and love were eternal and invincible; yet the greatest of all was love.

§ CLIX. PAUL'S MINISTRY AT EPHESUS

Paul at Ephesus (Acts 18¹⁹⁻²³)

When Priscilla and Aquila reached Ephesus, Paul left them there, but he went into the synagogue and argued with the Jews, who asked him to stay for a longer time, but he would not consent. Instead, taking leave of them, he said, I will come back to you, if it be the will of God. Then sailing from Ephesus and reaching Cæsarea, he went up to salute the church and then travelled down to Antioch. After spending some time there he went off on a journey through the Galatian and Phrygian region, strengthening all the disciples.

Apollos at Ephesus and Achaia (24-28)

Meanwhile a Jew by the name of Apollos came to Ephesus. He was a native of Alexandria, a man of culture, strong in his knowledge of the scriptures. He had been instructed in the way of the Lord, and he preached zealously and taught accurately about Jesus, though all the baptism he knew was that of John. He began to speak boldly in the synagogue; but after Priscilla and Aquila listened to him they took him home and explained more accurately to him the way of God. And as he wished to cross over to Achaia, the brothers wrote urging the disciples there to welcome him. And on his arrival he rendered great service to those who by God's grace had believed, for he powerfully and publicly refuted the Jews, showing from the scripture that Jesus was the Messiah.

Disciples of John at Ephesus (19¹⁻⁷)

It was while Apollos was in Corinth that Paul, after passing through the inland districts, came to Ephesus and found there certain disciples to whom he said, Did you receive the Holy Spirit when you believed? No, they replied, we have not even heard that there is a Holy Spirit. Then he said, In what were you baptized? They replied, In John's baptism. John, said Paul, baptized with a baptism of repentance, telling the people that they should believe him who was to come after him, that is in Jesus. When they heard this, they had themselves baptized in the name of the Lord Jesus. And after Paul laid his hands on them, the Holy Spirit came upon them, and they began speaking with tongues and prophesying. They were in all about twelve men.

Then Paul entered the synagogue and for three months spoke fearlessly, arguing and persuading people about the Kingdom of God. But as some grew stubborn and disobedient, defaming the way in the presence of the multitude, he left them, withdrew the disciples, and continued his argument every day from eleven to four in the lecture room of Tyrannus. This continued for two years, so that all the inhabitants of the province of Asia, both Jews and Greeks, heard the word of the Lord. Paul's method of work at Ephesus (8-10)

God also worked no ordinary miracles by means of Paul, so that even towels or aprons which he had used were carried to the sick and they were delivered from their diseases and evil spirits came out of them. Certain travelling Jewish exorcists also attempted to pronounce the name of the Lord Jesus over those who had evil spirits, saying, I adjure you by the Jesus whom Paul preaches. The seven sons of a certain Sceva, a Jewish high priest, were doing this; but the evil spirit answered and said, Jesus I know and Paul I know, but who are you? And the man in whom was the evil spirit, springing at them, overpowered two of them and treated them with such violence that they rushed out of the house stripped and wounded. This became known to all the inhabitants of Ephesus, Jews as well as Greeks; and awe fell on them all, and the name of the Lord Jesus was magnified. Many believers also came to confess and declare what they had done. And numbers who practised magic arts collected their books and burned them in the presence of Paul. When they added up their value they found that they were worth about ten thousand dollars. Thus the word of the Lord mightily increased and prevailed. Miracles performed by Paul (11-20)

After these events had transpired Paul resolved in the spirit to travel through Macedonia and Achaia to Jerusalem, saying, After I get there I must see Rome. So he sent two of his assistants to Macedonia, Timothy and Erastus, while he himself stayed on for a while in Asia. Paul's plans (21, 22)

The
silver-
smith's
attack
upon
Paul
(22 40)

It was about that time that no small commotion arose
over the way. For a silversmith by the name of Demetrius, by making silver shrines of Artemis, brought rich
profit to his workmen. Calling these together, along with
the workmen who followed similar trades, he said to them,
You men well know that this trade is the source of our
wealth. You also see and hear that not only at Ephesus
but over almost all the province of Asia this Paul has drawn
off a considerable number of people by persuading them
that hand-made gods are no gods at all. There is danger
therefore not only that this our trade will be discredited but
also that the temple of the great goddess Artemis will fall
into contempt and that she will be degraded from her
majestic rule, she whom all the province of Asia and the
inhabited world worship. When they heard this they were
filled with rage and kept crying out, Great is Artemis of
the Ephesians! So the city was filled with confusion, and
they rushed into the theater dragging with them Gaius
and Aristarchus, Macedonians who were travelling with
Paul. Paul also wanted to enter the popular assembly,
but the disciples would not permit him. Certain of the
Asiarchs, who were friends of his, also sent entreating him
not to venture into the theater. Now some of the people
were shouting one thing, and some another; for the assembly were in confusion, and most of them had no idea why
they had come together. Certain of the mob concluded
that it must be Alexander, since the Jews pushed him to
the front. So Alexander, motioning with his hand, desired
to defend himself before the people; but when they discovered that he was a Jew, one cry broke from them all,
and for about two hours they shouted, Great is Artemis of
the Ephesians! Then the recorder, quieting the mob, said,
Men of Ephesus, who is there among men that does not
know that the city of Ephesus is the guardian of the temple
of the great Artemis and of the image that fell from heaven?
Therefore, since these things are so, you should keep calm
and do nothing reckless. But instead you have brought
these men here who are neither robbers of temples nor
blasphemers of our goddess. If Demetrius and his fellow
tradesmen have a grievance against anybody, public ses-

sions of the courts are held and there are proconsuls; let both sides state their charges. If you desire anything further, it must be settled in the legal assembly of the citizens. Indeed we are in danger of being charged with riot in connection with to-day's proceedings, for there is no reason that we can give for this riot. After saying these words he dismissed the assembly.

When the tumult had ceased, Paul sent for the disciples and encouraged them. Then, taking leave of them, he went on his way to Macedonia. After passing through these districts and encouraging the people with many an address, he came to Greece, where he spent three months. Just as he was about to set sail for Syria, a plot was laid against him by the Jews. He therefore decided to return through Macedonia. And these accompanied him: Sopater of Berœa, the son of Pyrrhus, Aristarchus and Secundus from Thessalonica, Gaius of Derbe, Timothy and Tychicus and Trophimus from the province of Asia. These went on ahead to wait for us at Troas, while we sailed from Philippi after the days of unleavened bread and joined them at Troas, where we spent seven days. *Paul's journey through Greece (20¹⁻⁶)*

On the first day of the week, when we met for the breaking of bread, Paul was addressing them, for he was to leave on the next day. And he continued his address until midnight. Now there were a considerable number of lamps in the upper room where we met. In the window sat a young man named Eutychus and, while Paul preached on and on, he was overcome with drowsiness, went fast asleep, and fell from the third story, and was picked up dead. But Paul, going down, threw himself upon him and embraced him. Do not lament, he said, for his life is still in him. Then he went up stairs, broke bread and ate; at length after conversing with them until dawn he departed. As for the lad, they took him away alive and were greatly comforted. *Paul's restoration of Eutychus (7⁻¹²)*

Now we had gone on beforehand to the ship and set sail for Assos, planning there to take Paul on board, for this was his own arrangement, since he intended to travel by land. So when we met him at Assos, we took him on board and went to Mitylene. Sailing from there on the following day, we arrived opposite Chios. Next day we crossed over *Paul at the port of Ephesus (13⁻16)*

171

to Samos and went on the following day to Miletus, for
Paul had decided to sail past Ephesus in order that he might
lose no time in the province of Asia, for he was very eager
if possible to reach Jerusalem by the day of Pentecost.

His ad-
dress
to the
elders
(17-38)
From Miletus Paul sent to Ephesus and called to him the
elders of the church. When they came to him, he said,
You know well how I lived among you all the time since I
set foot in the province of Asia; how I served the Lord in
all humility and with tears and trials which came to me
through the plots of the Jews, how I never shrank from
declaring to you anything that was for your good or from
teaching you in public and in your houses, bearing my
testimony both to Jews and Greeks of repentance toward
God and faith in our Lord Jesus Christ. And now behold
I go to Jerusalem, impelled by the Spirit. What things
will befall me there I do not know. Only I know this,
that in every city the Holy Spirit testifies to me that bonds
and troubles are awaiting me. But I set no value on my
own life, if I may but finish my course and carry out the
commission that I received from the Lord Jesus to attest
the gospel of the grace of God.

And now behold I know that not one of you shall ever see
my face again—you among whom I went about preaching
the Kingdom of God. Therefore I protest before you this
day that I am not responsible for the blood of any of you,
for I never shrank from declaring to you the entire purpose
of God. Take heed to yourselves and to all the flock of
which the Holy Spirit has appointed you guardians that
you shepherd the church of the Lord which he has bought
with his own blood. I know that when I am gone, fierce
wolves will enter in among you, and they will not spare the
flock, and that many of your own number will arise who will
pervert the truth in order to draw away the disciples after
them. Therefore be on your guard, remember how for
three whole years I never ceased night and day admonish-
ing each of you with tears. And now I commend you to
God and the word of his grace. He is able to build you
up and give you your inheritance among all the consecrated.
I coveted no man's silver, gold, or apparel. You yourselves
know how these hands of mine provided everything for my

own needs and for those who were with me. In all things I set you an example that, working as I do, you should succor the needy and remember the word of the Lord Jesus, who said, It brings more happiness to give than to receive. Having spoken thus, Paul knelt down and prayed with them all. Then they all broke into loud lamentation and falling upon Paul's neck, kissed him lovingly, sorrowing most of all because he told them that they would never see his face again. Then they escorted him to the ship.

I. **Paul's Journey to Syria.** As has already been noted, Paul's original objective in his second missionary campaign was Ephesus. He apparently had intended to go there at once after leaving Achaia and to remain. Instead he made a hurried trip to Syria. His reason for so doing is not stated in the biblical narrative and evidently was an open question in the minds of the early narrators. The author of Acts inferred that his object was to salute the mother church at Jerusalem. Under the influence of this inference, Luke, in Acts 18[22], has not stated directly but left his readers to imply that Paul actually went to Jerusalem. Here one recognizes the influence of Luke's profound regard for the authority of the Jerusalem church. There is much evidence, however, that Paul did not revisit Jerusalem at this time. The account of the completion of his third missionary journey in Acts 21 clearly implies that he had not returned since the council at Jerusalem. At his private interview with the "pillar" apostles the one command which they had laid upon him was to remember the poor with gifts. That he would return to Jerusalem empty-handed is almost incredible. The evidence rather is that he went back to Antioch and there remained for some time. The situation suggests that the reasons which led him to do so, instead of going directly back to Ephesus, were twofold. The first was his need of rest after his exceedingly strenuous and in many ways discouraging work at Corinth. Paul, the native of the seaport town of Tarsus, was naturally fond of the sea and for him the sea journey was ordinarily restful rather than arduous. His remaining for some time at Antioch, even though the crying needs of the western fields were ringing in his ears, is best explained because of his need of rest. The other and probably the principal reason why he returned to Syria was that, after having rested for a time, he might revisit the churches of Galatia. Apparently the strenuous letter which he had written these Galatian churches was penned at Corinth and he was naturally desirous of following it in person. Inasmuch as the land journey was far more arduous, he wisely determined to make it, not on his return to Antioch, but as he, again refreshed, set out for his new field of activity. That he did then revisit the Galatian churches is stated by Luke. This time Paul followed the great Roman highway westward, from Antioch in Pisidia, taking the northern, more mountainous, route directly to Ephesus. Then at last, after having revisited the scenes of his earlier missionary activity, he found himself free for work in the chief emporium and political capital of the Roman province of Asia.

II. **The Political and Religious Importance of Ephesus.** The province of Asia was one of the largest, richest, and most closely knit of all the Roman provinces in Asia Minor. Here at Ephesus the Roman proconsul had his official residence. From Ephesus great commercial highways radiated to all the important cities of the province, and it was the chief gateway which led over the sea to Corinth and Rome. On the main highway to the east lay the cities of Colossæ and Laodicea. Northward, all within a radius of one hundred and fifty miles, were Sardis and Thyatira, the cities in which were established the important Christian churches mentioned in the opening chapters of Revelation. Ephesus was in many ways the most influential city in which Paul had as yet worked. Like most Greek cities, it encircled a hill rising about five hundred feet from the plain and crowned with an acropolis. The business and intellectual centre of the city was on the west of this hill looking toward the sea. On its northwestern slope above the River Cayster was the huge stadium capable of holding fully six thousand people. Here Paul with the Ephesian populace doubtless witnessed many of the popular games from which he draws some of his most effective figures of speech. Farther to the south on the western brow of the hill was the great theatre. The remarkably well-preserved ruins which have been excavated at this point probably represent a somewhat later theatre built on the site of the one which figures so prominently in the narrative of Acts. It marked the centre of the life of the ancient city. Just below it to the northwest was the Roman agora, while to the southwest was the famous Hellenistic agora, surrounded by beautiful porticos with public halls on the south. Not far from this point probably stood the Hall of Tyrannus.

According to tradition, Ephesus was settled by a Greek colony from Athens in the eleventh century B.C. Even before the Greeks appeared, the city was already famous as the shrine of a native nature-goddess, whose temple lay on the broad plain beside the Cayster to the northeast of the Græco-Roman Ephesus. Recent excavations have laid bare the foundations of this ancient sanctuary far below the huge platform of the great Greek temple of Artemis, which was built as early as the sixth century B.C. Out of the conflicts between the Greek colonists and the priestesses of the native temple grew the famous traditions of the Amazons who fought as men. In Paul's day the temple of Artemis stood seven feet above the plain on a great artificial platform, which had been built on the ruins of earlier temples. It is approached by ten steps, and covered an area of over eighty thousand square feet. Its huge columns rose more than sixty feet above the platform. Standing in solitary grandeur in the midst of the great plain, it appears to have well merited the signal honor of being reckoned as one of the seven wonders of the world. The oracles of the Greek goddess Artemis rivalled those even of Delphi, although they never appear to have exerted as wholesome a political or moral influence as did those of its more famous Hellenic rival. To the temple of Artemis came fugitives from all parts of Asia Minor, for within its sacred precincts they were immune from all pursuit or attack. It was also the great banking centre of that part of the Roman Empire, for kings as well as thousands of private individuals placed their wealth under the protection of the temple authorities, assured that it would be safely guarded. The gifts of thousands of pilgrims swelled the temple's income and supported the vast horde of virgin priestesses and celibate priests, of temple singers and hymn-writers, and of menial servants associated with this ancient shrine. The hierarchy of the temple and those whose income was dependent either directly or indirectly on the worship of the temple were always a powerful factor in the life of Ephesus. The city itself bore the coveted title of "Guardian (literally, Sweeper) of the temple."

III. **Conditions that Confronted Paul at Ephesus.** As early as 44 B.C. the Roman consul Dolabella had granted to the Jews of Ephesus the toleration of their religious rites, the privilege of Sabbath observance, and protection in making pilgrimages to Jerusalem (Jos., *Ant.*, XIV, 10[12, 25]). Augustus had later confirmed these privileges. Paul, therefore, found a strong Jewish colony at this great commercial metropolis. As at Corinth, he also found them unwilling to accept a religion which was offered to Jew and Gentile alike and which set aside as obsolete many of the inherited laws of their race. Ephesus was pre-eminently given up to magic and the religious quackeries inherited from the ancient religions. Many Jews were found in a cosmopolitan city like Ephesus who, for mercenary reasons, practised these magical arts. To this class belonged the strolling Jewish exorcists, the sons of Sceva, who figure in a popular tradition concerning Paul's work at Ephesus which the author of Acts has incorporated in his narrative. Ramsay is probably right in saying that "the writer is here rather a picker up of current gossip, like Herodotus, than a real historian" (*St. Paul*, p. 273). The story, however, records the indubitable fact that Paul here came into constant contact with this debased Judaism, in which popular demonology, angelology, and superstition were grotesquely commingled. Modern excavations have revealed hundreds of the magic papyri, or "Ephesian letters," as they are called because most of them were prepared in Ephesus. Although the prevailing religious life of Ephesus was shallow, the spirit of the city was on the whole tolerant. Here all religions of the East and West and of the North and South—Judaism, Gnosticism, the oriental mystery cults, Greek and Alexandrian philosophy, and nature-faiths—commingled; but the prevailing religious fashion was to single out and combine what was attractive in each. Hence, as long as Paul did not interfere with vested or financial interests, he was free to teach whatever and whenever and wherever he pleased and was sure of a liberal hearing.

IV. **Paul's Method of Work at Ephesus.** Again Paul's marvellous gift of adapting himself to any situation was well illustrated. The narrative in Acts states that he first went into the Jewish synagogue and endeavored by argument and persuasion to convince them that Jesus had inaugurated the Kingdom of God for which their race was longing, but that they rejected the way of thinking and living which he proclaimed. Then Paul adopted and followed a daily programme which evidently fitted the peculiar conditions of that ancient Ionian city in which the working hours for all classes began with sunrise and extended to eleven o'clock in the morning. The remainder of the day they spent in their homes or at public places. Paul apparently plied his trade of tent-maker during business hours. Then, when the lecture hours of the public philosophers and rhetoricians were over, he secured the lecture hall of one of them, a certain Tyrannus, and, as is recorded in the Beza text, argued publicly from eleven to four each day. In closely crowded Ephesus many were doubtless attracted to the lecture room of Paul the Christian philosopher. Jews and Greeks, and many visiting strangers from the neighboring cities of Asia listened to his fervid appeals. In Ephesus Paul himself must have become intimately acquainted with the mystery-religions of Asia Minor from which are drawn many of the figures of speech that appear in his later letters. His epistle to the near-by church of Colossæ is an excellent illustration of the way in which he probably combated the prevalent gnostic doctrines.

At Ephesus Paul built on foundations already laid by his co-workers Priscilla and Aquila, if not by earlier Christian apostles. In thus building he departed from his general rule of action because he recognized the great strategic importance of Ephesus. Evidently he made it the base for missionary activity throughout Asia. Epaphras and probably Timothy were sent to establish a Christian community in Colossæ (Col. 1¹⁻⁷). Tychicus possibly did similar pioneer work in Laodicea (Eph. 6²¹). The personal letter appended in chapter 16 to the Epistle to the Romans was evidently written to the Christians of Ephesus (cf., e. g., Rom. 16⁵) from Corinth, after Paul had left the capital city of Asia. In it are found warm personal greetings addressed to his fellow workers in Asia. Twenty-four in all are mentioned in this short letter. It suggests how well and how broadly Paul's work at Ephesus was organized and that Ephesus was but the centre through which he sought to reach all the important cities in southwestern Asia Minor.

V. **Paul's Conflict with the Pagan Cults.** For a considerable period Paul's work seems to have met with little opposition. In his contest with the Jewish exorcists the sympathy of a majority of the Ephesian populace was with him, for the anti-Jewish feeling was evidently strong. He does not appear to have come into direct conflict with the authorities of the temple of Artemis. The Asiarchs, some of whom sympathized with Paul, were the official local representatives in the province of the worship of the emperor and of Rome. Their task at this period was apparently more political than religious, for the bitter conflict between Christianity and the Roman emperor-worship still lay in the future. According to Acts, the first strong opposition to Paul's teaching came from organized labor and was due to the fact that his teachings had already gained a wide acceptance throughout the city. One of the favorite offerings of the pilgrims to the temple of Artemis was a votive image, which was presented to the goddess by the offerer and left within the temple precincts. These votive images represented the goddess seated on a throne. Those offered by the poorer people were usually made of terra-cotta. The wealthy brought images of silver. The guild of the silversmiths, of which Demetrius was the spokesman, evidently manufactured these silver images. Contemporary inscriptions indicate that there were many guilds of manual workers in ancient Ephesus. Thus, for example, the guilds of the wool-workers, of the surveyors, and of the workmen before the gate are mentioned in the inscriptions. They constituted, therefore, an important class in this commercial metropolis and were able by the cry of class interest to stir the mob to action. While subject to the strict supervision of Rome, Ephesus still enjoyed the democratic organization of a typical Greek city. It had its senate and in addition its popular assembly. In the peculiar civic organization of the cities of Asia Minor, the recorder or clerk was the leading official, as appears in the narrative of Acts. This narrative is probably correct in stating that he opposed the class uprising, fearing Roman suspicion and possible interposition. Either through ignorance of facts or intentionally the author of Acts has failed to speak of the greater misfortunes which overtook Paul. In fact, the exact order of events is not entirely clear, although it is obvious that the scene in the theatre, at which Paul was not present, occurred during the latter part of his sojourn at Ephesus and was probably one of the causes of his ultimate departure. Paul himself declared that he fought with wild beasts at Ephesus and many are inclined to interpret these words literally. It is possible, however, that he had in mind the infuriated mob which sought his life and that of his associates. In a later letter, written to the Corinthian Christians from Ephesus, he states that he nearly lost his life there (II Cor. 11[23]). There can be little doubt that the closing months of his activity were marked by bitter opposition and persecution.

VI. **The Results of Paul's Work at Ephesus.** Paul spent more time and apparently suffered more bitter persecution at Ephesus than at any other city that he visited except Rome, where he at last gave his life for the cause he served. At Ephesus also he had to contend against a complex of false philosophies, as well as pagan superstitions. And yet it proved a most fruitful field. In writing from there to the Corinthians he declared: "A great door is opened to me" (I Cor. 16[9]). There he was able to rally about him an exceedingly loyal band of helpers. In the Ephesian letter, appended to Romans, he speaks of "Priscilla and Aquila, my fellow workers in Jesus who for my life laid down their own necks" (Rom. 16[3, 4]). Two others,

Andronicus and Junius, shared a prison experience with him. Ephesus and the province of Asia in the succeeding centuries proved one of the great strongholds of Christianity, and yet the results of Paul's personal work there appear to have been far less permanent than elsewhere. We have no record that he ever again visited or wrote any other letter to the Ephesian Christians except the short personal note in Romans 16. Even in this he urges his fellow workers at Ephesus to keep their eye on "those who stir up dissensions and put hindrances in your way, contrary to the doctrine which you have been taught. Avoid them. Such creatures are no servants of Christ our Lord, they are slaves of their own base desires; with their plausible and pious talk they beguile the hearts of unsuspecting people." In Paul's later address to the Ephesian elders he is represented as warning them that "fierce wolves will get in among them, and they will not spare the flock"; also that "men of their own number will arise with perversions of the truth to draw the disciples after them" (Acts 21[29, 30]). These statements point to the many heretical and especially gnostic doctrines that sprang spontaneously from the already infected soil of Ephesus. In their earlier dealings with Rome the citizens of Ephesus had repeatedly shown themselves exceedingly fickle. The same impression regarding the Ephesian church is conveyed by the letter addressed to it in Revelation 2[4, 5]. The two letters to Timothy, to whose care the Christian communities in Asia were intrusted, indicate that the loyalty to Paul which had characterized the other churches of his planting was lacking here. II Timothy 1[15] contains the sweeping statement: "You know that all who are in Asia have turned away from me." While their nominal allegiance appears to have been transferred from Paul to John the presbyter and other apostolic leaders, the pioneer work of Paul remained the foundation of the church in Asia, and the principles laid down by him reappear in the rich Johannine literature that later sprang from Ephesus (§ CLXIX).

§ CLX. PAUL'S INTERPRETATION OF JESUS' SAVING WORK

Paul, a servant of Jesus Christ, called to be an apostle, set apart for the gospel of God concerning Jesus Christ our Lord, through whom I have received grace and a commission to promote obedience to the faith for his name's sake among all the Gentiles, among whom are you also, who are called to belong to Jesus Christ; to all in Rome who

Greeting (Rom. 1[1, 5-7])

179

are beloved by God, called to be saints, Grace and peace from God our Father and the Lord Jesus Christ.

Paul's relation to the Roman church (8-15)

First of all, I thank my God through Jesus Christ for you all, because your faith is reported throughout the whole world. God is my witness, the God whom I serve with my spirit in the gospel of his Son, how unceasingly I always mention you in my prayers, asking if at last the way may be opened to me by God's will to come to you. For I long to see you that I may impart to you some spiritual gift for your strengthening or, in other words, that I may be comforted by meeting you, I by your faith and you by mine. Brothers, I would not have you ignorant that I have often purposed to come to you (though hitherto I have been prevented) so as to have some results among you, as well as among the rest of the Gentiles. I have an obligation to Greeks and to barbarians, to wise and to foolish alike. Hence my eagerness to preach the gospel to you also who are in Rome.

Thesis: Righteousness comes alone through faith (16-17)

I indeed am not ashamed of the gospel, for it is God's saving power for everyone who has faith, for the Jew first and for the Greek as well. In that gospel God's righteousness is revealed by faith to develop faith, as it is written: Now the righteous shall live by faith.

Failure of the heathen world to obtain righteousness because of lack of faith in God (18-25)

For the wrath of God is revealed from heaven against all the impurity and wickedness of those who hinder the truth by their wickedness, for what is to be known of God is plain to them; for God himself hath made it plain. For, since the creation of the world, his invisible things, his everlasting power and divine nature, have been clearly perceptible in what he hath made, that they may have no excuse. Though they knew God, they have not glorified him as God nor given him thanks; they have given themselves up to futile speculations and let their senseless minds be darkened. Claiming to be wise, they have become fools; and they have exchanged the glory of the immortal God for the semblance of a likeness of mortal man, of birds, of four-footed beasts, and of reptiles. So God hath given them up in their heart's lust to sexual vice, to the dishonoring of their own bodies; for they have exchanged the truth for a lie and have worshipped and served the creature rather than the Creator, who is blessed forever.

180

THE LIKE REWARD FOR JEW AND GENTILE

He it is who will render to everyone according to his works, eternal life to those who by patiently doing good seek for glory, honor, and immortality, but wrath and indignation to those who are factious, who disobey the truth and obey wickedness. Trouble and anguish are for every human being who does evil, for the Jew first and for the Greek as well; but glory, honor, and peace for everyone who does good, for the Jew first and for the Greek as well. There is no partiality with God. All who sin outside the law will perish outside the law; and all who sin under the law will be condemned by the law. For it is not the hearers of the law who are just before God, it is those who obey the law who will be acquitted on the day when God judgeth the secret things of men.

What then, have we Jews any advantage? Not at all, for we have already charged both Jews and Greeks that they are under sin, as it is written, None is righteous, no, not one; no one understands, no one seeks for God. All have turned aside, one and all have become unprofitable; no one does good, not a single one. For no mortal will be acquitted in his sight by acts of obedience to the law, for through the law simply comes the consciousness of sin.

But now apart from the law a righteousness of God has been disclosed. It is attested by the law and the prophets, but it is a righteousness of God through faith in Jesus Christ. It is for all who have faith, for there is no distinction. All have sinned and fall short of the glory of God, but they are justified freely by his grace through the ransom provided by Jesus Christ. God set him forth as a means whereby men might, through faith in his blood, win divine forgiveness. This was to demonstrate the justice of God because he had passed over previously the sins committed during the period of God's forbearance, and to demonstrate the justice at the present epoch, showing that he himself is just and justifieth every man through faith in Jesus. Where then is the boast? It is excluded! By what law? Of works? No, by the law of faith. We hold that a man is justified by faith apart from the works of the law. Or is God only the God of the Jews? Is he not the God of the Gentiles also? Surely he is of the Gentiles also. Surely then there is one God, and he will justify the circumcised by faith, and the uncircumcised through faith. Do we then make the law of none effect through faith? No, indeed! We establish the law.

Abraham an illustration of this principle (4¹³⁻¹⁷ᵇ) For the promise to Abraham and to his offspring that he should inherit the world, was not made through the law, but through the righteousness of faith. For if they who are of the law are heirs, faith is without meaning, and the promise is made of none effect. What the law produces is wrath; but where there is no law, there is no transgression. For this reason inheritance depends upon faith, that it may be a matter of divine favor, to make the promise sure to all the offspring, not only to those who hold to the law but also to those who share the faith of Abraham, who is the father of us all, as is written: I have made thee a father of many nations.

The way peace with God is attained through Christ's self-sacrifice (5¹⁻¹¹) Therefore, since we are justified by faith, let us enjoy the peace we have with God through our Lord Jesus Christ. Through him we also have gained access to this grace wherein we stand, and we exult in the hope of God's glory. And not only so, but we also exult in our troubles, knowing that trouble produces stedfastness, and stedfastness produces tested character, and tested character produces hope. This hope never disappoints us, for God's love has flooded our hearts through the Holy Spirit which has been given to us. For while we were yet weak, in due season Christ died for the ungodly. Why, one will scarcely die for a righteous man, though one might perhaps dare to die for a good man. But God proveth his own love toward us, in that, while we were yet sinners, Christ died for us. Much more then, now that we are justified by his blood, shall we be saved from the wrath of God by him? For if, while we were enemies, we were reconciled to God by the death of his Son, much more, now that we are reconciled, shall we be saved by his life. Not only so, but we exult in God through our Lord Jesus Christ, through whom we now receive our reconciliation.

There is therefore no condemnation for those who are in Christ Jesus. For the law of the spirit of life in Christ Jesus has set me free from the law of sin and death. For what the law, weakened by the flesh, could not do, God hath done by sending his own son in the likeness of sinful flesh. And to deal with sin he condemned sin in the flesh, in order that the just requirements of the law might be fulfilled in our lives, as we walk not by the flesh but by the spirit. For those who are fleshly minded incline to the things of the flesh, but those who are spiritually minded incline to the things of the spirit. The inclinations of the flesh mean death, but the inclinations of the spirit life and peace. For the inclinations of the flesh are hostile to God, for they do not submit to the will of God (indeed they cannot). Those who are in the flesh cannot please God, but you are not in the flesh but in the spirit, if the Spirit of God dwells in you. Anyone who does not have the Spirit of Christ does not belong to him. But, if Christ is within you, though the body is dead as a result of sin, the spirit is living as a result of righteousness. And, if the Spirit of him who raised up Jesus from the dead dwells within you, then he who raised Christ Jesus from the dead will also make your mortal bodies live because his Spirit is dwelling within you.

So then, brothers, we are under no obligation to the flesh to live by the flesh. If you live by the flesh you must die, but, if by the spirit you put to death the deeds of the body, you will live. For as many as are led by the Spirit of God these are the sons of God. For you have not received a slavish spirit that would make you fear again; but you have received the spirit of sonship, whereby we cry, Abba Father! This Spirit bears witness with our own spirit that we are children of God; and if children then heirs, heirs of God and heirs with Christ also; for we share his suffering in order to share his glory.

I consider that the sufferings of this present life are not worthy to be compared to the glory which shall be revealed to us. Even the creation waits in eager expectation for the revealing of the sons of God. For the creation was subjected to vanity, not by its own choice but by him who thus subjected it, whose hope being that creation itself will also be delivered from the bondage of corruption and gain the glorious liberty of the children of God. For we know that

The new spiritual life open to the Christian (8:1-11)

Obligations and privileges of spiritual sonship (12-17)

Man's sonship in God the goal of creation (18-25)

even until now the whole creation sighs and throbs in pain; and not only so but we ourselves also, who have the first-fruits of the Spirit, sigh to ourselves as we wait for the deliverance of our body that means our adoption as sons. By this hope we were saved. But hope that is seen is not hope. Whoever hopes for what he sees already? But, if we hope for something that we do not see, we wait for it patiently.

Assistance of God's Spirit (26, 27)
So also the Spirit helps us in our weakness; for we do not know how to pray as we ought, but the Spirit pleads for us with sighs that cannot be uttered, and he who searcheth hearts knoweth what is in the mind of the Spirit, for the Spirit pleads for the saints according to the will of God.

Roll of those who love God (28-30)
We know also that to those who love God, even those who are called according to his purpose, all things work together for good. For those whom he knew beforehand he also appointed beforehand that they might be transformed into the likeness of his Son, that he might be the first-born of a great brotherhood. Then he also called those whom he had appointed beforehand, and those whom he called he also justified, and those whom he justified he also glorified.

Invulnerable security of those who trust in God's love revealed through Jesus (31-39)
What then shall we say to all this? If God is for us, who can be against us? Will not he who spared not his own Son but gave him up for us all freely give us all things? Who will lay a charge against those whom God hath chosen? When God acquitteth, who will condemn? Will Christ Jesus?—he who died, yes, and rather who was raised from the dead, who is at God's right hand, who also pleads for us! Who can ever separate us from Christ's love? Can tribulation, or anguish, or persecution, or famine, or nakedness, or peril, or the sword? For, as it is written, For thy sake we are killed all the day long, we are accounted as sheep to be slaughtered. No, in all these things we are more than conquerors through him who loved us. For I am convinced that neither death nor life, neither angels nor principalities, neither things present nor things to come, neither powers of the height or of the depth, nor any other created thing will be able to separate us from God's love in Jesus Christ our Lord.

Oh the inexhaustible wealth of God's wisdom and knowl-

edge ! How unsearchable his judgments ! I
ous his way ! Who ever knew the mind
Who has ever been his counsellor ? Who h
to him and has to be repaid ? All things co
live by him, and return to him. Glory to him forever. ⁽⁻⁻⁻⁻⁾
Amen.

I. **Date and Aim of Paul's Epistle to the Romans.** Paul's
letter to the Romans is the best New Testament illustration of an
epistle. Upon it Paul evidently expended great thought and care.
The Epistle to the Galatians reminds one of a rapid mountain torrent,
but in Romans Paul's thought flows more leisurely, winding here and
there, gathering a great variety and volume of figures as it flows on
to the practical applications with which the epistle closes. It was a
dramatic moment in Paul's life when he dictated this letter to the
Christian community at Rome. His work at Ephesus and Corinth,
and in fact in the Greek world, was nearing completion. Longingly
he looked at the great Roman ships setting out from Corinth for the
imperial city. As he tells his readers, to visit them was one of the chief
ambitions of his life. His long days and nights of labor with Priscilla and Aquila at Corinth and Ephesus had given him ample opportunity to become acquainted with the problems of the Roman church.
Doubtless many of his own converts, having gravitated toward the
imperial city, were included in its membership. It appears to have
comprised both Jewish and Gentile converts, for Paul in his letter evidently had both classes in mind. Even though his heart was in Rome,
his face was steadfastly set toward Jerusalem. He was well aware of
the opposition and perils which awaited him there, but nothing could
deflect him from his purpose to take back as a peace-offering to the
saints at Jerusalem the collections which he had gathered in response
to the request of the "pillar" apostles from the churches which he had
planted in the Western world. The Gentile problem which was still
insistent throughout the Eastern church was evidently prominent in
Paul's mind as he wrote his Epistle to the Romans. He also felt
strongly the call of that larger Gentile world which Rome represented.
He longed, as he tells his readers, to take up his evangelistic work
among them, but his primary aim was, as has been truly said: "A
restatement in the light of his experience, during the long mission now
closing, and in view of the fresh propaganda which he was contemplat-
ing in the West, of the principle of his Gospel to the Gentiles in its re-

lation to Judaism." Romans contains not a system of philosophy or theology, but Paul's great confession of faith. The situation called for the systematic setting forth of his mature convictions and the principles that had inspired him in his work. Here is revealed not Paul the theologian but Paul the Christian mystic and missionary.

II. **The Structure of the Epistle to the Romans.** Into the opening salutation (1^{1-7}) Paul puts not only his formal greeting but also his credentials as an apostle and the essence of his Gospel message. In 1^{8-17} is found the usual commendation of those to whom he wrote, a statement of his aim in writing to them, and the thesis which he later defends. Chapters 1^{18}–5^{21} contain his main teaching. Here he seeks to show what God has done through the work of Jesus to meet the needs of both Gentiles and Jews. In 6^{1}–7^{6} he makes certain practical applications of these principles and defines the obligations of those who enjoy the results of divine grace: it is to dedicate themselves to God and to live, like Jesus, a sinless life. In 7^{7-25} he reverts to the problems that gathered about the Jewish law and declares that it was simply preparatory to the work of Jesus but not able in itself to save men. Romans 8 is one of the great classical passages in Paul's writings. Here he speaks clearly out of the depths of his own spiritual experience and aims to show what Christ means in the inner life of the individual. "Christ" is not used here in the limited Jewish messianic sense. It stands not only for all that Jesus did and taught and was but also for the crucified yet living Christ whom Paul had beheld through his inner vision. Chapters 9–11 give the reason why the Jews, the favored people, had not been saved: through failure to believe in Jesus they had forfeited their birthright; but in God's plan they were yet to have a place with the Gentiles. Chapters 12–15 contain the practical application of the principles of the Gospel to Christian life and conduct. Chapter 16 is a personal letter that has been appended to the original Epistle to the Romans.

III. **Paul's Estimate of the Jewish Law.** In Paul's letter to the Roman Christians the historical student of religion recognizes the many and varied currents of influence which converged in the great apostle to the Gentiles. Most of the figures and many of the ideas expressed in this epistle are the product of his intensely legalistic training. His natural tendency to speak in legal terms was strengthened by the fact that he lived and worked in the rigidly legalistic atmosphere of the Roman Empire in which he proudly claimed citizenship. So often had he pleaded his own case before Jewish and Roman tribunals that it was second nature for him to speak in the language of the court-room. Whenever he referred to the Jewish law it was always in terms of highest respect. On its ethical side it still had for him a certain binding authority. He was keenly alive to its historical and practical value as a clear, concrete formulation of fundamental moral and religious principles. To Israel, during the childhood of the race, the law had been, like a Roman pedagogue, a wise guide directing the nation's moral and religious education. But Paul was also well aware of the limitations of the law. It had begotten in the majority of his countrymen self-pride and a sense of moral self-sufficiency which were fatal to all real religious progress. Moreover, Paul knew by painful experience that while the law developed in the mind of a conscientious man like himself a bitter consciousness of sin, it provided no practical way of escape from its consequences. Above all, the law emphasized the judicial side of God's character and provided no way of bringing man into that trusting, loyal fellowship with his divine Father which is the essence of true religion. Hence, Paul frankly declares that, while the ancient law had performed a great service in training men's moral sense, as a means of saving men from the consequences of their ignorance and misdeeds and of leading them into complete and joyous fellowship with God it was a failure. To this he adds the revolutionary but logical conclusion that the Jews who had staked their hope on keeping the law were, after all, on an equality with the Gentiles. Indeed, if their confidence in the efficacy of the law had dulled their consciousness of the need of the personal fellowship with God, their lot was even more pitiable than that of the great heathen world of Paul's day, which was longing and earnestly seeking for salvation and unity with God.

IV. **The Influences which Shaped Paul's Conception of Jesus.** Into Paul's life there had suddenly come a mighty transforming and satisfying spiritual experience. Psychology may explain the form of this experience, but it was regarded by Paul as a supreme miracle. Interpreted into the terms of the psychology of his own day, he had experienced what the contemporary mystery religions promised to their devotees: God (in the person of the crucified but risen Christ) had entered in and taken possession of him. This transcendent religious experience was repeated at many later crises of his life. That such experiences were possible was almost a commonplace of contemporary Greek or Roman religious thought. For centuries the teachers of the Jewish race also had taught that the Spirit of Jehovah at times

187

rushed upon and took possession of the true prophets and even of patriotic warriors like Gideon and Saul. The prophet Joel had predicted that this experience would be shared in common by all classes of men. The primitive church at Jerusalem had felt and seen the marvellous realization of this prediction.

In Paul's confession of faith (Rom. 1–11) the influence of many other inherited beliefs may also be recognized. Pharisaic Judaism had taught him to believe in the pre-existence and the supernatural character of the Messiah or Christ. In the light of Paul's own experience it was difficult for him to think of Christ, a spirit, as other than ever existent. In apocalyptic passages, like Daniel 7[13], "the one like to the Son of man" was represented as coming from the heavens and as standing beside the throne of God. On the other hand, legalistic Judaism, as interpreted by IV Ezra, represented the Messiah as an atoning sacrifice intended to propitiate the divine judge. Although not in the Old Testament, in the contemporary Jewish literature, such as the Wisdom of Solomon, II Baruch (48[42, 43]), and IV Ezra (3[7]), Adam, the traditional forefather of the human race, is regarded as the source of all the sin and woe which he has transmitted to his descendants. The burdening belief that all flesh was bowed to earth by a crushing, cumulative weight of sin was shared alike by Stoic philosophers and thoughtful Jews. In his own spiritual experience of Jesus and in that of his fellow Christians Paul found the fulfilment of all his inherited hopes and beliefs and the solution of all his spiritual problems. It was also inevitable that he should interpret Jesus and his work in the light of these varied inheritances. To ignore this fact is to misinterpret Paul and to fail to appreciate his permanent contributions to Christianity which are enmeshed in the figures and beliefs of a bygone age.

V. **Paul's Doctrine of Salvation through Faith in Christ.** To understand Paul's teachings it is also important to note that he is fond of using a great variety of figures to set forth the same ultimate truth. This method is a characteristic of most great religious teachers. The more important the truth the more important that it be viewed from many points. Paul, in his endeavor to make clear what Christ has done for him and could do for all men, used four familiar figures, each drawn from the legal vocabulary of his age. It is evident that they all represent the same vital experience in the life of the individual. The first, that of the redemption or emancipation of a slave from bondage, was grimly suggestive and familiar to every citizen of that

PAUL'S INT...

the Spirit of G
of Christ do
body is d
ness.
dw

ancient world.   It was probably sugge
in Mark 10[45]: "The Son of man has con
(as a slave) and to give his life as a ra
underlying idea is closely related to P
Christian liberty.   By its use he declar
from the bondage of that merely judica
Paul frequently speaks and which in his
Another figure was that of justificatior
course, was suggested by the ancient cou
was arraigned by the representatives of
assured only when his innocence could
stance adduced.   Here, as in each of these parallel figures, the dominating idea is that deliverance or salvation is attained as the result of
the divine love expressed in the work and death of Jesus.   A third
figure was that of forgiveness.   Here the sinner was thought of as a
debtor to whom God had granted full forgiveness, because of divine
love which Jesus supremely exemplified and proclaimed.   The fourth
parallel figure was that of reconciliation.   It implied that the sinner
by his acts had put himself in an attitude of enmity toward God.
Jesus is again the one who reconciles him to his divine Father.

It is significant that in each of these figures, by which Paul describes the salvation of the individual, the work of an intermediary
between God and man is implied, if not absolutely required.   It emphasizes the fundamental difference between Paul's own relation to
God and that of Jesus.   Jesus did not desire nor would he have tolerated any intermediary between himself and God.   Paul and the great
majority of his fellow Christians in the past, as in the present, crave
such an interpreter of God.   In supplying this practically universal need,
Paul and the early apostles made their supreme contribution to Christianity, for they proclaimed Jesus to be the great interpreter of God
to man.   Christ in man and man in Christ made personal fellowship
with God possible and easy.   Here Paul unconsciously joins hands
with the Greek mystics.   His doctrine of Christ in him and he in
Christ was not a mere figure of speech nor a dogma; it was a deep,
transforming, spiritual experience which freed him from his consciousness of sin and gave him instead a consciousness of fellowship with
God.   Sometimes Paul attributed this mystic experience to the presence of Christ, sometimes to the Spirit of Christ, and sometimes to
the Spirit of God within him.   In Romans 8[9-11] he uses these three
synonyms together: "But you are not in the flesh but in the spirit, if

od dwells in you. Any one who does not have the Spirit
es not belong to him; but if Christ is within you, though the
ead as a result of sin, the spirit is living as a result of righteous-
And if the Spirit of him who raised up Jesus from the dead
ls within you, then he who raised Christ Jesus from the dead will
so make your immortal bodies live because his Spirit is dwelling
within you." Like certain of the early writers in Acts, Paul evidently
uses the terms "Spirit of Jesus," "Holy Spirit," and "Spirit of God"
interchangeably. The ultimate basis of his mysticism is the contrast
between a life governed by the fleshly passions and a life governed by
the higher spiritual emotions which find their source and inspiration
in God. It is a life of fellowship and loyal co-operation with God
made possible as the individual is touched by the personality and inspired by the teachings of Jesus. It is this spiritual experience which
Paul describes by his favorite term "faith in Christ." It is not mere
subscription to articles of belief, but it is the effect of the Spirit of
Christ at work in the heart of the individual. It is the spirit of love
which Jesus proclaimed and exemplified, which transforms men into
his likeness and binds them together in loyal, devoted, self-sacrificing
service of the great brotherhood which he founded. When this Spirit
is at work in the heart of a man his past sins and his evil habits no
longer have power over him; he is conscious of God's forgiveness, and
is invincible against the pains and perils of life, for he is "more than a
conqueror through him who loved us." No power in heaven or earth
can separate him "from God's love in Jesus Christ our Lord." It is
thus that men are saved through faith in Christ. Well is this transforming spiritual process described in the primitive Christian prayer
preserved in the *Teaching of the Twelve Apostles:* "We thank thee,
our Father, for the life and the knowledge which thou hast made known
to us through Jesus thy Servant."

§ CLXI. PAUL'S SOCIAL TEACHINGS

Theme:
The
new
prin-
ciple
of self-
sacri-
fice
(Rom.
12$^{1, 2}$)

I beseech you, therefore, brothers, on account of the
mercies of God, dedicate your bodies as a living sacrifice,
holy and acceptable to God, for this is your reasonable
service. And do not be moulded in conformity to this world,
but be transformed through the complete renewal of your
mind, so that you may be able to make out what is the will
of God, even what is good and acceptable and perfect.

190

EACH TO DO HIS TASK

By virtue of the divine authority granted to me, I charge every one of you not to think of himself more than he ought to think; but so to think that he will attain a sane estimate of himself according to the degree of faith which God hath apportioned to each. For just as in our one body we have many members, and all the members do not have the same functions, so we, though many, are one body in Christ and we are each members one with another. We have different gifts according to the grace that is given us; if it is prophecy let us use it in proportion to our faith; if practical service, in practical service; the teacher must do the same in teaching; he who exhorts in his exhortation; he who gives must do it liberally; he who is an authority must be in earnest; he who does acts of mercy must do them cheerfully. *Each to do faithfully the task for which he is fitted (3-8)*

Let love be without hypocrisy; abhor what is evil, cleave to what is good. In your love for your brothers feel true affection for one another. In matters of honor yield to one another. Be not lacking in zeal; keep alive the spiritual glow; serve the Lord; rejoice in your hope; be steadfast in trouble, persistent in prayer; contribute to the needs of the saints, constantly practise hospitality. Rejoice with those who rejoice and weep with those who weep. Think in harmony one with another. Strive not for the high things, but associate with the humble. Do not be self-conceited. *In his social relation to his fellow Christians (9-13, 15, 16)*

Bless those who persecute you, bless and curse them not. Do not pay back evil for evil to anyone; take thought for what is seemly in the eyes of all. If possible, as far as it depends on you, live at peace with all men. Never revenge yourselves, beloved, but give place to the wrath of God; for it is written, Vengeance is mine, I will repay, saith the Lord. Rather, if your enemy is hungry feed him, if he is thirsty give him drink; for in so doing you will heap coals of fire on his head. Be not conquered by evil, but conquer evil by doing good. *The Christian's attitude toward all men (14, 17-21)*

Every individual must obey those who rule over him, for there is no authority apart from God; the existing authorities have been constituted by God. Therefore, whoever resists authority is resisting the order established by God, and they who oppose will bring judgment on themselves. For rulers are no terror to right-doers but to wrong-doers. *The Christian's duty to civil authority (13¹⁻⁷)*

191

You wish, do you not, to have no fear of authority? Then do what is right and you will be commended by it, for a ruler is the servant of God for your good. But if you do wrong, you have cause to fear, for he does not bear the sword for nothing, for he is God's servant to inflict divine punishment upon evil-doers. It is necessary, therefore, that we should obey, not only to avoid divine vengeance, but also for conscience' sake. For this same reason we pay taxes, for tax collectors are God's servants, devoting their energies to this very thing. Render to all their dues, tribute to whom tribute is due, taxes to whom taxes, respect to whom respect, and honor to whom honor is due.

To his fellow men (8-10)

Owe no man anything, except to love one another, for he who loves his fellow man has fulfilled the law. For the commands, Thou shalt not commit adultery, thou shalt not kill, thou shalt not steal, thou shalt not covet, these and all other commands are summed up in this one word, Thou shalt love thy neighbor as thyself. Love does no wrong to a neighbor; therefore love is the fulfillment of the law.

Obligations of the present crisis (12-14)

You also know what this crisis means: that it is high time to arouse ourselves from sleep, for salvation is nearer to us now than when we first believed. The night is far advanced, the day is near. Let us, therefore, lay aside the deeds of darkness and put on the armour of light. Let us behave ourselves becomingly, as in the light of day without revelry or drunkenness, without lust or sensuality, without quarrelling or jealousy. Rather let us put on the character of the Lord Jesus Christ and make no provision for gratifying the cravings of the flesh.

Toleration toward others (141-12)

Receive a man of weak faith, but not to pass judgment upon his scruples. One man has faith enough to eat all things; while the man of weak faith eats only vegetables. Let not the one who eats look down upon the one who does not eat, nor let the man who does not eat condemn him who eats all things, for God hath received him. Who are you that you should criticize the servant of another? Whether he stands or falls concerns only his own Master, and stand he will for the Master hath power to make him stand. One man rates one day above another, while another man rates all days alike. Let every man be fully convinced in his own mind. He who rates highly a certain day does it for the Lord. The eater also eats to the Lord, for he gives thanks to God; and he who refrains from eating, refrains for the Lord's sake and he also gives thanks to God. For none of us lives for himself and none of us dies for himself; for if we live, we live for the Lord, and if we die, we die for the Lord. Thus whether we live or whether we die, we are the Lord's. It was for this that Christ died and lives again in order that he might be the Lord both of the dead and of the living. And why do you criticize your brother? Or you, why do you look down upon your brother? All of us will have to stand before God's tribunal, for it is written:

As I live, saith the Lord,
Every knee shall bend before me,
And every tongue shall make confession to God.

Every one of us, therefore, will have to give an account of himself to God.

Therefore, let us no longer criticize one another. Rather make this decision, never to put any stumbling block or hindrance in your brother's way. I know and am convinced in Christ that nothing is in itself unclean, except that it is unclean to the man who considers it unclean. If your brother is being troubled because of food that you eat, then you are no longer living in accordance with the law of love. Do not by the food that you eat ruin that man for whom Christ died. Therefore let not what is good for you become a cause of reproach, for the Kingdom of God is not a matter of eating and drinking, but of righteousness, peace, and joy in the Holy Spirit. He who serves Christ in this way is acceptable to God and esteemed by men.

Consideration for another's conscientious scruples (13-18)

We who are strong ought to bear the infirmities of the weak, and not to please ourselves. Each of us should please his neighbor in order to do him good by building him up. And this is our duty, for Christ did not please himself, but, as it is written, The reproaches of those who reproached thee fell on me. For what was written of old was written for our instruction, that through our steadfastness and the encouragement of the scriptures, we might

Obligations toward the weak (15 1-6)

have hope. May the God who inspires steadfastness and encouragement grant to you that you may think in such harmony, one with another, after the example of Christ Jesus, that with one heart and voice you will glorify the God and Father of our Lord Jesus Christ.

The unity of both Jewish and Gentile believers (7-9)

Therefore, welcome one another, as Christ has welcomed you, for the glory of God. Christ, I say, became a servant to the circumcised in order to vindicate God's truthfulness in showing how sure are the promises given to our forefathers and also that the Gentiles might glorify God for his mercy. Even so it is written, For this reason I will praise thee among the Gentiles and sing to thy name.

The great aim in Paul's life-work (16b-21)

My aim has been to make the Gentiles an offering acceptable to God and consecrated by the Holy Spirit. Therefore, I have cause to be proud in Christ Jesus of the work which I have done for God, for I will not presume to speak of anything except what Christ has accomplished through me in securing the obedience of the Gentiles, by word and deed, by means of signs and miracles, and by the power of the Holy Spirit. The fact is that, from Jerusalem around as far as Illyricum, I have proclaimed fully the gospel of Christ. My ambition, however, has always been to preach the gospel only where Christ's name had not been mentioned lest I should be building on a foundation laid by another man, but, as it is written,

> That they might see to whom no report about him had come,
> That those who had not heard of him should understand.

I. **The Two Sides of Paul's Personality and Teaching.** Paul's breadth and greatness are attested by the fact that throughout the ages the most diverse types of mind have found in him their supreme inspiration. Ignatius, Luther, and Calvin are only a few of his many devoted, spiritual disciples. For eighteen centuries each generation has taken from Paul that which most appealed to its interests and needs and left the rest of his teachings almost untouched. A theological age found in Paul's writings the materials from which it reconstructed a complete metaphysical system. Now, in the present strongly social age, Paul promises still to hold his place as a moulder of Christian thought. The explanation of this marvel is Paul himself. At heart he was a mystic, but, unlike most mystics, he was intensely practical. This fact alone saved his theology from becoming mere vague mysticism or cold philosophy. His head was often in the clouds, but his feet were always planted squarely on earth. Faith meant everything to him, and yet in many of his writings he asserted in most practical terms that "faith without works is dead." This unique combination of mysticism and the strongly ethical and social interpretation of religion is undoubtedly the explanation of his continuous leadership. Men to-day may reject many of his theoretical doctrines, but they cannot escape the charm and inspiration of his practical ethics. This rare combination of the mystic and social teacher is due to Paul's personality and training. His peculiar type of mind and his unique psychological experiences made him a mystic. The apocalyptic tendencies of contemporary Pharisaism undoubtedly intensified this tendency. On the other hand, his early study of the Jewish law forever fixed in his mind the practical, social concept of religion. This precipitate remained long after he had rejected the ceremonial side of the law. This tendency was strengthened by his study of the ethical prophets and by his knowledge of the practical problems that were constantly arising in the lives of the Christians who looked to him for pastoral guidance.

II. **Paul's Reassertion of Jesus' Social Teachings.** The great force, however, which made Paul a strong social teacher was his familiarity with Jesus' social teachings. Paul was intensely interested in his own theories about Jesus; but it was in the field of practical social ethics that the great apostle stands closest to his Master. That this should be true was natural, for the heart of Jesus' teachings was ethical and social. Evidently Paul had a more extensive and intimate knowledge of these teachings than is generally recognized. His opportunities for gaining this knowledge were many, for he came into intimate and repeated contact with the disciples of Jesus while the first impression of their Master's work and teachings were still upon them. Evidently Paul also had in certain respects a more extensive acquaintance with certain of Jesus' teachings than is reflected in our gospel records. This fact is obscured, however, by Paul's peculiar method of quoting. Even his direct citations from the Old Testament are rarely reproduced with absolute accuracy. It was more natural for him to paraphrase and interpret than to quote verbatim. Ordinarily he did not believe it necessary to state that he was reproducing Jesus' teachings, for he assumed that practically all that he proclaimed was based on those teachings. Also he felt the living spirit of Jesus working in his mind and prompting his every word. It was only when he was in doubt as to whether or not he was reproducing his Master's teachings, as in I Corinthians 7, that he plainly states this fact. Hence, there are good grounds for believing that in the field of social ethics Paul is simply interpreting Jesus' teachings and that he has thus preserved certain elements not found in our four gospels. This conclusion is strongly confirmed by a careful examination of Romans 12 and 13, where in a majority of the cases the underlying principle can be directly traced to the lips of Jesus.

III. **Paul's Restatement of Jesus' Social Ideal.** Paul, like Jesus, began not with organized society but with the individual, and sought to develop socially minded citizens as the foundation for an ideal social order. Like his Master, he dealt primarily not with external acts, but with inner motives. He recognized that the individual must first be socially redeemed, transformed, and consecrated to the service of God and society. His thoughts and character must be moulded, not only by circumstances and social conventions, but above all by loyalty to the will of God and to the interests of the Christian community. After he has made this complete self-sacrifice to the service of God and his Kingdom, it is easy for each man to find his own individual task in the church and in society and to perform it efficiently. In Paul's mind the perfect social order is the "one body in Christ," of which all his faithful followers are members. It is unimportant that individual talents differ; the one essential is that each use his own for the largest profit of the community. Here, as in I Corinthians and Ephesians, he built on the foundations laid by Jesus in his parables regarding the Kingdom of God; but the details are determined by Paul's own personal experience. The Christian communities which he had founded had given him a vision of the perfect community, bound together by the spirit and principles of Christ. In his vision he saw this ideal community growing and extending, even as the Christian church was then rapidly extending, until it included all mankind. Paul, in his loyal service to the local communities, which were the prototype of the all-embracing community of the saints to be established in the future, had himself attained personal salvation, liberty, and fulness of life. Therefore he pointed out to his fellow Christians the same sure and satisfying way of salvation and life. He declared by implication that, instead of losing their life, they also could find it through loyalty to the ideal of the perfect community and in working for its establishment. In its glories each individual would attain the complete expression of his own highest aspirations; in its fellowship the full satisfaction of his social craving; in its service the development of his noblest gifts. This community of the socially redeemed, which Paul called the "Body of Christ," is not a mere mystical abstraction but a perfectly practical social ideal. In Paul's day each local Christian community gave to the individual Christian the field and the definite objective needed to develop his loyalty to the ideal community. Here, as always, Paul makes a complete and natural synthesis of the ideal and the practical. In so doing he has presented a working social programme as applicable to the needs of society to-day and in the future as it was in the first Christian century.

IV. **The Christian's Responsibility as a Member of Society.** Jesus simply presented social principles; but Paul in his fervent zeal to develop efficient loyalty to the ideal community (which occupied the central place in his vision of the future) lays down many definite laws and commands. He also sets forth his specific social teachings in systematic order and in a most condensed yet forceful form. In Romans 12^{9-16} he defines the Christian's responsibilities to the members of the Christian community. Verse [14] clearly belongs with the next section ($^{17-21}$), which describes the Christian's obligations to those outside the community. In 13^{1-7} he discusses the Christian's obligations to civil authorities. In verses $^{8-10}$ he stresses the underlying and all-comprehending principle of love. Love is indeed the golden strand that runs through all of Paul's social teachings. He begins with the command, "Let love be without hypocrisy," and ends with the quotation, "Love is the fulfillment of the law." His social teachings as a whole are simply a practical, detailed application of the Golden Rule to the problems of the individual in his relation to society. Jesus' beatitude, "Happy are the peacemakers," becomes on the lips of Paul a definite command: "Think in harmony one with another." "Happy are the humble" and "Happy are the poor in spirit" are also transformed into the definite commands: "Strive not for the high things but associate with the humble" and "Do not be self-conceited." The Master's command, "Love your enemies," on the lips of Paul becomes, "Bless those who persecute you, bless and curse them not." Paul also concludes his recapitulation of the Christian's responsibilities with the powerful, positive command: "Be not conquered by evil, but conquer evil by doing good," which is a splendid summary of the principles which underlie both Jesus' social teachings and method.

Throughout Paul's discussion of the Christian's obligations to organized society we recognize the influence of Jesus' broad principle: "Render to Cæsar the things that are Cæsar's and to God the things that are God's." In the concluding sentence Paul quotes almost verbatim the words of his Master, expanding them freely, however: "Render to all their dues, tribute to whom tribute is due, taxes to whom taxes, respect to whom respect and honor to whom honor is due." In his interpretation of Jesus' principle Paul shows the influence of his Roman citizenship, of his cosmopolitan training, and of his practical statesmanship. His assertion of the divine authority of rulers is in striking contrast with Jesus' rather contemptuous estimate of the men who play the tyrant over their subjects. The context implies that Paul had in mind simply those rulers who proved by their acts that they were "servants of God." His aim is evidently to deliver the Christians from conflict with the pagan authorities, but the working principles which he lays down are intensely practical through all ages. Nowhere can one find in such condensed form a more exact statement of a theory of government, of its obligations to the individual citizen, and of the duties of a citizen to the state.

V. **The Christian's Duties of Toleration and Consideration for Others.** It has been asserted that Paul's "outlook is almost devoid of social elements" and that the hope of the speedy second coming of Jesus destroyed his interest in society. Carried to its logical conclusion, this result would seem to a superficial reader inevitable; but exactly the opposite effect is discernible. Instead of encouraging his converts to sit with idle hands awaiting the great consummation, which he, as an heir to the Jewish apocalyptic hopes, regarded as imminent, Paul encouraged them to discharge all their social obligations with the greatest care and consideration. His belief that the "night is far advanced and that the day is near" only intensified his social consciousness. The explanation is that he regarded the Christian church already established and rapidly expanding as the foundation of the new world-wide community that was to be perfected at the second coming of Jesus.

Paul's breadth is also revealed in the principles which he laid down regarding toleration toward others. The man of weak faith, whom he had in mind, was the one limited by the conventional conceptions of religion. It was the type of man who regarded the observation of certain ritualistic forms and of days of feasting or fasting as absolutely essential. Evidently Paul himself did not share these beliefs; but he contended as earnestly for the liberty of personal judgment for the man with whom he did not agree as he did for his own. Each man, as he convincingly argues, is simply responsible to God. Here again it seems probable that Paul is standing squarely on principles proclaimed by Jesus and implied, though not recorded, in our gospels. It was this principle which determined the attitude of Jesus, as well as Paul, toward the ceremonial institutions of Judaism. Underlying Paul's command not to criticise nor look down upon a brother Christian one sees clearly Jesus' teaching: "Judge not that you be not judged." Also his command not to put a stumbling-block or hinderance in a brother's way is but Paul's free paraphrase of Jesus' words: "Woe to you who cause any of these little ones to stumble." With rare effectiveness and felicity Paul lays down the comprehensive Christian principle that the larger responsibility to show toleration and consideration to the brother of more limited vision rests upon the man of broader faith and outlook. He is the one who should be supremely governed by the law of love. The context also implies that the significant saying:

> The Kingdom of God is not a matter of eating and drinking,
> But of righteousness, peace, and joy,

came directly from the lips of Jesus.

VI. **The Christian's Obligation to Men of All Races.** In conclusion Paul suggests the Christian's larger missionary obligations to the Gentile world. He presents this responsibility, not in the form of a direct command, but first by pointing out the fact that Jesus' work was done that Gentiles as well as Jews "might glorify God for his mercy." He then adds that his own primary aim as an apostle has been to bring the Gentiles into harmony with God's purpose. He declares that his great ambition has been to preach the Gospel where before Christ's name had not been mentioned. Paul wisely leaves to each individual Christian the application of the principle so nobly illustrated by his own example and by that of his Master.

Thus, Paul's teachings regarding the social responsibilities of each Christian may be briefly summarized under six heads: (1) To give himself completely to the service of his divine Master. (2) To use each and all of his talents in behalf of "the body of Christ." (3) To show to his fellow citizens in this ideal commonwealth justice, love, consideration, and hospitality. (4) To regard all men of every shade of faith in the spirit of love and forgiveness and to serve them as opportunity offers. (5) To pay to the state its dues and to respect and obey its rulers. (6) To extend to the Gentiles everywhere the hand of Christian fellowship, to proclaim to them the Gospel of the Master, and by these means to attract them to the ranks of those who are loyally working for that perfect community which is ultimately to include all mankind. Thus, nobly and practically, in the concrete terms of love and loyalty and service, Paul interpreted Jesus' great social command to "seek first the Kingdom of God."

§ CLXII. PAUL'S LAST JOURNEY TO JERUSALEM

Paul's voyage to Ptolemais (Acts 21 1-7) When we had torn ourselves away from the presbyters of Ephesus and had set sail, we ran in a straight course to Cos; on the next day to Rhodes, and from there to Patera. Finding a ship bound for Phœnicia, we embarked and set sail. After sighting Cyprus and leaving it on our left, we sailed for Syria and landed at Tyre, for there the ship was to unload her cargo. After we had searched out the disciples, we remained there seven days. Certain of these disciples under the inspiration of the Spirit kept telling Paul not to set foot in Jerusalem; but when our time was up, we set out and went our way, escorted until we were out of the city by all of them, including women and children. Then kneeling on the beach we prayed and said good-bye to one another. While we went on board the ship, they returned home. Sailing from Tyre to Ptolemais, we completed our voyage. Then after we had saluted the brothers, we spent one day with them.

His experience at Cæsarea (8-14) Setting out the next morning, we came to Cæsarea and entered the house of Philip, the evangelist, who was one of the seven, and stayed with him. Now he had four unmarried daughters who prophesied. While we remained there many days a certain prophet by the name of Agabus came down from Judea. Coming to us, he took Paul's girdle and bound his own feet and hands, saying, Thus saith the Holy Spirit, ' So shall the Jews bind the owner of this girdle and hand him over to the Gentiles.' When we heard these words, we and those who dwelt at Cæsarea besought Paul not to go up to Jerusalem; but Paul replied, What do you mean by weeping and breaking my heart? For I am ready not only to be bound but to die in Jerusalem for the sake of the Lord Jesus. When he would not be persuaded, we ceased speaking, saying, May the Lord's will be done.

After some days, we packed up our baggage and set out for Jerusalem. And certain of the disciples from Cæsarea accompanied us, conducting us to the house of a certain Mnason, a native of Cyprus, one of the early disciples with whom we were to lodge. When we arrived at Jerusalem the brothers received us gladly. *His arrival at Jerusalem (15-17)*

On the next day Paul went with us to James. All the presbyters were present and, after saluting them, Paul told in detail all that God had done through his ministry among the Gentiles; and when they heard it they glorified God. *Reception at Jerusalem (17-20a)*

They also said to him, Brother, you see how many tens of thousands there are among the Jews who believe and that all of them zealously uphold the law. Now they have been told that you teach all Jews who live among the Gentiles to break away from Moses and that you tell them not to circumcise their children and not to follow the old customs. What now is to be done? They are sure to hear that you have arrived, therefore do what we say. We have four men here who have taken a vow upon themselves. Associate with them, purify yourself with them, and pay their expenses that they may shave their heads and all will know that there is no foundation for the stories about you but that you are orthodox and that you yourself keep the law. As for the Gentile believers, we have communicated to them our decision that they must abstain from those things which have been offered to idols, from blood, from the flesh of animals which have been strangled and from sexual vice. Then Paul associated himself with the men the next day, was purified along with them, and went into the temple, announcing when the days of purification would be completed, that is, when sacrifice could be offered for each of them. *The plan to conciliate the Jews (20b-26)*

Paul's
seizure
by the
mob
(27-30)

But when the seven days were almost over, certain Jews from the province of Asia, seeing Paul in the temple, stirred up all the crowd and laid hands on him, shouting, Men of Israel, help! This is the man who teaches all men everywhere against the Jewish people and the law and this place. And besides he has even brought Greeks into the temple and desecrated this holy place. (For they had previously seen Trophimus, the Ephesian, with him in the city whom they supposed Paul had taken into the temple.) The whole city was aroused and the people rushed together and seized Paul and dragged him outside the temple, and immediately the gates were closed.

His
deliv-
erance
by the
Roman
com-
mander
(31-40,
22²¹)

But while the people were seeking to kill Paul, word came to the commander of the garrison that all Jerusalem was in confusion. Immediately taking some soldiers and officers, he rushed down to them. But when they saw the commander and the soldiers they ceased beating Paul. Then the commander drew near and arrested him and ordered him to be bound with two chains. And he inquired, Who is he and what has he done? Some of the crowd shouted one thing, some another; but when he could not learn the exact truth on account of the uproar, he ordered Paul to be led into the barracks. But when Paul was at the steps, he had to be carried by the soldiers on account of the violence of the crowd, for the whole multitude of the people followed shouting, Away with him! Just as Paul was about to be led into the barracks, he said to the commander, May I say something to you? The commander replied, Do you know Greek? Then you are not the Egyptian who in former days stirred up the four thousand Assassins and led them out into the desert? Paul replied, I am a Jew, a native of Tarsus of Cilicia, a citizen of no insignificant city. I beg you, permit me to speak to the people. And as the commander gave permission, Paul stood on the steps and motioned with his hands to the people; and when there was perfect silence he addressed them in Hebrew, telling them of his vision on the way to Damascus and how the Lord said to him, Go, for I send you afar to the Gentiles.

Until he had said this the people had listened to Paul,

PAUL'S SCOURGING

but now they raised a great outcry saying, Away with such
a fellow from the earth, for he is not fit to live! They
shouted and threw their clothes into the air and flung dust
about until the commander ordered Paul to be led into the
barracks and to be examined under the lash in order to
ascertain the reason why the people had shouted at him.
But when they had tied him up with straps, Paul said to
the officer who was standing by, Are you permitted to
scourge a Roman citizen, and that without trial? When
the officer heard this he went to report the matter to the
commander, saying, What is this you are about to do? For
this man is a Roman citizen. Then the commander went to
him and said, Tell me, are you a Roman citizen? And he
answered, Yes. Then the commander replied, I paid a
large sum for this citizenship. But I was born a Roman
citizen, said Paul. Then the men who were about to examine him immediately left him. The commander also
was alarmed when he learned that Paul was a Roman
citizen and that he had bound him.

Scourg-
ing at
the in-
stiga-
tion
of the
mob
(22²²⁻
²⁹)

The next day the commander, wishing to know exactly
what charge was brought against Paul by the Jews, unbound
him and ordered the high priests and all the Sanhedrin to
assemble. Then bringing Paul down, he made him stand
before them. Whereupon, Paul looking straight at the
Sanhedrin, said, Brothers, I have lived before God with a
perfectly good conscience up to this day. Then the high
priest Ananias ordered those who were standing near Paul
to strike him on the mouth. Paul said to him, You white-
washed wall, God will strike you! Do you sit there to judge
me according to the law while you yourself break the law
by ordering me to be struck? But those who were standing by said, Would you rail at God's high priest? Paul
said, Brothers, I did not know that he was a high priest
(for it is written, ' Thou shalt not speak evil of a ruler of
thy people ').

Paul's
defense
before
the
San-
hedrin
(22³⁰⁻
23⁵)

Then Paul, knowing that part of the Sanhedrin consisted of Sadducees and the other part of Pharisees, shouted
to them, Brothers, I am a Pharisee, the son of Pharisees.
For the hope of the resurrection of the dead I am on trial!
When he said this, there was a quarrel between the Phari-

The dispute between the Sadducees and the Pharisees (6-10)

sees and the Sadducees, and the assembly was divided. For while the Sadducees say that there is no resurrection nor angel nor spirit, the Pharisees acknowledge all these things; hence there was a great uproar. And some of the scribes, who belonged to the party of the Pharisees, arose and contended, We find no harm in this man. What if some spirit or angel has spoken to him? When the quarrel became so violent that the commander feared that Paul would be torn in pieces by them, he ordered the troops to go down and take him from their midst by force and bring him into the barracks.

Paul's vision (11)

On the following night the Lord stood by Paul and said, Be of good courage, for as you have borne witness to me at Jerusalem so you must bear witness also at Rome.

The plot to kill him (12-15)

Now when daylight came, the Jews formed a conspiracy and solemnly swore not to eat or drink until they had killed Paul. Those who bound themselves by this oath were more than forty in all. Going to the high priests and elders they said, We have bound ourselves by a solemn oath not to taste anything until we have killed Paul. Now you, together with the Sanhedrin, must make it appear to the commander that you wish him to bring Paul down to you because you wish to investigate more minutely the charges brought against him. We will be ready to kill him before he comes near this place.

The disclosure of the plot (16-21a)

But Paul's nephew heard of the treacherous ambush and gained admission to the barracks and informed Paul. Then Paul called one of the officers and said, Take this young man to the commander for he has some information to give him. Accordingly the officer took and brought him to the commander and said, Paul the prisoner called me and asked me if I would bring this young man to you for he has something to say to you. Then the commander took him aside by the hand and inquired of him in private, What is the information you have to give me? He said, The Jews have agreed to ask you to bring Paul to-morrow down to the Sanhedrin for the avowed purpose of examining his case in detail. Now do not be persuaded by them, for more than forty of them are lying in wait for him.

Then the commander sent away the young man, enjoining him to 'tell no one that you informed me of these things.' He then summoned two of the officers and said, Make ready two hundred infantry, seventy horsemen, and two hundred spearmen by nine o'clock to-night to march as far as Cæsarea. Provide horses also to mount Paul so as to bring him safely to Felix the governor. He also wrote a letter to Felix.

Paul sent to Cæsarea (22-25a)

The soldiers, therefore, according to their instructions, took Paul and brought him by night to Antipatris. On the next day the infantry returned to the barracks, leaving the cavalry to go on with him. When they reached Cæsarea, they delivered the letter to the governor and also brought Paul to him. When he had read the letter, Felix asked from what province he was, and learning that it was Cilicia he said, I will hear all about your case whenever your accusers arrive. And he gave orders that Paul be kept in the pretorium of Herod.

Arrival at Cæsarea (31-35)

I. The Record of Paul's Journey to Jerusalem and Rome.

When Paul set out on his final journey to Jerusalem, the intermittent stream of narrative in Acts suddenly broadens, giving us a detailed picture of Paul's public activity. Fully one-fourth of the book of Acts is devoted to these journeys which finally led him to Rome. Only regarding Paul's two years' imprisonment at Cæsarea the narrative suddenly becomes silent. Two reasons probably explain this striking literary phenomenon. With the exception of the two years at Cæsarea, Luke was evidently drawing from his own personal experience and observation. Throughout most of this narrative he speaks in the first person plural. As has already been noted, the evidence is practically conclusive that Luke himself is the author of this journal of travel and that, even where he does not use the first person, he is in close personal touch with the facts. The second reason is because of the nature of the material here presented. Two of Luke's most important contentions are: (1) that practically all the opposition to Christianity came from the Jews, and (2) that the early attitude of the Roman officials toward Christianity was not only friendly but protective. It is probably under the influence of this motive that Luke has reproduced and expanded the speeches of Paul and the Roman officials and introduced even the supposed text of the letter sent by the Roman governor of Jerusalem to Felix, the procurator of

Judea. He also aimed to say as little as possible about the heart-burns and bitternesses of the past. Luke's concentration on these definite aims alone explains his silence regarding the real object of Paul's visit to Jerusalem and the realization of the apostle's great ambition.

II. **Paul's Reasons for Revisiting Jerusalem.** The narrative of Acts indicates clearly that Paul went up to Jerusalem in direct opposition to the earnest warnings of his friends. They knew well the bitterness of the opposition which he would meet in that centre of Judaism. The account of the warning of Agabus, who had just come from Judea and was therefore in close touch with conditions there, indicates that the old type of Hebrew prophet still survived in the Christian church. For the "Thus saith Jehovah" is substituted the equally impressive phrase "Thus saith the Holy Spirit." The over-mastering conviction that incites him to speak is evidently akin in every respect to that which in earlier days drew Amos from his flock and impelled him to speak before the assembled multitudes at the great sanctuary in Bethel. The methods whereby Agabus impressed his message upon Paul also recall the dramatic object-lessons which Ezekiel used to convince his irresolute countrymen. But neither the warnings of the Christian prophets nor Paul's own knowledge of the perils which confronted him at Jerusalem deterred him. What were the reasons which thus impelled him onward? The first was evidently his feeling that he must fulfil the parting injunction of the pillar apostles in their last interview at Jerusalem, when they urged him to remember the poor at Jerusalem. He also felt a deep obligation to discharge the trust placed in his hands by the Gentile churches and to deliver at Jerusalem in person the funds intrusted to his care. More important still, Paul desired in the presence of the mother church to vindicate his work among the Gentiles. He plainly declares this purpose in the conclusion of his letter to the Roman Christians: "Pray that I may be delivered from the unbelievers in Judea and also that my mission to Jerusalem may prove acceptable to the saints." Above all, Paul ardently hoped by this visit to establish the unity of the "Body of Christ." This achievement he hoped to make the crown of his life-work. All the influences of his Jewish inheritance led him to crave the approval and fellowship of his Jewish Christian brothers. If he could win these, all the bitterness of the Judaistic controversies would be but easily forgotten memories, and the Christian church would be in a position to face the Græco-Roman world with unbroken front. It was, therefore, as the first great apostle of Christian unity that Paul undertook this perilous adventure.

III. **Paul's Reception at Jerusalem.** The narrative of Acts indicates that Paul's reception by the leaders of the Jerusalem church was on the whole friendly, but it is ominously silent regarding the way in which they received the contributions of the Gentile churches. They were still chiefly concerned about Paul's attitude toward the Jewish law. It is evident that they were unable to rise above their intense Jewish environment. It is probable that already the storm of Jewish persecution was rising, which resulted a few years later in the death of James, the brother of Jesus, and in the scattering of the Jerusalem church. Even the optimistic Luke gives the impression that within the Christian brotherhood Paul met with bitter disappointment. While the leaders shared with him the joy inspired by his marvellous achievements in Gentile lands, they were unable to shake off their immediate fears. Their chief concern was still about his attitude toward the Jewish law. Was his action, as reported, in avowing publicly his personal loyalty to the Jewish law inconsistent with his earlier teachings and practices? It was certainly consistent with his avowed principle "of becoming like the Jews to win over the Jews and as one of themselves to those under the law." Moreover, his chief contention had been that the Jewish law was not binding on any Christians except as they freely chose to keep it in order not to offend the "weak." Against the action of the Jewish Christians, who continued for conscientious reasons to observe the laws of their fathers, he was the last to raise a voice of protest. The impression that he was opposed to the Mosaic law itself was also wrong. In the circumstances he probably felt amply justified, in order to remove false impressions, in associating with four poor men who had taken a vow and in defraying the expense of the sacrifices demanded by the Jewish ritual.

IV. **The Jewish Attack.** Paul's action probably satisfied the Jewish Christians, but in the end it proved disastrous. His presence in the temple aroused the smouldering antagonism of certain of the visiting Jews from the province of Asia, who had probably come into hostile contact with Paul during his long and strenuous ministry at Ephesus. The memory that Paul had earlier brought Titus, a Greek Christian, to Jerusalem, may still have lingered in the popular mind. If so, it tended to give credence to the charge of the Ephesian Jews that Paul had taken another Gentile Christian, Trophimus of Ephesus (who had journeyed to Jerusalem with Paul) into the sacred temple precincts. According to the Jewish law, confirmed by the tablets set up by Herod about the enclosure which shut in the inner courts of the temple, this was a capital offense. The charge was undoubtedly false, but it was sufficient to inflame the mind of the fanatical mob. The Romans were ordinarily inclined to support the Jewish law, but the Jews in their fury evidently intended to take justice in their own hands and to slay Paul on the charge of impiety. Uprisings of this character, even in the temple courts at this period, were evidently common, and the Roman guards, stationed at the tower of Antonia on the northwestern side of the temple area, were ever on the alert to put down an uprising. Their timely interference alone saved Paul's life. As ever in face of danger, he was cool and alert. It was characteristic of Paul to face the mob and to improve the dramatic opportunity thus offered to preach the faith for which he was ready to die. The variations in the account of his conversions indicate that the details of the speech here attributed to him are not the result of the verbatim report, for which the occasion offered no opportunity, but of Luke's tendency to present vividly and concretely the spirit and thought of the characters who figure in his narrative. Even in the hands of the Roman soldiers, Paul again proved himself master of the situation. Emperors like Augustus and Tiberius, keenly interested in the welfare of the provinces, had taught the Roman provincial officials to beware lest they misuse their power. Paul's assertions that he was a Roman citizen not only saved him from scourging but also insured him a fair hearing. Before the Roman official could take action, Paul, because of the nature of the charge brought against him, must be tried and condemned by the supreme Jewish court, the Sanhedrin. According to Luke's account, Paul, knowing well the constitution of this unique assembly, precipitated a dispute among its members which again brought in the Roman troops. The futility of the charge brought against Paul was evidently recognized by his bitterest foes. Baffled in their attempt to put an end to him at the hands of the mob, they formed a conspiracy to kill him secretly. Fortunately for Paul, he had Jewish kinsmen at Jerusalem, who revealed this plot to him. His ability and Roman citizenship had evidently made a deep impression upon the Roman commander, so that almost as a royal prisoner Paul was sent to Felix, the governor of Judea, whose official residence was at Cæsarea.

V. **The Results of Paul's Visit to Jerusalem.** Unfortunately, the details in Luke's account of Paul's visit to Jerusalem have obscured the main issue. Was his mission successful? Did the Jerusalem church accept the contributions of the Gentile Christians and in so doing cement the bond between the two branches of the Christian church? Whatever be the answer, the significant fact is established that Paul, who most nobly interpreted the spirit of Jesus, was such an ardent advocate of Christian unity that he was quite ready, if necessary, to die for this cause. The facts themselves are fugitive. Luke's narrative leaves us to infer that Paul's mission to Jerusalem was successful. Possibly there were details which Luke deemed best to omit. Early Christian tradition asserts that Luke himself was the one whom Paul describes in II Corinthians 8^{18-21} as "the brother who is praised by all the churches because of his services for the Gospel, and not only so, but who has been appointed by the churches to travel with us in charge of this contribution which we are administering for the glory of the Lord. His appointment was also in accord with our desire, for we want to take precaution lest any one should find fault with us regarding the administration of this charity, for we aim to do those things which are honorable, not only in the sight of God, but also in the sight of men." That Luke accompanied Paul to Jerusalem is clear. He appears also to have returned to Syria after the apostle's long imprisonment, for he was present to accompany him on his journey to Rome. It is strange that Luke says nothing in Acts concerning the realization of Paul's ardent hope that "his mission to Jerusalem might prove acceptable to the saints." Luke's account leaves us to infer that it was acceptable and that Paul's public proof of his personal regard for the Jewish law was one of the conditions under which they accepted it. If so, further light is thrown upon his reasons for submitting to what must to many of his friends have been regarded as a compromise. Possibly at the suggestion of the Jerusalem apostles part of the contributions from the Gentile churches was used to defray the expenses of the four Jewish Christians, who were thus enabled to fulfil their vows. Certainly Paul's later letters, and especially Philippians and Ephesians, resound with thanksgiving because the unity of the church of Christ had been established and the barriers, which had kept Gentile and Jew apart, had been removed. To the Gentiles of Asia Minor he writes (Eph. 2^{19-21}): "You are no longer strangers and foreigners, you share the membership of the saints, you belong to God's own household, you are a building which rests on the apostles and prophets as its foundation, with Jesus Christ as the corner-stone. In him the whole structure is welded together and rises into a sacred temple in the Lord."

§ CLXIII. THE AMBASSADOR IN BONDS

Paul's
im-
peach-
ment
(Acts
24¹⁻⁹)

Five days after Paul arrived at Cæsarea the high priest, Ananias, came down with some elders and an orator called Tertullus. They laid the case against Paul before the governor. After Paul had been summoned, Tertullus began to accuse him, saying, Inasmuch as it is owing to you, most excellent Felix, that we enjoy perfect peace and as it is through your wise provision that evils are corrected in this nation in every instance and in every place, we accept these with profound gratitude. But in order that I may not detain you too long, I beg you in your forbearance to hear a brief statement from us. For we have found this man Paul a pest and a disturber of the peace among all the Jews throughout the world and a ringleader of the Nazarene sect. He even tried to desecrate the temple, but we arrested him. By examining him yourself you will be able to find out about all these charges which we allege against him. The Jews also joined in the attack, declaring that these things were so.

Paul's
prot-
esta-
tion of
inno-
cence
(10-21)

Then at a signal from the governor, Paul made his reply: Knowing that you have administered justice in this nation for many years, I willingly make my defense, because, as you are able to ascertain, it is not more than twelve days since I went up to worship at Jerusalem. They neither found me arguing with any one in the temple nor stirring up a crowd either in the synagogues or in the city. They cannot prove the charges which they are now bringing against me. But this I confess to you that in the way, which they call a sect, I worship the God of our fathers, and I believe all that is written in the law and the prophets and I hold the same hope in God as they themselves entertain, that there is to be a resurrection of the just and the unjust. Therefore, I too am under obligation at all times to have a clear conscience before God and man. After several years I came up to bring alms and sacrifices for my nation. They found me while doing this in the temple, ceremonially pure and mixed up in no mob nor riot; but there were certain Jews from Asia who ought to be here before you to present whatever charge they may have against me. Or let those men there tell what fault they found in me when I stood before the Sanhedrin, unless it be that single sentence which I uttered when I shouted as I stood among them, 'It is for the resurrection of the dead that I am being tried to-day before you.'

But Felix, being accurately informed regarding the way, adjourned their case, saying to them, When Lysias the commander comes down, I will decide your case. He also gave orders to the officer to hold him in custody and to allow him some liberty and not to prevent his own friends from ministering to him. *Felix's decision regarding Paul (22, 23)*

Some days later, Felix came with Drusilla his wife, who was a Jewess, and sent for Paul and heard him speak regarding faith in Christ Jesus. But when he argued about justice, self-control, and future judgment, Felix became alarmed and replied, You may go for the present and when I find a convenient time I will send for you, though he hoped at the same time that Paul would give him money. For this reason he sent for him frequently and conversed with him. But when two full years had passed, Felix was succeeded by Porcius Festus. And as Felix wished to ingratiate himself with the Jews, he left Paul in custody. *Felix's delay of Paul's case (24-27)*

Now three days after Festus entered the province he went up from Cæsarea to Jerusalem. Then the high priests and the leading Jews brought a charge against Paul and begged Festus as a favor to send and have him brought to Jerusalem, for they were planning an ambush to kill him on the way. But Festus replied that Paul was in custody in Cæsarea and that he himself was about to go there in a short time. Therefore, he said, let those of you who are able go down with me and charge the man with whatever crime he has committed. After staying eight or ten days in Jerusalem he went down to Cæsarea. *The new plot of the Jews (25¹⁻⁶ᵃ)*

The next day Festus took his seat on the tribunal and ordered Paul to be brought in. When he arrived, the Jews who had come down from Jerusalem stood around him and brought many and grave charges against him which they were unable to prove. Paul said in reply, I have committed no offense against the Jewish law or the temple or Cæsar. *Paul's defense (6b-8)*

Paul's
appeal
to the
em-
peror
(9-12)

But Festus, wishing to win favor with the Jews, asked Paul, Are you willing to go up to Jerusalem and be tried there before me regarding these charges? Paul said, I am standing before Cæsar's tribunal, where I ought to be tried. I have done no wrong to the Jews, as you also know perfectly well. If, however, I have done wrong and have done anything worthy of death I do not object to dying. But if these men have brought no real charges against me, then no one has a right to favor them by giving me up to them. I appeal to Cæsar! Then after conferring with the council, Festus answered, You have appealed to Cæsar, to Cæsar you shall go.

Paul
before
Agrip-
pa
(13, 14,
23)

After some days had passed, King Agrippa and Bernice came down to Cæsarea to pay their respects to Festus. And since they were spending many days there, Festus laid Paul's case before the king. So on the next day Agrippa and Bernice came with much pomp and entered the audience hall, accompanied by the military commanders and by the chief men of the city. Then at the command of Festus Paul was brought in.

Paul's
defense
before
Agrip-
pa
(26¹⁻⁴,
22, 23)

Thereupon, Agrippa said to Paul, You have permission to speak in your own behalf. At this, Paul, stretching out his hand, began his defense: I consider myself fortunate, King Agrippa, in being able this day to defend myself before you against all the accusations with which I am charged by the Jews, for you are exceedingly well informed regarding all the Jewish customs and questions. Therefore, I beg of you hear me patiently. All the Jews know the kind of life I lived from my youth upwards among my nation and in Jerusalem. . . . Now to this day I have had the help of God and have stood firm, testifying to small and great, never saying a single word beyond what the prophets and Moses said would take place, namely, that the Christ was to suffer and be the first to rise from the dead and proclaim a message of light to the Jewish people and to the Gentiles.

The
replies
of
Festus
and
Agrip-
pa
(24-29)

When Paul thus made his defense, Festus said in a loud voice, Paul, you are stark mad! Your great learning is driving you insane! But Paul said, I am not mad, most noble Festus, but I am speaking words of truth and soberness. For the king to whom I can speak freely, knows about these things. Indeed, I cannot but believe that no detail has escaped his notice, for this thing was not done in a corner. King Agrippa, do you not believe the prophets? I know that you do. But Agrippa said to Paul, In a short time you will believe that you have made a Christian of me! Paul replied, Long or short, I pray to God that not only you but also all my hearers this day may be such as I am, excepting these chains.

Then the king arose with the governor and Bernice and those who had been sitting with them and withdrew to discuss the matter with one another. And they said, This man has done nothing deserving of death or imprisonment. Agrippa also said to Festus, This man might have been released if he had not appealed to Cæsar. *Declaration of Paul's innocence (30-32)*

Now when it was decided that we were to sail for Italy, they handed over Paul and certain other prisoners to an officer of the imperial regiment named Julius. Then going on board of a ship of Adramyttium, which was bound to the seaports of the province of Asia, we set sail, having with us Aristarchus, a Macedonian from Thessalonica. On the next day we put in at Sidon, where Julius treated Paul very kindly and allowed him to visit his friends and to avail himself of their generous care. Putting to sea from there, we sailed under the lee of Cyprus, because the wind was against us. Then, after sailing the whole length of the sea which lies off Cilicia and Pamphylia, we came to Myra in Lycia. There the officer found an Alexandrian ship bound for Italy and put us on board of her. For a number of days we made slow progress and came with great difficulty off Cnidus. Then, as the wind did not allow us to go on, we sailed under the lee of Crete, opposite Cape Salome, and coasting along with difficulty we reached a place called Fair Havens, near the city of Lasea. *Incidents of the voyage (27 1-8)*

Inasmuch as our voyage had taken considerable time and the sailing had become dangerous, and the autumn fast was already over, Paul warned them saying, Men, I perceive that this voyage will be attended with danger and much loss not only to the cargo and the ship but to our own lives. The officer, however, let himself be persuaded by the captain and the owner of the ship rather than by the *Paul's advice to the sailors (9-12)* things which Paul said. And as the harbor was inconvenient for wintering in, the majority advised putting to sea to try to reach Phœnix, a Cretan harbor facing southwest and northwest, in order to winter there.

The
storm
(13-20)
When a light southerly breeze sprung up, they thought that they had secured their object. After weighing anchor they ran close along the coast of Crete; but it was not long before a tempestuous wind called Euroklydon rushed down. The ship was caught and was not able to face the wind; so we gave up and let it drive. Then we ran along the lee of a little island called Cauda, where we managed with great difficulty to secure the ship's boat. After hoisting it on board, they used ropes to undergird the ship. Fearing lest they should be stranded on the Syrtis quicksands, they lowered the sail and lay to. But as we were being terribly battered by the storm, they began to lighten the ship the next day, and on the third day they threw the ship's tackle overboard with their own hands. Then for many days, neither sun nor stars were seen and a heavy gale still raged so that at last all hope of our being saved was taken away.

Paul's
words
of en-
cour-
age-
ment
(21-26)
Now when they had gone a long time without food, Paul stood forth in their midst and said, Men, you should have listened to me and not have set sail from Crete and thus spared yourself this hardship and loss. But now I bid you have courage, for there will be no loss of life, only of the ship, for last night an angel of the God to whom I belong and whom I serve, stood beside me and said, ' Fear not, Paul, for you must stand before Cæsar. Behold also, God hath granted you the lives of all those who are sailing with you.' Therefore, have courage, men ! For I believe God and that it will be just as I have been told. But we are to be stranded on a certain island.

Ap-
proach
to land
(27-32)
It was now the fourteenth night and we were drifting through the Sea of Adria, when the sailors in the middle of the night suspected that land was near. And when they cast the lead, they found twenty fathoms of water and a little further, when they cast the lead, they found fifteen. Then, fearing lest we should be stranded on the rocks, they threw out four anchors from the stern and longed for

the day. The sailors were trying to escape from the ship and had even lowered the boat in the sea, pretending that they were going to lay out anchors from the bow, when Paul said to the officers and the soldiers, Unless these men stay in the ship you cannot be saved. Then the soldiers cut away the ropes of the boat and let her fall off.

Just before daybreak, Paul begged them all to take some food, saying, To-day is the fourteenth day that you have been anxiously watching and fasting without taking food. Therefore I beg of you take some food, for this will keep you alive; indeed, not one hair of your heads will perish. After he had said these words, he took a loaf and, after giving thanks to God, he broke and began to eat it in the presence of them all. Then they were all encouraged and they themselves took food. There were about seventy-six souls of us on board. And when they had eaten enough, they lightened the ship by throwing the wheat into the sea. Paul's counsel (33-36)

When it was day, they could not recognize what land it was; but they noticed a certain inlet with a sandy beach on which they planned if possible to run the ship ashore. So cutting away the anchors, they left them in the sea. At the same time unloosing the ropes which tied the rudders and hoisting the foresail to the wind, they made for the beach. Coming to a place where two seas met, they stranded the ship. The prow, sticking fast, remained immovable, but the stern began to go to pieces on account of the beating of the waves. Then the soldiers counselled that they should kill the prisoners lest some one of them might swim ashore and escape. But the officer, desiring to save Paul, prevented them from carrying out their plan and commanded that those who were able to swim should jump overboard first and get to land and that the rest should follow, some on planks and the others on pieces of wreckage. Thus, they all got safely to land. The shipwreck (39-44)

Now, after we had escaped, we found that the island was called Malta. The rude natives showed us more than ordinary kindness, for they lighted a fire and welcomed us all because of the pouring rain and the cold. Now, when Paul had gathered a bundle of sticks and put them on the fire, a viper driven forth by the heat fastened itself on his Paul's experience with the viper (28 1-6) hand. When the natives saw the creature hanging from his hand, they said to one another, Undoubtedly this man is a murderer! Though he has escaped from the sea, justice will not let him live. He, however, shook off the creature into the fire and suffered no harm. But the natives waited for him to swell up or suddenly fall down dead; but after waiting a long time and seeing that no harm came to him, they changed their minds and said that he was a god.

Paul's acts of healing (7-10) In the same part of the island there was an estate belonging to the governor, whose name was Publius. He welcomed us and entertained us most hospitably for three days. Now it happened that the father of Publius was lying ill of fever and dysentery; so Paul went in to see him and after he had prayed, laid his hands on him and cured him. When this had happened, the other sick people in the island also came and were cured. Moreover, they loaded us with many honors and when we set sail they provided us with all those things which we needed.

Voyage to Puteoli (11-14) After three months we set sail in an Alexandrian ship called The Twin Brothers, which had wintered in the island. And touching at Syracuse, we remained there three days. Then tacking around we reached Rhegium. A day later a south wind sprang up and we arrived the second day at Puteoli where we found Christian brothers and were urged to spend a week with them.

Paul at Rome (15, 16, 30, 31) Thus, we reached Rome. From thence, brothers who had heard about us, came out to meet us as far as the Forum of Appius and the Three Taverns. And when Paul saw them, he thanked God and took courage. When we finally reached Rome, Paul was allowed to live by himself with a soldier to guard him. For two entire years he lived in his own hired house, receiving all who came to him, preaching the Kingdom of God and teaching about the Lord Jesus Christ, quite openly and without hindrance.

I. **Paul's Imprisonment under Felix.** Paul's transfer from Jerusalem to Cæsarea delivered him from assassination at the hands of the Jews but brought him under the power of Felix, one of the most unprincipled of the Roman procurators who ruled during this period over the troubled province of Judea. Like his brother Pallas, Felix

216

was probably once a slave of Antonia, the mother of the emperor Claudius. The conservative Roman historian Tacitus thus tersely describes him: "He exercised the prerogative of a king in the spirit of a slave, with superlative cruelty and licentiousness" (5⁹). His rule, as procurator, was in keeping with his character. He so exasperated his Jewish subjects that the Zealots and the Sicarii, the Nihilists of that period, fomented a series of rebellions which were mercilessly repressed by Felix. Popular messiahs, some of them secretly in league with Felix, also kindled false hopes among the common people and gave him further opportunity for pillage and confiscation. The statement, therefore, that Felix kept Paul in prison for two years, hoping to extract from him a bribe, is in perfect keeping with the character of this former slave, who by a turn of the wheel of fortune had been received into the imperial circle and had married, first a daughter of Mark Anthony and Cleopatra, and later Drusilla, the daughter of Herod Agrippa I.

The account of Paul's trial before Felix is probably based on Luke's memory of the event. The flattering words addressed to Felix by the orator, Tertullus, were well calculated to win a favorable hearing, but they were a parody upon the facts. In declaring that Paul was a disturber of the peace, Tertullus appealed to Felix on a point in regard to which he was exceedingly sensitive. Paul's reply is a notable example of direct, powerful oratory and probably represents the main points in the great apostle's address. His Roman citizenship probably alone saved him from an adverse decision. Felix had heard from Paul's own lips that his mission to Jerusalem was to bear funds from the Gentile churches. This fact was evidently the basis of his hope of securing a rich bribe. His mercenary purpose also explains the large degree of freedom which he granted to Paul. Instead of being incarcerated in a vile prison, the apostle was placed under the charge of a Roman military officer and allowed considerable liberty. The narrative of Acts is largely silent regarding the details of these two years. For Paul, however, they were years of intense intellectual and literary activity. His later letters suggest that he continued his correspondence with the Western churches and directed his lieutenants. Luke's silence regarding this period indicates that he returned to the Greek churches and possibly brought back at the end of the two years further contributions for Paul's support. Cæsarea was already one of the great intellectual centres of Syria, and Paul evidently improved the opportunities which it offered for further study. There is evidence in his later writing that during this period he read certain apocalyptic writings such as the *Assumption of Moses* and an otherwise unknown writing which Epiphanius designates as the *Apocalypse of Elias*. Also in the light of Paul's later letters it is evident that his conceptions of Jesus and of the significance of his work still further developed during these years so rich in their opportunities for meditation.

II. The Date of the Procuratorships of Felix and Festus.
The retirement of Felix and the succession of Festus to the procuratorship is one of the landmarks in New Testament chronology. Josephus states that "when Portius Festus was sent to succeed Felix, the leading Jewish inhabitants of Cæsarea went up to Rome to accuse Felix. He would certainly have been brought to punishment for his misdeeds toward the Jews had not Nero yielded to the importunate solicitations of Felix's brother, Pallas, whom he at that time held in the greatest honor." Tacitus in his *Annals* (13[23]) states that Pallas fell from Nero's favor in the year 55 A.D. This definite statement would fix very closely the date of the beginning of the procuratorship of Festus, did not Tacitus also add in the same context that Pallas was later tried and acquitted by an unprincipled judge by the name of Pætus, although, "the approved innocence of Pallas did not please men so much as his arrogance offended them." It is possible that this reference means that Pallas was later restored to Nero's favor. His restoration, however, is only a possibility. It is, on the whole, more probable that Felix was retired and Festus entered upon his proconsulship as early as 55 or 56 A.D.

III. Paul's Reasons for Appealing to Cæsar. Festus appears, on the whole, to have been one of the best of the Roman procurators. He was unfamiliar, however, with Jewish institutions. The accession of a new procurator encouraged Paul's Jewish foes to believe that they might secure a verdict against him, for Festus was naturally eager to win the favor of the leaders of the nation. The narrative of Acts suggests that Festus suspected their demand that Paul be transferred for trial to Jerusalem. At the same time, as a Roman ruler intent upon restoring peace to the province which had been torn by dissensions and riots as a result of the unprincipled rule of Felix, Festus naturally looked with suspicion upon the prisoner Paul. He evidently regarded him as a religious fanatic and therefore one to be carefully watched. Festus's desire to please the Jews evidently so overruled his Roman sense of justice that he was inclined to yield to the demands of the high priest and transfer Paul's trial to Jerusalem. This decision left Paul in a most critical position. To go to Jerusalem was to face the danger of secret assassination and the probability of ultimate condemnation, for a man like Paul, whose activity had so often aroused the mob, was regarded by the Roman officials as a criminal, even though he be innocent of any evil intent. On the other hand, as we know from Paul's letter to the Romans, his chief passion at this time was to visit the imperial city. Hence his appeal to Cæsar. As a Roman citizen he possessed the right of appeal and Festus had no valid grounds for refusing it.

Paul's later examination before King Agrippa II, the son of Herod Agrippa I, was an unimportant episode, except that it reveals still further the heroic spirit of the great apostle and his zeal to improve every possible opportunity to proclaim the religion of his Master. It was evidently introduced by Luke as a further illustration of the fact that the Roman officials found nothing in the work of Paul worthy of condemnation.

IV. **The Story of His Shipwreck.** The account of Paul's voyage and shipwreck is one of the classical passages of the New Testament. It gives us the most vivid picture in ancient literature of the life of the courageous mariners who defied in their little craft the perils of the sea. Most travellers bound from Palestine to Rome by the sea route embarked at Cæsarea, Accho, or Tyre. The small ships which plied from these ports sailed close to the shores of Syria and Asia Minor. There their passengers often transshipped, as did Paul at Myra in southern Lycia, in one of the larger Alexandrian grain ships, which sailed from the great Egyptian seaport directly to Rome. Thence the ordinary course ran past Rhodes, along the southern shore of Crete, where there were favorable harbors and thence northwesterly past the southern shores of Greece until they felt in their sails the northern winds which came down through the Adriatic and which bore them quickly to the eastern shores of Sicily. There they turned abruptly northward through the Straits of Messina and sailed directly to Puteoli or the mouth of the Tiber. The open season for navigation was ended by the 10th of November, although, according to the Latin writer Vegitius, the favorable season was limited to four short months between May 26 and September 14.

Paul was placed as a prisoner under the charge of the centurion Julius, who was apparently one of the many officers under the immediate direction of the emperor. With him went Aristarchus, whom Paul in Colossians 4[10] speaks of as his "fellow prisoner." According to the Western text, the journey from Sidon to Myra took fifteen days. The accepted text states that they met adverse winds which retarded their progress and compelled them to sail south of the Island of Cyprus, rather than skirt the shores of Syria and Asia Minor. From the first Paul seemed to have won the respect and later the genuine affection of the Roman official in whose charge he had been placed. With his usual enthusiasm and energy the apostle entered heartily into the discussion as to whether or not they should venture to continue their belated voyage along the southern shores of Crete. Paul's experience and good judgment led him to oppose this plan, but the counsel of the captain and the owner of the ship overruled his advice. The reference to the Feast of the Atonement indicates that they were venturing beyond the open season for sailing, and the event signally confirmed the wisdom of Paul's counsel. The vivid description of the storm and shipwreck needs no interpretation. Above it all Paul rises sane and serene, again the master of the situation. In the hour of crisis, as so often in his experience, his dauntless faith expressed itself first through a heavenly vision and then through words of cheer and inspiration. Here we see the reasons why Paul gained an invincible hold upon the affections and wills of men. Good faith, good fellowship, and unceasing confidence in the unlimited power and the constant guidance of a kindly Providence inspired him and all to whom he spoke. Even the venomous serpent, probably still paralyzed by the cold, seemed to the onlookers to have no power over this man who was in such close league with the Infinite. Even the sick were given new hope and health by his sympathetic touch. The miracles which Luke records seem but commonplaces in the life of Paul. As we have already seen, the apostle himself regarded them simply as incidental proofs of his divine commission. Before their three months' sojourn was over, not only the governor but also the entire population of the little island of Malta were vying with each other in showing hospitality to the Roman prisoner who had appealed to Cæsar.

V. **Paul's Journey to Rome.** After Paul and his strange company had spent three winter months in Malta they set out on an Alexandrian ship for Rome. Instead of going around to the mouth of the Tiber they entered the Bay of Naples and landed at Puteoli. It was a period when the beautiful Italian springtime was just bursting forth in its glory. Puteoli was at this time the favorite watering resort of the Roman nobility whose magnificent villas skirted the Bay of Naples. Dearer to the heart of Paul than the beauties of nature and the creations of man was the hearty welcome which he received from the Christian brothers residing there. His friend, the Roman centurion, allowed him to spend the week with them. On his arrival a messenger had evidently been sent to inform the Christians at Rome, for, as he proceeded on his journey, a deputation met him at the Forum of Appius, forty-three miles south of Rome. To Paul this evidence of their loyalty was a great inspiration. More as a triumphant conqueror than as a prisoner under a serious charge, he proceeded along the famous Appian Way toward the Imperial City which he entered at the Porta Capæna. Thence he probably proceeded through the heart of the city, viewing the Palatine with its stately palaces on the left, past the old Forum toward the northern side of the city where was situated the camp of the pretorian guard.

VI. **The End of the Race.** Luke states that for two years Paul lived in his own hired house, receiving all that came to him, preaching the Kingdom of God, and teaching about the Lord Jesus Christ, quite openly and without hinderance. This remarkable freedom may have been due to the influence of his friend the Roman centurion. It was entirely in keeping with the Roman custom of the period. Tacitus states in his *Annals* (6[3]) that Gallio, the brother of Seneca, who had been proconsul of Achaia during Paul's activity at Corinth and who, like the great apostle, met his death at the hands of Nero, was thus kept under guard, not in his own hired house but in the house of a Roman officer. One of Luke's chief aims was to show that, while the hand of Christian fellowship had been freely extended to the Jews, they had almost invariably taken the initiative in persecuting the Christians. He, therefore, departs from the direct narrative to tell us that Paul, soon after his arrival, called together the leading Jews of Rome, stated his case, and appealed to their sense of justice. Not having received any news from their fellow Jews in Palestine, they were at first inclined to accept his story, but the majority of them refused to accept his teachings. Luke's condensed narrative leads us to imply that Paul in the end failed to win that support from the Jews at Rome which he sorely needed. It was so contrary to his characteristic tact to upbraid them for their failure to accept the Christian faith that it is probable that this portion of the narrative has been somewhat colored by Luke's apologetic purpose. The significant fact underlying the narrative is that Paul fully recognized the peril of his position and the importance of conciliating, if possible, the Jews

at Rome. The abrupt ending of Luke's narrative is in itself ominous.
If Paul had been liberated by the Roman emperor, Luke would have
been the first to proclaim this fact, for it would have conserved as
nothing else could one of the chief aims for which he wrote. Luke,
on the other hand, was not writing a book of martyrs. Nothing is
said of the death of Peter, the other leading character in his history.
The death of James is passed over with the barest mention. The
martyrdom of Stephen alone is recorded in detail because of its powerful influence on the expansion of the Christian church. The tradition
that Paul was released to preach in the West cannot be traced earlier
than the end of the second Christian century and was probably based
on the apostle's expression of the hope, in Romans 15[24], that he might
live to visit Spain. The long delay of Paul's trial is in perfect keeping with all that we know about Nero and especially the early, irresponsible years of his reign when he spent practically all of his time in the
pursuit of pleasure and left the direction of public affairs to his old
teacher Seneca, the Stoic philosopher, and to Burrus, the pretorian
prefect. This long delay also gave Paul's Jewish foes, of whom the
heads of the priestly hierarchy at Jerusalem were the chief, an opportunity to collect ample evidence against him. There was much
that they could present to blacken his character in the eyes of the
Roman officials, who, in dealing with a prisoner charged with stirring
up sedition, were not so much concerned with motives as with acts.
Even Luke's narrative indicates that wherever Paul went he aroused
bitter opposition which frequently expressed itself in mob attack and
popular uproar. In II Timothy 4 we evidently have notes from the
closing days of Paul's life. In 4[14] the apostle speaks of Alexander
the blacksmith: "He has done me a great harm; the Lord will pay
him back for what he has done. Beware of him for he has been bitterly hostile to everything that I have said." It is not impossible that
this is Alexander the Jew of Ephesus, who, according to Acts 19[33],
was put forward as spokesman when the silversmiths and tradesmen
of that temple city rose up to mob Paul and his associates. In II
Timothy 4[16, 17] Paul adds pathetically: "The first time there was no
one to defend me, but all deserted me. May this not be brought up
against them! But the Lord supported me and gave me strength.
. . . I was rescued from the jaws of the lion." In the light of [11] we
see him alone, with only the faithful Luke to comfort him, fighting his
last great fight. Pitted against him were the same foes that had,
under the shadow of Roman authority a quarter of a century before,

hunted to death his innocent Master. The analogies between the two scenes are strikingly close. The actors and setting alone are different. Jesus faced death at the capital city of his nation. Paul the Roman citizen died at the capital of the empire to which he owed allegiance. Clement of Rome, who lived near the close of the first century, wrote: "Paul by his example pointed out the prize of patient endurance, . . . he won the noble renown, which was the reward of his faith, having taught righteousness to the whole world and having reached the farthest bounds of the West. And when he had borne his testimony before the rulers, he departed from the world and went into the holy place, having been found a notable example of patient endurance." Tertullian, who wrote in the second century, is more explicit: "Paul has for his crown the same death with John (the Baptist)." And Origen, early in the third century, states definitely that Paul "suffered martyrdom in Rome under Nero." Paul was probably beheaded at Rome in 57 or 58 A.D., early in the reign of Nero. In II Timothy 4[6-8] we have his final song of triumph: "I am already being poured out as a drink offering and my time to go has come. I have fought the good fight, I have run the race, I have kept the faith. Henceforth there is left for me the crown of righteousness which the Lord, the righteous judge, shall give me on that great day—and not only to me but to all who have loved the thought of his appearing."

§ CLXIV. THE LAST LETTERS OF THE AGED PRISONER

Paul, a prisoner of Jesus Christ and Timothy our brother, to our beloved fellow-worker, Philemon, to our sister Apphia, to our fellow-soldier, Archippus, and to the church which meets in your house. May grace and peace be granted you all from God our Father and the Lord Jesus Christ. *Greeting (Philemon 1-3)*

I always give thanks to my God when I mention you in my prayers; for as I hear of your love and faith which you manifest toward the Lord Jesus and to all the saints, I pray that their participation in your faith may result in their gaining a clear knowledge of all the good we enjoy through our relations to Christ. For I have had great joy and comfort in your love, my brother, because the hearts of the saints have been refreshed through you. *Thanksgiving (4-7)*

Therefore, although in Christ I might be quite free toward you to command you to do what is fitting, I appeal to

Appeal for clemency toward Onesimus (8-14)

you rather on the ground of love. So as Paul, the old man, who is now a prisoner for Christ Jesus, I appeal to you on behalf of my spiritual child who was born while I was in chains—Onesimus! Once you found him worthless, but now, true to his name (Profitable), he is worth something both to you and to me. I am sending him back to you, though it means parting with my very heart. I would have liked to keep him with me, that in your stead he might serve me during my imprisonment for the gospel; but I wish to do nothing without your consent, so that this kind act of yours might not be done under compulsion but of your own free will.

For consideration treatment (15-20)

Perhaps it was for this very reason that he was parted from you for a while, that you might receive him back for good, no longer as a slave but something more than a slave —a brother, peculiarly dear to me, but even dearer to you both as a human being and as a fellow Christian! Therefore if you regard me as a partner, then receive him as you would me. And if he has done anything dishonest or owes you any sum, put that down to my account: 'I, Paul, write this with my own hand, I will pay it back.' (I say nothing of the fact that you owe me, over and above, your very soul.) Yes, brother, let me have some return from you in the Lord! Refresh my heart in Christ.

Paul's hope (21-22)

I write you, trusting in your obedience. I know you will do even more than I say, and at the same time get quarters ready for me, for I hope that through your prayers I may be sent back to you!

Concluding salutation (23-25)

Epaphras, my fellow prisoner in Christ, salutes you, as do also Mark, Aristarchus, Demas and Luke, my fellow-workers.

May the grace of our Lord Jesus Christ be with your spirit. Amen.

Greeting (Col. 1¹, ²)

Paul, an apostle of Christ Jesus by the will of God, and Timothy, our brother, to the consecrated and faithful brothers in Christ at Colossæ. May grace and peace be granted to you from God our Father.

Thanksgiving (3-8)

We always give thanks to God, the Father of our Lord Jesus Christ, when we pray for you because we have heard of your faith in Christ Jesus and of the love which you cher-

224

ish for all the saints on account of the hope laid up for you
in heaven. You have heard of this hope in the message of
gospel truth which has come to you, as it spreads over all
the world, yielding fruit and increasing, as it also has done
among you from the day that you heard it and learned to
know what God's grace really is, as indeed you did learn
to know it from Epaphras, our beloved fellow servant.
He is a faithful minister of Christ in your behalf and it is
he who has informed us of your love in the Spirit.

Now I rejoice in my sufferings in your behalf, and I would Paul's
make up in my own person whatever is lacking of the suf- suffer-
ferings which Christ has to suffer in behalf of his body, the behalf
church. I have been appointed a minister of the church of the
in the position intrusted to me by God in your interests, tiles
to present God's message fully, even that secret which, (1^{24}—2^3)
though concealed from all ages and generations, now has
been disclosed to his saints. God willed that they should
understand the glorious wealth which this secret holds for
the Gentiles—this secret which is Christ in you as your
hope of glory. Him we proclaim, training and teaching
every man in all wisdom in order that we may present
every man before God, perfect in Christ. For this end I
labor, striving with a divine energy which is working mightily within me. Yes, I want you to know how severe is
the struggle in which I am engaged in behalf of you and
the brothers in Laodicea and for all who have never seen
my face, that their hearts may be encouraged, that they
may be welded together in love, that they may have all the
wealth of conviction that comes from insight, and that
they may know the secret of God which is Christ, in whom
all the treasures of wisdom and knowledge lie hidden!

Therefore, since you have received the Messiah, even Christ's
Jesus the Lord, live your life in him, being firmly rooted char-
and founded in him, confirmed in the faith, as you have and
been taught it, and filled to overflowing with gratitude to saving
God. Take care lest anyone lead you away prisoner by his (6-12)
philosophy or idle fancy based on human tradition, or on a
belief in the elemental spirits of the world and not on Christ.
For it is in Christ that the entire fullness of the divine nature dwells embodied and in him you are made perfect.

It is he who is the head of all rulers and powers; in him you have also been circumcised with a circumcision not performed by human hand, but with Christ's own circumcision, which consists in the putting off of the body of flesh, for you were buried with him in baptism and thereby raised with him through faith in the power of God which raised him from the dead.

What it means to be raised with Christ (3¹, ², ⁹⁻¹¹)

If, therefore, you have risen with Christ, seek those things which are above, where Christ is seated at the right hand of God. Mind what is above and not what is on the earth. Do not tell lies to one another, for you have stripped off the old mankind with its practices and have put on the new mankind, which is being renewed in knowledge in the likeness of its Creator. In that new creation there is neither Greek nor Jew, circumcised nor uncircumcised, barbarian, Scythian, slave nor freeman; but Christ is everything and in all of us.

The evidences of the Christ life (12-23)

Therefore, as God's own chosen, consecrated and beloved, be clothed with compassion, kindness, humility, gentleness, patience. Bear with one another and forgive one another, if anyone has a complaint against another. Just as the Lord forgave you, so you must forgive. And above all you must have love, for it is that which binds together the perfect life. Also let the peace which Christ gives reign supreme in your hearts. For this end you have been called to be members in one body. Also be thankful. Let the message of Christ dwell within you in rich measure. Teach and train one another in all wisdom by means of psalms, hymns and spiritual songs. Sing to God with thankfulness in your hearts, and whatever you do in word or deed, do all in the name of the Lord Jesus, giving thanks through him to God the Father. Children, obey your parents at every point, for this is right for those who belong to the Lord. Fathers, do not irritate your children lest you make them sullen. Servants, obey your earthly masters in everything, not only when their eye is on you, as those who aim simply to please men, but with single purpose, because you revere the Lord. Whatever you are doing, work at it heartily, as servants of the Lord and not of men.

Tychicus, that beloved brother and faithful minister and

fellow servant of the Lord, will give you all the information about me. It is for this reason that I am sending him to you that you may know how I am and to comfort your hearts. He is accompanied by that faithful and beloved brother, Onesimus, who is one of yourselves. They will inform you of everything here. And when this letter has been read by you, let it be read also in the church of the Laodiceans. Also see that you read the letter that reaches you from Laodicea. The salutation is in my own hand, from Paul. Remember me in my imprisonment. Grace be with you. *Personal notes (4[7, 16, 18])*

Paul, an apostle of Jesus Christ by the will of God, to the saints who are faithful in Christ Jesus. May grace and peace be granted to you from God our Father and the Lord Jesus Christ. *Greeting (Eph. 1[1, 2])*

Blessed be the God and Father of our Lord Jesus Christ who hath blessed us with every spiritual blessing in the heavenly realms through Christ! He chose us in him before the creation of the world that we might be consecrated and without blemish in his sight, destining us to be his sons through Jesus Christ. *Thanksgiving (3-5)*

Therefore, remember that once you were Gentiles in the flesh, who are called the 'Uncircumcision' by the so-called 'Circumcision,' which is the work of human hands in the flesh. Remember that you were at that time outside Christ, aliens to the commonwealth of Israel and strangers to the covenants of the promise, without hope and without God in the world. But now in Christ Jesus you, who were once far away, have been brought near by the blood of Christ. For he is our peace—he who united us both and broke down the hostile dividing wall. In his own flesh he set aside the law with its definite commands so as to make peace by uniting these two parts in himself into a new mankind. Thus in himself he put an end to that hostility by reconciling both Jew and Gentile to God in one body through the cross. And he came to proclaim a gospel of peace to you Gentiles who were far away and to the Jews who were near, for it is through him that we both have access by one Spirit to the Father. *The union of Jew and Gentile in Christ (2[11-18])*

Unity
of the
church
(4⁴⁻⁶)
There is one body and one spirit—one hope was held
out to you as the goal of your calling—one Lord, one faith,
one baptism, one God and Father of all, who is over us all,
acts through us all, and is in us all. But to each of us has
been given his own grace, according to the measure of the
gift of Christ.

The
one
body in
Christ
(11-16)
Christ himself granted some to be apostles, some to be
prophets, some to be evangelists, some to be pastors and
teachers, in order that the saints may be fully equipped for
the work of service, that is, for the upbuilding of the body
of Christ, until we all attain the unity of the faith and the
knowledge of God's son, even to the perfect manhood and
to the full measure of maturity which belongs to the fullness
of Christ, that we may no longer be babes, blown from
our course and carried here and there by every passing wind
of doctrine, by the adroitness of men who are skilful in making use of every evil device to mislead. Rather we are to
hold to the truth and by our love grow up wholly into union
with him who is our head, even Christ. Dependent on him,
the whole body is welded together and compacted by every
joint with which it is supplied, and by the due activity of
each part the body is enabled to grow so as to build itself
up in love.

The
broth-
erly
spirit
(4³¹⁻
5²)
Put away all bitterness and passion, anger, clamoring
and insults, together with all malice. Be kind to one another, tender hearted, forgiving one another, as God in
Christ has also forgiven you. Therefore, be imitators of
God, as his beloved children, and lead lives of love just as
Christ loved you and gave himself up for you to be a fragrant offering and sacrifice to God.

Arm-
ing
for the
long
con-
flict
(6¹⁰⁻²⁰)
In conclusion, be strong in the Lord and in the strength
of his might. Put on the complete armor of God, so as to
be able to stand against the stratagems of the devil. For
we have to struggle not with flesh and blood but against
rulers and authorities, against the forces which govern
this darkened world, against the spiritual hosts of evil arrayed against us in the heavens. Therefore put on the
complete armor of God that you may be able to stand on
the evil day and remain victors over all. Stand, therefore,
fastening the girdle of truth about your loins, putting on
the breastplate of righteousness, and having your feet shod

with the preparation of the gospel of peace. Above all, take the shield of faith by which you will be able to quench all the flaming darts of the evil one. Take the helmet of salvation and the sword of the Spirit, which is the word of God. Pray at all times in the Spirit, with all manner of prayer and entreaty. Be alert to seize every such opportunity, interceding in behalf of all the saints and in my behalf also, that speech may be given me, that I may expound fully and openly the mystery of the gospel on behalf of which I am an ambassador in bonds, that I may have freedom to speak boldly as I ought.

Our beloved brother Tychicus, a faithful minister in the Lord, will give you all the information about me, that you may know how I am doing; that is why I am sending him to you that you may know all about me and that he may encourage your hearts. *Personal notes (21-24)*

Peace and love with faith be to the brothers from God the Father and the Lord Jesus Christ. May grace be with all who love our Lord Jesus Christ sincerely.

Paul and Timothy, servants of Jesus Christ, to all the saints in Christ Jesus who are at Philippi, as well as to the bishops and deacons: Grace and peace to you from God our Father and the Lord Jesus Christ. *Greeting (Phil. 1 1, 2)*

I thank my God whenever I remember you; in all my prayers for you all I always pray with joy because of your co-operation in furthering the gospel from the very first day to this moment. For of this I am confident, that he who began the good work in you will go on to perfect it until the day of Jesus Christ. It is only right for me to be thus thinking of you all, for in my prison and as I defend and confirm the gospel, I recall how you all share with me the same grace. God is my witness that I yearn for you all with the tender affection of Christ Jesus himself. And this is my prayer that your love may become richer and richer in knowledge and in all manner of insight, that you may be able to make right distinctions, so that you may be men of transparent character and that you may do no harm to any one, in view of the day of Christ, and that you may be full of the fruits of righteousness, which come through Jesus Christ to the glory and praise of God. *Thanksgiving and protestation of affection (3-11)*

Now I would have you know, brothers, that the things

The
fortu-
nate
effects
of
Paul's
im-
prison-
ment
(12-14)

which have befallen me have really tended to advance the gospel; throughout the whole of the pretorian guard and everywhere else it is generally recognized that I am imprisoned for the sake of Christ, and most of the brothers have through my imprisonment gained greater confidence in the Lord to speak fearlessly the word of God.

His
calm
atti-
tude
toward
living
or
dying
(19-26)

I know that this will result in my release, because of your prayers and the supply of the Spirit of Jesus Christ, in fulfillment of my earnest expectation and hope that I may never feel ashamed, but that, now as ever, by my boldness Christ may be honored in my person, whether by life or by death. For me to live is Christ and to die is gain. But, if it is to live in the body, this means for me fruitful work; but what I should choose I know not. I am in a dilemma between the two. I have a strong desire to depart and be with Christ, for that is by far the best. But for your sakes it is more necessary that I should live on here in the flesh. And since I am sure of this, I know that I shall abide and remain with you all, to promote your progress and joy in the faith. Thus you will have ample cause to glory in Jesus Christ over me, as a result of my again being with you.

Exhor-
tation
to be
joyful
and
calm
(4¹-⁷)

Rejoice in the Lord always. Again I say, Rejoice. Let your forbearance be known to all men. The Lord is at hand. Be anxious about nothing; but in regard to everything make known your requests to God in prayer and supplication with thanksgiving; so shall the peace of God, which surpasses all understanding, keep guard over your hearts and your minds in Christ Jesus.

Cher-
ish
noble
thoughts
(8, 9)

Finally, brothers, whatsoever things are true, whatsoever things are honest, whatsoever things are just, whatsoever things are pure, whatsoever things are lovely, whatsoever things are of good repute—if there be any virtue or anything worthy of praise—think on these things. Practise also what you have learned and received and heard and seen in me; then the God of peace will be with you.

But I rejoice in the Lord greatly that now at length you have revived your thoughtfulness for me; for you were ever thoughtful, but you lacked opportunity. Not that I speak of want, for I have learned how to be content wherever I am. I know how to live humbly; I also know how to live amidst abundance. I have been initiated into each and every secret of life, both of plenty and of hunger, of abundance and of want. I can do all things in him who strengtheneth me. Yet it was beautiful of you to share in my affliction. You Philippians know well that, in the beginning of the gospel, when I departed from Macedonia, no church but yours had any communication with me about giving and receiving; even when I was in Thessalonica you sent money once and again for my needs. It is not the money I am anxious about, but what I am anxious about is the interest that accumulates in this way to your credit! I have enough of everything and more than enough. I am amply supplied with what you sent by Epaphroditus; it is a fragrant perfume, a sacrifice acceptable, well pleasing to God. And my God will supply all your own needs from his wealth in glory in Christ Jesus. Glory to God our Father for ever and ever. Amen.

I. **Paul's Last Letters.** Bound in chains and facing almost certain death, Paul continued to direct the churches of his planting by means of letters and faithful messengers. Five and possibly six of his surviving letters come from this period of imprisonment. They fall into two groups. The first group includes the letters to Philemon and the Colossians and the one which at present bears the name Ephesians. From references within them we learn that all three were sent at the same time in the care of Tychicus and Onesimus to Paul's friends in Asia Minor. The letter to the Philippians was written when Paul had already begun to feel the pinch of poverty. In this letter he promises to send Timothy to them ere long. In the closing chapter of II Timothy, which is unquestionably Pauline, his faithful fellow worker has already left him and, save for Luke, he is quite alone. This, therefore, represents the last of that remarkable series of letters which had come from the great apostle to the Gentiles. They contain Paul's dying testament. In them he has endeavored to formulate the heart of the message with which he has been intrusted and to explain the mystery of the gospel. As the result, they are, with the exception of Romans, the most doctrinal of his epistles. Under the shadow of his coming death he was evidently relaxing his hold on the detailed problems of individual churches. The distinctions between Jew and Gentile and the conflicts about the ceremonial law are but distant memories. Instead his thoughts are fixed on the eternal verities. As he himself tells us, he is now an old man. The reader sometimes misses the fiery vigor and the crisp incisiveness that characterize Paul's earlier controversial letters. The strength and charm of these letters lies in the wealth of rich and warm emotion which pervades them. The stream of love and brotherly kindness, which runs through all of his writings, now broadens and deepens. Paul is here intimately revealed as the friend and loving adviser of master and slave, of saint and sinner, of those strong in the Christian faith and of those perplexed with doubts. He is anxious about his own future only as it will affect his friends. Like his Master, he faces life and death unafraid. The peace of Christ completely fills his heart and brims over into these peerless love-letters. They also develop certain profound and important religious conceptions which he had only hinted at in his earlier letters.

II. **The Occasion of Paul's Letter to Philemon.** Paul's letter to Philemon and that in Romans 16 are the only personal notes that have survived from the apostle's voluminous correspondence. From Colossians 4⁹ we learn that Philemon was probably a native of the little town of Colossæ on the great highway that ran eastward from Ephesus. Paul's words imply that he was one of the converts won during the apostle's ministry at Ephesus. The letter is addressed to Philemon and his wife Apphia and to Archippus, who was probably their son. Philemon was evidently a wealthy and influential man. At this home the Christian church held its meetings, and Archippus was their leader. Among the many whom Paul had attracted to him through his personality and preaching, while a prisoner at Rome, was the runaway slave Onesimus—a part of the vast human wreckage that gravitated irresistibly to Rome. The confession of this genuinely converted slave revealed the fact that he had once belonged to Paul's friend Philemon and that he had not only run away but had probably stolen from his master. Both of these offenses, according to Roman law, were punishable by death. Paul's faith in the social efficiency of Christianity is signally illustrated by what he did. Into the hands of the runaway slave he put this letter and confidently sent him back to his master. It breathed the spirit of good-fellowship, mutual confidence, and brotherly kindness. It reveals a democracy that over-leaps all social distinctions. With kindly humor that is not the least of Paul's many attractions he makes a friendly pun on the name of Onesimus (Profitable). It is the letter of a courtly, noble-minded

Christian gentleman, forgetful of self and intent simply upon establishing goodwill between all men. It also well illustrates Paul's superlative tact. Not by command, but by an appeal to Philemon's generosity, he insures a hearty welcome and full forgiveness for the once dishonest, runaway slave. This homely little letter is, therefore, of large significance, for it presents Christianity not in theory but in practice, and introduces us to two worthy citizens of the ideal Christian community which Paul was seeking to make world-wide.

III. The Purpose and Thought of Paul's Epistle to the Colossians. Like the Epistle to the Romans, this letter was apparently written to the members of a church which Paul had never visited. Its general structure closely resembles that of the larger epistle. It begins with the usual greeting and thanksgiving (1^{1-23}). The doctrinal and most important section is found in $1^{24}-2^{23}$, the practical applications in 3^1-4^6, and the concluding notes and salutations in 4^{7-18}. The occasion of the letter was a visit of Epaphras, a faithful Christian, who laid before Paul the complex problems which were troubling the Christians of Colossæ. Colossæ, by virtue of its geographical situation was peculiarly exposed to the gnostic and Greek influences which emanated from Ephesus on the west, and to the popular doctrines of the mystic religions which came pouring in from the East. Certain Jewish exorcists, who still insisted on the importance of ceremonial rites, such as circumcision and strict Sabbath observance, apparently contributed to the confusion of religious ideas and so completed the bewilderment of the simple-minded Christians of Colossæ. In this epistle Paul is evidently fighting the current gnostic and mystical religions with their own weapons. It is another graphic illustration of his being "all things to all men." His language and teachings clearly show the influence of his talks with Epaphras. Here beliefs partially suggested in earlier epistles are expanded. It is also possible that during his imprisonment Paul had been reading certain current Jewish apocalyptic books. The result is that in this epistle and in its companion, Ephesians, the historical Jesus largely disappears and the Christ is interpreted in the language of the Jewish apocalypses. Like all the Jews of his age, Paul firmly believed in hierarchies of angelic beings both good and bad. Through the Jewish belief in personified Wisdom his mind had been opened to the doctrine of the Logos, set forth by the Greek philosophers and Philo. He also appreciated the attractions of the mystery-religions, which offered personal salvation through mystical unity with the Deity.

The terms in which Paul sets forth his Christology in these epistles are, therefore, not peculiar to him but a part of his varied inheritance. His aim is to make clear to all types of readers his profound conviction that Christ is absolutely supreme above all the elemental spirits of earth and heaven and thus to furnish a practical basis for unity and to prevent discord and factiousness. To those familiar with Greek philosophy he declared: "In Christ the entire fulness of the divine nature dwells in the body." To those who inclined toward the pagan mystery-religions, he said in terms already familiar to them: "You have been buried with him in baptism and thereby raised with him through faith in the power of God which raised him from the dead." The key to the interpretation of his statements is found in his profound and original conception of the mystical social solidarity of the race and of Jesus' unique relation to the ultimate ideal community which he calls the "Body of Christ." With prophetic insight he sees this "new creation in which there is neither Greek nor Jew, circumcised nor uncircumcised, barbarian, Scythian, slave nor freeman; but Christ is everything and in all of us." This new mankind is a product of the mind and work of Jesus. His life, his heroic sacrifice, and his abiding spirit are the essential creative forces. Paul evidently has these facts in mind when he declares that "Christ is everything and in all of us." Every noble emotion, every spiritual aspiration, and every prompting of loyalty to the ideal community are felt by Paul to be "Christ in him." Christ represents in Paul's thought those eternal forces at work in the world and in the hearts of men that have already broken down the hostile dividing wall between Jew and Gentile and are uniting by the bonds of love and brotherhood all mankind into one universal community. In the light of this profound conviction the Pauline Christology, with all its poetic, old-world imagery, becomes the symbol of eternal and intelligible verities.

IV. **The Identity of the So=called "Epistle to the Ephe= sians."** One of the perplexing New Testament problems is the strikingly close analogy both in structure and thought between the epistle to the Colossians and that addressed (in its present superscription) to the Ephesians. The absence of any reference to specific conditions in the Ephesian church and the relative lateness of the tradition embodied in the superscription make it exceedingly improbable that this epistle was originally sent to the Christian community at Ephesus. In Colossians 4[16] Paul refers to a letter which he was sending to the Laodiceans and which he wished the Christians of Colossæ also to read. Just why he wrote two letters dealing with practically the same themes in very much the same way is not clear; but that he did so is on the whole the best explanation of the existence of Ephesians. Laodicea was only six miles from Colossæ, and Hierapolis across the Lycus River was the home of another Christian community. Each of these Christian churches was confronted by the same problems. Realizing how great was the peril and possibly fearing lest the letter to the Colossians might be lost, Paul apparently, in the enforced leisure of his imprisonment, wrote a duplicate letter, at the same time modifying and expanding the original. It is possible that this second letter bore the superscription, "To the Laodiceans," as is suggested by Marcion and other early authorities. This explanation is, on the whole, more satisfactory than that it is the work of an unknown Christian who used Paul's letter to the Colossians as a foundation on which to build later doctrines. Even though, like Colossians, it reflects many beliefs only hinted at in earlier epistles but found in the complex of religions which was the background of Paul's work and thought, its ideas are distinctively Pauline.

V. **Paul's Love=Letter to the Philippians.** The occasion of Paul's letter to the Philippians was the visit of one of their number, Epaphroditus, who had brought from them to Paul in prison a gift of much-needed money. The messenger had been seriously ill and homesick at Rome. He accordingly is to be Paul's messenger to the Philippian Christians. The apostle's aim is to express his thanks and love, not only for this gift but for the many which had endeared their friendship and bound him peculiarly close to them. It is, therefore, one of the most intimate of his letters. His larger aim is to set forth his faith under trial and thereby to strengthen that of his loyal friends so that they may enjoy in largest measure the peace and happiness that the Christian life affords. Paul's approaching death sanctifies and glorifies this letter. Its detailed allusions light up the darkness which otherwise shrouds the closing days of his Roman imprisonment. All anxieties and polemics have disappeared. "Rejoice" is its key-note. In fact Paul uses this word so often that in 3[1] he exclaims, with a characteristic flash of kindly humor: "Well then, my brothers, rejoice in the Lord. I am repeating this word 'rejoice' in my letter, but that does not tire me and it is for you a safe precaution." Here is spontaneously revealed the joy of a runner who has nearly completed his race—the joy of one who speaks out of his own rich experience. He is still hoping that he may be released in order to visit them, but regarding the outcome of his trial he is indifferent, assured that, whether it be life or death, either is gain. In his closing he expresses the wealth of his love for them and reveals his burning zeal to inspire each of them with the serene faith which made life or death for him a joy.

VI. **Paul's Contribution to Christianity.** Chief among the many difficult tasks which the present generation has undertaken is the evaluation of the work of Paul. Many have contended that he has concealed rather than revealed the personality and teachings of the Master whom he professed to serve. For a generation the question of whether Jesus or Paul is the real founder of Christianity has been hotly discussed. That Paul's beliefs, especially regarding the Christ, were influenced by his Jewish and Hellenic inheritances cannot be questioned. His pictures of a pre-existent, supernatural Messiah who is to come again from heaven to judge mankind and to establish a new kingdom on earth, is very different from the simple portraits of Jesus in the oldest gospel records; but he shared these beliefs with the primitive church. They are not his unique or permanent contributions to Christianity. It is, therefore, unfortunate that Christian theology in the past has been built more on the teachings of Paul than on those of Jesus. The chief reason is because the material which has come from Paul is far more abundant. His great historic work was the breaking of the bonds of Judaism. In this task he did not work alone, for Stephen and many others shared in this labor; but it was Paul who formulated the declaration of independence and commanded the forces that effected the revolution. He grasped most clearly Jesus' great teaching of individual liberty and made it an accepted tenet in the Christian church. Paul also found the results of Jesus' work and teachings enmeshed in a narrow Jewish environment. He brought them out and held them up before the enraptured gaze of humanity. Moreover, he interpreted the principles of Jesus and the beliefs of his immediate followers into the language and figures current in the larger Graeco-Roman world of his day. Thus Paul was the chief leader in that band of enthusiastic, devoted missionaries who transplanted Christianity from Jewish to Gentile soil. While he was not the first Christian missionary, he inspired and directed the great missionary movement of the first century until, through his wise statesmanship and tireless activity, Christianity had been established in all the great cities of the empire. Paul also reared up a large band of efficient Christian preachers and teachers, who multiplied his work and carried its influence to all civilized races.

In his life, as well as in his teachings, Paul interpreted Christianity as a personal, spiritual fellowship between God and the individual; at the same time he placed a profound emphasis upon the ethical and social aspects of religion. All generations have recognized that Paul's warm, religious life, his devotion to his Master, and his self-sacrificing heroism are to be counted among the richest heritages of Christendom. The present generation, however, is beginning to appreciate the supreme value of his contribution to the practical interpretation of Jesus' social teachings. He it was who developed the logical and concrete implications of his Master's ideal of the Kingdom of God. On the basis of his work with the Christian communities which he established in the fields of his missionary effort he perfected the plan of an ideal community that would include all mankind, that would give every man an opportunity through loyal, loving service to attain fulness of life and happiness and would realize in definite form on earth the lofty, social teachings of his Master. It is, therefore, not as a theologian but as a Christian missionary, statesman, and social organizer that Paul has made his greatest and most permanent contributions to Christianity. The external structure and the creeds of historic Christianity are largely the results of his building; but, as he always asserted, the foundation on which it is laid is Jesus Christ.

CHRISTIANITY DURING THE SECOND HALF OF THE FIRST CENTURY

§ CLXV. THE MESSAGE OF HOPE AND INSPIRATION IN I PETER

Greeting (I Peter 1:1, 2)

Peter, an apostle of Jesus Christ to God's chosen people, the exiles of the dispersion in Pontus, Galatia, Cappadocia, Asia, and Bithynia, chosen in accordance with the foreknowledge of God the Father through the sanctifying work of the Spirit to obey Jesus Christ and to be sprinkled with his blood. May grace and peace be multiplied to you.

Thanksgiving for their future hope (3-9)

Blessed be the God and Father of our Lord Jesus Christ! In accordance with his great mercy he hath caused us to be born anew to a living hope through the resurrection of Jesus Christ from the dead, to an inheritance imperishable, undefiled, and unfading. It has been reserved in heaven for you who are guarded by the power of God through faith for a salvation which is ready to be revealed at the last hour. Rejoice, therefore, in this, even though now for a short time you may need to suffer various trials. This suffering is only for the testing of your faith (far more precious than gold which perishes and yet is tested by fire), and it will be found to result in praise and glory and honor at the reappearing of Jesus Christ. Him you love, although you have not looked upon him. Though at present you cannot see him, you nevertheless believe in him and you will exult with an unspeakable and glorious joy when you obtain, as the object of your faith, the salvation of your souls.

The fruits of this new birth (22, 23, 2:1-3)

Now that through your obedience to the truth you have purified your souls for a brotherly love that is sincere, love one another heartily and fervently; for you have been born anew, not of mortal but of immortal seed by God's everliving and enduring word. So put away all malice, all deceit and insincerity and envy and slander of every kind!

238

FRUITS OF THE NEW BIRTH

Like newly born infants, thirst for the pure spiritual milk, that by it you may grow up to salvation.

You are the chosen race, the royal priesthood, the holy nation, the people who belong to God, that you may proclaim the excellencies of him who called you out of darkness into his marvelous light. Once you were no people but now you are God's people. Once you were unpitied but now you are pitied. The true Israel (9, 10)

Beloved, I entreat you as sojourners and exiles not to indulge the fleshly passions which wage war upon the soul. Conduct yourselves properly before the heathen, so that, although they now defame you as evil-doers, they may yet glorify God, when you are put on trial, because they see your good deeds. To attract the heathen to God (11, 12)

Submit for the Lord's sake to every human authority, whether it be the emperor as supreme or governors sent by him for the punishment of evil-doers and the encouragement of those who do what is right. For it is God's will that by doing what is right you should silence the ignorant charges of foolish persons. Be free men, but do not make your freedom an excuse for evil conduct; rather be God's true servants. Honor everyone, love the brotherhood, reverence God, honor the emperor. To submit to human rulers (13-17)

Household servants, be submissive to your masters with all respect, not only to those who are kind and considerate but also to those who are surly; for it is a merit, when from a sense of a duty to God one patiently endures the pains of suffering unjustly inflicted. For if you do wrong and receive a blow for it, what credit is there in your bearing it patiently? But if, when you do right and suffer for it, you bear it patiently this counts as a merit in God's sight. Duty of servants (18-20)

It is for this that you were called, for when Christ also suffered in your behalf, he left you an example that you should follow in his footsteps. He committed no sin nor was guile found in his mouth. When he was reviled he reviled not again; when he suffered he never threatened, but left everything to him who judgeth justly. He it was who bore our sins in his own body on the cross that we, having died as far as our sins are concerned, may live for righteousness. By his wounds you have been healed. For you were Jesus' example (21-25) straying like lost sheep, but now you have come back to the Shepherd and Guardian of your souls.

Duties of wives (3¹⁻⁴) In the same way you wives must be submissive to your husbands so that, even if some of these husbands do not believe the word, they may be won over, apart from the word, through the behavior of their wives when they see how reverent and blameless your behavior is. Let not your adornment be merely outward, one of plaiting the hair, putting on ornaments of gold, or wearing apparel. Instead, it should be a new nature in the heart with the incorruptible beauty of a gentle and peaceful spirit which is of rare value in the sight of God.

Of husbands (7) Likewise, you husbands, be considerate, as you live together with your wives, recognizing that they belong to the weaker sex. Also treat them as heirs, equally with you, of the gift of life, so that your prayers may not be hindered.

The Christian spirit and its reward (5⁻¹²) Finally, you should all be of one mind, sympathetic, kind to the brothers, compassionate, humble, not paying back evil for evil nor reviling when you are reviled, but on the contrary giving a blessing in return, for to this end you have been called that you may inherit a blessing, for,

> He who would love life,
> And see good days,
> Let him restrain his tongue from evil,
> And his lips from speaking guile;
> Let him turn from evil and do good,
> Let him seek peace and pursue it.
> For the eyes of the Lord are on the upright,
> And his ears are open to their cry;
> But the face of the Lord is set against evil-doers.

The blessing awaiting the faithful in persecution (13⁻18) And who will wrong you, if you are zealous for that which is good? Even if you have to suffer for what is right, you are happy. So have no fear of their threats nor be troubled; but in your hearts reverence Christ as Lord, being always ready with an answer for any one who asks you for a reason for the hope which you cherish. Yet answer with meekness and fear, preserving a good conscience, so that, when you are assailed, those who slander your good Christian behavior may be put to shame. For it is better for you to suffer for doing right, if that be the will of God, than for doing wrong; for Christ also, once for all, died for sins, a just man for unjust men, that he might bring us to God.

Therefore, since Christ has suffered in the flesh, you must arm yourselves with a determination to do the same (for he who has suffered in the flesh has done with sin) that for the rest of your life in the flesh you may be governed not by human passions but by the will of God. For in the past you have given time enough to doing what the heathen choose to do ! You used to live lives of unbridled license, lust, hard drinking, revelry, dissipation and illicit idolatry; therefore, they think it strange that you will not plunge with them into the same flood of profligacy; so they abuse you. But they will have to give account to him who stands ready to judge the living and the dead. *The inspiration of Christ's example (4:1-6)*

Now the end of all things is near. Therefore, keep a cool head, be calm, and pray. Above all be intent upon loving one another, for love hides a multitude of sins. Be hospitable to one another without grudging. You must serve one another, each with the talents which he has received, as excellent stewards of God's manifold goodness. If anyone preaches, let it be as one who utters the word of God. If anyone renders a service, let it be in the strength which God supplieth, so that in everything God may be glorified through Jesus Christ to whom belongs the glory and the dominion forever and ever. Amen. *Call to love and service (7-11)*

Beloved, do not be surprised at the fiery ordeal, which has come to test you, as though a strange experience had befallen you. Rather, since you are sharing Christ's sufferings, rejoice that when his glory is revealed you may also rejoice and exult. If you are reproached for the sake of Christ, you are happy, for then the Spirit of glory, even the Spirit of God himself, is resting upon you. Let none of you suffer as a murderer or a thief or an evil-doer or as one who meddles with other people's affairs; but if a man suffers for being a Christian, let him not be ashamed; let him rather glorify God for being permitted to bear this name. *To patient suffering (12-16)*

The time is come for the judgment to begin with the

<table>
<tr>
<td>The impending day of judgment (17-19)</td>
<td>household of God; and if it begins with us, what will be the end of those who reject God's gospel! If the righteous man is scarcely saved, what will become of the impious and sinful! Therefore, let those who are suffering in accordance with the will of God, while they continue in their well-doing, intrust their souls to him, their faithful Creator.</td>
</tr>
<tr>
<td>Responsibilities of elders (5¹⁻⁴)</td>
<td>Now, I exhort the elders among you—I who am also an elder and a witness of the sufferings of Christ and a sharer in the glory to be revealed—be shepherds of your flock of God. Take charge of them, not under compulsion but willingly, in accordance with the will of God, not for base gain but freely, not by way of lording it over your charges but proving yourselves patterns for the flock. Then when the chief Shepherd appears, you will receive the unfading crown of glory.</td>
</tr>
<tr>
<td>Of young men (5-7)</td>
<td>In the same way you younger men must also submit to the elders. Indeed, all of you must gird yourselves with humility toward one another, for God opposeth the proud but giveth grace to the humble. Humble yourself, therefore, under the strong hand of God, so that when it is time, he will raise you. Cast all your anxiety upon him, for he careth for you.</td>
</tr>
<tr>
<td>All to be firm while being tested (8-11)</td>
<td>Be calm, keep awake. Your enemy, the devil, is going about like a roaring lion, seeking whom he can devour. Resist him, be steadfast in the faith, knowing that your brothers in other parts of the world are passing through the same sufferings. And the God of all grace who hath called you to his eternal glory in Christ, after you have suffered for a short time, will restore, establish, and strengthen you. The dominion is his forever and ever. Amen.</td>
</tr>
<tr>
<td>Personal notes (12-14)</td>
<td>Through the agency of Silvanus, our faithful brother (as I consider him), I have written these few lines in order to encourage you and to testify that this is what the true grace of God is. Stand fast in it. The church in Babylon, chosen by God like yourselves, salutes you, as does also my son, Mark. Salute one another with a kiss of love. Peace be to you all who are in Christ.</td>
</tr>
</table>

I. The Later Years of the Apostle Peter. Unfortunately, Luke's interest is transferred in the latter part of the book of Acts so

242

completely to Paul that we are left in almost complete ignorance regarding Peter's later activity. From Paul's letter to the Galatians it is evident that James, the brother of Jesus, with his zeal for the Jewish law, best interpreted the spirit of the Jerusalem Christians. Peter's inclination to extend to the Gentile Christians the hand of fellowship, as has been noted on one memorable occasion, was openly rebuked by James. This inclination probably explains (1) why Peter did not remain at the head of the Jerusalem church and (2) why he sought other missionary fields. Acts 9^{32}–11^{18} indicates that he first turned his attention to the cities along the Mediterranean seaboard. There is no evidence that he ever returned to make his permanent home at Jerusalem. He was not there on the occasion of Paul's final visit. Early tradition says that he became the head of the Antioch church. It is exceedingly probable that he made this the centre of his work in Syria. Paul's eagerness to push westward was perhaps in part due to his desire, or possibly his formal agreement, to leave this field to Peter and his associates. It is evident that Peter's reputation and authority steadily increased. In I Corinthians 1^{12} Paul refers to the Cephas or Peter faction in the church at distant Corinth. Paul's other later reference to Peter is incidental but suggestive. He claims, although he evidently did not avail himself of the right, "to travel with a Christian wife like the rest of the apostles, like the brothers of the Lord, like Cephas himself." It is indeed unfortunate that he did not tell us where Peter was wont to travel, but the statement does imply that, like Paul and most of the early Christian apostles, Peter himself had entered upon the work of an itinerant missionary. The complete absence of any reference to Peter in Paul's detailed letters written during his imprisonment indicates that, as late as 57 or 58, "the apostle to the circumcision" had not as yet transferred the field of his activities to Rome.

II. **Peter's Martyrdom.** There are indications, however, even in Acts that Peter became a missionary in later years to the Gentiles as well as to the Jews. Early and late Christian traditions are all agreed that he spent his last days in the Imperial City and there met his death at the hands of Nero. Clement of Rome, writing about 100, says: "Peter, who on account of unrighteous jealousy, endured not one or two, but many sufferings, and so, having borne his testimony, went to his deserved place of glory," is, like Paul, "a notable pattern of patient endurance." He adds: "To these men who lived lives of holiness was gathered a vast multitude of the elect, who by many indignities and tortures, being the victims of jealousy, set the finest examples among us." Eusebius, quoting from Dionysius, bishop of Corinth during the second half of the second century, states that Peter and Paul both taught in Italy and suffered martyrdom at the same time. He quotes also from a certain Caius, who lived during the last half of the second century: "I am able to show the trophies of the apostles; for if you will go to the Vatican or to the Ostian Way, you will find the trophies of those who laid the foundation of this church." In the light of this early and cumulative testimony, there can be little doubt that Peter went to Rome and there met his death. It seems certain, however, that these events were subsequent to the martyrdom of Paul in 57 or 58. Indeed, the needs of the Roman church may well have drawn him to the Imperial City soon after Paul's death. If Peter went to Rome in 58 and met his death during the persecutions of Nero in 64, he had ample time in which to reorganize the Roman church and to establish the basis of the traditions which have grown up about his work. Peter's irenical spirit was well calculated to conciliate the large Jewish element in the Roman church and to unite them with the ardent followers of Paul. Thus there is every reason to believe that at last the most impulsive, the most unstable, the most outspoken, and in many ways the most devoted of Jesus' disciples, by his earnestness and his eagerness to serve, not only received but merited the highest honors that the later church had to bestow; also that he was finally united with his Master through martyrdom, not at Jerusalem, the centre of Judaism, but at Rome, the new religious capital of Christendom.

III. **The Growth of the Western Church.** The momentum given to the spread of the Christian church by Peter and Paul and their associates increased rather than declined during the last half of the first century. Before 60 A.D. Christianity is said to have been preached throughout the inhabited world. For the most part the heroic activity which resulted in this marvellous growth is an unwritten chapter in human history. The biblical record does not carry us far beyond the death of Paul, and the extra-biblical Christian historians furnish few details regarding this important period. We know it chiefly through the results which were clearly apparent during the next century. Christianity, like a kindling flame, had swept along the northern shores of Africa from Egypt to Carthage. In all the important cities of Spain, of southern Gaul, of Asia Minor, as well as Greece and Italy, strong and growing Christian communities were established. In Rome Christianity had become such a prominent force that it commanded the attention of the Roman as well as the Christian historians. As Luke asserts in his apostolic history, Christianity in its earliest days had been fostered rather than persecuted by the Roman authorities. The first active persecution began under Nero in 64. It was apparently confined to Rome, or at least to Italy, and there is no evidence that it spread to the provinces. It tended, however, to bring the Christians into prominence. Doubtless to them was transferred much of the popular disfavor that had hitherto been reserved for the Jews. Tacitus in his *Annals* (15⁴⁴) has painted a gruesomely vivid picture of this persecution. He states that in order to overcome the persistent rumor that Rome had been set on fire by the command of Nero, the emperor "put in his own place as culprits and punished with most ingenious cruelty, men whom the common people hated for their shameful crimes and called Christians. Christ, from whom the name was derived, had been put to death in the reign of Tiberius by the procurator Pontius Pilate. The deadly superstition, having been checked for a while, began to break out again, not only throughout Judea, where this mischief first arose, but also at Rome, where from all sides all things scandalous and shameful meet and become fashionable. Therefore, at the beginning, some were seized who made confessions; then, on their information, a vast multitude was convicted, not so much of arson as of hatred of the human race. And they were not only put to death, but subjected to insults, in that they were either dressed up in the skins of wild beasts and perished by the cruel mangling of dogs or else put on crosses, to be set on fire, and, as day declined, to be burned, being used as lights by night. Nero had thrown open his gardens for that spectacle and gave a circus play, mingling with the people dressed with charioteer's costume or driving in a chariot. From this arose, however, toward men who were indeed criminals and deserving extreme penalties, sympathy, on the ground that they were destroyed not for the public good, but to satisfy the cruelty of an individual." Under the growing insistence of Rome that all her subjects prove their loyalty by joining in the common worship of the emperors, the lot of the faithful Christians became increasingly difficult. Under such emperors, however, as Vespasian and Titus, there was no open persecution.

IV. **The Persecution of the Christians by Domitian.** Domitian, who came to the throne in 81 A.D., was an autocrat by nature and relentlessly crushed anything which suggested opposition to his absolute authority. Certain members of the growing Christian sect soon became the object of his bitter persecution. Originally Christianity appears to have spread among the slaves and poorer classes of the empire, but in the reign of Domitian it mounted almost to the throne itself. According to the Roman historian Cassius Dio, in 95, the last year of Domitian's reign, he put to death his cousin Flavius Clemens and banished his wife, Flavia Domitilla, who was also related to the emperor. "The charge of atheism was made against both of them, in consequence of which many others also who had adopted the customs of the Jews were condemned. Some were put to death, others lost their property." One of the Christian catacombs to-day bears the name of Domitilla, and many members of her household lie buried there. Strikingly significant of the place which Christianity had already won in the empire is the fact that the two sons of Clemens and Domitilla had been adopted by Domitian and named as his successors. Had not their parents' heresy been discovered, a Christian emperor would probably have been crowned at Rome within less than seventy years after the death of Jesus. Domitian does not appear to have instituted a wholesale persecution of the Christians, but the beliefs of the individual Christians rendered it almost impossible for them to be loyal to their Master and to the rigorous demands of the emperor. The result was that active persecution broke out at many points throughout the empire. Its severity was dependent to a great extent upon the policy of the local Roman rulers. Pliny, the famous Roman writer, in his letter to the Emperor Trajan, written about 112 A.D., throws much light upon the earlier persecutions and especially upon the character of the Christians and their numbers and prominence even in the distant parts of the empire. Pliny had been appointed governor of the province of Bithynia in northwestern Asia Minor. His letter also reveals the policy of Rome under the lenient rule of Trajan. Pliny prefaces his letter with the statement: "It is my custom, my lord, to refer to you all questions about which I have doubts." Then he goes on to speak of the many Christians who had been brought before him, had confessed their beliefs, and had persisted in holding them, until he had been compelled to order them away to execution. He adds: "There were others of like insanity, but, because they were Roman citizens, I noted them down to be sent to Rome. Soon after this, as it often happens, because the matter had been brought to notice, the crime became wide-spread and many cases arose. . . . Others who had been named by an informer said that they were Christians and soon after denied it, saying, indeed, that they had been, but had ceased to be Christians, some three years ago, some many years, and one even twenty years ago. . . . They asserted, however, that the amount of their fault or error was this: that they had been accustomed to assemble on a fixed day before daylight and sing by turns a hymn to Christ as a god; and that they bound themselves with an oath, not for any crime, but rather not to commit a theft, or robbery, or adultery, not to break their word, and not to deny a deposit when demanded. After these things were done it was their custom to depart and meet together again to take food, but ordinary and harmless food; and they said that even this had ceased after my edict was issued, by which, according to your commands, I had forbidden the existence of clubs. On this account I believed it the more necessary to find out from two maid-servants, who were called deaconesses, and that by torture, what was the truth. I found nothing else than a perverse and excessive superstition. I therefore adjourned the examination and hastened to consult you. The matter seemed to me to be worthy of deliberation, especially on account of the number of those in danger. For many of every age, every rank, and even of both sexes, are brought into danger, and will be in the future. The contagion of that superstition has penetrated not only the cities but also the villages and country places." To this letter Trajan replied, commending Pliny's policy and stating that the Christians were not to be sought out but if they were accused and convicted, they were to be punished. He also commanded that every opportunity be given them for repentance and that anonymous accusations should not be admitted. These remarkable letters make vividly clear the painful condition in which the Christians found themselves throughout the Roman Empire from the days of Domitian and give the reader a definite conception of the background of the first epistle of Peter, of Hebrews, and of the book of Revelation, all of which are the outgrowth of a period of bitter and prolonged persecution.

V. **The Aim and Contents of I Peter.** It is a striking fact that I Peter, according to its superscription, was written to certain of the Christians of Bithynia, regarding which Pliny writes in his letter to Trajan. Like Paul's epistles to the Colossians and Laodiceans, I Peter was intended to be passed on from one Christian community to another. The provinces to which it is addressed lie in northwestern Asia Minor. The order in which they are mentioned probably represents the natural itinerary of the messenger who bore the epistle. If so, he would land first at Pontus on the southern side of the Black Sea and thence go southward through Galatia, turning westward toward Cappadocia and Asia, and thence northward through Bithynia, whence he could return by water or the direct highway overland to Rome. The opening paragraph, following the greeting, states the aim of the letter. It was to keep alive the hopes and to encourage the Christians in the presence of strong temptations and bitter persecutions. The general introduction, which ends with 2^{10}, is intended to set forth the beliefs which are the inspiration of the persecuted Christians. In 2^{11}–3^{12} the author aims to define their duties toward unbelievers and toward each other in their social relations. This is all summed up in $3^{8, 9}$. Chapters 3^{13}–4^{11} picture the blessings awaiting those who do right and patiently endure suffering for the sake of their faith. The thesis is presented in the opening verses ($3^{13, 14}$) and summed up in 4^{7-11}. The section 4^{12}–5^{11} contains an exhortation to be courageous in suffering and places special emphasis upon the obligations of the elders and the young men in the Christian communities. Again the opening verses ($^{12, 13}$) contain the thesis and the concluding verses (5^{8-11}) the summary. Brief personal notes are found in 5^{12-14}. The epistle is characterized by its complex yet classical Greek style, by its remarkably symmetrical structure, and by its broad, hopeful, courageous spirit. It was well calculated to calm and steady the terrified, wavering Christians, for whom it is written. From the allusions in the opening verses of chapter 4 it appears that those to whom the epistle or homily is addressed were converts from paganism who were familiar, through bitter personal experience, with the hideous vices which were prevalent throughout the Græco-Roman world.

VI. Authorship and Date of I Peter. The superscription, "Peter an apostle of Jesus Christ," appears to answer at once the question of authorship, but the epistle itself contains data which present one of the most difficult problems with which the New Testament reader is confronted. Certain indications point directly to Peter, the disciple, as the author. Many phrases and ideas, as, for example, the assertion, in 1^{17}, that God judges every one impartially is a reassertion of the apostle's word as reported in Acts 10^{34}. So, also, the privilege of sharing Christ's sufferings is emphasized both in I Peter $4^{13, 16}$ and in Acts 5^{41}. The beliefs set forth in this homily, and especially the expectations regarding the speedy reappearance of Jesus to judge all mankind, suggest the simple faith of the primitive Christian church. On the other hand, it is difficult to believe that Peter, the Galilean peasant, accustomed to the Aramaic tongue, could acquire the relatively finished Greek style which is found in this homily. As has also been shown in a detailed study (*cf.* Foster, *The Literary Relations of I Peter*), two hundred and eighteen passages in this short book are either directly dependent upon or closely related to three of Paul's epistles (Rom., Eph., and I Cor.). These references represent half of the book. As has been definitely demonstrated, I Peter is a literary mosaic. It quotes largely from the Greek version of the Old Testament. The author was also intimately acquainted with the Wisdom of Solomon (*cf.*, *e. g.*, 2^{25} and Wisd. 1^6 and 31^3, or 3^{20} and Wisd. $14^{5, 6}$) and with II Maccabees. There are also many points of contact with the Epistle to the Hebrews, and it seems probable that the dependence is on the side of I Peter. On the other hand, this homily is quoted by the author of James and also by Clement of Rome, who wrote about 100 A.D. Even more significant are the repeated allusions to the persistent persecutions to which the "exiles of the dispersion," that is, the Christians scattered throughout the Roman Empire, are subjected. The only historical situation which fully meets these conditions is furnished by the reign of Domitian, 81–96. They are in exact accord with those which Pliny found in Bithynia a decade or two later. While it would have been chronologically possible for Peter to have written this homily before his death, the persecutions of Nero, as reported by the Roman and Christian historians, do not present the background implied in I Peter. Pliny's reference to a Christian who declared that he had recanted twenty years before may well be a direct allusion to the persecution which our author contemplated. In the light of all the facts, therefore, it seems probable that I Peter was written between 90 and 95 A.D., although an earlier dating in the reign of Nero is not absolutely excluded.

In certain respects this homily presents a striking analogy to the first half of the book of Acts. In both books Paul is clearly the more original, pioneer spirit. His convictions and energy dominate the situation; but the authors of each of these writings reveal a strong desire to give to Peter a certain pre-eminence. In each writing the aim also is to reconcile the thought of these two great leaders in the apostolic church. In Acts the earlier differences were passed over in silence. In I Peter many of the ideas and striking phrases of Paul reappear under the name of the Galilean apostle. The explanation of this surprising phenomenon is perhaps to be found in the unusual phrase, "through Silvanus," which is found in the postscript to the epistle.

The identity of Silvanus is not certain. This postscript indicates that he was Peter's scribe. The preposition that is used, as well as the context, implies that he was more. If the epistle was dictated by the Galilean apostle the present Greek form of the epistle is probably the work of the amanuensis. Furthermore, if Silvanus or Silas is the one who accompanied Paul in his second missionary journey, the prominence of Pauline ideas and phrases is easily explained. The broad outlook of the epistle, the mention of "my son Mark" in the concluding verses, and, above all, of the church in Babylon, as the church which sends greetings, point to Rome as the place where this epistle was written. Tradition furnishes not the least evidence that Peter ever visited Babylon or that Christianity by the middle of the first century had penetrated the valley of the Tigris and Euphrates. As in later Christian literature, Babylon is beyond reasonable doubt a symbolic designation for corrupt Rome, even as "my son" is applied to Mark, not literally but symbolically. The conclusion which on the whole best satisfies these complex facts is that the central teachings in the epistle came originally from the lips of Peter, but that the letter in its present form is largely the work of Silvanus or Silas. Writing as he probably did at the beginning of the last decade of the first century, when the controversy between Jew and Gentile Christian, between Peter and Paul, was practically forgotten and when Paul's teachings had broadened and deepened the current of Christian thought, he unconsciously, if not deliberately, blended the teachings of the two great apostles and sent the epistle forth in the name of Peter as a practical message of hope and encouragement to the persecuted Christians in the distant provinces.

§ CLXVI. THE EARLY CHRISTIAN SERMON IN HEBREWS

God's supreme revelation through Christ (Heb. 1^{1-4})

God, who in ancient days spoke to our forefathers in many forms and fashions through the prophets, has at the end of these days spoken to us through a Son whom he appointed heir of all things, as it was through him that he created the universe. He, reflecting the brightness of God's glory and being the exact image of God's own character, upholds all things by his word of power. After he had secured our purification from sins, he sat down at the right hand of the majesty on high, having become as far superior to the angels as the name he has inherited is superior to theirs.

For to what angel did God ever say,

> Thou art my son,
> I have this day become thy Father?

Or again,

> I will be a father to him,
> And he will be my son.

He says to the Son,

> Thou didst found the earth at the beginning, O Lord,
> And the heavens are the work of thy hand.
> They will perish, but thou remainest,
> They will all grow old like a garment,
> And thou wilt roll them up like a mantle,
> And like a garment they shall be changed,
> But thou art the same,
> And thy years will never fail.

For it was fitting that God, for whom and by whom all things exist, after he had brought many sons to glory, should perfect by suffering, the Pioneer of their salvation, for both he who sanctifies and those who are sanctified all have one Father. It was necessary that he should resemble his brothers in every respect in order to prove a merciful and faithful high priest in all things divine, and in order to atone for the sins of the people. For, inasmuch as he has suffered by his temptations, he is able to help those who are tempted.

Signifi-
cance
of
Christ's
suffer-
ing
(2¹⁰, ¹¹,
¹⁷, ¹⁸)

Therefore, holy brothers, you who share a heavenly calling, fix your thoughts on Jesus, the apostle and high priest of our confession. He was faithful to those who appointed him, just as Moses also was faithful in all God's house. For Jesus has been counted worthy of greater glory than Moses, inasmuch as the founder of the house enjoys greater honor than the house itself. For every house is founded by some one, but God is the founder of all things. Moreover, Moses was faithful in all God's house as an attendant, in order to bear witness to the things which are to be revealed; but Christ was faithful as a Son over God's house, and we are that house, if we hold firm to the end the confidence and the pride in our hope.

Our sympathetic high priest (4¹⁴⁻¹⁶) Inasmuch, therefore, as we have a great high priest who has passed through the heavens, Jesus the Son of God, let us hold firmly our confession of faith. For we have not a high priest who is incapable of sympathizing with our weaknesses, but one who has been tempted in all ways like ourselves, yet without sinning. So let us approach the throne of grace with confidence, that we may receive mercy and find grace to help us in the hour of need.

The fellowship with God thus established (10¹⁹⁻²⁴) Therefore, brothers, since we have confidence to enter the holy Presence by virtue of the blood of Jesus, by the new and living way which he has opened up for us by rending the veil, that is, of his earthly nature, and since we have a great priest over the house of God, let us draw near with a true heart and full assurance of faith, having had our hearts sprinkled clean from an evil conscience and our bodies bathed in pure water. Let us hold the hope which we avow without wavering, for he is faithful who gave us the promise. Let us consider how we can stir up one another to love and to good deeds.

Encouragement from the past (32⁻³⁶) Recall the former days, when, after you were enlightened, you endured a hard struggle and much suffering. This was partly because you yourselves were being held up as objects of reproach and persecution and partly because you made a common cause with those who were thus treated; for you not only sympathized with the prisoners but you also accepted the confiscation of your own possessions cheerfully, knowing that you have for yourselves more valuable and lasting possessions. Therefore, do not cast aside your confident hope, for it carries with it great reward. For you stand in need of patient endurance, so that, after doing the will of God, you may receive what you have been promised.

Examples of the power of faith (11¹⁻³) Now faith is the assurance that we will receive that for which we hope, the conviction of the reality of those things which we do not see. It was for this that the men of olden time were attested. Through faith we understand that the world was fashioned by the word of God so that what is seen was made out of the invisible.

By faith Abel offered God a more acceptable sacrifice than Cain and thus was attested to be righteous. For God gave the attestation by accepting his gifts and through this faith, though dead, he still speaks. Abel (4)

By faith Enoch was taken to heaven, so that he did not die and could not be found, because God had taken him away. For before he was taken to heaven he was attested to be well pleasing to God; but without faith it is impossible to be well pleasing to him, for the man who draws near to God must believe that he doth exist and that he doth reward those who earnestly try to find him. Enoch (5, 6)

By faith Noah, after having been taught by God about things still unseen, reverently constructed an ark to save his household; thus he condemned the world and became heir of the righteousness that depends on faith. Noah (7)

By faith, Abraham obeyed, when he was called to go forth to a place which he would receive as an inheritance, and he went forth not knowing where he was to go. By faith he came and made his home in the promised land as in a foreign country, living in tents, as did Isaac and Jacob who were co-heirs with him of the same promise. For he was waiting for the city which has the foundations, whose builder and maker is God. By faith, when Abraham was tested he sacrificed Isaac and was ready to sacrifice his only son, although he had received the promise and had been told, It is through Isaac that your offspring shall be reckoned; yet he considered that God was able to raise men even from the dead. Abraham (8-10, 17-19)

By faith, Moses was hidden for three months after birth by his parents, because they saw that the child was beautiful and they did not fear the royal decree. By faith Moses when he had grown up refused to be called the son of Pharaoh's daughter, preferring to endure ill-treatment with God's people rather than to have the passing pleasures of sin, because he considered reproaches with the Messiah to be richer wealth than all the treasures of Egypt; for he was looking for the reward. By faith he left Egypt, not because he feared the king's wrath, for he held on his course as one who saw him who is invisible. By faith he instituted the passover that the destroying angel might not touch the first- Moses (23-29) born of the Israelites. By faith they crossed the Red Sea, as through dry land; but when the Egyptians made the attempt, they were drowned.

Rahab (31)

By faith, Rahab, the harlot, did not perish with those who were disobedient for she had welcomed the spies peaceably.

Other ancient heroes of the faith (32-34)

What more shall I say? For time would fail me to tell of Gideon and Barak and Samson and Jephthah, of David and Samuel and the prophets—they who by faith conquered kingdoms, administered justice, obtained promises, shut the mouths of lions, quenched the power of fire, escaped the edge of the sword, from weakness were made strong, proved valiant in war and put to flight foreign armies.

Later martyrs for their faith (35-40)

Women received back some as though raised from the dead; others were broken on the wheel, refusing release that they might secure a better resurrection. Others again were tested by scoffs and scourgings; yes, and by chains and imprisonment. They were stoned, they were sawn in two, they were tried by temptation, they were killed by the sword. They went about in sheepskins and goatskins, enduring want, oppressed, ill-treated (men of whom the world was not worthy), wanderers in the desert and among the hills, in caves and in holes in the ground. Through faith, these all were attested, but they did not obtain the promise. God had something better in store for us, so that apart from us they were not to attain full perfection.

Therefore be brave and stand (12¹⁻⁸)

Therefore, surrounded as we are by such a great crowd of witnesses, let us lay aside every handicap and the sin, which clings so closely to us, and let us run with patient endurance our appointed course, fixing our eyes on Jesus, the Pioneer and Perfecter of faith. He, for the sake of the joy which lay before him, patiently endured the cross, looking with contempt upon the shame, and is now seated at the right hand of the throne of God. Therefore consider him who steadily endures all that hostility from sinful men, so as to keep your own hearts from fainting and failing. In your struggle against sin you have not yet shed your blood. Have you forgotten the comforting message that reasons with you as with sons?

My son, do not think lightly of the Lord's discipline,
And do not faint when he correcteth you,

For whom the Lord loveth he disciplineth,
And scourgeth every son whom he receiveth.
Patiently endure for the sake of discipline,
God is dealing with you as with sons;
For where is the son whom his father does not discipline?
And if you are left without that discipline which all share,
Then you are not sons but bastards.

Moreover, we had our earthly fathers to discipline us, and we yielded to them! Shall we not much more patiently submit to the Father of our spirits, and so live? For while their discipline was only for a time and according to their judgment, he disciplines us for our profit that we may share in his holiness. All discipline seems for the present to be painful not joyous; but to those who are trained by it, it afterwards yields the fruit of peace and righteousness. Therefore, strengthen your drooping hands and weak knees and make straight the paths for your feet, so that what is lame may not be dislocated but rather be made whole. *Therefore submit to God's discipline (9-13)*

Persistently strive for peace with all men and for that consecration without which no man will ever see the Lord. Carefully guard lest anyone misses the grace of God, that no root of bitterness grow up to trouble you and through it many be defiled; also that there be no fornicator or ungodly person like Esau, who for a single meal parted with his birthright. For you know how, when later on he wanted to secure the blessing, he was set aside, for he found no opportunity to repent, though he sought it earnestly with tears. *Avoid moral backsliding (14-17)*

For you have not come to what you can touch, to flaming fire, to gloom and darkness and to storm and the blare of the trumpet, and the sound of words, such that those who heard it begged that no more should be added (for they could not bear the command, If a beast touches the mountain it must be stoned). So terrible was the sight that even Moses said, I am terrified and trembling. Rather you have come to Mount Sion, the city of the living God, the heavenly Jerusalem, to myriads of angels, to the festal *The contrast between the old and the new covenant (18-23)*

255

gathering, and to the assembly of the first-born whose names are recorded in heaven, to the spirits of righteous men made perfect, to Jesus who mediates the new covenant, and to the sprinkled blood which speaks a nobler message than Abel's.

Therefore be obedient to your divine Master (24-29)

See to it that you do not refuse to listen to him who is speaking to you, for if they who refuse to listen to their earthly instructors fail to escape, how much less shall we escape if we turn a deaf ear to him who speaketh from heaven. Then God's voice shook the earth, but now he promiseth, saying, Once again I will cause not only the earth but the heavens to quake. The phrase 'once again' denotes the removal of those things which can be shaken as created things, in order that those things only which cannot be shaken may remain. Therefore, let us render thanks that we are receiving a kingdom that cannot be shaken, and in this way let us worship God acceptably with godly reverence and awe, for our God is indeed a consuming fire.

Jesus, our spiritual and everlasting sacrifice (13 8-15)

· Jesus Christ is the same yesterday, to-day and forever. Do not let yourselves be drawn aside by all sorts of strange teachings, for it is well to have one's heart strengthened by God's grace and not by special kinds of food which have never been of any use to those who scrupulously attend to them. We have an altar from which the worshippers at the Jewish tabernacle have no right to eat. For the bodies of those animals whose blood is taken by the high priest into the holy place as a sin offering are burned outside the camp. And for this reason Jesus also suffered outside the gate in order to sanctify the people by his blood. Therefore, let us go to him outside the camp, sharing his reproach, for we have no lasting city here below, but we seek for the city to come. Through him, then, let us constantly offer to God our sacrifice of praise, namely, the fruit of lips which make confession in his name.

Benediction (20, 21)

Now may the God of peace, who brought up from the dead our Lord Jesus, who by the blood of the eternal covenant is the great Shepherd of the sheep, fully equip you with every good thing that you may do his will, creating in us, through Christ Jesus, what is acceptable in his sight. To him be the glory for ever and ever. Amen.

THE LITERARY FORM OF HEBREWS

I. **The Literary Form of the Epistle to the Hebrews.** In its literary form and thought the so-called "Epistle to the Hebrews" stands in solitary grandeur among New Testament writings. Its only kinsmen are the speeches of Peter, Stephen, and Paul reported in Acts. It was evidently written by a Greek Christian. Its involved, often redundant sentences reveal the student rather than the man trained in the active stream of life. Its traditional title and the personal notes in the last chapter give it the semblance of an epistle; but there can be little doubt that it was originally addressed by word of mouth to a definite assembly of Christians, for it has all the characteristics of a sermon. It is faultlessly constructed as an oration according to the canons of the Greek rhetoricians. The impressive introduction is found in 1^1–4^{13}. The formal argument, which develops the thought that Jesus is our great high priest who enables us to enter the divine presence with confidence, is presented in 4^{13}–10^{31}. The ideas are here prevailingly expressed in the first person. The short passage, 10^{32-39}, marks the sharp transition to the direct personal application. The pronoun "you" henceforth takes the place of "we." The examples of the men of faith who have endured sufferings are massed impressively and dramatically in chapter 11. The generalizations, the logical conclusions, and the practical exhortations follow in 12^{1-29} and 13^{8-15}. The elaborate benediction, which furnishes the appropriate conclusion to this noble sermon, is found in $13^{20, 21}$. The indications that the contents of this epistle were first presented to an audience within the physical as well as the mental vision of the preacher are many. In 5^{11}, for example, when he began to develop the intricate allegory of "the high priest with the rank of Melchizedek," some of his audience may well have yawned. With the intuitions of the true preacher he felt that their interests were suddenly relaxed, for he adds: "On this point I have a great deal to say which it is hard to make clear to you, for you have grown dull of hearing." Indeed, there is a trace of impatience in his words: "You still need someone to teach you once more the elementary principles of the divine revelation. You are in need of milk not of solid food!" But in the next paragraph he recovers his buoyant optimism and probably also the attention of his audience: "Let us go on then to what is mature, leaving elementary Christian doctrine behind." In 11^{32} he exclaims: "Time would fail me to tell of Gideon" and the other heroes of the faith. It is the preacher, not the writer, who feels the imperative limitations of time. The bonds of sympathy and interest between the speaker and his audience were evidently very close. He constantly addresses them as "beloved" or as "brothers." In 10^{32-34} he asks them to "recall the former days when, after you were enlightened, you endured a hard struggle and much suffering." He goes on to speak of the reproaches which they endured, of their sympathy for those who were in prison, and of the cheerfulness with which they bore the confiscation of their possessions. Here we listen to a pastor praising and exhorting members of the flock which he has led through much tribulation and which is again facing persecution. As several scholars have observed, the personal notes in $13^{1-7,\ 16-19,\ 22-24}$, destroy the otherwise close-knit unity of the book (cf. Torrey, *Journal of Bib. Lit.*, XXX, 137–156). The interest, the vocabulary, and the literary style are fundamentally different from those which characterize the rest of the sermon. It is exceedingly probable that the notes were later added to this address in order to give it the appearance of an epistle and to imply that it came from the great apostle to the Gentiles. The reference to brother Timothy and the salutation from the Italians support the inference without definitely stating that what preceded was written by Paul from Rome.

II. **The Authorship and History of Hebrews.** Notwithstanding the implication of the personal notes in chapter 13, the Pauline authorship of Hebrews was early questioned, even by the church at Rome. That he is not its author is now almost universally recognized. While Hebrews has many points of contact with Paul's epistles, its thought moves on an entirely different level. Its author was a theologian, a finished orator, and a master of the Greek idiom. He was acquainted with the writings of Philo and the Alexandrian type of thought. The early conflict between Jew and Gentile had completely disappeared from his horizon. All the institutions and events of Old Testament history were to him but prophetic types of heavenly and future realities. He adopted without question the apostolic teaching that the Christians were the seed of Abraham (2^{16}) and the true people of God (4^9). He quotes at length from the Greek version of the Old Testament, and his quotations are very exact, but he follows guilelessly the mistakes of the Greek translators. Like most of the apostles, he regards the Old Testament primarily as a collection of predictions regarding Jesus and the triumphant progress of Christianity. As has been truly said, the author is "a man of deep sincerity and great richness of soul." His interest in Christ, however, is more intellectual and not so personal as Paul's. For him Christ is the great high priest who has made it possible for his followers to attain forgiveness of their sins and direct access to God. And yet the author of Hebrews has an intensely practical rather than a merely theological interest. He was endeavoring to inspire and help his fellow Christians who were facing bitter persecution. In the latter part of the famous eleventh chapter he apparently has in mind the persecutions of Nero in 64, as well as the earlier attempt of Antiochus Epiphanes to wipe out Judaism. When he spoke, these events lay in the distant past. The persecutions which he immediately faced were probably those under Domitian. A date about 85 A.D. also satisfies in every respect the literary relationships of Hebrews. Its use by Clement of Rome about 100 fixes its origin in the first century. Alexandria at this time undoubtedly had a large Christian community and this strongly Græco-Roman city furnishes the most natural background for the original sermon contained in Hebrews. Either by chance or definite intention it was carried in time to Rome. Its high intellectual and spiritual values undoubtedly from the first gave it an accepted position in the rapidly growing collection of early Christian writings. When later in the second Christian century the New Testament canon was beginning to be definitely fixed, Hebrews lacked but one thing and that was the apostolic (Pauline) authority which, by implication, the personal notes in 13 supply. It is probable that by the middle of the second century Hebrews was current in its present form and had won its place side by side with the other New Testament epistles.

III. **The Aim of the Sermon in Hebrews.** Pliny's famous letter to Hadrian makes clear the peril which the author of Hebrews was seeking to avert. The Roman governor tells of many who were or had been Christians, who at his dictation prayed to the gods and made supplication with incense and wine to the emperor's statue, which Pliny had ordered to be brought into the court for this purpose. He also says: "In addition to this they cursed Christ, none of which things, it is said, those who are really Christians can be made to do." In $6^{11,\ 12}$ the author of Hebrews states his aim: "It is my earnest desire that each of you should show his zeal to realize your full hope to the very end, so that instead of being slack you may imitate those who inherit the promises by their unswerving faith." His purpose is to strengthen the faith of the Christians so that they will hold fast to it amidst the trying temptations and persecutions that impend. All of his thought and teaching are focused on this definite end. In this respect the epistle of I Peter and Hebrews are in close accord.

They are probably the outgrowth of the same great struggle. In preserving the faith of Christendom during this severe ordeal they each performed an inestimable service.

IV. The Theme and the Development of the Thought of Hebrews. The text from which the sermon in Hebrews was preached was apparently taken from Jeremiah 31[31]. It is quoted not at the beginning but in the heart of the sermon (8[10]):

> This is the covenant I will make with the house of Israel;
> I will set my laws within their mind,
> And I will inscribe them upon their hearts,
> I will be a God to them,
> And they shall be a people to me.

The author's thesis is that Christ, superior to all other agents sent by God to man, is the culmination of all preceding revelation and the one who has established the new and everlasting covenant between God and the individual. In 12[2] he describes Jesus as the Pioneer and Perfecter of our faith. The foundations of this sermon are the primitive Christian beliefs and the teachings of Paul. To these are added the distinctive contributions of the Alexandrian type of thought. While there are few traces of rabbinical influence, there are many points of contact with the noble homily in IV Maccabees which at about the same period was either preached as a sermon or sent out as a general epistle. Possibly both emanate from Alexandria. Both accept the belief in atonement for sin. This doctrine was in fact a fixed tenet of contemporary Judaism. In both of these homilies faith is conceived of, not in the Pauline sense of mystical fellowship with God, but as a belief in the providential rulership of the world (*cf.* IV Mac. 15[24], 16[22]). Both also illustrate their teachings by the example of the Old Testament heroes.

To a modern reader the first, the doctrinal part of the sermon in Hebrews, is the least convincing. The picture of the exalted Christ in the opening paragraphs undoubtedly represents the beliefs of a majority of the Christian church at the close of the first century. Already the roots of this doctrine have been traced through Paul and the early apostles back to the Jewish apocalypses. The author of Hebrews has evidently arrived at the same beliefs by a different way. Following the Alexandrian teachers and especially Philo, who interpreted the entire Old Testament allegorically, he drew chiefly from the Psalms the proofs of Jesus' divine nature. The present age is particularly impatient with the use of proof texts, especially when they are torn from their context and given an interpretation entirely foreign to that in the mind of the original writer. Thus, for example, in 1¹⁰⁻¹² he quotes from Psalm 102²⁵⁻²⁷, which was clearly addressed to Jehovah, for the original psalm begins in ¹²:

> Thou, Jehovah, art enthroned forever,
> And thy fame is to all generations.

As uniformly in the Greek text (which the author of Hebrews followed) "Jehovah" was translated "Lord." This fact alone explains his interpretation of the psalm as a description of Christ's character and creative work. The passage is significant because it throws clear light on one of the ways in which the creed of the later church developed. It also explains why there is such a vast difference between the simple, vivid picture of Jesus in the Synoptic Gospels and the elaborate Christology of these later writers. Throughout the opening chapters of Hebrews the logic is largely that of the Alexandrian allegorical school, which was inclined to find a symbolic meaning in every Old Testament phrase and figure. Even though the author of Hebrews feared that his audience might fall asleep in the process, he developed at length his allegory regarding Melchizedek, the king of Salem, finding in the meaning of each of these titles symbolic suggestions of the character and work of the future Messiah. To his hearers, however, this allegorical method of interpretation was undoubtedly as convincing as that of the modern biblical interpreter is to the present generation. In estimating the permanent value of Hebrews, it is important to remember that the author's aim was not doctrinal but practical. In describing the character and work of Jesus he used the terms and figures which were most intelligible and impressive to his hearers. The conclusion of his doctrinal introduction is found in 10¹⁹⁻³¹. Its great central teaching is in perfect harmony with the teaching of Paul and the gospel narratives, and is as true as it is significant: Jesus by his work has rendered unnecessary all the complicated rites which were associated with the ancient covenant and has made it possible for each individual to enter into personal, intimate fellowship with God himself. The thought in the remainder of the sermon moves on a high intellectual and spiritual plane. The author's noble array of the heroes of the faith has been the inspiration of millions of tried and tempted souls through the ages. With the true instincts of the preacher he has included women as well as men in this list. Even Rahab, the harlot, rises to bear testimony to the power of faith to transform a wasted, impure life. Faith, as thus concretely defined, is not only intellectual belief but trust and loyalty expressed in life and acts. Thus it is that our author supplements Paul's mystical, though more spiritual conception of faith, and imparts to it a practical, kinetic quality.

V. The Charm and Power of Hebrews. Undoubtedly the sermon in Hebrews brought conviction and inspiration to the persecuted Christians who first heard it. It has also contributed much to the beliefs of the Christian church. It is to-day one of the ten or twelve great books of the New Testament. Its charm lies not merely in its majestic rolling sentences. Its power is certainly not dependent upon its logic. Unlike many of Paul's epistles, its appeal is not primarily to the emotions. Its charm and power lie rather in its dauntless, courageous spirit and in the marvellously effective way in which the author has rallied the forces which engender faith and steadfast endurance in the presence of temptation and trial. It is interesting to analyze these forces. The first is Christ's triumphant exaltation and his superiority to angels and men. The second is his sympathy with our trials and temptations, for he himself has shared them. The third is his supreme achievement in having made access to and fellowship with God possible and easy for every individual, however burdened with sins. The fourth is that he has swept away the cumbersome forms of the old covenant and established a new and simpler relation between God and man. The fifth is that the Christian, if he proves faithless, will forfeit thereby all hope for the future. The sixth is that past experience has shown that Christ's followers have the power to endure even the most terrible trials and persecutions. The seventh is the inspiring example of the long list of heroes who, through faith, have achieved. The eighth is the supreme example of Jesus himself. Thus the ultimate charm and power of Hebrews lie not in its theology nor its rhetoric but in its ability to inspire heroic, self-sacrificing faith in God and undying loyalty to the principles of Jesus.

§ CLXVII. THE VISIONS OF THE ULTIMATE VICTORY OF CHRISTIANITY IN THE BOOK OF REVELATION

The purpose of this revelation (Rev. 1⁻³)

A revelation by Jesus Christ, which God granted him that he might make known to his servants what must quickly come to pass. He disclosed it by sending it through his angel, to his servant John, who bore witness as to what is the Word of God and the testimony of Jesus Christ, even to what he saw. Blessed is he who reads and blessed are they who hear the words of this prophecy and lay to heart the things which are written in it, for the time is near.

John to the seven churches in the province of Asia. May grace be granted to you and peace from him who is and was and is forevermore, and from the seven spirits before his throne and from Jesus Christ who is the faithful witness, the first-born from the dead and the ruler of the kings of the earth. *Greeting (4, 5a)*

To him who loves us and who has freed us from our sins by his own blood and made us a Kingdom, to be priests to his God and Father, to him be glory and power for ever and ever. Amen. Lo, he is coming on the clouds and every eye will see him, even those who pierced him, and the tribes of earth will mourn over him. Even so. Amen. I am the Alpha and the Omega, saith the Lord God, he who is and was and is forevermore the Almighty. *Ascription of praise to Christ (5b-8)*

On the Lord's day I was in the Spirit, and I heard a loud voice behind me like a trumpet calling, Write what you see in a book and send it to the seven churches. *The command to write (10, 11a)*

To the angel at the church at Ephesus write: I know your deeds, your toil and your patient endurance. 'And I know that you cannot tolerate wicked men and that you have tested those who called themselves apostles but are not and have found them to be liars. And I know that you are enduring patiently and have borne up for my sake and have not grown weary. Yet I have this against you: you have given up your first love. Let anyone who has ears listen to what the Spirit says to the churches: To him who overcomes I will grant to eat from the tree of life which is in the paradise of God.' *The letter to the Ephesians (2¹ᵃ⁻⁵ᵃ, 7)*

To the angel of the church at Smyrna write: These are the words of the First and Last, he who is dead and has returned to life: 'I know your distress and poverty (but you are rich!). I know how you are being slandered by those who call themselves Jews and are not, but are a mere synagogue of Satan. Do not fear what you are about to suffer. The devil, indeed is going to throw some of you into prison, that you may be tested, and for ten days you will *To the church at Smyrna (8-11)* have to endure distress. Be faithful even to death and I will give you the crown of life. Let anyone who has ears listen to what the Spirit says to the churches: He who overcomes shall not be injured by the second death.'

To the church at Per-gamum (12, 13)

To the angel of the church at Pergamum write: These are the words of him who has the sharp, two-edged sword: 'I know where you dwell. Satan's throne is there; and yet you are loyal to my name and have not renounced your faith in me, even in the days of Antipas, my witness and faithful servant, who was put to death among you in the place where Satan dwells.'

To the church at Thy-atira (18, 19 26)

To the angel of the church at Thyatira write: These are the words of the Son of God who has eyes like a flame of fire and whose feet are like burnished brass: 'I know your deeds, your love, your faith, your service, and your patient endurance. I know that of late you are doing more than you did at first. Only hold fast to what you have until I come.'

To the church at Sardis (3¹⁻⁴)

To the angel of the church at Sardis write: These are the words of him who holds the seven spirits of God and the seven stars: 'I know your deeds; you have the name of being alive but are dead. Be watchful, rally what is still left, though it is about to perish; for I have found none of your deeds complete in the eyes of God. Now, re-member, those teachings which you have received and heard, hold to them and repent. If you will not be watch-ful, I will come like a thief and you will not know at what hour I will come upon you. Still you have a few names in Sardis of those who have not soiled their garments. They will walk beside me in white, for they are worthy.'

To the church at Phil-adel-phia (7, 8, 10)

To the angel of the church at Philadelphia write: These are the words of the faithful and Holy One who has the key of David, who opens and none shall shut and shuts and none shall open: 'I know your deeds. See, I have set an open door before you which no one is able to shut, for though you have little strength, you have kept my word, you have not renounced my name. Because you have kept my word through your patient endurance, I will keep you safe from the hour of trial which is coming upon the whole world to test the dwellers on earth.'

LETTER TO THE CHURCH AT LAODICEA

To the angel of the church at Laodicea write: These are the words of the Amen, the faithful and true witness, the beginning of God's creation: ' I know your deeds; you are neither cold nor hot—would that you were either cold or hot! So because you are luke-warm, neither hot nor cold, I am going to spit you out of my mouth. I reprove and discipline those whom I love; therefore be in earnest and repent. Lo, I stand at the door and knock. If anyone listens to my voice and opens the door, I will come in to him and sup with him and he with me. To him who overcomes I will grant to sit beside me on my throne, as I myself have overcome and sat down with my Father on his throne. Let anyone who has ears listen to what the Spirit says to the churches.' To the church at Laodicea (14-16, 19-22)

After this I looked, and there was a door standing open in heaven. And the first voice which I had heard talking with me like a trumpet said, Come up here, and I will show you what must come to pass after these things. Immediately I found myself in the Spirit, and lo, a throne stood in heaven and One sitting on the throne who resembled in appearance jasper and sardius. And around the throne there was a rainbow, resembling emeralds in appearance, and also around the throne were twenty-four other thrones and on these thrones were seated twenty-four elders, clad in white robes with golden crowns upon their heads. From the throne there come flashes of lightning and peals of thunder, while in front of the throne seven blazing torches are burning, which are the seven spirits of God. And in front of the throne there appears to be a sea of glass, resembling crystal, and on each side of the throne all around it are four living creatures, full of eyes before and behind. And day and night they never cease saying, The vision of God seated on his heavenly throne (4 1-6, 8b)

Holy, holy, holy, is the Lord God Almighty,
Who was and is and ever more shall be.

Then in the midst of the throne and before the living creatures I saw a Lamb standing among the elders. And I looked and heard the voice of many angels round the throne and the living creatures and the elders, numbering The power and glory of the Lamb (5 6a, 11-14) myriads of myriads and thousands of thousands, crying aloud, Worthy is the Lamb that has been slain to receive power and wealth and wisdom and might and honor and glory and blessing. And I heard every creature in heaven and on earth and under the earth and on the sea and all things that are in them, crying, To him who is seated on the throne and to the Lamb be blessing and honor and glory and dominion for ever and ever. And the four living creatures said, Amen. And the elders fell down and worshipped.

The gratitude and blessedness of the triumphant saints (7⁹, ¹⁰, ¹³, ¹⁴, ¹⁷) After that I looked, and there was a vast host which no one could count, from every nation and tribe and people and tongue, standing before the throne and before the Lamb, clad in white robes, with palm branches in their hands. And they cried aloud, saying, It is to our God who is seated on the throne and to the Lamb that we owe our salvation! Then one of the elders addressed me, saying, Who are these clad in white robes, whence have they come? I said to him, You know, my Lord. So he told me, These are the people who have come out of the great distress and washed their robes and made them white in the blood of the Lamb. For this reason they are now before the throne of God and serve him day and night within his temple.

> He who is sitting on the throne will shelter them in his tent;
> Never again will they be hungry or thirsty,
> Never again will the sun or any scorching heat smite them;
> For the Lamb in the midst of the throne will be their shepherd,
> And will guide them to fountains of living water;
> And God will wipe away every tear from their eyes.

The fate of Babylon and of those who worshipped the beast (14⁶⁻¹²) Then I saw another angel flying in mid-heaven, with an eternal gospel to proclaim to the inhabitants of the earth, to every nation, tribe, language and people. He cried aloud, Fear God, give him glory, for the hour of his judgment is come. Worship him who made heaven and earth, the sea and the fountains of water. And another, a second

266

angel followed, crying, Fallen, fallen is Babylon, the great. She who made all nations drink the wine of wrath provoked by her vice! And then another, a third angel followed these, crying aloud, Whoever worships the Beast and his image or receives a mark on his forehead or on his hand shall drink the wine of God's wrath which stands ready unmixed in the cup of his fury and shall be tortured with fire and brimstone before the holy angels and the Lamb. And the smoke of their torture goes up for ever and ever, and they get no rest from it day and night—the worshippers of the Beast and his statue and all who receive the mark of his name. This is what reveals the patient endurance of the saints who keep God's commands and the faith of Jesus!

Then I heard a voice from heaven saying, Write this: Blessed are the dead who die in the Lord from henceforth! Even so, says the Spirit; let them rest from their labors; for what they have done goes with them. *The reward of the faithful (13)*

Then I saw heaven open wide and there was a white horse. Its rider was named Faithful and True, and he righteously judges and makes war. His eyes are a flame of fire and on his head are many diadems. He has a name inscribed upon him, known to no one but himself. He is clad in a robe dipped in blood, and his name is the Word of God. The armies of heaven follow him on white horses, clothed in fine linen, white and spotless. From his mouth proceeds a sharp sword wherewith to smite the nations, and he will shepherd them with a rod of iron and tread the wine-press with the fierce anger of God Almighty. On his robe and on his thigh his name is written: *The Redeemer King (19¹¹⁻¹⁶)*

KING OF KINGS AND LORD OF LORDS

And I saw the Beast and the kings of earth and their armies assembled to make war on him who was seated on a horse and against his army. But the Beast was seized, together with the false prophet who had done signs before him by means of which he seduced those who received the mark of the Beast and worshipped his statue. Both of them were cast alive into the lake of fire that burns with brimstone, and the rest were killed by the sword which *The destruction of his human enemies (19-21a)* came forth from the mouth of him who was seated on the horse.

Final resurrection and judgment (20¹¹⁻¹⁵) Then I saw a great white throne and One was seated on it from whose presence earth and sky fled away and no place was found for them; and I saw the dead, great and small, standing before the throne. And the books were open—also another book, the book of life, was open. And the dead were judged by what was written in these books according to their deeds. And the sea also gave up its corpses and Death and Hades gave up their dead; and all were judged according to their deeds. Then Death and Hades were cast into the lake of fire (this is the second death—the lake of fire). And everyone who was not found enrolled in the book of life was cast into the lake of fire.

God's coming down to dwell among men (21¹⁻⁵) Then I saw a new heaven and a new earth, for the first heaven and the first earth had passed away and the sea is no more. And I saw the Holy City, the New Jerusalem, coming down from God out of heaven, all ready like a bride arrayed for her husband, and I heard a loud voice out of the throne saying,

> Behold God's dwelling place is with men,
> And he will dwell among them,
> And they shall be his people.
> Yea, God himself will be among them,
> And he will wipe away every tear from their eyes,
> And death shall be no more;
> No sorrow nor wailing nor pain,
> For the first things have passed away.
> And he who was seated on the throne said,
> Behold, I am making all things new!
> And he added, Write this:
> These words are faithful and true.

The divine presence within the city (22⁻²⁷)
> I saw no temple in the city,
> For its temple is the Lord Almighty and the Lamb.
> The city has no need of the sun,
> Nor of the moon to give it light,
> For the glory of God illumines it,
> And the lamp thereof is the Lamb.

268

THE DIVINE PRESENCE

By its light will the nations walk,
And into it will the kings of earth bring their glory.
Its gates will never be shut by day,
For there will be no night there.
They will bring into it the glory and honor of nations,
But nothing unclean shall ever enter it,
Nor any one who practises abomination or falsehood,
Only those whose names are written in the Lamb's
    book of life.

Then he showed me the river of the water of life, bright The
river
and
tree of
life
(22¹,²) as crystal, flowing through the streets of the city from the throne of God and of the Lamb. On both sides of the river grew the tree of life, bearing twelve kinds of fruit, each month yielding its own fruit. And the leaves of the tree serve to heal the nations.

None who was accursed will remain there; The
glories
of the
new
city
(3-5)
But the throne of God and of the Lamb will be in it,
And his servants will render him holy service,
And they will look upon his face,
And his name will be on their foreheads.
And there will be no more night there,
And they will have no need of the light of lamp or sun,
For the Lord God will illumine them;
And they will reign for ever and ever.

Then he said to me, do not seal up the word of the Its
speedy
coming
(10-15) prophecy of this book, for the time is near.

Let the wicked still be wicked,
Let the filthy still be filthy,
Let the righteous still do right,
Let the holy still be holy.
Behold I am coming quickly,
And my reward is with me,
To reward each one for what he has done.
I am the Alpha and the Omega,
The First and the Last,
The Beginning and the End.
Blessed are those who wash their robes,

269

That theirs may be the right to the tree of life,
That they may go through the gates into the city.
Without are the dogs and the sorcerers,
The fornicators, the murderers, and the idolaters,
And everyone who loves and practises falsehood.

The world-wide invitation (16, 17)

I, Jesus, have sent my angel to testify these things to you for the churches.

I am the Root and the Offspring of David,
The bright, the morning Star.
The Spirit and the Bride say, Come,
And he who hears, let him say, Come;
And let the thirsty come,
Whoever will, let him take the water of life freely.

I. **The Aim of the Book of Revelation.** Through the ages the book of Revelation has been the stumbling-block of the realist and the delight of the mystic. Hundreds of volumes have been written interpreting its symbolism. Its magic phrases have been interwoven in Christian hymns and the devotional life of the church; but for the majority of men and women to-day it is a sealed book—sealed so tightly that they pass it by with calm unconcern. It represents the opposite pole of thought from that of the present historical, scientific age. Its literary antecedents are the apocalypses of Ezekiel, Zechariah, and the closing chapters of Daniel. Its author was a poet and a dreamer; but, like the authors of I Peter and Hebrews, his aim was intensely practical. The hopes, which he clothes in his highly symbolic visions, were the common property of the primitive church. Paul frequently alluded to them. In the second chapter of II Thessalonians he presents these hopes in detail. The authors of I Peter and Hebrews were constantly reminding their readers that "the end of all is near." These apocalyptic hopes, as have been noted, were a part of their Jewish inheritance. But the attitude of the Græco-Roman world was also that of expectancy. The greater the prevailing vice and suffering, the more ardently Jew and Gentile hoped and believed that a great world upheaval was near. In his preface the author of Revelation states that his purpose was to "show what must soon come to pass." But his aim was not merely to satisfy the curiosity of his fellow Christians; it was to prevent their accepting the false teachings and teachers to which he refers in his opening exhortations

to the seven churches. It was to keep the tempted Christians throughout the world from bowing down to the Beast which represented
Rome and the emperor-worship. It was to hold up so vividly before
them the rewards of future blessedness awaiting the faithful that they
would resist persecution even to death. This strange book is saturated
with the spirit and the ideals that actuated the early Christian martyrs.
It dramatizes the mighty conflict between Christianity and heathen-
dom. Its appeal is not primarily to the reason but to the emotions.
It was well calculated to stir the enthusiasms, to call forth deeds of
heroic self-sacrifice, and to buoy up the martyr at the stake. The
author, like all the other apocalyptic writers, was also inspired by an
ethical aim. In the bitter conflict between Christianity and heathen-
dom the righteousness of the divine Ruler of the universe was at the
stake. Our author, like the immortal poet who has given us the book
of Job, asserts his invincible conviction that God is just and good
and that he will in the end vindicate, not only his righteous servants,
but his own eternal justice.

II. **The Theme and Literary Character of the Book of Revelation.** In this book we have a stupendous world drama set forth in
the form of an epistle. Under the influence of Paul's brilliant example,
later Christian authors and editors evidently felt that this was the
only acceptable way in which to gain authority and general acceptance for their teachings. The personal notes in the introduction (1-3)
and in the epilogue (22^{18-21}) are loosely connected with the rest of the
book. After 1-3 the geographical background of the book is not
Asia Minor but Palestine. These introductory and concluding notes
were apparently added to give to the book the semblance of an epistle.
Its theme is Christianity's long and painful struggle with paganism
and the organized forces of evil and its ultimate triumph. Revelation
also objectifies and dramatizes the great truth that the supreme power
at work in the regeneration of human society is the spirit and work of
the Christ and the heroic self-sacrifice which he exemplifies and in
turn inspires. Such a dramatic foreshortening of history possesses a
unique value, for it enables us to see the great historic movements in
their genetic relations and in their real significance. The book of
Revelation is, therefore, a fitting conclusion to the Bible, which begins with a description of the creation of the universe and a setting forth
of the divine purpose, for it gives a glorious picture of the ultimate
realization of that purpose. The book is a composite of dissolving
visions, all blended together like the different motifs in a grand ora-

torio. Bold figures and strange symbols, with which we have become partially familiar in the Old Testament prophecies and in contemporary Jewish literature, confront us at every point. The picture of a woman arrayed with the sun, with the moon under her feet, and on her head a crown of twelve stars, seems but the dream of a mere visionary unless we are acquainted with the literary and intellectual atmosphere which produced it. A leading characteristic of the apocalyptic literature is that historic forces and movements are represented largely by symbols drawn from the animal or natural world. Not only is the imagery exceedingly dramatic, but the action is rapid and on a broad scale. The whole is distinctly impressionistic. It is impossible to visualize many of these pictures notwithstanding their seeming concreteness. If we could see in our mental vision an objective city of gold with walls of jasper and twelve huge gates, each made of a single pearl, and yet the whole transparent like glass, we would fail completely to appreciate the author's purpose. The language is that of mysticism and it speaks almost wholly to the feelings. As the late Professor James has said, in commenting upon these visions: "They stir chords within us which music and language touch in common."

III. The Authorship and Date of the Book of Revelation. Another marked characteristic of the apocalyptic writings is that they were all (except the *Shepherd of Hermas*) published anonymously or rather under the pseudonym of some earlier saint who was supposed to have possessed the power of predicting the future. Thus the score or more of extant Jewish apocalypses are all later than 200 B.C., but bear the names of Enoch, Noah, Daniel, Baruch, and Ezra, who lived long before. From Christian sources comes the Apocalypse of Peter, of which a fragment has recently been discovered. Although at one period it nearly gained a place in the New Testament canon, it is now universally recognized as pseudonymous. It is probable that the book of Revelation is no exception to this otherwise universal rule. The account in Mark 11[37, 38] of a request of the disciples James and John that they be allowed to sit one on Jesus' right hand and the other on his left in his glory, reveals an apocalyptic interest which would naturally lead a later Christian writer to single out these two disciples as the most natural medium for revelations regarding the future. The early death of the apostle James was a well-known fact of primitive Christian history. The martyrdom of his brother John, though clearly implied by the early traditions, was not so firmly established. Hence he who was Jesus' favorite disciple would most naturally be selected from the Twelve as the one to whom to ascribe later visions. That he is the author of the book of Revelation is not clearly stated but strongly implied in its opening chapters. The possibility, of course, remains that it was the work of another John. John, the presbyter of Ephesus, is held by many scholars to be its author. It is probable that the book was written in Ephesus, but the internal evidence is decisive that it is not from the same author that wrote the Fourth Gospel. The language and idioms of the two books are fundamentally different. Revelation is an Hebraic writing transcribed rather than translated into popular, Hellenistic Greek. As Dionysius, bishop of Alexandria in the middle of the third century, says, after describing the distinctive characteristics of the Gospel of John: "Utterly diverse and strange is the apocalypse in comparison with all this, hardly touching or even approximating to any of these things, having no common relation to them." The God of Revelation is not the loving Father of the Fourth Gospel but a majestic King sitting in solemn state to receive the homage of his human subjects. Very different also is the portrait of Jesus. In the book of Revelation the note of love is almost lacking. It reverses the words of Jesus in John 15[15]: "I call you servants no longer. . . . I call you friends." The indications that the book was written near the close of the first Christian century are cumulative. It probably contains fragments of an earlier Christian apocalypse coming from the reign of Nero, but it also reflects the popular belief, current in the latter part of the century, that Nero, the arch persecutor of the Christians, had again come back to life and was instigating a new and more horrible persecution (17[8]). The dark and ominous horizon revealed in this book has all the characteristics of the latter part of the reign of Domitian. Then not only the Christians of Rome but all throughout the empire were exposed to constant temptation and many to active persecution. The Beast and his statue, which had many worshippers (*cf.* 14[11]), are apparently but veiled allusions to Domitian and to his vigorous campaign against all Christians who refused publicly to acknowledge his divine authority. The book of Revelation, therefore, may with reasonable confidence be attributed to an otherwise unknown Christian prophet who wrote about 95 B.C., and like the writers of the Gospel and epistles of John belonged to the Johannine school, who were strongly influenced by John, the presbyter of Ephesus.

IV. **The Contents and Sources of Revelation.** The general divisions of the book of Revelation are obvious. Chapters 1–3 contain letters to seven important churches in the province of Asia. In 4^1–11^{13} are found preliminary visions of coming judgment. Chapters 11^{14}–20^{15} describe in vivid apocalyptic form the overthrow of Rome and of Satan. The culmination of the book is a description, in 21, 22, of the new and heavenly reign which is to be instituted on earth when the preliminary work of destruction has been completed. Into the body of the book have been woven many older apocalypses and apocalyptic themes, but they all lead up to one grand, final crescendo. Thus, for example, the vision in 4 of Jehovah seated high on his throne, guarded by four beasts, each with six wings, who cry, "Holy, holy, holy, Lord God Almighty," is an expansion of Isaiah's magnificent vision (recorded in Isaiah 6). The Old Testament student also recognizes in the succeeding visions the four living beings of Ezekiel 1, the four horns of Zechariah 1; in 14, vivid descriptions of the day of judgment drawn from Zephaniah and Joel. The glowing picture of the New Jerusalem is suggested by Isaiah 49–54. The figures and symbols of Daniel 7–12 also reappear at many points. In Revelation 11–13 and 18 there are traces of older Jewish apocalypses, which have been only slightly revised and adjusted to their new Christian setting. Thus, for example, the command in $11^{1, 2}$ "to rise up and measure the temple of God and the altar" strongly implies that this was first written before the destruction of the Jewish temple in 70 A.D. Furthermore, in the symbolism there are unmistakable traces of older Babylonian and Persian myths. The sun and moon and the five planets are probably to be identified with the seven astral deities of the Babylonian pantheon. Corresponding to these are the seven spirits in 1^4 and the seven angels in 8^2. The huge red dragon, with its seven heads and seven horns and seven diadems upon its heads, which "with his tail swept away a third of the stars of heaven and flung them to the earth," probably represents the later Jewish version of the old Babylonian story of Tiamat, personified chaos, that contended against the gods. In Revelation 12, "that old serpent is called the Devil and Satan, the seducer of the whole earth." He is overthrown by the angels of heaven, led by Michael, who in the book of Daniel figures as Israel's patron angel.

V. **The Interpretation of the Book of Revelation.** Interpreters of Revelation are divided into two distinct groups. The first includes those who disregard the fact that a fundamental characteristic of the apocalyptic type of literature is the presentation of past and present history as though it were still future. Therefore, they regard the visions as predictions yet to be fulfilled and interpret them liter-alistically. The second group interpret the visions in the light of the conditions that obtained during the first Christian century and seek to find the underlying principles which they illustrate. The first group rarely agree in their detailed interpretations, for they ignore the historical background and are guided almost wholly by ingenious con-jecture. Their followers are usually of the mystical, enigmatical type of mind that scorns scientific methods of research. The second group follow the only method that promises to give a true understanding of the thought and purpose of the original writer. The selection of seven churches is probably because seven is a part of the prevailing sym-bolism of the book. The churches mentioned first are situated in the three leading cities along the eastern Ægean. The order is from south to north: Ephesus, Smyrna, and Pergamum; then from north to south, including representative inland towns. Each of these churches had on the whole proved faithful. The allusion to "Satan's throne" is probably due to the fact that Pergamum was the old capital of the province of Asia and was therefore the traditional centre of the emperor-worship. Since 29 B.C. it had also had a flourishing temple dedicated to Augustus or Rome.

Chapters 4–6 contain the impressive introduction to the great world drama. In 5 the Almighty is pictured, seated on his throne, attended by angels and worshipped by the representatives of the church. In 5 the figure of the "Lion of the tribe of Judah and the Scion of David" looms up impressively. He proves to be none other than "the Lamb that seemed to have been slain." This unique description of the Messiah is evidently taken from Isaiah 53[7] ("as a lamb that is led to the slaughter"). In 6 the agents of death appear. In these opening chapters the poet brings out with great dramatic effectiveness the tremendous contrast between the bitter conflict that was then raging and that was destined to rage between the church and the empire, and the peace and majesty in heaven above. Chapter 7, which represents a digression from the main theme, introduces another element of con-trast, for it gives an anticipatory vision of the countless hosts of the servants of God. It is evidently introduced to give the reader an assurance of the ultimate outcome of the great conflict.

The recurrence of the number seven gives a certain literary unity to the book. Not only are there seven letters to seven churches from the seven spirits before the divine throne, but the scroll which con-tains the record apparently of the sins of mankind is sealed by seven seals. At the breaking of each of these seals a new judgment is visited upon the earth. The breaking of the seventh seal (8^{1-5}) is the prelude to the blowing of seven trumpets that announce the world judgment. Each blast introduces one of the natural portents, which were associated in apocalyptic thought with the end of the world. The blowing of the sixth trumpet marked the destruction of Jerusalem (11^{1-14}). With the blowing of the seventh trumpet, the scene is transferred temporarily from earth to heaven. This last blast inaugurates the titanic struggle between the hosts of good and evil. Here the author weaves in many of the figures of the old mythology and it is difficult to be absolutely sure of his meaning at every point. Chapter 12 is the most difficult in the book. The people of promise, of whom the Christians are the lineal heirs, is apparently represented by the woman clad in the sun with the moon under her feet. The male child to whom she gives birth, who is to "shepherd all the nations with an iron flail and who was caught up to God and to his throne," is clearly the Messiah or Lamb whose victorious rôle is later described. The first of the two Beasts, which emerge in 13, represents Rome and the emperor-worship; the second Beast her zealous provincial priesthood that had "every one put to death who would not worship the statue of the Beast and obliges all men low and high, rich and poor, freemen and slaves alike, to have a mark put upon their right hand or forehead so that no one can buy or sell unless he bears the mark, that is the name of the Beast." The cipher 666 is the total of the numerical values represented by the Hebrew letters of the name Cæsar Neron (k = 100, s = 60, r = 200, n = 50, r = 200, w = 6, and n = 50; making 666). This identification is confirmed by the fact that in the old Latin version, where Nero is written without the final n (which equals 50), the number is 616, representing again the exact total of the Hebrew letters. Chapter 14^{1-5} is another of those marvellous digressions which stir the imagination and hope of the reader and anticipate the final victory recorded in 21 and 22. In 14^{6-20} the theme of judgment is again taken up, and in 14^{-20} the final judgment recorded in the succeeding chapters is anticipated. In 15^1-16^1 the scene is transferred again to earth. The seven angels with seven bowls represent the seven plagues which are poured out upon earth. Again the seventh is the culmination. This last bowl is emptied upon Rome, the woman with seven heads, which represented the seven hills on which she was seated and the seven kings who ruled over her ($17^{9, 10}$). The eighth head is apparently to be identified with Domitian. The ten horns possibly stand for the angelic being which will fight for her at the great final conflict. The vivid description of the overthrow of Rome in 18 was largely suggested by the II Isaiah's lament over fallen Babylon (Isaiah 47), and that of Ezekiel over Tyre (Ezek. 26, 27). Chapter 19^{1-10} contains another of the wonderful anticipatory visions of the certain vindication of the faithful. It furnishes an effective contrast to the powerful description of the final overthrow of the Beast and of Satan in $19^{11}-20^{15}$.

The culminating scene of this tremendous drama (21^1-22^{17}) is one of the most poetic and powerful passages in literature. Here all the noblest promises found in the Old Testament prophets are presented in one stupendous, concrete picture. The underlying thought is that after all the evil in the earth has been swept away by the purifying fires of judgment, God himself will come to dwell among his faithful people and to satisfy their every want. Jew and Gentile will share alike in the privileges of this ideal commonwealth in which "nothing unclean shall enter, nor any one who practises abomination or falsehood." Like Paul, the author of Revelation is endeavoring to portray objectively the ideal of the Kingdom of God, the community of the morally and socially redeemed, that Jesus held up before his followers. It is this picture of the perfect social state, as the final goal of creation, which gives to the book its perennial value for all generations.

§ CLXVIII. THE CHRISTIAN WISDOM OF THE EPISTLE OF JAMES

James, a servant of God and of the Lord Jesus Christ to the twelve tribes in the dispersion, greeting.

Greeting
(James
1^1)

Count it as pure joy, my brothers, whenever you find yourselves hedged about by various trials. Be sure that the testing of your faith produces endurance; only let your endurance be a finished product that you may be perfect and complete, lacking in nothing. If any of you lack wisdom, let him ask God who giveth to all men liberally and without reproach, and it shall be given him. Only let him ask in faith, with never a doubt; for the man who doubts is like a surge of the sea driven and tossed by the wind. Let not that man think that from the Lord he will receive anything, double-minded that he is, unstable in all his ways.

The testing of faith $(2-8)$

Let a brother of low position rejoice when he is raised up;

277

The uncertainty of riches (9-11)

but also let one who is rich rejoice in being brought low, for he will pass away like the flower of the grass, for the sun rises with the scorching wind and the grass withers, its flower drops off, and the beauty of its appearance perishes. So shall the rich fade away in the midst of their undertakings.

The real nature of temptation (12-15)

Happy is the man who endures under trial; for when he has stood the test he will receive the crown of life which is promised to all who love God. Let no one say, when he is being tried by temptation, I am being tempted by God; for God is incapable of being tempted by evil and he tempts no one. Everyone is tempted as he is carried away and lured by his own desire; then desire conceives and bears sin and when sin is fully matured it gives birth to death.

God's gifts only good (16-18)

My beloved brothers, do not be deceived: every gift is good and every endowment is perfect, coming down from above, from the Father who is the source of all love, with whom there is no variation nor shadow of change. In accordance with his own will he brought us forth by the word of truth, in order that we might be a kind of first-fruits among his creatures.

The necessity of self-control (19-21)

Know this, my beloved brothers. Therefore, let every man be quick to hear, slow to speak, slow to be angry; for human anger does not lead to what God regards as right. So ridding yourselves of all that is vile and of the evil that abounds, receive humbly the message implanted within you which is able to save your souls.

Of obedience (22-25)

Act on the word instead of merely hearing it and deluding yourselves. For, if any one hears but does not act, he is like a man who looks at his natural face in a mirror, for he looks at himself, goes off and at once forgets what he was like. But he who looks intently at the perfect law of freedom and continues looking, proving himself to be no forgetful hearer, but an active doer, will be blessed in his activity.

The essence of religion (26, 27)

If any one thinks he is religious and does not bridle his tongue but deceives himself, his religion is worthless. The religion that is pure and stainless in the sight of God the Father is this: to care personally for orphans and widows in their trouble and to keep oneself unspotted from the world.

My brothers, as you believe in our Lord Jesus Christ, who

is our glory, do not show favoritism. For suppose a man comes into one of your meetings, wearing gold rings and handsome clothes, and there also comes in a poor man in dirty clothes. If you attend to the one who wears handsome clothes and say, Sit here, this is a good place, and say to the poor man, Stand there, or Sit at my feet, are you not making distinctions among yourselves and judging people with wrong standards? Listen, my beloved brothers, hath not God chosen the poor of this world to be rich in faith and to inherit the Kingdom which he has promised to those who love him? Yet you insult the poor man. Is it not the rich who lord it over you and themselves drag you into law courts? Is it not they who revile the noble name you bear? If, however, you are fulfilling the royal law according to scripture, which says, You must love your neighbor as yourself, you are doing well; but if you show partiality you are committing sin and are convicted by the law as offenders. *True democracy (2¹⁻⁹)*

For whoever obeys the law as a whole, but makes a single slip is guilty of everything. For he who said, Do not commit adultery, also said, Do not kill. Now, if you do not commit adultery but do kill, you have transgressed the law. Speak and act as those who are to be judged by the law of freedom; for a merciless judgment will be meted out to him who shows no mercy; but mercy triumphs in the face of judgment. *The necessity of complete obedience (10-13)*

What use is it, my brothers, if a man says he has faith and yet has no works? Can his faith save him? Suppose a brother or a sister is ill-clad or lacks daily food, and one of you says to them, Depart in peace; be warmed and well fed, but does not give them what their body needs, what use is that? So faith without deeds is dead in itself. But some one will say, You have faith! Yes, and I have deeds as well. You show me your faith without works and I will show you by works what faith is! You believe in one God? You are quite right; evil spirits also believe and shudder. *The futility of faith without works (14-19)*

My brothers, let not many become teachers, for you know that we teachers shall be subjected to severe judgment. We all make many slips; if any one does not make a slip in speech that man is perfect; he is able to curb his whole nature. In the case of horses we put the bridles into their *The necessity of controlling the tongue (3¹⁻¹²)*

279

mouths to make them obey us and so we move the whole
of their bodies. See also the ships; though of great size
and driven by stiff winds, they are turned by a tiny rudder,
wherever the mind of the steersman wishes. So the tongue
is a small member of the body, but it can boast of great
achievements! See how a little spark may set a vast
forest on fire! The tongue also is a fire. It is a world of
mischief. The tongue is set among our members, stain-
ing the whole body and setting fire to the whole circle of
existence and is itself set on fire by hell. For every kind of
beast and bird, of creeping animals and creatures of the sea
may be tamed and has been tamed by mankind; but no
man can tame the tongue. It is an incessant evil, full of
deadly venom! With it we bless the Lord and Father, and
with it we curse men made in the likeness of God. Blesses
and curses come from the same mouth. My brothers,
this ought not to be. Does a fountain pour out fresh water
and bitter from the same opening? Can a fig tree, my
brothers, bear olives? Or a vine, figs? No more can salt
water yield fresh.

Noble deeds the evidence of true wisdom (12-18) — Who among you is wise and intelligent? Let him show
by wise conduct that his deeds are inspired by a wise
modesty. But if you are cherishing in your hearts bitter
jealousy and rivalry, do not speak boastfully and falsely
against the truth. That is not the wisdom which comes
down from above, but it is earthly, sensuous and devilish.
For wherever jealousy and rivalry are there is disorder
and every kind of vile deed. The wisdom from above is
first of all pure, then peaceable, forbearing, well-wishing,
full of mercy, and good fruits, impartial and sincere. For
the peacemakers who sow in peace there is a harvest of
righteousness.

Causes of war (41-3) — What causes wars and contentions in your midst? Is it
not from the cravings which are at war in your members?
You crave things and yet cannot get them. You envy and
covet, yet you cannot obtain your end. You fight and make
war; you do not get what you want because you do not
ask God for it. You do ask, but you do not receive because
you ask with the wicked intent that you may spend it on your
pleasures.

THE CURSE UPON ILL-GOTTEN RICHES

Come now, you rich men, weep and howl over your impending miseries. Your riches are rotting, your clothes are moth-eaten, your gold and silver are covered with rust and their rust will be evidence against you and it will devour your flesh like fire. You have been storing up treasures in these last days. See the wages due those who have reaped your fields—the wages of which you have defrauded them—are calling out against you and the cries of the harvesters have reached the ears of the Lord of hosts. You have revelled here on earth and given yourselves to pleasure; you have fattened yourselves as for the day of slaughter; you have condemned, you have murdered the righteous man who does not resist you. _{The curse upon ill-gotten riches (5¹⁻⁶)}

Be patient therefore, brothers, until the Lord arrives. See how the farmer waits for the precious fruit of the earth, waiting patiently over it until it receives the early and latter rain. So you must be patient. Strengthen your hearts, for the coming of the Lord is near. Do not murmur against one another, brothers, lest you be judged. See, the judge is standing at the door! Take, brothers, as an example of fortitude and patience the prophets who have spoken in the name of the Lord. Remember, we call those blessed who patiently endure. You have heard of Job's patient endurance and you have seen the issue of the Lord's dealing with him, how the Lord is full of compassion and pity. _{The advent of the Lord (7-11)}

But above all, my brothers, swear not, neither by heaven nor by earth, nor by anything else. Let your 'Yes' be a simple 'Yes' and your 'No' a simple 'No,' that you may not fall under condemnation. _{To avoid all oaths (12)}

Is any one of you suffering? Let him pray. Is any one in good spirits? Let him sing praise. Is any one among you sick? Let him send for the elders of the church and let them pray over him, anointing him with oil in the name of the Lord. And the prayer of faith will restore the sick man, and the Lord will raise him up; even if he has committed sins they will be forgiven him. So confess your sins to one another, and pray for one another that you may be healed. The prayers of a righteous man exert a powerful influence. Elijah was a man with a nature like _{The value of prayer (13-18)}

281

ours; and he earnestly prayed that there might be no rain
and for three years and six months there was no rain. Then
he prayed again, and the sky gave forth rain and the earth
yielded its fruit.

The Christian's opportunity (19-20)

My brothers, if any of you goes away from the truth
and some one brings him back, know that he who brings
the sinner back from the error of his way saves his soul
from death and covers a multitude of sins.

I. **The Literary Form of the Epistle of James.** The epistle
of James stands unique among the New Testament writers. In literary form it resembles more closely the collection of Jesus' sayings
found in the so-called "Sermon on the Mount" (Matt. 5–7) than any
other New Testament book. Like the proverbs and gnomic essays
in Ben Sira and the book of Proverbs, it is a string of pearls loosely
strung together and sent forth as an epistle. At many points the
author shows intimate familiarity with the writings of the famous old
Jewish sage, Ben Sira (e. g., 1¹², and B. Sir. 31⁸⁻¹⁰). The author's comparison of the words of a teacher to a stream flowing from a fountain
is taken from Ben Sira 24³⁰. In 5⁴⁻⁶ he evidently had in mind the words
of that famous wise man, found in 34³²: "He who deprives the hireling
of his hire is a shedder of blood." The literary characteristics of the
epistle of James are those of the Jewish wisdom literature, which found
its later counterparts in the writings of Epictetus and Marcus Aurelius.
The thought gathers about certain themes, such as temptation, the
value of riches, the use of the tongue, and the relation of faith and
works. The themes discussed throughout are those which especially
interested the sages and moralists of all ages. The tone is that of a
practical, ethical teacher. Fifty-four imperatives are found in the one
hundred and eight verses. The style is vivid, the literary figures
fresh and striking, and the illustrations are drawn from nature and
every-day life. Although there is a distinctly Jewish coloring, the
language is that of a finished Greek writer. There are no traces of
the strong Aramaic influence which is clearly apparent in many other
New Testament writings.

II. **The Aim of the Epistle of James.** The forceful literary
form in which the thought is expressed strongly suggests that this
epistle contains teachings which had often been communicated orally
before they were committed to writing. In 3¹ the author plainly
states that he was a teacher. Like Ben Sira, his aim was evidently to

THE AIM OF THE EPISTLE OF JAMES

put in permanent form the most important of his practical teachings. His abrupt ending also recalls that of Ben Sira and the book of Proverbs. The indications of logical order are more evident in the first part of the book; the latter part contains loosely arranged supplemental teachings. The author's aim was to correct certain false interpretations of Christianity that were then current. Paul's doctrine of justification through faith had evidently been misinterpreted and misused by many who claimed, in practice at least, that intellectual beliefs or mystical religious experiences were the essentials in the Christian life, and that their moral acts were relatively unimportant. It is not entirely clear whether the author is taking direct issue with Paul's assertion, for example, in Galatians 2^{16}, " that a man is justified simply by faith in Jesus Christ" or with the misinterpreters of Paul. In any case, it is obvious that the entire aim of the book is practical rather than theological. The author and Paul live in different intellectual worlds. Evidently the author of the epistle of James was familiar with Galatians, I Corinthians, and Romans, and did not wholly approve of Paul's emphasis on faith in contrast to works; but he had no desire nor intention to enter into a controversy with the great apostle. His chief concern was to deliver the church from the abuses which, in his day, were bringing disgrace upon the name of Christ. In addressing his teachings to "the twelve tribes in the dispersion," it is clear that he was not speaking to Jews but to Christendom. When he wrote it was the universally accepted belief throughout the church that the Christians were the lineal heirs of the chosen people. Like the Jews after the exile, they were scattered widely throughout the world. In the light of his teachings it is also evident that he was addressing not Jews nor the heathen, but backsliding members of the Christian commonwealth and that, as has well been said, his aim was "to hold a mirror before his brethren that they might see their sorry figures and be lastingly ashamed."

III. **The Authorship and Date of James.** The gnomic form of the book and its strong social interest suggest at once a kinship with the teachings of Jesus. The emphasis on law, as opposed to faith, also seems to point to James, the stanch supporter of the Jewish law. He it was who, according to Paul, forced even Peter and Barnabas to recant from the broad position which they had taken in their relation to Gentile Christians (Gal. 2^{12-14}). Josephus in his *Antiquities* (XX, 9^1) states that Ananus, or Annas, the son of the corrupt high priest of the same name who had been chiefly instrumental in causing the crucifixion of Jesus, succeeded his father in the priesthood. After the death of the procurator Festus he put to death James, the brother of Jesus. Josephus says that this younger Ananus "was a bold man in his temper and very insolent. He also belonged to the sect of the Sadducees, who were more rigorous than the rest of the Jews in judging offenders. Accordingly (while Albinus, the new procurator, was still on his way to Judea), he assembled the court of the Sanhedrin and brought before them James, the brother of Jesus, who was called Christ, and certain others, and, when he had preferred an accusation against them as breakers of the law, he delivered them to be stoned."

Josephus adds that this act did not meet with the approval of the better-minded Jews and that as a result Ananus was speedily removed from the high-priesthood. The date of the death of James, the brother of Jesus, was therefore about 62 A.D., under the reign of Nero. The real cause of his death was probably the fear of the Sadducees lest the Christian doctrine of the Messiah might compromise them with Rome. Symeon, a nephew of Joseph and a cousin of Jesus, was placed at the head of the Christian church in Palestine; but even before the death of James the centre of thought and influence had passed to the Western Church. From the occasional references to James, the brother of Jesus, it is evident that he was a strong character, zealous for the Jewish law and eager to prevent a breach between Christianity and Judaism. In the light of his historical relations to Paul, opposition to the teachings of the great apostle, such as is implied in the epistle of James, might be expected. The date of James's martyrdom would give time for him to become acquainted with the epistles as well as with the teachings of Paul. It is not entirely impossible that some of the teachings of James, the brother of Jesus, have been incorporated in this epistle, but the evidence that he is not its author is overwhelming. The practical impossibility that a Galilean peasant, constantly using Aramaic, could write in a rhetorical Greek style, free from all Aramaisms, has long been recognized. The legal emphasis in this epistle is not upon the Jewish law but upon a body of Christian principles which had begun to take definite form near the close of the first Christian century. Not a single reference is found in the epistle to the earlier conflict between Judaism and Christianity. When its author wrote, entirely new problems were on the horizon. Paul's teachings and work are not in the near but remote background. It is practically incredible that a writing coming from the brother of Jesus could have been so completely without personal references to the Master and to his teachings as is the epistle of James. Its problems and interests are practically the same as those that figure in the epistle to the Hebrews, in the writings of Clement of Rome, and in the *Shepherd of Hermas*, which belong to the last two decades of the first and opening years of the second century. The evidence is also reasonably convincing that the author was familiar with I Peter. Add to this the peculiar problems with which he is dealing, and the proof becomes cumulative that he was probably a Greek Christian, by the name of James, who wrote from Rome during the closing years of the first or the opening years of the second century. This conclusion is in full accord with the testimony of the superscription, as well as with the contents of the epistle. The earliest church traditions also support this dating. Eusebius placed this epistle among the controverted books. Jerome says that it was probably written by a different James from the brother of Jesus, though it gradually acquired authority. It is not found in the earliest lists of New Testament books, and not until the third century did it gain an established place in the canon. Its place there is probably due to the later belief that it was written by the brother of Jesus; but its contents and contribution to the history of Christianity amply justify its position in the canon. The New Testament, like the Old, reflects many diverse points of view and beliefs. Not the least of its charms and values is that it presents not merely one but all sides of truth.

IV. **The Contributions of the Book of James to Developing Christianity.** It is evident that this epistle, like all the New Testament writings, grew out of practical needs. The author, in his spirit and theme, reminds us in many ways of the old Hebrew prophet Amos. He evidently had a warm heart, but an exceedingly brusque exterior. He was so intent upon making his points that he did not stop to present the other side of the truth which he was emphasizing. In the days of Amos religion had been interpreted as mere conformity to certain ceremonial rites. When the epistle of James was written the danger that threatened Christianity was that faith might be interpreted narrowly as the mere acceptance of certain doctrines, or as nominal allegiance to its Founder, or as the sharing of certain mystical experiences which failed to transform the individual character or to lead to right acts. Christianity, like Judaism and all great religions, faced this peril at the end of the first Christian century, even as it has at many later periods in its history. In sounding a sharp note of warning, this otherwise unknown James has made a large contribution to Christianity. In his interpretation of the principles of Jesus he undoubtedly was not the equal of Paul. The great apostle declared that the first and absolute essential in the Christian life was to establish an intimate, spiritual fellowship with God. At the same time, he always affirmed that the fruits of the Spirit, that is, of that genuinely spiritual fellowship with God which he described as faith, were the only certain proofs that a man had this faith. These are precisely the characteristics and the acts for which the author of James was contending. As we have seen, Paul devoted nearly as much attention to describing and emphasizing these fruits of the Spirit as he did to his analysis of the individual spiritual experience of which they were but the external evidence.

The author of James was the forerunner of the modern ethical-culture movement. In his emphasis on personal dependence upon God and of unwavering faith he also laid a sound foundation for morals; but he lacked the profound spiritual experience of the great apostle to the Gentiles and therefore the power to interpret Christianity as a whole rather than in its parts. His epistle is not, however, as Luther asserted, "an epistle of straw." It is a noble and practical homily on a text which Jesus himself propounded: "By their fruits you shall know them." It was a strong protest against the tendencies which during the Middle Ages obscured the real essence of Christianity. It is a protest to which Christianity in the present age is listening with results which are most practicable and commendable. At the same time, it is equally important to remember that the epistle of James presents not all but only a part of Christianity.

V. **The Democracy of the Epistle of James.** The historical student of religion naturally classifies many of the tendencies in the epistle of James as Ebionite. Its denunciation of riches, its disparagement of worldly wisdom, and its emphasis on deeds of mercy are all characteristic tenets of that Palestinian Christian sect. But they are not due to the influence of a particular sect. They are the natural corollaries of the great social principles laid down by Jesus. Like Paul, its author was seeking to define the duties of citizens in the Kingdom of God. The book of James is the most democratic of all the New Testament writings except the Gospels of Matthew and Luke, which present most fully the teachings of the Master. Simply and concretely James interprets into every-day life Jesus' social teachings and acts, which acknowledge no superiority except that established by service. The resentment which he feels toward the rich who defraud those who labor for them is closely akin to Jesus' hot indignation against the grafting high priests who in legalized ways were putting their hands in the pockets of the poor. His vivid picture of the deference paid to the rich and the neglect shown to the poor brother (2^{1-9}) is unfortunately not entirely inapplicable to certain Christian churches to-day. If the epistle of James had not found a place in the New Testament real Christianity would never have been committed so absolutely and irrevocably to practical democracy. It is not "an epistle of straw," but of practical power, for it contributes many important details to the plan of the ideal community, the establishment of which is the goal of Christianity.

§ CLXIX. THE RULE OF LOVE IN THE EARLY CHRISTIAN CHURCH

That you may share our fellowship, we now declare to you that which existed from the very beginning, which we have heard and which we have seen with our eyes and touched with our own hands, namely, the Word of Life. The Life has appeared and we saw it and bear witness and announce to you that eternal Life which was with the Father and was manifested to us. And our fellowship is with the Father and with his Son Jesus Christ. And we are writing these things that our own joy may be complete. *The Christian fellowship (I John 1^{1-4})*

This is the message which we heard from the Lord Jesus and now announce to you: God is light and in him there is no darkness at all. If we say, We have fellowship with him while we walk in darkness, we are lying and do not act sincerely; but if we walk in the light, as he is in the light, we have fellowship with one another, and the blood of Jesus his Son cleanses us from every sin. If we say we have no sin, we are deceiving ourselves and the truth is not in us. If we confess our sins, he is so faithful and just that he forgives our sins and cleanses us from all unrighteousness. If we say we have not sinned, we make him a liar and his word is not in us. *The evidence of this fellowship ($5-10$)*

My dear children, I am writing this to you that you may not sin; but if anyone does sin, we have an advocate with the Father in Jesus Christ, the righteous. He himself is an atoning sacrifice for our sins, though not for ours alone but also for the sins of the whole world. *The universal Saviour ($2^{1, 2}$)*

287

The evidence of being a Christian (3-6)   And by this we may be sure that we know him—if we obey his commands. He who says, I know him, but does not obey his commands is a liar and the truth is not in him. But whoever obeys his word, in him love for God has really reached perfection. By this means we may be sure that we are in him; whoever says he remains in him ought himself to walk even as he walked.

Of walking in the light (7-11)   Beloved, I am not writing you any new command, but an old command which you have had from the beginning: the old command is the word which you have heard. And yet I am writing you a new command, which is realized in him and also in you, for the darkness is passing away and the true light is already shining. He who says he is in the light but hates his brother is still in darkness. He who loves his brother remains in the light, and in the light there is no stumbling block. But he who hates his brother is in darkness, he is walking in darkness and does not know where he is going, for the darkness is blinding his eyes.

The new command of love (12, 13, 15-17)   My dear children, I am writing to you because for his sake your sins are forgiven. Fathers, I am writing to you because you know him who has been from the very beginning. Young men, I am writing to you because you have conquered the evil one. Children, I have written to you because you know the Father. Love not the world nor the things in the world. If anyone loves the world, love for the Father is not in him. For all that is in the world, the cravings of the flesh and the cravings of the eyes and the vainglory of life, belongs not to the Father but to the world. And the world with its cravings is passing away, but he who does the will of God remains forever.

God's love toward his children (31-3)   See what a marvelous love the Father hath bestowed upon us in letting us be called the children of God! And that we are. For this reason the world does not recognize us: because it has not known him. Beloved, we are now children of God, but what we are to be has not been revealed. We do know that when Christ appears, we shall be like him, for we shall see him as he is. And everyone who has this hope fixed on him keeps himself pure just as he is pure.

  Anyone who is born of God does not commit sin, for a

divine seed remains in him and he cannot sin because he is born a child of God. By this the children of God and the children of the devil are recognized: anyone who does not do right is not a child of God nor is he who does not love his brother. For this is the message you have heard from the very beginning, that you are to love one another. Do not wonder, brothers, that the world hates you. We know that we have passed over from death to life because we love our brothers. He who has no love remains in death. Anyone who hates his brother is a murderer, and you know that no murderer has eternal life remaining in him.

Their love for their brothers (9-11, 13-15)

We know what love is by this, that Christ laid down his life for us; so we ought to lay down our lives for the brothers. But if anyone has this world's wealth and sees his brother in need and restrains his sympathy for him, how can love for God remain in him. My children, let us show our love not in words nor with lips only, but by deed and sincerity.

The measure of Christian love (16-18)

Beloved, let us love one another for love comes from God and everyone who loves is born of God and knows God. He who does not love, does not know God, for God is love. God's love for us has been manifested by his sending his only Son into the world that through him we might live. Love consists in this, not in our love for him but in his love for us and in his sending his Son to be an atoning sacrifice for our sins.

God is love (4 7-10)

Beloved, since God so loved us, then we ought to love one another. No one has ever seen God; but if we love one another, then God remaineth in us and the love for him is perfect within us. By this we know that we remain in him and he remaineth in us because he hath given us a portion of his own Spirit. And we have seen and bear witness that the Father hath sent the Son as a Saviour of the world. Whoever confesses that Jesus is the Son of God, God remaineth in him and he remains in God, and we ourselves know the love God hath for us and we believe in it. God is love, and he who remains in love remains in God and God remaineth in him. Love is perfect with us when we have full confidence about the day of judgment, for we

The proofs of God's love in man (11-21)

are just as he is in respect to this world. In love there is no fear. Instead of that, perfect love drives out all fear, for fear has to do with punishment; he who fears has not attained perfect love. We love because he first loved us. If anyone declares, I love God and yet hates his brother, he is a liar; for he who does not love his brother whom he has seen, cannot love God whom he has never seen. And we have this command from him, that he who loves God is to love his brother also.

The life and fellowship of the early Christians (Apology of Aristides 15)

The Christians know and trust God, the Creator of heaven and earth in whom are all things and from whom are all things, and who hath no other God beside him. From him they have received the commandments which they have engraved on their minds and keep in the hope and expectation of the world to come. Therefore they do not commit adultery nor fornication; they do not bear false witness; they do not deny what has been deposited with them, nor covet what is not theirs. They honor father and mother and show kindness to their neighbors. If they are judges, they judge uprightly. They do not worship idols made in human form, and whatever they do not wish that others should do to them, they do not to others. They do not eat of food offered to idols because they are undefiled. They placate those who oppress them and make them their friends; they do good to their enemies. Their wives are absolutely pure and their daughters modest. Their men abstain from every unlawful marriage and from all impurity in the hope of future recompense. If any of them have bondmen, bondwomen or children, they persuade them to become Christians for the love that they have towards them; and when they become so they call them without distinction, brothers. They do not worship strange gods. They walk in all humility and kindness, and falsehood is not found among them. They love one another. They do not refuse to help the widows. They rescue the orphan from him who does him violence. He who has gives ungrudgingly to him who has not. If they see a stranger, they take him to their dwellings and rejoice over him as over a real brother; for they do not call themselves brothers after the flesh but after the Spirit and in God. When one of their poor passes from the world, any one of them who sees it provides for his burial according to his ability. And if they hear that any one of their number is in prison or oppressed for the name of their Messiah, all of them provide for his needs. And if it is possible to redeem him, they deliver him. If any one among them is poor and needy and they do not have food to spare, they fast two or three days that they may supply him with the necessary food. They scrupulously observe the commands of their Messiah. They live honestly and soberly as the Lord their God commanded them. Every morning and every hour they thank and praise God for his loving kindnesses toward them; and for their food and drink they give thanks to him. If any righteous man among them passes from this world, they rejoice and give thanks to God, and they escort his body as if he were setting out on a journey from one place to another. If, on the other hand, they see that one of their number has died in his ungodliness or in his sins, they weep bitterly and sigh as over one who is about to go to punishment.

As men who know God, they ask from him what is proper for him to give and for them to receive. Thus they do throughout their entire life. And inasmuch as they acknowledge the loving kindnesses of God toward them, lo, because of them, there flows forth all the beauty that is in the world! But the good deeds which they do, they do not proclaim in the ears of the multitude, but they take care that no one shall perceive them. They hide their gift as one who has found a treasure hides it. Thus they labor to become righteous as those who expect to see their Messiah and to receive from him the glorious fulfillment of the promises made to them. Truly this is a new people and there is something divine in them! The uniqueness of the life of the Christians (16)

I. **The Aim and Thought of I John.** First John occupies a unique place among the New Testament writings. Although one of the latest, it presents in simplest form the essence of Christianity. In its literary character and in its conception of Jesus and his work, it is closely related to Hebrews. While it is nominally an epistle, it is in reality a brief homily, containing a series of meditations and exhortations. In its loosely connected structure, in its epigrammatic style, and in its profound emphasis on life and deeds, as well as upon belief, it is closely akin to the book of James. The reader also recognizes many echoes of Paul's distinctive teachings. All non-essentials, however, are cast aside and the eternal principle of love, first clearly proclaimed by the prophet Hosea, and declared by Jesus to be the supreme motive power in religion and morals, is given the central place. What the earlier prophets and Jesus had assumed, the author plainly states, namely, that God is love. The logic that underlies I John is simple and compelling: love, being the chief attribute of God, is the supreme force in the universe. It inspired Jesus to do that saving work for men which is the highest expression of divine love. True love for God begets love for men. It is this love which overcomes all fear, all hatred, and even the power of sin and death, and binds together God, the individual, and mankind into one divine fellowship. The author of I John clearly states in his opening paragraph that his purpose is to enable his readers to enjoy that divine fellowship which has been made possible through the self-sacrificing work of Jesus. He also aims to guard them against certain Docetic teachings, which led to a practical denial of Jesus' human existence ($4^{2, 3}$) and substituted for the simple belief in the Friend and Teacher of mankind a vague, metaphysical mysticism. In the concluding notes (5^{13}) he reasserts his dominant aim: "I have written in this way to you who believe in the Son of God, that you may be sure that you have eternal life." It was, therefore, to promote love and trust and fellowship among the followers of Jesus that this wonderful homily was committed to writing and sent forth as a tract.

II. **The Authorship and Date of I John.** The bonds which bind together this epistle and the Fourth Gospel are both many and close. In each the point of view is that of eternity, rather than any specific moment in history. Each was inspired by a practical, evangelical aim. That of the Fourth Gospel is plainly stated in 20^{31}: it is "that you may believe that Jesus is the Messiah, the Son of God, and that believing you may have life in his name." The Fourth Gospel is apparently addressed to both believers and unbelievers, while I John is an intimate message to those who have already felt the love of God inspired by Jesus. Both writings come from a mystic who regards the facts of history and ordinary experience as but symbols of deeper, spiritual realities. To him the material world, with its pomps and its passions, is but a passing panorama. He who does the will of God is the only abiding factor in the phenomena of human life. Many striking phrases also bind together these two writings (e. g., "to walk in the light," or, "in darkness," "to be born of God," "to do the truth," and "God is light"). There are also equally striking points of difference. For example, the epistle does not use the Old Testament, while the gospel does so frequently. In the epistle man's relation to God is direct, while in the gospel it is through Christ. In one the thesis is that the Christ is Jesus, in the other that Jesus is the Christ. While these points of contact and difference may not point to absolute identity of authorship, they can be explained only on the hypothesis that both writings come from the same school and are inspired by the same deeply spiritual mind. The maturity of the thought points to a relatively late period in the apostolic age. The absence of any references to persecution suggests that they come from the brief but bright period between the persecution of Domitian, which ended in 96, and the reign of Trajan, which began in 98. At least a date very close to the beginning of the second Christian century fully satisfies all the implications of I John. The author, like that of the Fourth Gospel, reveals the influence of the Alexandrian type of thought. He identifies Jesus with the Logos or Word of Life, eternal and ever existent with God, yet incarnated so that he was seen with the eyes and touched by the hands of his followers. Here the Stoic doctrine of the Logos, the Jewish belief in a pre-existent Messiah, and the Christian memories of the historic Jesus blend. In the light of the oldest historic evidence, it is probable that not John, the son of Zebedee, who, the earliest traditions state, was martyred about the middle of the first century, but John, the presbyter of Ephesus, speaks to us, if not through his own pen, through that of one of his faithful followers. If this generally accepted conclusion of modern scholarship be true, we probably have here not merely the richly spiritual message of a later Christian writer, but a luminous reflection of the teachings of the Master himself.

III. **The Personality back of the Johannine Writings.** John, the presbyter of Ephesus, was in all probability "the beloved disciple," who, according to the gospel that bears his name, was intimately associated with Jesus during the closing days of his ministry. He is described in the epilogue of the Fourth Gospel (21^{24}) as, "the disciple who bears testimony to these facts and who wrote them down; his testimony we know is true." It is significant that the early Christian writer, Papias, also calls this John, the presbyter, a disciple of

Jesus, even though he was not one of the Twelve. The brief letters known as II John and III John come directly from his hand. The first is a friendly note of warning, sent to an important Christian community (addressed as "the elect lady and her children") which the presbyter hopes in the near future to visit personally. The warning is directed against certain travelling preachers who are advocating Docetic teachings similar to those referred to in I John 4[2, 3]. Third John is a private letter to Gaius, who was probably a member of the same community to which the letter in II John was sent. It reveals the fact that another leader of the Christian church, Diotrephes, had refused to submit to the authority of the presbyter and had threatened to excommunicate Gaius. It is clear that both of these letters were written by one accustomed to exercise authority over the local Christian communities. He is strenuous for the truth which has evidently crystallized in his mind into a definite body of doctrines. Thus he speaks in II John [2] of "the truth which remains within us and will be with us forever." But the dominant note in all this thinking, as in I John, is love: "It is the command which we have had from the very beginning—'Let us love one another.' To live by his commands, that is what love means. And the command is, 'Live in love as you have learned to do from the beginning.'"

The personality revealed in these letters is that of an old man who calls the members of the community under his care "children," and who can remember the historic beginnings of their faith. He, therefore, speaks with the authority of one who had personally heard the commands of the Master. These implications correspond to the beautiful portrait preserved in a fourth-century tradition, recounted by Jerome in his commentary on Galatians: "When the holy evangelist, John, had lived to extreme old age in Ephesus, he could be carried only with difficulty by the hands of the disciples, and as he was not able to pronounce more words, he was accustomed to say at every assembly: 'Little children, love one another.' At length the disciples and brothers, being tired of hearing always the same thing, said: 'Master, why do you always say this?' Thereupon John gave an answer worthy of himself: 'Because this is the command of the Lord, and if it is observed, then it is enough.'"

The John who is revealed in this tradition, and especially through the three epistles and the gospel which bear his name and the imprint of his profound thinking, has a distinct and consistent personality. Even though we know practically nothing about the details of his

THE PERSONALITY OF JOHN

life, he must be counted with Peter and Paul as one of the three great forces in the apostolic church. The influence of the Alexandrian Greek atmosphere amidst which he spent at least his later years may be recognized not only in his free use of allegory but also in his peculiar type of thought. He has much in common with Philo of Alexandria, who interpreted the thought of the Greek philosophers in the light of his Jewish inheritance. When John declared in the prologue of his gospel, "In the beginning the Logos (or Word) was with God," he spoke as a Jew, familiar with the personification of Wisdom in Proverbs 8^{22}. When he declared that "the Logos was God," he echoed a familiar Stoic teaching. The two great teachers, however, who influenced John and his disciples most were Paul and Jesus. He fully accepted, for example, Paul's doctrine of the eternal, pre-existent Christ, and of his exaltation in the presence of the Father and the belief that he was to come again to judge the world. He also reasserted Paul's great principle of Christian liberty through Christ. In his allegory of the vine and its branches he taught Paul's social ideal of the "Body of Christ." From both Jesus and Paul he drew his central teaching that love is the ruling principle in the universe and that service for the Christian community is the only valid basis of reward. In all of his writings he is evidently combating on the one side the belief that Jesus was nothing more than a great teacher and prophet, and on the other the fatal tendency to deny altogether Jesus' humanity. The Fourth Gospel asserts in strongest terms Jesus' divinity and seeks to establish it by seven great signs of which the account of the raising of Lazarus is the culmination. At the same time it emphasizes Jesus' human side: his hunger, his weariness, his changing emotions, and his warm personal affection for his disciples. Thus John established the identity of the exalted Christ, which Paul and the other apostles revered, with the historical Jesus of the Synoptic Gospels. While he harmonized different currents of Christian thought and combated others, John's great contribution was the emphasis which he placed on Christian love and liberty and upon service for the universal brotherhood, which Jesus gave his life to establish. The New Testament would be incomplete without the immortal declaration of faith contained in the words: "God is Love. God so loved the world that he gave his only Son, that every one who believes in him might not perish but have eternal life. We love because he first loved us."

IV. **The Life of the Early Christians.** Aristides, the Athenian philosopher, in his defense of the Christians before the Emperor Hadrian (117–138), has given a remarkably vivid picture of the life of the early followers of Jesus. It is a picture which is confirmed and supplemented by the testimony of scores of contemporary witnesses. Christianity proved an open door of hope and opportunity not only to the "lost sheep of the house of Israel" but also to the lost sheep of the pagan world. Even Celsus, its bitterest enemy, exclaims: "What sort of people do the Christians invite to their religious rites? 'Any one who is a sinner,' they say, 'or devoid of understanding, or simple-minded— in short, whoever is unfortunate will be received in the Kingdom of God.'" To the despondent sinner, to the homeless stranger, to the helpless slave, and to the hopeless outcast Christianity extended the hand of fellowship and a cordial invitation to join the brotherhood of those who were living in accordance with the spirit and teaching of him who declared: "One is your Master, and you all are brothers. Let him who would be first among you be the servant of all." Brotherliness, as illustrated in the life of the early Christian church, has well been defined as "love on a footing of equality." In the presence of the early Christians hostile pagan critics were forced to cry out: "Look, how they love one another!" All this varied cloud of witnesses bear testimony that primitive Christianity was not primarily a creed but a life of love and service. Its rites were very simple. Baptism was conceived of as a bath of purification, "to restore the health of the soul," and to endue the individual with the spirit of Jesus. It meant adoption as a son of God and admission into the Christian fellowship which Jesus had established. During the first century the Lord's Supper was the evening meal which each local community shared in common. Not until the days of Trajan was it transferred (as a result of the imperial decree) to the morning and made a distinctly liturgical act. In the apostolic church it symbolized Jesus' self-sacrificing, triumphant service for his followers. It was also the expressive rite which bound together the members of each local Christian community and kept forever alive within them their Master's spirit of love and fellowship. Prayers were spontaneous, being inspired by the direct influence of the Spirit. Speaking with tongues was common. The enthusiasm begotten by the consciousness of being enlisted in a great cause stirred all hearts. These Christian communities were also potent educational forces. All their members were trained by constant practice, as well as by precept, to govern their every act by the spirit of love and loyalty to the interests of the great brotherhood and to labor for its extension throughout the world.

THE LIFE OF THE EARLY CHRISTIANS

The organization of these communities was simple and for practical service. At the head of each community stood the bishop who directed its religious life and especially its work for the sick and needy. Next to him, as the responsible directors of the Christian community, were the presbyters or elders. Under the immediate direction of the bishop were the deacons, who are described in an early Christian writing as "doers of good works, looking after all by day and by night." In another Christian writing they are directed "to act as eyes for the bishop, carefully inquiring into the actions of every church member . . . in order to find out those who are sick in the flesh and to bring such to the notice of the main body, who know nothing of them, that they may visit them and supply their wants." In the early church, widows were appointed to perform the services which later devolved upon the deaconesses. Thus we are told in a second-century document that "in every congregation at least one widow is to be appointed to take care of sick women; she is to be obliging and sober; she is to report cases of need to the elders." Definite contributions were provided for the needy. Justin Martyr in his *Apology* (LXVII) states: "Those who are well-to-do give as they choose, each as he himself purposes. The collection is then deposited with the president, who succors orphans, widows, those who are in want owing to sickness or any other cause, those who are in prison, and strangers who are on a journey." All gifts were voluntary and were simply and directly applied to the needs of each community.

Not every Christian proved loyal to the spirit and teachings of his Master, but every effort was made by the members of the community to care for its morally delinquent. The lofty yet practical moral ideals of Jesus and Paul were constantly held up before them; not only through the words, but in the lives of their fellow Christians. The second chapter of the *First Epistle of Clement*, which was written to the Corinthian Christians near the close of the first century, bears eloquent testimony to this fact: "Day and night you agonized for all the brotherhood, that by means of compassion and care the number of God's elect might be saved. You were sincere, guileless, and void of malice among yourselves. Every sedition and every schism was an abomination to you. You lamented the transgressions of your neighbors and judged their shortcomings to be your own."

Visiting Christians were entertained for three or four days as guests of the local community. Then, if they remained, work was secured for them. Visiting evangelists, prophets, and laymen bound the Christian

THE CHRISTIAN RULE OF LOVE

communities together into one great brotherhood. These bonds were strengthened by the exchange of letters and in time by common supervision. The Roman church ultimately won its position of pre-eminence and authority through its kindly reception of all Christians visiting the Imperial City and through its valuable services to the local Christian communities far and near. Thus Paul's great ideal of the unity of the "Body of Christ" was in a measure concretely realized and the social principles of Jesus became the most powerful and abiding forces in the empire.

V. **The Essence of Christianity.** The Apostolic Age is pre-eminently significant because it reveals in concrete, historical terms the essence of Christianity. Obviously, it is not a system of dogmas, nor a complex ecclesiastical organization, but a living historic movement. From the point of view of the individual, Christianity is not only a faith but an attitude and a way of living. Objectively, it is the expansion of the unique brotherhood which Jesus established during his Galilean ministry. It is the community of those who, under the impulse of his teaching and example, recognize God as their Father and all men as brothers. It is a world-wide fraternity of men and women, young and old, who, in their loyalty to God and in their service for their fellows, are being socially and morally redeemed. It is a movement which, during the first century, spread throughout the world unfettered by creeds or rules or complex organization and, therefore, free to adapt itself to the varied needs of humanity. The heroic death of Jesus, instead of destroying this brotherhood, transferred its centre to Jerusalem. There his invincible faith, his divine enthusiasm, and his burning zeal to redeem and serve humanity so inspired his followers that their numbers increased with incredible rapidity. Persecution only fanned the flame of love and loyalty into a conflagration that scattered its firebrands throughout the great cities of the empire. The love and zeal of the scattered disciples quickly attracted others to this divine brotherhood, so that before the generation which had felt the immediate touch of Jesus' personality had passed away, a chain of Christian communities extended from Jerusalem to Rome. Each citizen of this new commonwealth, that had suddenly sprung into existence, felt himself bound to every other member by the bonds of love and common endeavor. Fraternal co-operation took the place of hostile competition. The will of God, as interpreted by Jesus and the divine Spirit within them, became their supreme rule of life. Thus in a large measure the spiritual and social ideal, which Jesus called "the Kingdom of God" and Paul the "Body of Christ," became in the Apostolic Age an historic reality. In the succeeding centuries many influences tended to arrest Christianity's normal development; but its ideal of loving fellowship with God and of complete loyalty to the perfect community, which Jesus aimed to establish, remains for the individual and humanity "the way, the truth and the life."

APPENDIX

I

A PRACTICAL REFERENCE LIBRARY

Books for Constant Reference. The literature on the Apostolic Age is exceedingly voluminous. Moffatt's *Introduction to the Literature of the New Testament* presents in easily accessible form the important bibliography in connection with the New Testament books and the results of modern critical scholarship. McGiffert's *Apostolic Age* remains the most thoroughgoing and satisfactory history of this important period. The general student will find many valuable suggestions in Bacon's *Story of St. Paul*. The first part is devoted to the history of Paul and the second part to a discussion of the contents of his letters. Wood's *Life and Ministry of Paul, the Apostle,* is an exceedingly compact, well-proportioned study of the work and teachings of the great apostle in the light of their historical setting. Ramsay's *St. Paul the Traveller and Roman Citizen* is in reality a historical and geographical commentary on the records of Paul's journeys found in the book of Acts. Upon the problems which these narratives present Professor Ramsay has focused the results of his important investigations in Asia Minor and Greece. Deissmann's *St. Paul—A Study in Social and Religious History* is an exceedingly fresh and stimulating interpretation of Paul not only in the light of his geographical but also of his intellectual and religious environment. For the study of individual books, the volumes of the *Century Bible*, and especially the compact yet scholarly commentaries in *The Bible for Home and School*, are reliable and usable. For more detailed study the volumes of the *International Critical Commentaries* are the best authorities.

Additional Books of Reference: Introductions. The brief, compact introductions to the New Testament by Peake and Bacon present the results of critical yet constructive scholarship. Jülicher's *Introduction to the New Testament* is more detailed and yet is exceedingly luminous and stimulating. Harnack's *Acts of the Apostles* contains a minute study of the literary structure and sources of Acts. Even

APPENDIX

though the facts and conclusions here presented may not be accepted by the reader, they are exceedingly suggestive. The monograph by Torrey, entitled *The Aramaic Source in the Book of Acts*, throws much new light upon the origin and historical value of Luke's great epic of conquering Christianity. Lake's *Earlier Epistles of St. Paul* deals not only with the critical questions presented by Paul's major epistles but also with their interpretation and harmonization with the parallel records contained in Acts. In his *Light from the Ancient East* Professor Deissmann has placed at the disposal of the reader a wealth of contemporary Greek literature and archæological material which illuminates the New Testament writings.

Contemporary Religions. In his *Evolution of Early Christianity* Professor Case has presented in compact but masterly form the different currents of religious life and thought amidst which Christianity developed and has traced their influence upon Christian thought during the formative Apostolic Age. In a more minute, painstaking, and yet on the whole less satisfying manner, Clemen deals with the same problem in his *Primitive Christianity and its Non-Jewish Sources.* Kennedy in his *St. Paul and the Mystery Religions* and Gardner in his *Religious Experiences of St. Paul* discuss the influence of Paul's religious environment upon the development of his faith.

Histories of the Apostolic Age. Weizsächer's *The Apostolic Age and the Christian Church* (I, II) presents a vivid and detailed picture of the development of the early church. Bartlet's *The Apostolic Age* is a well-proportioned sketch of the period. Ropes's *Apostolic Age* is not a complete history but rather a discussion of certain important problems and phases in the life of this important era. It contains many valuable suggestions for the more advanced student. Scott's *The Beginnings of the Church* is a detailed study of the life of the Christian community at Jerusalem in the days preceding the work of Paul. Ramsay, in his *Church in the Roman Empire*, presents the larger political environment of Christianity. Dobschütz, in his *Apostolic Age*, treats briefly but vividly the life of the Christian communities, beginning with the death of Jesus and extending down into the Post-Apostolic Age. This volume is paralleled by his larger and more detailed *Christian Life in the Primitive Church.* This volume contains a wealth of data which make exceedingly real the life and problems of the early Christian communities. Similar in scope and aim is Harnack's *Expansion of Christianity* (I, II). The student who desires to consult the extra-canonical authorities regarding the Apostolic and Post-Apostolic Age will find a careful selection of the more important passages in Ayer's *Source Book for Ancient Church History*.

Lives of Paul. A fascinating, concise sketch of the personality and thought of Paul, written from a critical but sympathetic point of view, is found in Wrede's *Paul*. Equally critical, but in many respects more satisfying, is Weinel's *St. Paul—The Man and His Work*. Each of these writers is a severe yet appreciative critic of the great apostle. To this same class belongs Clemen's *Paul, His Life and Work*. Two stimulating volumes, which are the outgrowth of the hotly contested controversy as to whether Jesus or Paul was the real founder of Christianity, are Meyer's *Jesus or Paul* and Weiss's *Paul and Jesus*. Jones, in his *Paul, the Orator*, discusses at length the forensic side of the great apostle's activity. Ramsay, in his *Cities of St. Paul*, presents a rich abundance of historical and archæological data regarding the scenes amidst which Paul carried on his epoch-making missionary campaigns in Asia Minor.

II

GENERAL QUESTIONS AND SUBJECTS FOR SPECIAL RESEARCH

The GENERAL QUESTIONS, as in the preceding volumes, follow the main divisions of the book and aim to guide the student in collecting and co-ordinating the more important facts presented in the biblical texts or in the notes.

The SUBJECTS FOR SPECIAL RESEARCH are intended as a guide for further study in related lines, and aim, by means of detailed references, to introduce the student and the teacher to the more important passages in the best English books of reference. In classroom work many of these topics may profitably be assigned for individual research. The references are to pages, unless otherwise indicated. Ordinarily, several parallel references are given, that the student may be able to utilize the book at hand.

INTRODUCTION: THE RECORDS AND BACKGROUND OF THE APOSTOLIC AGE

I. The Records of the Work and Teachings of the Apostles.
GENERAL QUESTIONS: 1. Describe the duration and importance of the Apostolic Age. 2. The historical value of the New Testament letters

and epistles. 3. Reasons that led the author to write the book of Acts. 4. Evidence that the author was Luke, the physician. 5. His personality and equipment. 6. Nature of the sources incorporated in Acts 1^1–15^{35}. 7. Historical value of the journal of travel in 15^{35}–28^{31}. 8. Conclusions regarding the historical value of the records of the Apostolic Age.

SUBJECTS FOR SPECIAL RESEARCH: 1. Luke's use of medical terms in Acts. Moffatt, *Introd. to N. T.*, 289, 290; Harnack, *Luke the Physician*, 175–198; Hobart, *The Medical Language of St Paul*. 2. The historical accuracy of Acts. Moffatt, *Introd. to N. T.*, 304–8; Lightfoot, *Essay on "Supernatural Religions,"* 291–302; Ramsay, *Christianity in the Roman Empire*, chaps. II–VIII.

II. The Historical and Religious Background of the Apostolic Age. GENERAL QUESTIONS: 1. Describe the personality and policy of each of the Roman emperors from Tiberius to Trajan. 2. The ways in which Rome prepared the world for Christianity. 3. The history of the Jews of Palestine from 36 to 90 A.D. 4. Compare the Jews of Palestine with those of the dispersion. 5. Describe the ways in which the Jews attempted to win the heathen to Judaism. 6. The teachings of Epicureanism, Cynicism, and Stoicism. 7. The ideas underlying emperor-worship, and their significance for Christianity. 8. The characteristics of the mystery-religions. 9. The social and religious needs of the Roman world.

SUBJECTS FOR SPECIAL RESEARCH: 1. The history and tenets of Stoicism. Case, *Evolution of Christianity*, 267–283; Article, "Stoicism," in *Encyc. Brit.* 2. Origin of the Roman emperor-worship. Case, *Evolution of Christianity*, 195–222; Deissmann, *Light from the Ancient East*, 342–384. 3. Contemporary mystery-religions. Case, *Evolution of Christianity*, 284–330; Cumont, *Oriental Religions in Roman Paganism;* Mead, *Thrice Greatest Hermes;* Reitzenstein, *Poimandres;* Jacoby, *Die antiken Mysterienreligionen und das Christentum.*

PRIMITIVE CHRISTIANITY IN PALESTINE AND SYRIA

§ CXLVI. **The Origin of the Jerusalem Christian Community.** GENERAL QUESTIONS: 1. Why did Jesus' followers immediately after his death make Jerusalem their home? 2. Describe the personnel of the Jerusalem Christian community. 3. The motives that led the disciples to elect Matthias. 4. The historical and traditional elements in the story of the day of Pentecost. 5. The psychological ex-

APPENDIX

perience that then came to the members of the Jerusalem community. 6. The central ideas in Peter's sermon. 7. The beliefs of the primitive Christians.

SUBJECTS FOR SPECIAL RESEARCH: 1. Speaking with tongues in the early Christian church. Scott, *The Beginnings of the Church*, 57–83; Lake, *Earlier Epistles of St. Paul*, 241–252; Cutten, *Psych. Phenomena of Christianity*, 37–59. 2. The use of the title "Lord." Scott, *Beginnings of the Church*, 84–108; Weiss, *Kurios*. 3. Mediæval and modern faith-cures. Cutten, *Psych. Phenomena of Christianity*, 196–231.

§ CXLVII. **The Life of the Primitive Christian Community.** GENERAL QUESTIONS: 1. Describe the circumstances and the significance of the healing of the lame man in the temple. 2. The leading ideas in Peter's address to the multitude. 3. The reasons why the apostles were arrested and the basis of their defense before the Sanhedrin. 4. Economic and social principles governing the Christian community at Jerusalem. 5. The sin of Ananias and Sapphira. 6. How far and in what respects was the community at Jerusalem a local realization of Jesus' ideal of the Kingdom of God?

SUBJECTS FOR SPECIAL RESEARCH: 1. The origin and history of the Ecclesia or Church. Scott, *Beginnings of the Church*, 28–56; Hastings, *D. B.*, I, 425, 426. 2. Communistic tendencies in early Christianity. McGiffert, *Apostolic Age*, 66–70; Dobschütz, *Christian Life in the Prim. Church*, 143–6; Rauschenbush, *Christianity and the Social Crisis* 120–3.

§ CXLVIII. **The Work and Death of Stephen.** GENERAL QUESTIONS: 1. Why did Christianity appeal especially to the Jews of the dispersion? 2. Describe the reasons which led to the appointment of the seven, and their personnel. 3. The personality of Stephen. 4. The subjects discussed by him with the Hellenistic Jews. 5. His attitude toward Judaism and his claims for Christianity. 6. His contributions to the new faith through his teachings and martyrdom.

SUBJECTS FOR SPECIAL RESEARCH: 1. The religious and social life of the Jewish synagogue. Hastings, *D. B.*, IV, 640–3; Oesterley and Box, *Religion and Worship of the Synagogue*. 2. The Jewish proselyting movement. McGiffert, *Apostolic Age*, 157–160; Dobschütz, *Life in the Primitive Church*, 160–7; Harnack, *Expansion of Christianity*, I, 11–18; Thatcher, *The Apostolic Church*, 19–33.

§ CXLIX. **The Expansion of Christianity after the Death of Stephen.** GENERAL QUESTIONS: 1. Describe the effect of Stephen's martyrdom upon Jesus' followers. 2. The personality and teachings

APPENDIX

of Philip the evangelist. 3. The results and limitations of his work among the Samaritans. 4. The basis and significance of the conversion of the Ethiopian eunuch. 5. The steps which led to the establishment of Christianity at Antioch. 6. The historical origin of the term "Christian." 7. The nature of the persecution of the Christians under Herod Agrippa I. 8. Influences that transformed Peter's attitude toward the Gentiles. 9. The permanent contributions of the Palestinian Christians to Christianity.

SUBJECTS FOR SPECIAL RESEARCH: 1. Antioch at the middle of the first Christian century. Hastings, *D. B.*, I, 103, 104; Ramsay, *Church in the Roman Empire*, chaps. II–VII. 2. The reign of Herod Agrippa I. Hastings, *D. B.*, II, 359, 360; Mathews, *Hist. of N. T. Times*, 181–7; Schürer, *Jewish People in the Time of Jesus Christ*, Div. I, II, 150–165.

PAUL'S WORK AND TEACHINGS

§ CL. **Paul's Early Training and Conversion.** GENERAL QUESTIONS: 1. Describe Paul's physical and family inheritance. 2. His personal characteristics. 3. His intellectual and religious environment at Tarsus. 4. His educational opportunities at Jerusalem. 5. The motives that led him to persecute the followers of Jesus. 6. The differences and points of agreement in the four accounts of his conversion. 7. The experience that made him a devoted follower of Jesus. 8. The first fifteen years of his missionary activity. 9. His opportunities to become acquainted with the life and teachings of Jesus.

SUBJECTS FOR SPECIAL RESEARCH: 1. The situation and history of Tarsus. Wood, *Life and Ministry of Paul*, 23–30; Ramsay, *Cities of St. Paul*, 85–244. 2. Paul's conversion. Wood, *Life and Ministry of Paul*, 49–53; Bacon, *Story of St. Paul*, 34–67; Deissmann, *St. Paul*, 115–124; Gardner, *Religious Experiences of St. Paul*, 20–56.

§ CLI. **Paul's First Missionary Campaign.** GENERAL QUESTIONS: 1. Significance of Paul's year of work with the Antioch community. 2. The reasons why he and Barnabas set out on their first missionary campaign. 3. The limitations and results of their work at Cyprus. 4. Paul's reasons for going to southern Asia Minor. 5. The conditions which confronted Paul and Barnabas in Galatian Antioch. 6. Their experiences at Iconium and Lystra. 7. The results of their first campaign in Asia Minor.

SUBJECTS FOR SPECIAL RESEARCH: 1. The situation and strategic importance of Galatian Antioch. *En. Bib.*, I, 184; Ramsay, *Cities of*

APPENDIX

St. Paul, 247–295. 2. The situation of Iconium. *En. Bib.*, II, 2144–6; Ramsay, *Cities of St. Paul*, 317–382.

§ CLII. **The Breaking of Jewish Bonds.** GENERAL QUESTIONS: 1. Why did the missionary campaign of Paul and Barnabas present a difficult problem to the Christian church, and what was the nature of that problem? 2. Discuss the date and significance of Paul's conference with the "pillar" apostles at Jerusalem. 3. Peter's vacillation in regard to associating with Gentile Christians. 4. The attitude of the Judaistic party in the church. 5. The proposed compromise. 6. Paul's contributions to the ultimate solution of the problem.

SUBJECTS FOR SPECIAL RESEARCH: 1. The chronology of Paul's life. Moffatt, *Introd. to N. T.*, 62–64; Hastings, *D. B.*, I, 423–5; *En. Bib.*, I, 809–817; Deissmann, *St. Paul*, 235–260. 2. The charges which the Jews brought against the Christians. Case, *Evolution of Christianity*, 123–146; McGiffert, *Apostolic Age*, 192–211.

§ CLIII. **Paul's Second Visit and Later Letter to the Churches of Galatia.** GENERAL QUESTIONS: 1. Describe Paul's immediate and ultimate objective in his second missionary campaign. 2. The communities to which the epistle to the Galatians was written. 3. Its date and aim. 4. Paul's method of presenting his convictions. 5. His estimate of the relative importance of the Jewish law and of the work of Jesus. 6. The meaning and responsibilities of Christian freedom.

SUBJECTS FOR SPECIAL RESEARCH: 1. The North and South Galatian theories. Moffatt, *Introd. to N. T.*, 90–101; McGiffert, *Apostolic Age*, 178–181; Ramsay, *St. Paul the Traveller*, 178–184. 2. Date of Paul's letter to the Galatians. Moffatt, *Introd. to N. T.*, 101–6; Ramsay, *St. Paul the Traveller*, 189–192; Lake, *Earlier Epistles of St. Paul*, 253–273.

§ CLIV. **Paul's Missionary Work in Macedonia.** GENERAL QUESTIONS: 1. Describe the probable reasons why Paul did not at once continue his work in Asia Minor. 2. The psychological antecedents and significance of his vision at Troas. 3. The conditions under which he worked at Philippi. 4. The results of his work there. 5. Conditions at Thessalonica. 6. The character of the Christian community which he there established. 7. The significance of his work in Macedonia.

SUBJECTS FOR SPECIAL RESEARCH: 1. The nature of Paul's visions. Weinel, *St. Paul*, 80–84; Cutten, *Psych. Phenomena of Christianity*, 60–70. 2. The situation and history of Philippi. Hastings, *D. B.*, III, 837; *En. Bib.*, III, 3701–3.

APPENDIX

§ CLV. Paul's Letters to the Christians at Thessalonica.
GENERAL QUESTIONS: 1. Describe the general structure and the five distinctive divisions found in the majority of Paul's letters. 2. The characteristics and the charm of Paul's literary style. 3. The reasons why Paul wrote his first letter to the Thessalonians. 4. Its structure. 5. Its leading ideas. 6. The structure of II Thessalonians. 7. The evidence that it was written by Paul. 8. Its important teachings.

SUBJECTS FOR SPECIAL RESEARCH: 1. Contemporary Greek letters. Deissmann, *Light from the Ancient East*, 107–400. 2. Evidence for and against the authenticity of II Thessalonians. Moffatt, *Introd. to N. T.*, 81, 82; Bacon, *St. Paul*, 243–251. 3. The situation and history of Thessalonica. *En. Bib.*, IV, 5046–8; Hastings, *D. B.*, IV, 749, 750.

§ CLVI. Paul's Work at Athens and Corinth. GENERAL QUESTIONS: 1. Draw a general plan indicating the situation of the important public buildings at Athens when Paul visited it. 2. Describe its intellectual and religious life and Paul's attitude toward it. 3. Express in the form of a paraphrase the leading ideas in his address to the Athenian crowd. 4. The way in which it was received. 5. In what did Paul's skill as an orator consist? 6. What peculiar and difficult problems confronted Paul at Corinth? 7. What new methods did he there employ? 8. In what respects was his work at Corinth successful?

SUBJECTS FOR SPECIAL RESEARCH: 1. Philosophical schools in Athens in Paul's day. Ramsay, *St. Paul the Traveller*, 238–244; Zeller, *The Stoics, Epicureans, and Skeptics;* Windelband, *Hist. of Ancient Philosophy;* Gomperz, *Greek Thinkers*, II, III. 2. The geographical and commercial importance of Corinth. Dobschütz, *Life in the Primitive Church*, 11–13; Frazer, *Pausanias*, II, 1, 2; *En. Bib.*, I, 897–9.

§ CLVII. Paul's Correspondence with the Corinthian Church.
GENERAL QUESTIONS: 1. Describe the intellectual and moral conditions in Corinth when Paul visited it. 2. The peculiar problems in the Christian church at Corinth. 3. The contents of Paul's first letter to the Corinthian Christians. 4. The structure and contents of his second letter: I Corinthians. 5. Paul's method of dealing with factions in the Christian church. 6. His teachings regarding personal immorality. 7. The occasion and contents of his third letter to the Corinthians. 8. The structure and leading ideas of his fourth letter.

SUBJECTS FOR SPECIAL RESEARCH: 1. Paul's teachings regarding the death and resurrection of Jesus. Deissmann, *St. Paul*, 173–9; Weinel, *St. Paul*, 300–312. 2. The later history of the Corinthian

APPENDIX

church reflected in *I Clement*. Dobschütz, *Life in the Primitive Church*, 211–7; *Ante-Nicene Fathers*, I, 1–21.

§ CLVIII. **Paul's Principles of Christian Living.** GENERAL QUESTIONS: 1. Formulate in your own words Paul's statement of a Christian's duty in case a dispute arises with a fellow Christian. 2. Describe his conception of the moral responsibilities of those who enjoyed Christian liberty. 3. Compare his teachings and those of Jesus regarding marriage and divorce. 4. Describe his practical interpretation of Jesus' law of love. 5. His teachings regarding the "Body of Christ." 6. The setting of his hymn to love in I Corinthians 13. 7. Express in the form of a paraphrase the leading ideas in this hymn.

SUBJECTS FOR SPECIAL RESEARCH: 1. A comparison of the Roman and Christian attitude toward divorce. Westermarck, *Hist. of Human Marriage;* Howard, *Hist. of Matrimonial Institutions*, I. 2. The literary charm of Paul's hymn in praise of love. Weinel, *St. Paul*, 137; Von Norden, *Antik. Kunstprosa*, II, 506.

§ CLIX. **Paul's Ministry at Ephesus.** GENERAL QUESTIONS: 1. Trace on the map Paul's probable itinerary from Ephesus to Antioch. 2. Describe the situation of Ephesus. 3. Its political and religious importance. 4. Its intellectual life in Paul's day. 5. The ways in which Paul adapted his methods to local conditions. 6. The pagan opposition which he aroused. 7. The limitations and the results of his work at Ephesus.

SUBJECTS FOR SPECIAL RESEARCH: 1. The history of Ephesus and the results of recent excavation. *En. Bib.*, II, 1302–5; Hastings, *D. B.*, I, 720–4; Wood, *Discoveries at Ephesus*. 2. The temple of Artemis. Hastings, *D. B.*, I, 605, 606, 724; *En. Bib.*, I, 1098–1100.

§ CLX. **Paul's Interpretation of Jesus' Saving Work.** GENERAL QUESTIONS: 1. Describe the reasons which led Paul to write his epistle to the Romans. 2. Its structure and important divisions. 3. The practical value and limitations of the Jewish legal system. 4. What Jesus and his teaching had done for Paul. 5. The inherited ideas which shaped Paul's conception of Jesus. 6. The different figures which he employed to describe Jesus' saving work, and their meaning. 7. The way in which Jesus, according to Paul, saves men.

SUBJECTS FOR SPECIAL RESEARCH: 1. The Christian church at Rome. McGiffert, *Apostolic Age*, 325, 328, 588–593; Dobschütz, *Life in the Primitive Church*, 121–3, 203, 204. 2. Paul's theology. Deissmann, *St. Paul*, 143–192; Ropes, *Apostolic Age*, 134–168; Wrede, *Paul*, 84–119; Weinel, *St. Paul*, 286–352.

APPENDIX

§ CLXI. **Paul's Social Teachings.** GENERAL QUESTIONS: 1. Describe Paul's interest in ethical and social questions. 2. The evidence that he had a wide and first-hand knowledge of many of Jesus' social teachings. 3. Paul's statement of Jesus' principle of self-sacrifice. 4. The Christian's duty to his fellow Christians. 5. To civil authorities and organized society. 6. Paul's principle of tolera-tion. 7. The influence of his belief in the speedy second coming of Jesus upon his social teaching and activity. 8. Compare Jesus' teach-ings regarding the Kingdom of God and Paul's regarding the "Body of Christ."

SUBJECTS FOR SPECIAL RESEARCH: 1. Social life in the Roman Em-pire. Fowler, *Social Life at Rome in the Age of Cicero;* Tucker, *Life in the Roman World of Nero and St. Paul.* 2. The social life of the early Christian churches. Harnack, *Expansion of Christianity*, I, 181–249. 3. Royce's interpretation of Paul's social teachings, *The Problem of Christianity*, I, II.

§ CLXII. **Paul's Last Journey to Jerusalem.** GENERAL QUES-TIONS: 1. Describe the incidents of Paul's journey to Jerusalem. 2. The reasons that led him to revisit the home of Judaism. 3. The extent to which his mission to the Jerusalem church appears to have been successful. 4. The reasons why the Jews hated him. 5. The basis and nature of their attack. 6. Was Paul's visit to Jerusalem a mistake?

SUBJECTS FOR SPECIAL RESEARCH: 1. Paul's skill and methods as an organizer. Wrede, *Paul*, 56–62; Weinel, *St. Paul*, 200–217. 2. The finances of the early Christian churches. Dobschütz, *Life in the Primi-tive Church*, 58, 59; Harnack, *Expansion of Christianity*, I, 227–230.

§ CLXIII. **The Ambassador in Bonds.** GENERAL QUESTIONS: 1. Describe the reasons why Felix kept Paul in prison for two years. 2. The charge of Tertullus, and Paul's defense before Felix. 3. The intellectual atmosphere of Cæsarea. 4. The evidence regarding the date of the proconsulship of Festus. 5. Paul's reasons for appealing to Cæsar. 6. Trace on a map Paul's journey from Jerusalem to Rome. 7. The story of his shipwreck. 8. His life as a prisoner at Rome.

SUBJECTS FOR SPECIAL RESEARCH: 1. The personal history of Felix. *En. Bib.*, II, 1516, 1517; Schürer, *Hist. of the Jew. People*, Div. I, II, 174–183. 2. Roman ships and methods of sailing. *En. Bib.*, IV, 4480–4; Smith, *Voyage and Shipwreck of St. Paul;* Torr, *An-cient Ships.*

§ CLXIV. **The Last Letters of the Aged Prisoner.** GENERAL QUESTIONS: 1. Describe the letters which Paul wrote during his imprisonment at Rome. 2. His aim in writing to Philemon and the way in which he endeavored to accomplish it. 3. The occasion of his letter to the Colossians. 4. The teachings which it presents. 5. The evidence that the so-called epistle to the Ephesians was written by Paul. 6. Its leading ideas. 7. The aim of Paul's letter to the Philippians. 8. The light which it throws upon Paul's condition at the time. 9. Paul's leading contributions to the beliefs, the organization, and the social ideals of Christianity.

SUBJECTS FOR SPECIAL RESEARCH: 1. Origin and distinctive beliefs of Gnosticism. Dobschütz, *Life in the Primitive Church*, 251–276; *En. Bib.*, II, 1738–42; Mansel, *Gnostic Heresies*. 2. Polycarp's Epistle to the Philippians. *Ante-Nicene Fathers*, I, 31–36. 3. Paul's contributions to the faith of Christianity. Wrede, *Paul*, 155–182.

CHRISTIANITY DURING THE SECOND HALF OF THE FIRST CENTURY

§ CLXV. **The Message of Hope and Inspiration in I Peter.** GENERAL QUESTIONS: 1. What is known regarding Peter's later activity? 2. What evidence is there that he died a martyr at Rome? 3. Describe the extension of Christianity throughout the Roman world during the first century. 4. How far did it penetrate the imperial household? 5. What does Pliny state regarding the character of the Christians in Bithynia? 6. Describe Domitian's persecutions of the Christians. 7. The aim of I Peter. 8. Its probable authorship and date. 9. Its leading ideas.

SUBJECTS FOR SPECIAL RESEARCH: 1. Domitian's policy toward his subjects. Ayer, *Source Book for Ancient Church History*, 11, 12; Ramsay, *The Church in the Roman Empire*. 2. The thought and authorship of II Peter. Moffatt, *Introd. to N. T.*, 359–371; Jülicher, *Introd. to N. T.*, 232–241.

§ CLXVI. **The Early Christian Sermon in Hebrews.** GENERAL QUESTIONS: 1. Describe the evidence that the so-called epistle to the Hebrews was originally uttered as a sermon. 2. The character and point of view of its author. 3. The class to which it was addressed. 4. The temptations which confronted them. 5. The aim of the author of Hebrews. 6. The way in which he develops his theme. 7. The literary charm of Hebrews. 8. Its contribution to the faith of Christianity.

APPENDIX

SUBJECTS FOR SPECIAL RESEARCH: 1. The characteristics of Alexandrian life and philosophy. *Encyc. Brit.* I, 573–5; Kingsley, *Alexandria and Her Schools;* Zeller, *History of Philosophy;* Knaack, *Alexandrische Litteratur.* 2. A comparison of Paul's interpretation of the character and work of Jesus with that of the author of Hebrews.

§ CLXVII. **The Visions of the Ultimate Victory of Christianity in the Book of Revelation.** GENERAL QUESTIONS: 1. Describe the aims of the author of the book of Revelation. 2. The practical problems with which the author is dealing. 3. The class of literature to which it belongs. 4. Point of view and date at which it was written. 5. Its use of figures drawn from early apocalyptic writings. 6. The meaning of its dramatic pictures. 7. The social significance of its description of the new Jerusalem.

SUBJECTS FOR SPECIAL RESEARCH: 1. The apocalypse contained in IV Ezra. Charles, *The Apocryphal and Pseudepigrapha of the O. T.,* 542–624. 2. Christian beliefs regarding the end of the world. Clemen, *Primitive Christianity and its Non-Jewish Sources,* 117–174.

§ CLXVIII. **The Christian Wisdom of the Epistle of James.** GENERAL QUESTIONS: 1. Describe the literary peculiarities of the epistle of James. 2. The motives which influenced its author to write. 3. The history of James, the brother of Jesus. 4. The probable date of the epistle of James. 5. The point of view and character of its author. 6. Its distinctive teachings. 7. Its emphasis on democracy. 8. Its practical value.

SUBJECTS FOR SPECIAL RESEARCH: 1. History of the Palestinian Christian communities. Harnack, *Expansion of Christianity,* II, 247–276. 2. The *Teaching of the Twelve Apostles.* Ayer, *Source Book for Ancient Church History,* 37–41; Hastings, *D. B.,* Extra Vol., 438–451.

§ CLXIX. **The Rule of Love in the Early Christian Church.** GENERAL QUESTIONS: 1. Describe the aim of the author of I John. 2. Its teaching regarding love. 3. Its probable author and date. 4. The evidence that I John and the Fourth Gospel come from the same ultimate source. 5. The personality revealed in the Johannine writings. 6. Evidences that the principles of love prevailed in the early Christian communities. 7. The organization and institutions of the early churches. 8. What is Christianity?

SUBJECTS FOR SPECIAL RESEARCH: 1. The picture of early Christian life in the *Shepherd of Hermas.* Dobschütz, *Life in the Primitive Church,* 309–362. 2. The treatment of the sick and needy in the early church. Dobschütz, *Life in the Primitive Church,* 368–370; Harnack,

APPENDIX

Expansion of Christianity, I, 131–151, 230–236; Ulhorn, *Christian Charity in the Ancient Church.* 3. Baptism and the Lord's Supper in the early church. Scott, *Beginnings of the Church*, 162–223; Clemen, *Primitive Christianity and its Non-Jewish Sources*, 212–266; Heitmüller, *Taufe und Abendmahl im Urchristentum.*